BLACK LIBERATION THROUGH THE MARKETPLACE

HOPE, HEARTBREAK, and the PROMISE of AMERICA

RACHEL S. FERGUSON
MARCUS M. WITCHER

EMANCIPATION
BOOKS

An EMPANCIPATION BOOKS BOOK
An Imprint of Post Hill Press
ISBN: 978-1-63758-344-9
ISBN (eBook): 978-1-63758-345-6

Black Liberation Through the Marketplace:
Hope, Heartbreak, and the Promise of America

Cover design by Cody Corcoran

Cover art: © 2021 The Jacob and Gwendolyn Knight Lawrence Foundation,
Seattle / Artists Rights Society (ARS), New York

Post Hill Press
New York • Nashville
posthillpress.com

Published in the United States of America
1 2 3 4 5 6 7 8 9 10

This book is dedicated to the thinkers, lawyers, entrepreneurs, teachers, and artists who insisted in the face of crushing obstacles that America is for Black people too. Phillis Wheatley, Lysander Spooner, Frederick Douglass, Booker T. Washington, Oswald Garrison Villard, John H. Johnson, Madame C.J. Walker, Rose Wilder Lane, Zora Neale Hurston, T.R.M. Howard, Nat Hentoff, Stanley Crouch, Albert Murray, and so many others. May their dream never die.

Contents

Introduction

At a recent visit to the International Civil Rights Center & Museum in Greensboro, North Carolina, Rachel was struck by the opening image depicting a beautiful hand-sewn American flag with the words of Thomas Jefferson's Declaration superimposed: "We hold these truths to be self-evident, that all men are created equal, that they are endowed by their Creator with certain unalienable rights, that among these are life, liberty, and the pursuit of happiness." The tour guide, a stunning older Black lady named Robin with dreadlocks down to her knees, then pressed a button and the image changed, with the faint shadow of the flag behind, to images of slave auction signs and whites-only, no-colored-allowed signs. Robin spoke of the unfulfilled promise of the Declaration as she led the group through the dreadful review of Black lynching, economic exclusion, school segregation, and the many of other forms that Jim Crow took. After letting the group view a copy of a *Green Book* (the secret travel guides that Black Americans used to navigate the Jim Crow South), Robin declared that "our answer to the racism and segregation that we experienced was entrepreneurship." She then listed dozens of Black inventions, walked the group through a room full of images of Black businesses, banks, newspapers, and churches. This story—the story of a high ideal, often unrealized but still inspiring, and a struggle for independence and economic power—is the story of Black liberation through the marketplace.

As Americans, addressing past racial injustices and ensuring that the promises of our founding are extended to every citizen are of the utmost importance. Jefferson accused the British of "a long train of abuses," and the Black experience in America has certainly been that. We have a duty to understand this and to address these injustices to whatever extent possible. Our political culture, however, often undoes such efforts.

Tribalism. Polarization. Contempt. This reality haunts the American conversation. The Right blames the Left's identity politics. The Left blames Trump. Trump blames the media. Experts blame smartphones, social media, and the twenty-four-hour news cycle. Whatever the cause, unless you are an apolitical digital minimalist or in a coma, you're feeling the pressure to take a side. And you also can't avoid the fact that many (though not all) of our most contentious cultural and political conversations revolve around issues of racial justice.

Fair enough. Our social and political disputes are real, and they matter. There are right and wrong answers to the pressing questions of the day. The problem is not that we are incapable of thinking through difficult cultural and policy issues. Rather, the problem is a phenomenon we will call "bundling."[1] Social and political problems are complicated, and practical politics requires the formation of a platform. The process forces us to lump together positions on a wide variety of topics—from climate change, abortion, and tariffs to Afghanistan—in order to form parties and mobilize a base. Furthermore, the psychology research shows that we get a hit of positive hormones when we feel like part of a group.[2] Taken together, bundling positions on a wide variety of issues in order to form a party is just too hard to resist.

Unfortunately, reality doesn't actually conform to the traditional political platforms, and often positions are bundled together that don't necessarily follow from the same principles.[3] That's just one reason why we argue here that we cannot fruitfully address issues of racial justice without first committing ourselves to a process of unbundling. We also argue that various details of Black American life and history make racial justice a particularly bad fit for politics as usual in America. The Black American experience does not fit well into majority culture's political categories, and it's not right to try to make it fit. Here, we take a classical liberal approach to the history of Black oppression in America because we think it offers insights that are often overlooked: a kind of third way that breaks out of a stultifying two-sided conversation. Nor have classical liberals themselves done a great job of communicating with the public how a philosophy that limits government to a defense of individual rights, encourages markets, and values civil society can speak into the lives of Black Americans in a powerful way. And yet, we think that it can and that it does. Finally, we think that Black American culture overlaps with classical liberal values in ways that ought to be explored more. We hope to begin the process of addressing this failure in our ranks with this work.

In this book, we'll be taking a look at certain episodes in Black history here in America, including several truly stunning stories of Black success. We pick out several episodes in which the state excluded Blacks from the institutions that underlie healthy economic activity, just as progressive scholars have highlighted.[4] We pick out other episodes in which state intervention on behalf of Blacks (and other marginalized groups) has undermined their economic and cultural flourishing, just as conservative scholars have argued. We make some surprising and counterintuitive discoveries along the way that don't fit either narrative very well. We suggest that certain practical policy changes and cultural shifts that address the root causes of marginalization can do more to address the pain of our past than many on-the-nose solutions on offer.

We want to show that neither political tribe has a very good grasp on America's racial situation and that this distorts our understanding of American history as well. We offer an alternative account—one that takes the truest insights from both conservative and progressive scholars but is also willing to jettison the elements of their accounts that have misled their supporters. Research shows that most Black Americans don't fit comfortably in either camp, anyway, so it makes sense to reframe and reorient our account of the Black experience.[5]

We anticipate that our readers will experience this book as a bit of a roller-coaster ride. You might find yourself quite comfortable with the claims in one chapter but deeply anxious about those in the next. We hope you'll stick with us and perhaps even experience something we've come to enjoy—a sense of freedom gained by a certain distance from the demands of political tribes. Maybe this sort of approach could generate a tribe of its own!

We open the reframing project with a discussion of the terms "classical liberalism" and "social justice" as they each relate to the Black American experience. Classical liberalism captures America's dedication to four distinct institutions: property rights (including the right to bodily integrity), freedom of contract, equal protection under the law, and a cultural affirmation of trade and entrepreneurship. The great classical liberal F. A. Hayek famously critiqued the term social justice. While we find his critique of the term as he understands it successful, we argue that its meaning has broadened to include some principles that classical liberals can affirm, and frankly always have affirmed. Many of the historical injustices against Black Americans (which we discuss in detail in later chapters) can only be understood as violations of the very institutions that Hayek requires as the foundation for a successful social and economic order. So classical liberalism can and should have a good grasp on the significance of historical, systemic injustices for flourishing now. At the same time, Hayek's famous idea of the "information problem" helps us to avoid ineffective solutions and move toward more productive approaches to how historical injustices can truly be made right. We deal with solutions at the end of the chapters that are particularly relevant to that strategy, such as addressing transitional justice at the end of the chapter on atrocities against Black Americans, or addressing criminal justice reform at the end of the chapter on the drug war and mass incarceration.

The greatest challenge to a classical liberal understanding of the oppression of Black Americans comes from the claims of critical race theory, in which liberal institutions in their very nature perpetuate the inequalities that arise from historic oppression. Central to this account is the claim that capitalism is inextricably tied up with systems of oppression, both historic and contemporary. This claim, if true, would certainly be damning to any classical liberal contributions to the discussion of race in America. By mapping the careful debates over two central essays in the Pulitzer Prize–winning 1619 Project, we demonstrate that such claims are deeply confused on a number of levels. First, they stumble into fallacious historical reasoning by slipping back and forth between various definitions of "capitalism" and "liberalism." Second, they misunderstand the economic data around slavery as well as the deep differences in the economic philosophies of the North and the South in the antebellum period. Third, they unwisely jettison the Black American tradition of holding in tension admiration for the political principles of the founding with lament for our failures to live up to those ideals. Unlike critical race theory, which starts from a place of deep suspicion about our liberal legal institutions, classical liberals agree with Frederick Douglass that a liberal system of law based on our current Constitution is our best hope for a flourishing polity.

In Chapter 3, we start in earnest to think about the history of Black people in America in terms of the most fundamental classical liberal values: property, contract rights, and the rule of law. We demonstrate the deep desire of newly emancipated Black people to own their own farms while enduring the multifarious attempts of whites—through social strictures, laws, and cartels—to stop this from happening. We also see the freedmen overcoming these obstacles by appealing to the rule of law regarding their own property rights, as well as their freedom of contract, of movement, and of association. Appeals to the Freedmen's Bureau allowed some to sidestep the lack of reliable courts in the South. When whites attempted to collude to fix wages and keep workers in bondage, they played farmers off of each other in order to break the cartels. They used their freedom of movement by leaving for the Delta where there were better opportunities. And they formed their own internal associations to accomplish the greatest leap forward in literacy of any society on earth thus far. Presented with a constant stream of obstacles, Black Americans were yet able to improve noticeably in income, diet, and housing, growing the Black economy at twice the pace of the white economy during the late nineteenth century. While this still left them in deeply unequal material circumstances in comparison to whites, it demonstrates an impressive gain while under serious duress.

In Chapter 4, we choose not to look away from the many atrocities carried out by whites against whole Black communities. Any classical liberal account ought to assiduously acknowledge failures in the rule of law and all that such failure can mean for the flourishing of individuals and communities. Not only were constant harassment, subjection to the corrupt practice of convict leasing, full-fledged violent communal attacks, and thousands of lynchings a failure of the law to protect the basic liberty of Black Americans, but supposed "law enforcement" officers were often actively involved in these crimes. Whites who fought for equal justice could be lynched themselves. While these episodes, such as the burning of Black Wall Street in Tulsa, are becoming better known nowadays, we want to emphasize that they are not just random atrocities. Instead, we must also conceive of these episodes as a kind of focused lawlessness. While it's easy to see that a lawless society will not develop much economically (and in many other ways as well), we should also note that systems of law that function well in general can be dysfunctional or even nonfunctional with regard to a particular population, retarding their economic development severely. Since several of these episodes amounted to whites particularly targeting well-off Blacks, we also note that any well-functioning commercial society is incompatible with the vice of envy, an evil disposition of character that will wreak havoc and destruction on a society and an economy. We also begin our "Looking for Solutions" series here with Transitional Justice. One of the most important things we can do in response to historical injustice is properly honor the survivors in our institutional memory. These focused, local efforts at appropriate recognition can be effective where sloppy, sweeping statements made at too high a level seem both disingenuous and ineffective.

In Chapter 5 we turn to a discussion of the Black church, a lodestar of civil society in American history. We appeal to the global history of Black Christianity, as well as to the uniqueness of Black church practice and doctrine in America, to dispel the old trope of Black subjugation through the "white man's religion." Black Christianity develops in a robustly independent way from white Christianity, though it also offers the possibility of connection and reconciliation between the two groups. Sadly, many white Christians chose the culture of white supremacy over their own brothers and sisters in the faith, leaving a scar across American society and politics that is evident to this day. We review the ways in which the Black church created a realm of freedom, healthy Black identity, and empowerment. The deep and continued religiosity of Black Americans, statistically speaking, also explains much of their confusing place in American political categories. While eminently practical in matters of politics, Black Americans are fairly socially conservative, making them an odd fit for today's progressive movement. At the same time, their deep and thoughtful integration of the social gospel with a historically orthodox understanding of personal salvation makes them an odd fit for today's conservatives as well. This central part of many Black Americans' lives is least understood or appreciated by progressives and conservatives alike—even so-called conservative Christians. A better understanding of the Black church tradition and the potential to revitalize it as a center of cultural productivity also presents an exciting opportunity to break out of the dead and stultifying tribalism that has imprisoned us in this cultural moment.

In Chapter 6 we continue with the theme of Black civil society, focusing on self-empowerment efforts from within the Black community. We find that there was more overlap between W. E. B. Du Bois's and Booker T. Washington's visions of Black empowerment than has been generally believed. Black notions of "uplift" and "self-help" have nothing to do with a hyper-individualist, bootstrap mentality that the same words might evoke today. Rather, they refer to the pooling of resources within the Black community for the shared goal of Black economic improvement: networking, mentorship, and institution building. This tradition is most impressively exemplified in the fraternal association movement, a kind of collection of small societies that functioned as both club and social insurance program. With almost half of all Black American men involved, fraternal societies formed a core of Black civic life that, though diminished, still lives on today. Furthermore, these fraternal associations allowed for economic cooperation and economic flourishing that seems almost miraculous in light of the obstacles that had to be overcome. We tell the stories of John Johnson, Madam C. J. Walker, T. R. M. Howard, and other wildly successful Black entrepreneurs whose economic success always translated into infrastructure for the burgeoning movement for Black legal equality. In fact, without their economic support, the accomplishments of the civil rights movement are simply unthinkable.

In contrast to the hope and achievement embodied in the Black church, Black fraternal societies, Black business, and Black political organizations, we review in Chapters 7 and 8 the deplorable history of progressive eugenics, racist unions, housing segregation and exclusion, so-called "urban renewal," and highway construction. These ambitious attempts at socially engineering the populace undermined and destroyed Black property and contract rights at every turn. Minimum wage policies targeted Blacks, immigrants, and women to keep them out of the so-called healthy "Aryan," and male workforce idealized by turn-of-the-century progressives. An economically innumerate understanding of trade as a space of class conflict drove union policy to pit racial groups against one another. Backwards notions of racial superiority and inferiority, and condemnations of racial mixing helped progressive central planners at the federal level justify to themselves exclusionary policies that left urban Blacks with very few places to live and high rents as a result of the shortage. Finally, federal urban renewal (slum clearance) and highway projects were carried out in such a way that local municipal governments were funded to entirely destroy whole communities—many of which, though poor, were healthy centers of cultural life and of an upwardly mobile working class. The placement of highways further segregated already divided cities, subsidized "vanilla suburbs," and hastened the economic hollowing out of the inner cities. In short, these efforts at top-down social engineering of white-Black economic relations was an unmitigated disaster, destroying Black wealth, community, and economic momentum. At the end of Chapter 7, in the "Looking for Solutions" section, we highlight the importance of economic freedom and discuss how these principles can be applied to the struggles of lower-income folks in particular. At the end of Chapter 8, we focus on one of the most important in our series of "Looking for Solutions": neighborhood stabilization. Dealing with the havoc that has been wreaked by state-sponsored social engineering will be a holistic, hyper-local, long-term project. However, there is much hope to be found in the prophets of neighborhood stabilization whose superior philanthropic model is finally making an impact on the way we do charity.

In Chapter 9, the story of failed central planning continues with the Great Society, except this time Black Americans were disparately affected by programs that were applied to all poor

Americans. Failed public housing projects, failing (and still segregated) schools, and the unintended consequences of poorly constructed welfare programs destroyed so much of what Black America—and now rural white America, as well—had built up in social capital. We record in horror the plummeting marriage and employment rates, immobile poverty rates, and skyrocketing violence and drug addiction in post–Great Migration inner-city communities. Avoiding entirely a "blame-the-victim" account, we appeal to the basic concepts of neoclassical economics to show how this sort of micromanaging public policy creates perverse incentives, making decisions that every stable society should discourage into the only economically rational choice for the poor. The predictable outcomes of such policies are not at all unique to government dependency in America but are uniform across the globe. In "Looking for Solutions" here, we focus on educational freedom, an important step in breaking the cycle of poverty and geographic isolation.

In Chapter 10, we take a look at the root causes of our current mass incarceration crisis, which currently involves more than a third of Black men in the criminal justice system at some time in their lives. While the current crisis cannot (mostly) be traced to overtly racist policy, the injustice of the system as it has evolved since 1970 makes all poor and marginalized people especially vulnerable to oppression. We carefully analyze the implementation of immunity for public officials, the War on Drugs, the push for aggressive prosecution, the rise of mandatory minimums, the militarization of the police and the rise of SWAT, and many other factors in the current crisis. America's criminal justice system has become deeply corrupt, and its official lawlessness is the gravest threat to the American dream of a peaceful and prosperous multiethnic polity. Of course, we are "Looking for Solutions" in the criminal justice reform arena, where good, data-driven debate has led to serious policy solutions, some of which we can observe as they are happening in real time.

Throughout in our "Looking for Solutions" sections, we discuss practical steps for the healing of our nation's deepest wounds. Straightforward fixes like affirmative action or housing subsidies have proven ineffective and sometimes disastrously counterproductive. Instead, we sadly admit that the state can cause many problems that it cannot itself repair. Instead of continuing to wrangle over plans for new forms of social engineering beleaguered by politics, we focus on removing the greatest obstacles to justice that the state has created: ending the War on Drugs, reforming the criminal justice system, addressing the "welfare cliff," and attaching school funding to the student and not to the school.

We recommend those policies that will spur on economic growth, the one most effective program for advancing the poor that is also most easily overlooked. Positive programs to address historical injustice include transitional justice, aspects of which have been implemented internationally where great atrocities and apartheid have existed within a polity. Transitional justice is superior to social justice because it straightforwardly addresses the actual violations of the rule of law by aggressors, and its requirements are clear and limited. Replacing the clumsy tool of government entitlement, we look to the prophets of neighborhood stabilization, thinkers like John Perkins and his Christian Community Development Association, Robert L. Woodson Sr.'s grassroots movement, and Robert Lupton's Focused Community Strategies. The new possibilities for school funding opened up by recent Supreme Court rulings have the potential to empower the Black church again, as a healthy Afro-American-centric form of Christian education could do the same work for struggling Black children that the Catholic parochial system did for so many immigrant children.

The great filmmaker Akira Kurosawa once said, "The role of the artist is to not look away." We believe that this is also the role of every reflective American citizen who has not given up on the dream of a thriving Black America and of the healing of our racial wounds. We believe that classical liberalism—the very philosophy of America's founding—provides more insight and positive tools for this project than has been generally understood. We hope that in the pages of this book, you will not look away and that you will find the hope for the future that we, too, discovered as we explored the pain and promise of Black America.

Chapter 1

Classical Liberalism, Social Justice, and Black America

Much of the tension between today's conservatives and today's progressives can be characterized as an argument over the concept of social justice.

Progressives complain that conservatives are hyper-individualists, ascribing to a pull-yourself-up-by-your-bootstraps mentality that denies the reality of social constraints and privileges that determine most social outcomes. Were you or I to have grown up in a certain kind of low-income, high-crime neighborhood, for instance, a keen sociologist could, fairly easily and fairly accurately, predict the probability that we end up in poverty, are un- or under-employed, are a single parent, or are involved in the criminal justice system. Similarly, accurate predictions can be made for a child of wealth and privilege. It's absurd, they say, to act like individuals are totally self-determining, or that if some demographic suffers from certain social pathologies such as addiction or poor health outcomes, it's simply because they all, by some amazing coincidence, made bad choices. The solution, say the progressives, is to admit that these outcomes are socially, not individually, determined, and therefore must be addressed by public means. Government planners can ameliorate the suffering of downtrodden communities through a plethora of programs for income, health, and education, and conservatives' objections to these programs belie a heartlessness and disdain for the marginalized. Social justice, then, is comprised of a collection of government programs that will redistribute wealth, nationalize services such as health care, and address social inequalities.

Conservatives, on the other hand, complain about social justice advocates—who, they argue, oversimplify complicated social problems by assuming they can all be solved through government intervention. It's not so much that individuals simply make bad choices, they say, but rather that the underlying culture in which an individual grows up will shape her character in a way that will then, in turn, shape her life and outcomes. Does the culture encourage stability through marriage, for instance? Are children taught the value of hard work? Are church and other community organizations an important part of their lives? Conservatives complain that no amount of money transfers, extra funding for dysfunctional schools, or other bureaucratic, one-size-fits-all, centrally planned solutions can make up for a loss of the kind of stable family and community life that develops character and ultimately leads to decent outcomes. Conservatives argue that by blaming the system and relying on centralized, political solutions that crowd out local and culturally specific efforts, social justice advocates undermine the very institutions that those on the edges of society desperately need to cultivate and maintain in order to flourish, those of family and community.

CLASSICAL LIBERALISM

Perhaps our readers have never heard the term classical liberalism or have only a vague outline of what this political philosophy entails. We argue here that it ought to be more commonly linked with the history of Black America, whose liberation was the concern of many serious classical liberals, including most, if not all, of the abolitionists, Frederick Douglass in particular, and Oswald Garrison Villard, a co-founder of the NAACP. Rose Wilder Lane (the daughter of Laura Ingalls Wilder of *Little House on the Prairie* fame) is considered one of the three "mothers of libertarianism"—the term "libertarianism" being invented in the early twentieth century as a revival of classical liberalism. She wrote extensively for the largest Black newspaper in America at the time, the *Pittsburgh Courier*, arguing for Black equality from a libertarian perspective. Zora Neale Hurston, the great anthropologist and novelist, agreed with Lane, George Schuyler (the newspaper's editor), and others in her opposition to the New Deal.[6] Sadly, she died in obscurity after being marginalized, at least in part, for her anti-communist and individualist views.[7] We will highlight many others who fought for Black dignity and equality by appealing to classical liberal values.

Nor is classical liberalism generally associated with social justice; in fact, the two movements are often considered antithetical. If someone thinks of social justice as the massive redistribution of wealth to equalize material outcomes, then it is antithetical to classical liberalism. But is this really how most people use the term? Or do most people, when saying that they care about social justice, simply imply that we ought to go out of our way to care for those least well-off in our society, those most marginalized, and those most vulnerable to oppression? If so, the debate between classical liberals and social justice advocates will be one of means, not ends, because the empowerment of the least well-off has been an important focus of classical liberal thought from its very inception. The task ahead of us is not to determine whether the plight of the marginalized ought to concern us but rather to determine what justice for them really entails in practical terms.

Americans over the last fifty years or so have begun to use the term "liberal" in a completely different way from the rest of the world and from its use in political philosophy. Originally, the term "liberal" arose from the Latin root *liber*, meaning "free." Ancient city-states, being small and generally quite homogenous, could organize themselves around some vision of a good human life, which always included a shared religion, shared customs, and shared language. But the rise of large, pluralistic modern states meant that people needed to live together in peace with others who did not necessarily share all these background assumptions. Rather than focus the task of the state on making people virtuous practitioners of a particular conception of the good human life, classical liberals insisted that the state ought to simply guarantee certain basic freedoms to individuals, who could then be free to form their own voluntary communities of virtue. Thus, people of various backgrounds could learn to tolerate one another.

What's more, there began to emerge a concept of individualism as well, which claimed that individuals should be free to determine what they believe and why, what they do for a living, where they live, and how they use their property. In fact, many classical liberals like Adam Smith and John Locke claimed that each individual person is actually the owner of their own selves, meaning that they are the ones properly in charge of deciding what they do with themselves.[8] But they didn't take that to mean that individuals can do whatever they want. After all, the people around them also hold this high and dignified title of "self-owner." Others' rights to determine their lives for themselves are just as important as one's own, and so everybody must limit their own activities so that they don't violate anyone else's bodily integrity or property, and so that they don't fail to keep the promises they've made to them in contractual agreements. Even if certain classical liberals, like David Hume and John Stuart Mill,[9] didn't believe in this grand idea of natural rights, they still believed that societies work best when people treat one another according to certain basic freedoms.[10]

Don't let this emphasis on individualism give the false impression that classical liberals act as though each person is an island, subsistent unto themselves. Some of the best work on the collective wisdom built up over generations through custom and tradition was done by classical liberals of the Scottish Enlightenment. This limited and reasoned concept of individual freedom has always been upheld by classical liberals as the basis for the economic interdependence of the marketplace as well as the social and spiritual interdependence of a healthy and robust set of civil society institutions. In fact, one of the things the great French sociologist Alexis de Tocqueville noticed about Americans is that they are the first to try to solve problems, not by the power and influence of a great lord or a government official, but by forming a club![11] Tocqueville's insight is an important reminder that liberalism is a political philosophy, not a philosophy of life. It won't answer our deepest and most pressing human questions about God, the soul, or the best way to live. A liberal society self-consciously relies on other, nonpolitical institutions to provide the transcendence all humans seek, such as houses of worship, clubs and organizations, the neighborhood, and the family. We refer to these institutions as *civil society*. In contrast to a totalitarian society, in which the state sees such intermediary institutions as competition to its power, the true classical liberal knows that the kind of tolerance and peace we enjoy in a free society would crumble without thick, stable civil society institutions. A liberal society needs more of this, not less, and that's why it's so important that this book includes in-depth discussions of the Black church, Black fraternal societies, and Black business organizations.

So if liberalism defends basic freedoms, what should these basic freedoms be? Well, one way to avoid hatred and intolerance among diverse neighbors is to allow them to be beneficial to one another. If each of us respects others' rights to use their own labor as they wish, we must also respect their ownership of what they gain from that labor, as well as the agreements they make with others about what they do with what they gain. The product of this mutual respect is the commercial society—a society based on making and trading rather than violent taking through war and political conquest. So liberal law is built on *property rights* and *freedom of contract*, the underlying institutions of a free and economically flourishing society.

But neither of these important freedoms will get anyone very far if we can't trust that they will be defended when push comes to shove. If you own a house, but no one will stop your neighbor from burning it down or a powerful political entity from taking it and giving it to someone else, then your property right is meaningless. If you make a contract with someone but they refuse to pay you, and when you take them to court they simply bribe the judge to decide in their favor, then your freedom of contract is meaningless too. If you try to sell your house but are told that you are not allowed to sell to certain people or that the government told the bank that they're not allowed to give you a loan, your freedom of contract is meaningless. And neighbors will not enter into creative endeavors and mutually advantageous exchanges with one another if they can't trust one another or the system! As we can see in development economics, high-trust societies tend to get richer faster because people can take creative risks knowing that their rights will be defended should something go wrong. This fundamental institution is called *the rule of law*, and no talk of rights is meaningful if citizens do not enjoy the equal protection of the law.

Do the examples we cited above sound eerily familiar? Savvy readers will already hear echoes of the abuses we outlined in the introduction: collusion of the police with crimes committed against Black citizens under Jim Crow (Chapter 4); so-called urban renewal and highway construction, in which Black homes were confiscated through the abuse of eminent domain and whole neighborhoods were destroyed (Chapter 8); the inability of post-emancipation Black Americans to find a court that would defend their property rights against whites who took their land (Chapter 3); covenant deeds and FHA red-lining practices that disallowed voluntary exchange between Black and white homeowners or Black citizens and their mortgage lenders (Chapter 8). We will go into far more detail in the coming chapters, but hopefully we can see right away how so much of the story of the oppression of Black Americans has consisted of the violations of the three basic institutions of liberal law favored by classical liberals: property rights, freedom of contract, and the rule of law.

There's still one piece missing though. Just prior to 1800, something dramatic occurred. Some call it the "Great Enrichment," or the "Great Fact." It's expressed in what *Reason* magazine calls "the most important graph in the world."[12]

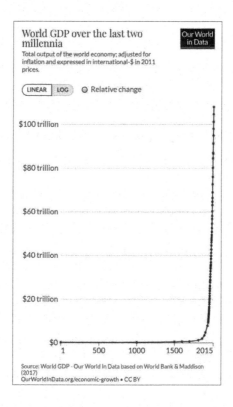

World GDP over the last two millennia
Total output of the world economy; adjusted for inflation and expressed in international-$ in 2011 prices.

Our World in Data

LINEAR | LOG | Relative change

$100 trillion
$80 trillion
$60 trillion
$40 trillion
$20 trillion
$0

1   500   1000   1500   2015

Source: World GDP - Our World In Data based on World Bank & Maddison (2017)
OurWorldInData.org/economic-growth • CC BY

For the first time in the history of the human race, regular people in Europe and America, working-class craftsmen, farmers, and shopkeepers, began to get richer. In one century, their incomes shot up to the point that their populations began to expand exponentially. Instead of dying off in famines as usually happened, they were surviving and living long enough to reproduce, causing a population boom. This made some, like Thomas Malthus, think that we would run out of food, but we didn't. People invented faster machines, used better techniques, and bred bigger seeds. Then the wealth started to spread, as the rest of the world began to adopt the same approach. Unbelievably, the condition of most human beings for most of human history, scratching one's living out of the earth from morning till night, surviving on less than the equivalent of three dollars a day, has completely changed in the last two hundred years. Today, only 8 percent of the world's population lives at this level, what the World Bank calls "extreme poverty."[13] By 2018, Brookings recorded that a majority of people across the globe are middle class, an event they called "a global tipping point."[14] As societies get richer, women become more educated and delay marriage and childbirth, so population has begun to level off too. But even though the world's population has *septupled* in the last two hundred years (from one billion people to over seven billion), people are, on average, getting richer and richer. A humble bike messenger can now listen to symphonies on his phone while getting immediate notification of the location for his next delivery. For lunch he can choose from among dozens of types of food from all over the world. In the evening he can enjoy one of thousands of choices in entertainment or listen to the greatest thinkers in the world discuss their ideas. In a way, he enjoys more wealth than the kings of old. He sits comfortably in a well-heated or air-conditioned home, with access to antibiotics should he get an infection and highly precise surgical techniques when other health issues arise. What would have killed us not one century ago now fails to even concern us. But where did this explosion of innovation, wealth, trade, and distribution come from? And why did it happen when it did?

Surely, these three basic institutions—private property, freedom of contract, and the rule of law—are part of this story. But these were all in fairly good condition a few hundred years before the Great Enrichment. Back then, many people looked down on trade and on the vocation of business. Businesspeople were seen as out of place: too rich for the peasants and too low-born for the aristocracy. They were seen as engaging in an activity vaguely unnatural—making money from lending money as bankers do, or somehow getting a higher price for a good that they bought at a lower price, as merchants do.[15] But aren't things just worth whatever they're worth? How does the trader make money unless he's cheating people? And what about guilds and trade unions? These businesspeople were always pushing to change cherished techniques, charge different prices, pay different wages, use different labor, and in many other ways disturb the status quo.

What shifted in the mid-eighteenth century was the attitude toward the *entrepreneur*.[16] Slowly, people were beginning to realize that while innovative ways of doing things and free trade across national borders could create difficulties in the short-term, allowing for these practices created far more tolerance and wealth than forcing people to stick to the old ways. Praise began to arise for the entrepreneur's willingness to take on risk in order to bring us wonderful items from far away, or clever machines that saved us from back-breaking labor. As the discipline of economics developed, it became clear that the traders, bankers, and merchants were not (usually) making money by cheating people. They encountered risks and dangers to bring items from where they were common to where they were rare. They exchanged the current enjoyment of wealth for the future payoff by investing in other people's projects. They often laid their entire personal fortunes— and the personal fortunes of their friends and families too—on the line to achieve a vision of building something that would serve consumers much better than what they had before. This new understanding of economics, this praise for the entrepreneur and the tradesmen's role in enriching our lives, was the final piece of the puzzle, the catalyst for the Great Enrichment. Thus, the vast majority of people living on the planet today are enjoying a life of flourishing about which their ancestors could hardly have dreamed.[17] If you were under the impression that global poverty is getting worse, set down the book for a moment and head over to Gapminder.org or HumanProgress.org. Be encouraged!

Why tack the term "classical" onto liberal? It's not really necessary, but it helps to distinguish classical liberals from the term "liberal" as it is used in American politics. While the American "liberal" leans politically left, classical liberals are neither left nor right. Twenty years ago, we would have said that they do not wish to interfere with economic exchange, as those on the left do, nor do they wish to interfere in your personal moral choices, as those on the right do. Today, both the Left and the Right seem to want to interfere in both of these arenas, as long as it's their pet issues that are taken up by the law. Classical liberals have always known that there are a few cases that might require extra state interference. Classical liberal David Hume discussed what economists now refer to as "public goods problems" (like providing national defense) and "externalities problems" (like pollution) in the mid-eighteenth century.[18] While classical liberals acknowledge these areas in need of state intervention, they resist as much as possible expanding the state beyond its narrow purpose of defending rights and handling a few needs that markets can't address. That's because "power tends to corrupt," and what's more, state action isn't subject to the discipline of market competition, which means that state provision of goods will always be frustratingly inefficient and fraught with cronyism, a form of political privilege seeking.[19]

While classical liberals universally praise the fruits of free market exchange as a stunning outcome of a free society, they also believe in the intrinsic value of liberty: the freedom of conscience to investigate life's biggest questions of meaning and purpose, the freedom of movement to move wherever one believes will benefit oneself and one's family the most, the equal protection of laws such that peaceful people can live in peace with their neighbors, and all of the unnamed but assumed liberties we enjoy in a free society. In other words, while classical liberals are glad that freedom leads to so much economic flourishing, it's also just plain wrong to push other people around. So classical liberalism is a political philosophy that insists on the legal equality of every citizen—that upholds the rights of individuals in the defense of their property (including the integrity of their own bodies), their freedom of contract, and the equal enjoyment of state protection in these rights. Classical liberalism values the insights of economics and appreciates entrepreneurship broadly construed. It encourages the communities of virtue that emerge through civil society institutions.

WHAT ABOUT SOCIAL JUSTICE?

In John Tomasi's *Free Market Fairness*, he lays out classical liberal thinker after classical liberal thinker arguing that the liberal revolution is by far the greatest thing that could happen to poor people, marginalized people, and oppressed people since it restricts the power of government to oppress you, requires that the law protect you from the oppression of your neighbors, and frees you up to participate in really effective systems of voluntary cooperation, whether these be economic or social. There's John Locke's concern for the "day labourer in England," Bernard Mandeville's "the very Poor" who "Live'd better than the Rich before," and Adam Smith's diatribes against the way economic protectionism benefits the rich and is established at the expense of the poor.[20] Tomasi goes on to find similar examples throughout the works of the American Founders, such as James Madison's defense of "thick economic liberty" because it results in a "great dispersion of property ownership across the entire population."[21]

If classical liberalism is so great for the poor and marginalized, why is it depicted as the enemy of social justice? Actually, it depends on what we mean by social justice.[22] The great classical liberal economist F.A. Hayek pointed out that we cannot engineer a free society and the economy that emerges out of it, and therefore we cannot force certain outcomes, such as the material equality of the citizens, even though their legal equality is the very foundation of the liberal system. If social justice advocates think of material inequality as inherently unjust, they will disapprove of the unpredictable outcomes of free market exchange. Nobody is seriously claiming that people in a society with market exchange deserve what they have in some cosmic sense of the word. They may have worked hard, certainly, but they also definitely benefit from being part of a system that encourages new wealth creation, and they may also benefit from sheer luck; timing, circumstances, or who you know can easily play a part in economic success as well. A free market system doesn't rely on the claim that everyone's property holdings are cosmically just. Classical liberals probably deny that there is any such thing as a cosmically just distribution of property, or if there is, that we could figure it out, or if we could figure it out, that we could make it happen without state tyranny crushing individuals' freedoms and the productive system that arises from them. The point of respecting property rights is to have a system that's relatively obvious and psychologically compelling for everyone, that draws a bright enough line in the sand between our stuff and their stuff that we can live together in peace, and that generally encourages people to be productive by letting them keep their gains from trade.

Surprisingly, socialist thinkers like G. A. Cohen, author of *Why Not Socialism?*, admit as much. Lamenting what he sees as a predatory system, he concedes that "we do not know how to honour personal choice, consistently with equality and community, on a large social scale."[23] Cohen concedes that we don't know how to allocate resources without prices, we don't know how to encourage productivity without private incentives, and we don't know how to have a deeply redistributive state without constant violations of personal freedom. He simply hopes that someday we will somehow overcome these difficulties. However, the idea that technological advancement, for instance, could someday allow for a planned economy is wrongheaded for one simple reason. To quote Hayek, "competition [is] a discovery procedure."[24] That is, the reason that the price system in a free market is the only way to get reliable decisions upon which we can base rational economic choices is because people don't actually know what they prefer until they get the chance to decide. We don't know what needs to be made, which restaurants ought to stay open, how much people will buy, or what they'll be willing to pay for it until we actually let the competitive process that entrepreneurs undergo take place. To really get our heads around the wonders of the price system, see our "Lesson from Classical Liberalism #2" at the end of this chapter, or watch the delightful short animated poem online, "A Wonderful Loaf."

We imagine, however, that we're preaching to the choir. While there are a few die-hard socialists out there, most Americans who care about social justice are not at all interested in perfect material equality. Wisely, they instinctively grasp that a concern about equality isn't really about whether some rich people are richer than other rich people, but rather whether there are people so disadvantaged that they become vulnerable to oppression. Here, classical liberals and social justice advocates can agree that a morally praiseworthy system of justice must be as good as possible for the marginalized. This is one reason why it's so common to see classical liberals and social justice advocates coming together to fight for things like criminal justice reform, educational freedom, easing immigration processes, and neighborhood development. When they disagree on other things, like tax policy or the best form of anti-racism, it's because they disagree on what really works and what doesn't.

THE CLASSICAL LIBERAL TRADITION IN BLACK AMERICA

If the priorities of classical liberals had been opposed to the struggle for Black liberation in America, we wouldn't have a leg to stand on in writing this book, no matter how grand our principles. But nothing could be further from the truth of our history.

Adam Smith's endorsement of free trade in *The Wealth of Nations* necessarily included a powerful condemnation of slavery, on both moral and economic grounds. Inscribed on Smith's grave in Edinburgh are his words: "The property which every man has in his own labour, as it is the original foundation of all other property, so it is the most sacred and inviolable."[25]

It turns out that free market thinkers of the mid-nineteenth century were fiercely anti-slavery, including William Lloyd Garrison, Henry Ward Beecher, Joshua Leavitt, and Ralph Waldo Emerson. These thinkers were followers of "Victorian England's apostle of free trade," Richard Cobden. For these, free trade and abolitionism were both expressions of their Christian commitment to nonviolence. Garrison, the famous publisher of *The Liberator*, described himself as a "radical free trader" who even went so far as desiring the abolition of "all custom-houses [tariff-collection centers], as now constituted, throughout the world"! The Anti-Corn Law League and the Anti-Slavery Society both appealed to a fundamental right of human beings to control their own labor and exchange their wages for whatever they chose.[26] Frederick Douglass met Cobden in England and used his Anti-Corn Law League as a model for abolitionism, and radical Republican anti-slavery senator, Charles Sumner, corresponded with Cobden as well (yes, that Sumner, the one who got caned in the middle of the

Senate after accusing the senator from South Carolina of having an affair with an ugly mistress, that is, slavery).[27]

Classical liberal economist John Stuart Mill was so famous for his anti-slavery and anti-racist views, as a matter of fact, that Thomas Carlyle nicknamed economics "the dismal science" for this very reason. As David Levy explains, "...Carlyle's target was not Malthus [the thinker who predicted mass starvation], but economists such as John Stuart Mill, who argued that it was institutions, not race, that explained why some nations were rich and others poor. Carlyle attacked Mill, not for supporting Malthus's predictions about the dire consequences of population growth, but for supporting the emancipation of slaves. It was this fact—that economics assumed that people were basically all the same, and thus all entitled to liberty—that led Carlyle to label economics 'the dismal science.' Carlyle was not alone in denouncing economics for making its radical claims about the equality of all men. Others who joined him included Charles Dickens and John Ruskin. The connection was so well known throughout the 19th century, that even cartoonists could refer to it, knowing that their audience would get the reference."[28]

Frederick Douglass was a loud and proud classical liberal in every way.[29] He was fully aware of the philosophical alternatives, with both anarchists and socialists mixing in the anti-slavery societies of his day, but he chose liberalism. Douglass was deeply impressed by his first experience in making a contract for work and getting paid, only to have to hand his pay over to his slaveholder. That experience solidified in his mind the idea that one belongs to oneself, along with one's labor, and that to take the fruits of a man's labor away is theft. In his famous speech, "What to a Slave is the Fourth of July?"[30] Douglass asks the crowd if they would have him argue that "man is entitled to liberty? That he is the rightful owner of his own body?... There is not a man beneath the canopy of heaven, that does not know that slavery is wrong for him." Douglass argued explicitly against his socialist friends that property is a natural right and that the main problem with unionism is that it assumes that workers and owners are playing a zero-sum game when they're actually in a mutually beneficial relationship. As to property: "So far from being a sin to accumulate property, it is the plain duty of every man to lay up something for the future." As to the mentality of the unions of his day, their idea that "every piece of bread that goes into the mouth of one man, is so much bread taken out of the mouth of another" was not "villainy" but rather merely "honest stupidity,"[31] since a productive economic system creates new wealth rather than simply redistributing what already exists. Finally, Douglass's push for Black land grants and universal education for Black Americans was framed, not in the language of general welfare, but in the language of straightforward restitution for theft of labor and other crimes against formerly enslaved people.[32]

"Give the Negro fair play," Douglass declared in 1893, "and let him alone." But that was just the issue; the Southern Black codes would not give the Black people fair play, limiting gun rights, voting rights, and economic rights based on color. Douglass's frustration increased as he grew older, but he always said that "[t]he trouble never was in the Constitution, but in the administration of the Constitution."[33]

Oswald Garrison Villard and Moorfield Storey co-founded (along with Du Bois and others) the National Association for the Advancement of Colored People. As a young man and after some disappointing experiences with journalistic ethics, Villard celebrated finding a few papers for which to write in which his colleagues were "…radical on peace and war and on the Negro question; radical in our insistence that the United States stay at home and not go to war abroad and impose its imperialistic will upon Latin-American republics, often with great slaughter. We were radical in our demand for free trade and our complete opposition to the whole protective system."[34] While commentators of our day often seem confused by Villard's and his colleagues' philosophical commitments, they are nothing but a consistently classical liberal commitment to freedom, which includes refraining from violating the freedom of other countries through military involvement with them. Classical liberals oppose both slavery at home and imperialism abroad.

In the late nineteenth century he and Storey both participated in the last gasps of a party straightforwardly aligned with classical liberalism, the Gold Democrats, who "believed 'in the ability of every individual, unassisted, if unfettered by law, to achieve his own happiness' and had upheld his 'right and opportunity peaceably to pursue whatever course of conduct he would, provided such conduct deprived no other individual of the equal enjoyment of the same right and opportunity.' They had stood for 'freedom of speech, freedom of conscience, freedom of trade, and freedom of contract, all of which are implied by the century-old battle-cry of the Democratic Party, 'Individual Liberty.'" Villard and Booker T. Washington worked together to convince President Wilson to turn back his policy of resegregating federal offices and to defend Blacks' rights in the South but were sorely disappointed by Wilson's refusal. Villard wrote a popular biography of John Brown, and his memoirs were called *Fighting Years: Memoirs of a Liberal Editor*, although in later decades of his life he was not as laissez-faire in his economic views as he had been as a young man. On the other hand, Moorfield Storey, a co-founder and the first president of the NAACP, stuck to his classical liberal views with regard to economic rights, civil rights, and just war theory for his whole life. He believed in "pacifism, anti-imperialism, and racial egalitarianism" as well as "laissez-faire," the old term for free trade. As one can imagine, this became increasingly difficult to do, as the rise of New Deal legislation and confidence in big government reached its highest levels in American history. While many were convinced to abandon the laissez-faire, free market perspective, new economic research has shown that Roosevelt's efforts invariably made the Depression last far longer than necessary, and some of the worst offenses against Black property rights and freedom of contract occurred as part of the administration of the New Deal. There is now a hot debate about whether the New Deal was intrinsically or only incidentally racist, but we know for sure that it increased racial disparities unnecessarily by slowing economic growth, excluding the poor, paying farmers not to farm, and flooding farms for the Tennessee Valley Authority (the latter two offenses crushed Black tenant farmers).[35] While it's rarely mentioned today, historian David Beito has chronicled that many prominent Black Republicans persisted in opposing the New Deal, including Zora Neale Hurston. Surely it made some difference that it was the Republicans at that time who were sponsoring anti-lynching legislation while Roosevelt and the Democrats stood by and did nothing.[36]

As the term liberalism began to shift in American politics, the old classical liberal ideas were revived—perhaps in an increasingly simplified form—under the term "libertarian." Rose Wilder Lane helped launch this movement with her book *The Discovery of Freedom* as well as her work in journalism. Lane was converted from communism to libertarianism after a visit to Russia, where a peasant told her that the replacement of his village's tradition of communal values with central planning would never work. He said that "in Moscow there are only men, and man is not God. A man has only a man's head, and one hundred heads together do not make one great head."[37] For many years she wrote for the largest Black newspaper in the nation, the *Pittsburgh Courier*. She was excited to join this diverse set of writers, especially their editor, George S. Schuyler, sometimes known as "the Black H. L. Mencken." Like Lane, Schuyler had also converted from socialist leanings to conservative and libertarian ones, fighting hard against communist infiltration into Black organizations. The *Courier's* "Double V" campaign stood for "victory against fascism abroad and Jim Crow at home." In support of the Double V campaign, Lane claimed that she had finally found "the place where I belong.... Here are Americans who know the meaning of equality and freedom." Like Adam Smith before her, Lane praised the wonder of the market but kept a cold and suspicious eye on "the big boys"—capitalists who gain from their political connections, which we refer to as *cronies* in this book. Ironically, given what we now know about its effects on racial disparities in housing, Lane was fired from the *Courier* for a too-hotly worded column on the evils of zoning. She went on to inspire and help organize many of the mainstays of classical liberal thought still in existence today, such as the Institute for Humane Studies and the Foundation for Economic Education.[38]

We don't have time here to discuss so many others, such as T. R. M. Howard and his influence in the civil rights movement or civil libertarian Nat Hentoff's writing and activism on behalf of Black Americans and other voiceless groups. It's true that in the '70s and '80s anti-communism (a value classical liberals shared with the vast majority of Black Americans) seemed to take center stage. However, libertarians were among the earliest to push back against the drug war, as well as investing heavily in the fight against the rise of mass incarceration, both issues that affect all Americans, but Blacks disproportionately. There was also a split in sensibilities among civil rights activists themselves: those who felt that economic government programs constituted the natural next step for Black Americans to take in the fight for civil rights (MLK was moving in this direction), and those who emphasized the older model of Black economic empowerment and strong civil society institutions such as religious involvement and family (the view of Malcolm X, for instance). The emphasis that we will place on solutions such as the neighborhood-stabilization movement follows the latter approach, appealing to civil rights activists like John M. Perkins and Robert Woodson, who became heroes of holistic neighborhood development and community anti-violence efforts.

Perhaps the idea of classical liberalism and Black liberation seems like an awkward mash-up of two disparate traditions, but we believe we can demonstrate in the following chapters two central claims: that classical liberalism is a prominent player in America's history of Black liberation, and that it also guides us toward the best solutions for today and tomorrow too.

Lessons in Classical Liberalism #1: Emergent Order and the Information Problem

Hayek takes it for granted that, in a free society, there are as many personal aims being pursued as there are people. Everybody has their own personal goals, but they're also coordinating with one another in order to achieve them. This sounds like total chaos, and in fact, some classic critiques of the free society, such as that of Karl Marx, do claim that it's too messy and disorganized. But Hayek (following his teacher Ludwig von Mises, as well as Scottish Enlightenment figures like Adam Ferguson[39]) counters that the pursuit of disparate aims can lead to a highly complex web of orderly interactions, as long as a few basic, abstract rules are in place. Everybody needs to follow certain basic social rules that are general in nature, like honoring one's contracts and respecting others' property rights. Abstract rules aren't there to achieve any concrete goals of particular people or groups of people. Rather, they form a kind of infrastructure within which every person or group can pursue their own aspirations.

When Hayek talks about individual aims, he's not necessarily referring to the big disagreements we have with one another over religion or the good life or politics. He means mundane things, like how different individuals want to be teachers or start a bakery or form a club or join a church. Hayek means that the most basic, everyday features of our lives require some set of general rules by which we all operate together in society so that we can go about our business. While it may be true that we can't agree on our conception of the good human life, what's more to the point is that we can't agree on how many teachers, bakeries, clubs, or churches there should be, where they should be located, and what they should busy themselves doing. Rather than trying to get us all to agree on such a huge variety of things, a free society simply allows us to pursue these things ourselves, as long as we're peaceful in doing so.

What's so special about this idea? In the earlier part of the twentieth century, it was taken for granted within the progressive movement that the increasing complexity of modern life required more and more central planning by experts.[40] Hayek's insight leads to the opposite view: the more complex a system becomes, the more general and abstract the rules must be. This is what frees up individuals and groups to innovate, adapt, and evolve in order to navigate their ever-changing world. Hayek used the term "spontaneous order" for the beautiful and complex web of peaceful human interaction that arises from the right set of underlying rules. The order that ordinary people bring about is not spontaneous in the sense that it comes out of nowhere; we make plans and thoughtfully carry them out. It's spontaneous in that it arises from the bottom up rather than from the top down. In order to avoid confusion over this point, many social scientists have shifted to the term "emergent order," which better captures how a set of abstract rules allows the order to emerge: people can evolve and adapt to changes in the most agile way, without the necessity of any one central organizer to make it happen.

In contrast to this emergent order, Hayek cites the communist and socialist experiments in command and control economies that were then being tried in the USSR and China, and in more limited ways elsewhere as well. In these experiments, the assumed chaos, waste, and inequality that arises in a system of free association were supposed to be overcome by the scientific planning of benevolent comrades.

We're all familiar with the moral arguments against these systems: in order to plan an economy, you've got to plan people's lives—what they learn, where they work, where they live, and so on: a great offense against human dignity. But Hayek's genius was to show that there's a purely practical argument against these systems as well. That is, centrally planned economies, whether they'd end up being bad or good for people in theory, just aren't possible. In fact, it's not possible to plan an economy to achieve some conception of a good or scientific or perfectly egalitarian society, because the central planner doesn't have the information to do so. This is Hayek's "information problem."

Lessons in Classical Liberalism #2: The Information Problem

The easiest way to understand the information problem is to ask yourself how you make decisions. If someone owned a bakery, for instance, how would she decide how much to make, which types of pastries, whether to increase or decrease advertising, or whether to continue in business? Those can be tough questions for any baker! But whatever she's considering, we know she has to start with two fundamental questions: How much will it cost, and will it pay off? So, it turns out that when doing any kind of economic planning, we always start with prices. That baker will be asking herself about her customer base, their favorite things, how the business is doing so far, and ultimately, whether she's covering all her costs. If she's spending more than she's bringing in, and she already tried new pastries or different advertisements or a different location but it hasn't worked, she should probably just close up shop and try something else. Without these numbers on hand, though, she actually can't tell what she should do. These numbers, these incredible little conveyors of important information, these data for our economic calculations we call "prices." And if the baker cannot plan her bakery without prices, how can the central planner plan an entire economy without them?

One more thing. We all learned in our eighth-grade economics courses that prices are generated by supply and demand. But think just a little more deeply about what that means. In order to find out what the relevant price is for their planning purposes, people's exchanges have to create prices in the first place. They must be able to freely trade items with one another at rates to which they voluntarily agree. And in order to have that ability, they have to be able to own the things they are exchanging, so that the exchanges are genuinely up to them. This gets us to something more profound than we might have expected from a discussion of a baker using prices to figure out her bottom line. What we've discovered is that the institution of private property, as well as all the freedoms involved in making exchanges of our property with other people, is totally fundamental to the generation of prices. Prices, in turn, are the information hidden in our complex web of economic exchanges, the very information, in fact, that the central planner does not, and cannot, have. Without private property and free exchange then, there is no such thing as a free or prosperous society.

This point will come up over and over again in our discussion of the history of Black Americans as well as their hopes for the future. While political rights such as voting are certainly important, economic freedom weaves more immediately into all our day-to-day business. It's economic freedom—the freedom to own things, trade them or keep them as you wish, and labor where you will—that defines much of the story of Black oppression through exclusion from economic freedoms, as well as Black liberation through economic freedom and empowerment.

Lessons in Classical Liberalism #3: The Great Enrichment

It's hard for modern people in developed economies to imagine the life of an average human prior to a few hundred years ago. Life expectancy was low, mothers died in childbirth, children died in infancy, plagues and famine decimated whole populations, and the combination of all these factors with intense violence between neighboring societies kept the earth's population at a minimum. It is no exaggeration at all to say that the last 200 to 250 years constitute something miraculous. The septupling of human population (from around one billion to now far over seven billion people) has coincided with the near-elimination of abject poverty (from basically 100 percent of the population to now around 8 percent). We've seen plummeting child and maternal death rates, skyrocketing life expectancy, and the emergence of the global middle class. That's right: global inequality has never been lower, as 50 percent of the world's population falls into the category of the middle class within their own economies. To say that this is historically unheard of is a gross understatement; better to say that it exceeds our ancestor's wildest imaginations.

Surely there is no better explanation for all this than the rise of global markets. Free trade across borders has launched the world into a new era of the division of labor and specialization. This increased economic efficiency has, quite frankly, made the entire world quite rich. In many Asian countries, for instance, the last forty years represent a paradigm shift, as families have moved in just two generations from subsistence farming to a modern economy with schools, hospitals, technology, and creature comforts. Even those areas, such as sub-Saharan Africa, that had long struggled to participate in the global economy are now seeing wages and life expectancy rise at an astonishing rate.

We do not deny that humans have, wrongly, oppressed and exploited one another. What we do claim, however, is that the common association of these activities with free markets is entirely wrongheaded. That's why the world's long history of colonialism and imperialism never pulled anybody out of the grinding poverty of the human experience; great rulers died of diseases that you or I would treat with antibiotics. Louis the XIV of France, who famously said, "I am the State!" couldn't keep his wine from freezing in his wine glass at dinner—there was no such thing as a central heating system. The areas that struggle the most economically are those that lack Hayek's underlying institutions. Economic development experts tell us that unstable institutions and political corruption undermine social trust and block the efforts of entrepreneurs, causing the persistence of poverty in these places.

We argue that the peaceful exchange of the market is a high-water mark of civilization and that the creativity unleashed in commercial societies puts to bed many of humanity's most vicious tendencies toward violent domination, theft, and deceit.

In light of these three lessons, our great complaint against progressives, many (though not all) purveyors of social justice, and socialists is that they have not honestly grappled with the concept of an emergent order, the impossibility of central planning because of the information problem, the problem of unintended consequences of well-intentioned policy, or the incompatibility of their plans with the freedoms that arise from the legal and institutional mechanisms that lead to prosperity. This is not a mere quibble. We maintain, both as a matter of theory and with regard to the empirical evidence we offer in this book, that the very institutions that some of these theorists abhor are the keys to human flourishing in the Black American community, and that their plans to compromise and undermine those institutions have been, and continue to be, one of the causes of Black oppression and suffering. That is, we are not merely saying that massive redistribution would be nice but that it won't work; we are saying that the empowerment of historically marginalized communities through the removal of government oppression in the criminal justice and education systems, through property ownership, asset accumulation, and freedom of contract, and through cultural repair of their social institutions—the great values of a classical liberal social order—constitute a substantive plan for genuine liberation.

America and Black America overlap in such a way that they can never really be conceptualized apart from one another. The greatness of Black America is the greatness of America itself. We call on every American, of every race, color, or creed, to advocate for and get personally involved in the recommendations we make below. Rather than get into the weeds of particular policies and programs, we outline broad areas of reform and point the reader to helpful resources should they wish to go deeper, peppering these hopeful plans for moving forward in those chapters where they seemed to be most relevant. We discuss:

I.   leaving failed solutions behind,
II. doing justice to our past,
III. creating a more inclusive economy,
IV. reforming our criminal justice system,
V.   setting our education system free, and
VI. stabilizing struggling neighborhoods.

We have demonstrated in this work that the Black community has already developed within itself deep and abiding resources for cultural, economic, and spiritual advancement. We don't need to invent any wheels here. We need to free and empower what already exists.

Chapter 2

Liberation Through Abolition: The Black American Pro-Constitutional Tradition

Should you, my lord, while you peruse my song,
Wonder from whence my love of Freedom sprung,
Whence flow these wishes for the common good,
By feeling hearts alone best understood,
I, young in life, by seeming cruel fate
Was snatch'd from Afric's fancy'd happy seat:
What pangs excruciating must molest,
What sorrows labour in my parent's breast?
Steel'd was that soul and by no misery mov'd
That from a father seiz'd his babe belov'd:
Such, such my case. And can I then but pray
Others may never feel tyrannic sway?
—Phillis Wheatley, 1772

The spirit of our age is reactionary. Contenders ping-pong ever more absolutist accounts of history and sociology to shore up their deepest commitments, creating a snowball effect of overstatement, dismissiveness, and rage. Nuance and complexity are not on the menu.

Let us compare two efforts at educating young people about America's history: the textbook *Virginia: History, Government, Geography* (1956) was in use in the public school system as late as the 1970s. Slave life is described as a "happy and prosperous" improvement on life in Africa, with loving, familial relationships between master and slave (p. 373). The accompanying picture depicts a Black man in a suit with a beautifully dressed family surrounding him, shaking the hand of a white master in a top hat in front of the fine-looking boat from which he presumably just disembarked.[41]

In fact, the Middle Passage was a harrowing death trap, and America's slave system depended on the ever-present threat of violence to control the slave population—hardly a picture of beloved rescuers and their grateful servants. Even a "benevolent" master, who saw his role as one of caretaker, could rarely avoid the financial temptation to separate enslaved families, a central trauma of the slave experience. Not only does the claim to ownership of persons violate human dignity in and of itself, but the American system left enslaved Blacks without the protection of the law in any way, vulnerable to the constant threat of rape, beatings, family separation, and the maws of the hounds that chased runaways. Viable plans for rebellions against this oppression, and several large-scale attempts, though ultimately unsuccessful, caused waves of terror among the slaveholding class, who contorted their legal and economic systems to maintain their power.

The 1619 Project, a series of essays in the *New York Times* that serves as the basis for some public school curriculum today, attempts to correct the kind of academic fraud described above by centering the Black experience in American history. Unfortunately, it, too, makes historically inaccurate claims in order to weave a narrative that makes maintaining slavery the central concern of America's Founders as well as its economic system.

We hope in this volume to counter the reactionary tendency to pick one's favorite facts (or worse, distort the facts) in order to weave an oversimplified story. Instead, we try to squarely face what is true and false in each extreme in order to tell the truth, however messy. But perhaps more to the point, telling the messy story describes the approach of the greatest heroes of Black America and of the movements to which they subscribed in the hope of Black liberation. Albert Murray claimed that Black Americans have produced "the most complicated culture, and therefore the most complicated sensibility in the western world."[42] When it came to the question of America's unique legacy of freedom versus America's unjust and cruel treatment of Blacks, these icons of Black liberation chose a both/and rather than an either/or approach, in keeping with the complexity of the Black American experience. Men like Frederick Douglass, Ralph Ellison, and Martin Luther King Jr., and women like Phillis Wheatley and Zora Neale Hurston asserted that the explicit principles of the American founding experiment were eminently praiseworthy, while at the same time existing in painful contradiction to the legal and practical realities of slavery and Jim Crow. As Douglass put it, the problem has not been the Constitution, but rather "whether the American people have honesty enough, loyalty enough, honor enough, patriotism enough, to live up to their own Constitution."

In an understandable desire to give a just account of the victims of oppression in American history, many progressive narratives attempt to entirely re-center the story on oppression. But in doing so, they lose the very tension that made the treatment of Black Americans stand out as morally unacceptable. They lose the moral leverage upon which both the abolitionists and the civil rights movement appealed to the broader population. An important question in any historical analysis is, "Compared to what?" Most human societies have enslaved other humans, for instance, and many continued to do so both during the period in which slavery was legal in America and right up to the current day. By insisting on such high ideals of liberty and equality, the Founders forced themselves, Americans, and outside observers of America to compare its tangled reality with its unique and exemplary political claims. Only by reference to these standards could the hypocrisy of the American system draw the moral ire it did.

A separate but related arena for contention involves America's deeply commercial economy and culture. What if oppression is profitable? The plain truth is that it often is, and oppression of Black people, particularly under slavery and the neo-slavery of convict leasing, made some people very rich. As owners of legal capital in other persons, these people can in some sense be accurately referred to as "capitalists," creating an association between the worst sorts of injustice and an entire economic system. Today, the term "capitalism" is often contrasted with socialism, but we won't be able to make sense of our current debates without introducing an older dichotomy: free trade versus protectionism.[43]

Lessons in Classical Liberalism #4: Adam Smith, Economic Protectionism, and Slavery

Adam Smith wasn't contemplating socialism in 1776 when he published *An Inquiry into the Nature and Causes of the Wealth of Nations*. Rather, he simply tried to account for the stunning gains in wealth that regular, everyday people were just then beginning to experience. Normal people—workers, peasants, nobodies— had always been so desperately poor, scratching their living out of the earth from sunup to sundown. How was it that their wages were improving, that they were eating better, that they had better shelter and better clothes? What could possibly explain this shift in their fortunes? In addressing this question, Smith conveyed some of the most fundamental principles of economics: the division of labor, price theory, and free trade.

In Smith's day, the most prominent economic theory was "mercantilism," or to use a more familiar term, protectionism. In this view, a government raises all sorts of barriers or "protections," such as tariffs, to ensure that the country exports more than it imports and piles up the money gained in the form of gold and silver. Protectionists believed that these barriers kept a state strong by protecting its domestic industries from competition. Smith countered that protectionist policies such as tariffs block the efficiency created by the division of labor by making it harder for people to trade across borders. This, in turn, limits their ability to adjust in an agile way to changing circumstances of supply and demand. Instead of making the nation strong and rich, these policies make the nation poorer.

As mentioned previously, Adam Smith was an abolitionist, because he considered the most basic form of property to be that which we hold in our own selves. Furthermore, like all forms of economic protectionism and theft, slavery enriches a few while impoverishing the economy more broadly. The term "capitalism" has only confused our national conversation, as to some it connotes support of whatever is good for owners, while to others it refers to Smith's notion of free trade. In fact, free trade often presents a threat to owners as entrepreneurs are allowed to enter the market to compete with them and political protections in their favor are denied. In this volume, we use the terms *free trade* or *free markets* to refer to a system of rights to one's bodily integrity, one's property, and freedom of contract, as well as to a cultural appreciation for the role of the entrepreneur and the vocation of business. Special legal protections for owners may benefit particular people at everyone else's expense, but there's a better term for that than "capitalism." That's called "cronyism." It's a kind of political entrepreneurship, a way of seeking privilege through political connection. These are not just quibbles over terminology; rather, these distinctions get at the very heart of economic wisdom.

THE NEW HISTORY OF CAPITALISM

In one of the most historically contentious pieces in the 1619 Project's collection, Matthew Desmond appeals to the work of a school of historians variously referred to as the Slavery and Capitalism school, or the New History of Capitalism school. In his article "In order to understand the brutality of American capitalism, you have to start on the plantation," Desmond relates modern corporate oversight of employees to the claim that the 400 percent improvement in cotton yields between 1800 and 1860 were the result of improved torture techniques—a direct reference to the work of Ed Baptist in *The Half Has Never Been Told*. Desmond does not mention that Baptist was deeply and consistently criticized for serious economic mistakes throughout this work, including by the very authors from whom he got his 400 percent statistic: Alan Olmstead and Paul Rhode. They countered that these gains were accomplished through improved agricultural techniques, including the breeding of seeds that created much larger cotton bolls. In their withering review, these experts on the economics of slavery declared Baptist's whole book "flawed beyond repair" and other economics of slavery experts agreed.[44] The most egregious claim they criticize involves miscalculating the proportion of the cotton industry to the American economy. Baptist claims that cotton was a full 50 percent of the entire American economy in this period. The reality is closer to 5 percent, meaning that Baptist was off by tenfold.[45] Others in the same literature habitually overstate the significance of slave labor to the overall economy, while refusing to engage with the economists pressing them on their claims.[46] As a matter of fact, the entire New History of Capitalism school, whose main thesis is the inextricable association of capitalism with slavery, has been roundly criticized by experts as being woefully unfamiliar with the economic literature on slavery.[47] Their unwillingness to correct these figures in light of serious scholarly challenges is no longer just a matter of esoteric academic debate. Ta-Nehisi Coates, for instance, famously quoted the 50 percent line in a congressional hearing on reparations in 2019, referencing Baptist by name.

Some have accused commentators on the 1619 Project of nitpicking when it comes to these historical mistakes. They argue that scholars want to use these issues to discredit the entire project because they don't like the shift in narrative that the project suggests. Instead, we want to ask why just some of the claims made in the project seem so liable to historical blunders, while others fare quite well under scrutiny. One cannot properly understand American history without understanding slavery! This is transparently correct. So why exaggerate the role of slavery beyond the prominent place it ought already to hold? One possibility is that the authors of the controversial articles are leveraging the American Black experience for a separate ideological agenda. In this case, Desmond and the New History of Capitalism scholars pursue an anti–free market agenda, blaming slavery for the parts of contemporary American economic policy that are less politically progressive than Europe's. In their efforts to malign the free market by associating it with slavery, they have failed to engage with the economic literature, thus making serious mistakes that undermine the narrative they're advancing. We propose to reject and replace a narrative that slavery is essential for understanding the American economic system. We argue that this narrative belies a profound misunderstanding of the principles of free market economics, which must regard slavery as a particularly tragic form of the protectionism that free marketers condemn. Instead, nations that pursue economic freedom *for every person* consistently create more wealth and better outcomes for the well-being of their members.

SLAVERY WAS PROFITABLE BUT FOR WHOM?

To be fair to the critics, it's true that many classical liberal economists thought slavery is, in and of itself, unprofitable, but this is not always the case. In their logic, enslaved people have no incentive to work hard except the lash; they receive none of the gains from harder or smarter work. Free laborers, on the other hand, will be more inventive and better motivated by the opportunity for greater reward. Furthermore, free laborers are far more likely to be well-matched to their work, since they can move around in order to find the best employment for their talents. In search of higher wages, they will increase their human capital by educating themselves and learning to operate productive machinery. To Smith and his fellow travelers, it looked like an open and shut case: free labor is not only the moral option, it's also more efficient and more productive.

They weren't exactly wrong either. It just depends on who gets to enjoy the profits. The distinction between slaveholder's profits on the one hand and productivity for the whole economy on the other has been a source of major confusion in the literature on this topic. When Robert Fogel and Stanley Engerman published *Time on the Cross*, demonstrating without any real doubt that plantation owners did quite well for themselves and that the plantation system was incredibly productive, it inspired real dismay, sending shock waves through academia and even in the popular news. We knew slavery was immoral, but we thought it was inefficient too—that it was just a bad way of arranging one's economic system. Over time, the main thrust of the analysis from *Time on the Cross*, that slavery was fairly productive, has been upheld, while other claims from the book are more doubtful.[48] What does that mean for an economic argument against slavery?

It turns out that it doesn't mean much. In retrospect, we might not have been so surprised that slavery could produce a lot of cotton and make plantation owners rich.[49] After all, planters could force enslaved people to work far longer hours than a free laborer would be willing to do, or if he was willing, he would require significant overtime pay. Slaves also worked at far younger ages and kept the elderly busy with any work they were able to do. Furthermore, all women worked, even just before and just after childbirth. Indeed, "[t]wo thirds of slaves participated in the labor force, compared with only one-third for free populations, North and South."[50] Planters could get away with very low costs by giving enslaved people in-kind goods like food and extremely basic clothes and housing. The costs of this upkeep fell far below the wages they would have had to pay a free laborer.[51] Some have objected that this fails to account for the upfront expense of paying the slave trader for the value of the slave. That's true, but it's also true that planters treated their slave property as a form of speculation: the economic value of the slave was a huge part of the way they built the investment portfolio that they hoped to hand down to their heirs. In other words, they treated slave property in much the same way that many people today treat home ownership: not as a liability but as an investment asset.[52]

Since picking cotton doesn't require much education or differentiation of skills, the fact that the slaves weren't allowed to learn and couldn't shift jobs according to their talents had little effect on the planters. Cotton picking also required large gangs of laborers that could be immediately available at particular times of the year, making slavery an exploitative but economically viable option for running a cotton business.

But economists aren't actually all that interested in how to make particular businesses run well. As a matter of fact, they don't even care if any particular business continues to exist. They're interested in how to make an entire economy run well. That includes thinking about which institutions we need in order to encourage efficiency and innovation so that people who are not especially wealthy or powerful can have good lives. As Adam Smith would say, "Little else is requisite to carry a state to the highest degree of opulence from the lowest barbarism but peace, easy taxes, and a tolerable administration of justice: all the rest being brought about by the natural course of things."[53] And as Nathan Nunn, an expert in the economics of slavery, succinctly concluded after tracking slave use and the economy of the following decades Southern county by Southern county, "[t]he data shows that slave use is negatively correlated with subsequent economic development."[54]

Lessons in Classical Liberalism #5: The Broken Window Fallacy

When it comes to systems that lack a "tolerable administration of justice," economists ask us to compare what is to what could have been. The nineteenth-century economic journalist, Frédéric Bastiat, explained this technique in his famous essay, "That Which is Seen and That Which is Unseen." We see the benefit to the contractor when he gets a bunch of work fixing windows after a riot. What we don't see are all the ways those families could have spent that money if they hadn't had to deal with the destruction of their windows. We don't see the new shoes for the kids or savings in the bank and earning interest. Those are just a few of the possibilities that families had to forego when they were forced to spend money on repairs. This is where we get the term "the broken window fallacy." Bastiat wanted to help people see that just because *someone* in an economy is benefitting from a particular circumstance that does not mean that the circumstance is beneficial overall. Someone else is losing: the shoe store, the banker, or an entrepreneur who went to that bank for a loan. At the same time, the family who had to forego the shoes or the savings to pay for the new window loses as well. (And we haven't even mentioned the costs of increased policing to deal with future riotous window breakers.) If the window had never been broken at all, more people would have gotten what they wanted. We see what the contractor gains, but we don't see what all the others lose. That makes it easy to conclude that there was something positive about the window getting broken in the riot, when in reality it's exactly what it sounds like: costly destruction.

This is just what must be done when we consider whether slavery is profitable. Most slaveholders in antebellum America made money, and some became the richest men in the country. Taking up the economic way of thinking, however, we ask ourselves whether slavery, as an institution, was more efficient and productive for the whole economy than a system of free labor would have been.

We're taking a purely economic approach for the moment, but we'll soon see that the underlying moral questions are more deeply connected to the economic question than it might appear. For now, forgive the cold, calculated language of economics. It rightly disturbs us to talk in this cavalier way about traffic in human persons, but the upshot of doing so is to show that oppressing people is no way to build a prosperous economy. Slavery is morally condemnable no matter its economic consequences, but it's still worthwhile to correct the record: its economic consequences are bad for almost every single person involved.

First, we make sure to recall that even if the loss of slave labor had cost the South its cotton business, Southerners still would have busied themselves doing something, probably growing flax or wool. While these crops may not have been as profitable as cotton, remember that the relevant difference is the difference in profitability between cotton and flax or wool, not the difference between having a cotton business and having nothing. The same goes for the slave trade. Absent the possibility of trading in human persons, merchants would have busied themselves buying and selling the next most valuable commodity. In this way, we can roughly calculate the marginal value of slavery, as economists put it. Marginal value is the value of something in comparison to the next best alternative. Let us assume that there would be some real economic loss in growing something besides cotton. It was very popular, after all. Now we must compare that loss in profits to the costs of slavery itself and ask ourselves which is greater. The costs of slavery can be categorized under deadweight loss, privilege seeking, and negative externalities, although there are certainly more types of loss we could explore if we had the space to do so.

DEADWEIGHT LOSS[55]

In his article, "Deadweight Loss and the American Civil War," Jeffrey Hummel argues that:

> [t]wo broad positions have dominated the history of economic thought with respect to chattel slavery. The view of the classical economists, dating back as far as Adam Smith and including a good many abolitionists, was that slavery was inefficient and therefore unprofitable. The contrasting position of the new economic historians, most closely identified with Robert Fogel and Stanley Engerman, is that slavery was profitable and therefore efficient. Both positions are partly wrong (as well as partly right). Southern slavery was indeed profitable but nevertheless inefficient; it operated like other obvious practices—from piracy through monopoly to government subsidies—where individual gains do not translate into social benefits. In the terminology of economics, it was a system that

imposed significant "deadweight loss" on the southern economy, despite being lucrative for slaveholders.

The term "deadweight loss" refers to situations in which too much or too little is produced.[56] It must be taken into account that slaves were coerced into working far longer hours than they would have done if they had been free wage laborers (we can confirm this by paying attention to their preference for more leisure after the war).[57] However, this does not mean that these long hours were spent efficiently; after all, enslaved people could not invest in their own human capital (education) nor could they go where their labor was most sought after and earn more. Since the enslaved resented their enslavement, they would often purposefully underproduce. After all, slaveholders made them work as many hours as possible anyway and for no greater reward. So the slave system created losses all around by taking enslaved people away from better uses for their labor, making them give up leisure they would have preferred had they been free to choose, forbidding improvement of their human capital, and incentivizing them to create fewer or worse products with the effort they did put out. Remember that "efficiency" is always in terms of some goal. For economists, the goal is always the maximization of people's preferences. And the preferences of the enslaved count just as much as anyone else's preferences in the economic calculus.

Furthermore, they were "compensated" only in terms of food, clothing, and shelter. While it may be true that, due to the immediate availability of food on Southern farms, most slaves ate fairly well,[58] there is every reason to think that their compensation under a system of wage labor would have been much higher, particularly since difficult and risky jobs usually extract a higher wage. The desperation of white planters after the war to bid laborers away from other planters or try to limit workers' movement (we'll hear more about this phenomenon in the next chapter) just goes to show that had they been free to move around and make enforceable contracts, they could have bid up their wages. Hummel estimates that the deadweight loss of income (or the income-equivalent of preferred leisure) can be calculated at somewhere between $52 million and $190 million. For some sense of reference, 1860 dollars would now be worth thirty-one times this amount, or between $1.6 billion and $5.9 billion today. Economic costs caused by the trauma of being enslaved, both during and after legal slavery, are beyond calculation. Enslaved people experience high rates of PTSD, addiction, illness, and suicide, all of which crush economic flourishing for them personally, removing their contributions from the economy, and some of which fall on the community in costs of care.[59] As Henry George put it, "The enslavement of part of their number could not increase the wealth of a people, for more than the slaveholders gained the enslaved would lose."[60]

The cost to the state of enforcing a coercive system Hummel estimates at between $64 and $210 million ($2 billion and $6.5 billion today). This might include: overseers, man hunters, slave codes (made particularly confusing and complicated by the nonsensical legal situation of "property" that has his or her own volition), legal costs of both those laws and the prosecution of slave rescuers, military defenses against acts of sabotage and rebellion as well as the destruction of the acts themselves, police costs for protecting free Blacks from re-enslavement, commerce bans on abolitionists or potential abolitionists, and colonization schemes.[61] We must remember here that these costs were borne by everyone in the country, but the gains from such enforcement redounded only to slaveholders. Between 1791 and 1861, the US federal government alone spent $51 million on enforcement, or 2.8 percent of federal government expenditures, according to political scientist David Ericson.[62]

Finally, there remained a cost to poor whites in the South, even though it is incomparable with the losses experienced by the enslaved. The Southern economy suffered such that the free labor wages of whites were bid down by being in competition with slave labor. These non-slaveholders also overwhelmingly paid the costs of the slave patrols (going after runaways, breaking up gatherings, conducting random searches, and suppressing insurrections), as participation was compulsory for all able-bodied males. Increasingly, the plight of those who were, even then, referred to as "poor white trash" is getting more attention from historians. There is increasing evidence of friendship and cooperation among poor white and enslaved Black people in endeavors such as underground markets. These partnerships posed a constant threat to the planter class and their "plain folk" middle-class allies. We now know that elites purposefully alienated poor whites and Blacks from one another as a form of social control.[63] So there's significant income loss to poor white Southerners, the loss of their own freedom to military demands that had no benefit for them, and the imposition of a cultural system that undermined their voluntary economic networks. Poor white and Black Southerners would go on to suffer economically during and after the Civil War. Sherman's scorched-earth policies wrought—even according to his own claims—$100 million in damage ($1.6 billion in 2020 dollars), and economists estimate that the consequences persisted until at least 1920.[64]

If we add up the various forms of loss described here, they account for more than a fifth of the Southern economy, according to Hummel.

PRIVILEGE SEEKING

There's a category of economic waste that economists unhelpfully have named "rent-seeking," but which we will refer to here as privilege seeking, although in popular parlance we might just say "cronyism."[65] Assuming a generally just system in which the rules are applied consistently to everyone, privilege seeking is the phenomenon in which some try to rig the political rules or the economic environment in their own favor, not by creating a better widget, so to speak, but by messing with the system of rights. Mostly, when we think of privilege seeking we think of lobbying, whether one is lobbying to get government subsidies, to establish regulations that one's smaller competitors won't be able to keep up with, to put in place protective tariffs for one's products, and so on. The counter-lobbying is wasteful too, as those who are being oppressed or extorted by an unfair privilege have to lobby to defend themselves, rather than just being able to go about their business. In the case of slavery, the rules were deeply unjust from the get-go, and the Southern planters were dug in enough that only rarely did anyone deem it worth their time to try to change them through political channels. But the existence of this persistent injustice created the constant need to shield the privilege against slaves' inevitable desire for freedom. On the one hand, these efforts include beatings and other punishments, the hiring of cruel overseers, the expense of slave catchers, the twisting of religion to justify these practices, energy spent on persuading others that slavery was acceptable, and more. On the other hand, the enslaved as well as the abolitionists expended resources to try to escape, to sabotage the enslavers' projects, to run the Underground Railroad, to finance rebellions, and to publish and persuade on abolitionism.

The main privilege-seeking cost associated with the institution of slavery, however, was the cost of the Civil War. Direct military costs combined with the cost of the associated economic destruction (for both sides) are estimated by economists at around $9.5 billion in 1861 dollars, or $285 billion in 2021 dollars.[66] While a few have argued that the war somehow helped America economically, say, by speeding up the industrialization process, economists respond that such changes were already well underway and that the war made little difference. Instead, the extended costs of economic destruction, especially in the South, persisted for a century. Tragically, Sherman's slash-and-burn vengeance contributed to the impoverishment of the newly emancipated Black population by leaving them in a destroyed economy. We ought to keep this privilege-seeking insight in mind as we move forward in history as well. The energy and resources expended to assert white supremacy in the South were immense. Whites lobbied for an endless train of legal changes, including Black-only gun laws, laws that required employers' permission to change jobs, extra voting restrictions, pig laws, vagrancy laws, and eventually, the whole infrastructure of Jim Crow's apartheid-like system. The entire civil rights movement can be understood as a grand counter-lobbying effort as well. The relevant thought here is to imagine all the possible uses of the resources spent on these efforts had the legal situation of Black Americans been settled justly. In comparison to a baseline of settled justice, all these expenses count as waste.

NEGATIVE EXTERNALITIES

"Whatever of mechanical talent or
intellect, capable of illustrating a nation,
there is in the three millions of slaves is
lost for ever for want of education...."
—Cassius Clay, 1848

In his excellent work on worldwide slavery, *The Poverty of Slavery: How Unfree Labor Pollutes the Economy*, Robert E. Wright presents a detailed accounting of the negative externalities imposed by slavery. Negative externalities are costs of an exchange that are borne by someone other than the parties to the exchange. Pollution is the classic example, which is why Wright appeals to the metaphor in his book's title. Wright's work not only adds to an appropriate accounting of slavery's costs in American history, but it reminds us that the economic analysis of American slavery will not be so different from slavery elsewhere in the world. Although American slavery was especially brutal, it operated similarly as far as economics is concerned. American slavery created the same expropriated profits for slaveholders and the same society-wide costs for the American South as it did—and still does—in other slave economies. Wright divides the negative externalities into several categories. The first deals with the negative impacts on descendants of the enslaved, on potentially enslaved people, on enslaved people's place of origin, and on slaveholder culture. The second deals with effects on population growth and free labor. Third, he claims that the slave system stymies the development of agriculture, education, infrastructure, and technology. Finally, he argues that it increases wealth disparity, and degrades governance and institutional quality. Wright is most discouraged by the contemplation of opportunity costs, though. The term "opportunity cost" refers to the things we could have done if we hadn't decided to take the particular course that we chose. When we imagine a free America in which Black people were confident in their rights and free to live as they chose, we see the creativity, the invention, the social contribution of a huge number of people that we surely missed out on because they were not free. Who can know what might have been?

We've already mentioned psychological effects on the enslaved themselves in our section on deadweight losses, since those were a direct cost of the enslavement. Indirectly, formerly enslaved people and the descendants of slaves were adversely affected by a lack of capital, racism, and social stigma. These had clear economic effects, as both the Freedmen's Bureau and Northern religious organizations spent millions to educate them, only to have their investment dashed by the iron grip former slaveholders reasserted on the legal and political system. Without material capital, newly freed Black Americans could not buy land, and racism made it almost impossible even if they did have money.

Remaining economically dependent on their former slaveholders, and without real legal protections, American Blacks entered a period of quasi-slavery.

Those who are thinking of the planters' defense that slaves were better off here than they had been in Africa, consider this: the development of the African economy was itself more decelerated by slavery than any other continent. One economist, Nathan Nunn, has even demonstrated that the greater the number of people kidnapped for the slave trade in a particular region, the lower its economic prosperity *today*.[67] The population of Africa was devastated by the slave trade, retarding its economic growth long after the trade became technically illegal. In Western Africa, where males were preferred for trade to the New World, the sex ratio dropped to as low as fifty to one hundred. (The opposite was true in East Africa, where women were preferred to men and shipped to Arab nations.) This kind of massive and lopsided depopulation completely destabilized institutions and led to famine, thus exacerbating the dependence on the slave trade, creating yet more inter-ethnic violence, and creating a vicious cycle of economic backwardness. Once-proud crops of oranges, limes, plantains, cotton, sugar, indigo, and sugar cane were abandoned to pursue slaving. Slave modes of production persisted even after the slave trade died down, as huge leaps forward in development had been entirely missed by portions of the African population. To this very day, former slaving centers have "less schooling, less literacy, less formal employment, lower levels of economic freedom, and lower per capita output."[68] Not only do these costs affect the well-being of huge portions of Africa, but think of the missed opportunities for wholesome trade, and the billions of dollars in the efforts of nongovernmental organizations and state-to-state aid that have been spent on the continent. After escaping the bonds of colonialism in the twentieth century but associating their slave history with capitalism, many African countries adopted disastrous socialist policies, sinking into worse economic decline and social unrest. Finally, today, Africa's economic prospects look truly hopeful.[69]

Slaveholders themselves were also negatively impacted by the practice, as Frederick Douglass starkly presents in the figure of his mistress, Mrs. Auld, who at their first meeting was so well-mannered: "But, alas! this kind heart had but a short time to remain such. The fatal poison of irresponsible power was already in her hands, and soon commenced its infernal work. That cheerful eye, under the influence of slavery, soon became red with rage; that voice, made all of sweet accord, changed to one of harsh and horrid discord; and that angelic face gave place to that of a demon."[70] John Newton describes the loss of the "moral sense," with hearts hardened like "steel." And Thomas Jefferson admitted as much as well, stating that there must "be an unhappy influence on the manners of our people, produced by the existence of slavery among us."[71] The high incidence of rape enabled by the power of slaveholders over their female slaves fed a culture of sexual compulsivity among slaveholders. The sexually transmitted diseases, jealous and enraged planter wives and enslaved husbands, and children separated from their half-siblings bred a culture of anger and violence. Southerners carried weapons with them at all times, and the South had a homicide rate many times that of the North.[72]

Slavery twisted Southern culture. As to STDs in particular, sailors participating in the slave trade actually died at a rate greater than the enslaved themselves due to disease. As we will see in greater detail in Chapter 5, white Southern Christianity was skewed and distorted deeply in order to justify the institution—scars that persist and cause acrimony to this day in southern denominations. Finally, as Booker T. Washington noted, "The slave system...in a large measure, took the spirit of self-reliance and self-help out of the white people," creating among slaveholders a spoiled and idle culture.[73] While the economic effects of health problems may seem more obvious, economists are also deeply interested in the moral and cultural fabric that upholds a healthy economy. Cruelty, violence, self-deception, and idleness do not lend themselves to a flourishing economic life. Good manners, honesty, frugality, and a strong work ethic often appear in lists of the "commercial virtues" because, given the right legal institutions, they result in a low-crime, high-trust, highly productive society.[74] Perhaps here someone in the tradition of the Southern agrarians may object that these are simply differences between Northern and Southern culture. If Southerners simply preferred a slower, less materialistic way of life, this would be no problem for a true economist who measures success according to people's real preferences, not just gross domestic product. We refer here to costs imposed on the majority by a tiny minority of planters, as well as cultural costs that developed to sustain the coercive system. There isn't a thing in the world wrong with a poorer but more relaxed way of life if that is voluntarily chosen, but it is morally unacceptable to impose economic and cultural costs through force.

Next, Wright looks at population growth and the effect on free labor. First, it's true that America's slaves were far better fed than most slaves. With the slave trade ended and cotton booming, the value of slaves as an investment climbed in the first half of the nineteenth century, and food was fairly cheap. Nevertheless, diets were low in protein, causing late menarche in females and malnutrition in children. Working so close to mothers' due dates caused low birth weights, and an early end to breastfeeding so mothers could get back to work didn't help the situation. Ultimately, even given the incentives of slaveholders, infant mortality rates among enslaved women were twice that of white women at the time.[75] Since slaveholders didn't need children to work on the farm, they also had low birth rates. Benjamin Franklin argued that slavery also reduced the population of other free citizens, since the South was averse to immigration, and free whites in the South had low wages because of the availability of slave labor, causing many of them to emigrate. Such low population density discouraged infrastructure investments and made financial services more expensive.

Readily available credit is absolutely necessary to robust economic growth. As such, the South lagged behind the North—one of the major reasons that it lost the Civil War.

One of the most obvious negative externalities of the slave system was the way that it disincentivized economic development. The Southern economy lost out on improvements that would have come from greater investments in education, infrastructure, and technology both because of the availability of slave labor and a cultural resistance to modernization. Slaves themselves had no incentive to innovate for the benefit of their slaveholders. Although the extremely wealthy were highly educated in the South, per capita literacy rates were relatively low.[76] Very few patents were awarded in the South, and industrial techniques remained embarrassingly backward because unskilled laborers were tied to the work. In some cases, Southern industrial mining efforts were using leased convicts to remove water by bucket almost a century after steam engines were applied to such efforts elsewhere. Because of the constant supply of cheap labor, planters rarely attempted to economize by technological improvement. Schools, bridges, and roads were kept at a minimum throughout the South, as many lived almost entirely on the produce of their plantations and only had to go to market once or twice a year.[77]

Southern elites also actively fought against modernization and industrialization, which conflicted with their idea of themselves as lords of feudal manors. Eugene Genovese confirms that "hardly a southern intellectual could be found, no matter how passionately proslavery, who did not point to [the planters' 'aristocratic ethos'] as being fundamental to the southern ethic.... Some wrote with sorrow and fear of the military and political consequences; others wrote with joy and expressions of superior virtue. But almost all agreed on the fact." This is not to say that the South should have been mostly industrial like the North. Southerners had a comparative advantage in agriculture. However, agriculture is an economic sector like any other; it can take advantage of improved breeding, irrigation, and crop-rotation techniques, among other types of improvement. And the South did take on far more industrialization after the war as well, so one can assume that perverse incentives limited earlier adoption. Once again, think of the opportunity costs. The South had a large economy on global terms, but the relevant question is whether it did as well as it could have done without the institution of slavery.

Finally, slavery increased wealth disparity and degraded governance and institutional quality. Today, it's popular to be concerned with wealth inequality—the gap between the richest and the poorest people. Economists rightly point out that this might not be the most interesting data on which to focus our attention. After all, in an age of immense technological growth, it's possible for a few innovators to reach stratospheric heights of wealth while the poor continue to improve steadily or even rapidly. Looking at wealth disparity, however, brings out a different dynamic: the spread of wealth across the whole economy. It is a truism that economies with significant middle classes are more stable and more prosperous than ones with some very rich and most very poor, even if average per capita income looks the same at a particular point in time. A society with this sort of wealth bell curve is economically hopeful because the majority has a sense of ambition and independence. As markets have become freer and freer across the world, the majority poor have turned into the majority middle class, a welcome change.[78] While the North experienced this change, the South lagged badly behind, with the small number in the middle class owning a slave or two. In other words, people in the South were not rising out of poverty unless they participated in slavery, and very few could do so.[79]

Under legal slavery, there were pieces of "property" that could make choices, plying the court system with puzzling and expensive cases: Can slaves be married? Can they own property? Can they own another slave? What happens if they travel to a place where slavery isn't legal? In spite of the claim that slaveholders had full property rights over their slaves, many in the political class pressed for laws to prohibit manumission and slave self-purchase. As we can see from comparisons with other places like Mexico (where self-purchase effectively ended slavery before the law did), slave self-purchase is often in the interests of both slaveholder and enslaved. But the existence of a thriving free Black community was seen by state legislatures as too much of a temptation for runaways.[80] Racial control in general, including the suppression of education, was a way for planters to shift the costs of a coercive system onto others while simultaneously making everyone poorer by lowering human capital and limiting mutually advantageous exchanges. After slavery was legally ended, we cannot exaggerate the extent to which the courts and political institutions were corrupted by the need to keep Black people in quasi-slavery. The South continued to lag economically as a result of these exploitative measures.

Even the idea that the planters themselves benefitted from all this exploitation depends on a thought experiment about what they might have done otherwise. Hummel concludes that "[w]ealthy planters, extracting enormous transfers from Black slaves and smaller transfers from poor whites, earned rates of return no greater than northern merchants and manufacturers." But with so much of their capital invested in slaves, slaveholders could envision no way to shift to a new system without massive capital losses.

Weighing the deadweight losses, the waste of privilege seeking, the negative externalities, and the opportunity costs against the difference between a cotton market and the next best alternative market, we see without any doubt that the situation in the American South was no different from economists' evaluation of slave societies worldwide. The marginal value of slavery is negative. The loss of economic freedom for individuals always leads to a loss of prosperity for the whole.

Moral costs are not possible to quantify. Think of the loss of the ability to act on one's own free will for those who were enslaved or the moral stain on a nation that had thoroughly controverted its founding principles. We are not indulging in "historical presentism" here by applying our own moral values to a different age. As we have shown, the hypocrisy of slavery was well-recognized throughout the entire founding period, and deeply criticized from both a religious and a political perspective throughout its tenure. The economic, social, cultural, theological, technological, and moral confusion of the slave system infected the American experiment profoundly.

THE FREE MARKETERS WERE RIGHT AFTER ALL

So slaveholders benefitted—at least, economically—from slavery, but no more than they might have from participation in other industries had their economic history evolved differently. It also matters a lot that they lost out culturally. The economy more broadly suffered badly from the institution. As we mentioned in Chapter 1, the abolitionist movement was populated with free traders, including some of its most famous leaders, such as William Lloyd Garrison and Harriet Beecher Stowe.[81] John Stuart Mill was reviled for following the "dismal science" of economics because the discipline is inherently anti-slavery. The entire enterprise of economics is based on the concept of private property, especially in one's labor, and Mill economists at the time believed that slavery makes nations poorer and more unhappy than freedom would. Mill took as his starting point the assumption that each person's preferences (no matter their ethnicity) were to be considered equally in his utilitarian calculus and believed that an entirely free society led to the greatest happiness for the greatest number of people. The concept of free trade is inextricably tied up with the ownership of oneself and the freedom to contract out one's labor as one wishes. After all, how could free traders say that changes in wages draw labor to its most efficient use, if the laborers aren't allowed to move or develop their talents? The thought of a well-functioning price system under slavery is absurd.

Correspondingly, vehement defenders of the slave system hated the philosophy of free trade, positioning themselves as a kind of old-world aristocracy standing against the ravages of economic disruption. Southern slavery apologist George Fitzhugh argued that free trade was "tainted with abolition, and at war with our institutions," and that Southerners must "throw Adam Smith, Say, Ricardo & Co., [free market economists] in the fire."[82] Fitzhugh's frustration with the political economy of his time arose from its association with notions of individual freedom, which he saw as a cover for a kind of industrial enslavement in which the capitalist avoids having to provide for his workers: "Political economy is the science of free society. Its theory and its history alike establish this position. Its fundamental maxim Laissez-faire and 'Pas trop gouverner,' [Don't govern too much] are at war with all kinds of slavery, for they in fact assert that individuals and peoples prosper most when governed least." Since Fitzhugh thought slave governance a benevolent form of socialism, he considered it only logical to extend the institution to poor white factory workers as well.[83]

Historian Joyce Chaplin describes the planters' vision of themselves as a golden mean between the "rudeness" of the Indians and "an impersonal, luxurious, and immoral commercial society." Instead, their way of life "obeyed the human passions essential to societal cohesion" such as the desire to be part of a natural hierarchy.[84] Often accused by outsiders of backwardness because of the persistence of slavery, Southerners offered "a defense of the archaisms of their way of life (redolent of praise for the classical, biblical, and feudal ages) against a money-grubbing and impersonal capitalist order."[85] Many Southerners took great pride in the vision of their economy as a benevolent feudalism. They made enough improvements to keep up their way of life but generally scorned the habits inculcated by commerce.

Ironically, Desmond and the New History of Capitalism scholars have rehabilitated the old Southern "King Cotton" economic view that the slave system was a productive way to organize an economy and that Northern industry flourished because of its dependence on Southern cotton. But cotton might have been grown by non-slave laborers; cotton could be gotten elsewhere (as it was during the war, or by the French all along); it wasn't the only fabric available for clothing (wool and linen were both popular as well); and most of all, at 5 percent, it just wasn't a large enough portion of the American economy to be treated as the driver of economic growth.[86] As is always the case, the really stunning economic growth during this period arose from widespread innovation, not exploitation.[87] If we consider the astronomical rise in wealth during this time period, it becomes obvious that trade-tested innovation is driving growth, since slavery and imperialism are ubiquitous elements of human history, but tenfold gains in wealth for regular, everyday people is not.

One of the most disturbing things about the resurrection of this view by some of the writers involved in the 1619 Project is the message that it sends: that a whole economy really does become better off by exploiting an underclass of some kind. If that were true, we would be living in an incredibly depressing reality—one might wonder how contemporary slavery will ever be overcome. Thankfully, it's not true. Indeed, it is patently false. We have a more hopeful message, and we think that throughout this volume, we can make a compelling case for it: we'll always become far better off by peaceful, voluntary exchange with other free people than we ever would by stealing from them or coercing them. The more people understand this, the more we can benefit one another without rancor.

We've established that while Black slave labor did build a significant portion of the American economy, America could have achieved a much healthier economy using only free labor. Overstating the percentage of the economy that involved slave labor only feeds into the damaging idea that America somehow needed slavery to flourish economically. We do not correct these claims in order to downplay the role of Black Americans in economic history but rather to condemn the institution of slavery as an inefficient economic system that creates deadweight losses, the waste of privilege seeking, negative externalities, and perverse path dependencies.

Consider some of the economic concepts discussed in our sections on the losses incurred under the slave system. Many of them arose simply from restrictions on choice. The whole economy lost out because enslaved people weren't allowed to learn, to move around for better opportunities, to find the work that fit their talents, and to spend wages to buy the things they wanted. We showed that other participants in the slave system also lost out on the opportunity to pursue economic flourishing in a system that didn't require distortion of their family commitments, religion, politics, courts, police systems, and personal character. These distortions came at great costs, costs that we continue to pay today. Classical liberals do not in any way deny the long-lasting consequences of slavery. What we deny is the particular analysis of Desmond's essay in the 1619 Project and his attempt to inextricably tie free markets to this painful history. Instead, slavery undermined our system of liberal law and violated the basic principles of free market economics, wreaking havoc for the American experiment.

Economics is the study of human choice. The generation of real prices as pieces of information requires freedom in terms of secure private property and free exchange. The adjustment of labor and goods to fluctuating supply and demand requires freedom of movement and freedom of contract. The development of new ideas and more efficient ways of meeting our needs requires freedom of thought and association. Over time, flourishing through exchange with others replaces war and coercion as a means of acquisition and makes us all freer. There is, at base, no way to disconnect the realities of economic flourishing from the robust protection of human freedom.

THE IDEALS OF THE AMERICAN REVOLUTION

If slavery didn't fit in well with America's (generally) free market economic system, it didn't fit in well with its system of government either. That doesn't mean that slavery didn't influence the American system of government in certain ways; it absolutely did. The particular wording of both the Declaration of Independence and the Constitution had to be changed to accommodate the institution. In the original version of the Declaration, Jefferson blamed King George for sticking the Americans with the institution and then turning around and using the slaves against them. King George "waged cruel war against human nature itself, violating its most sacred rights of life and liberty in the persons of a distant people who never offended him, captivating and carrying them into slavery in another hemisphere or to incur miserable death in their transportation thither."[88] These phrases could not be allowed to remain in the final draft because of the offense they would cause to slaveholders.

The records of the Constitutional Convention as well as the published debates between the federalists and the anti-federalists also contain extensive discussion of slavery, possibly the most divisive issue in the proceedings. One anti-federalist letter objected to the adoption of the Constitution on the basis of its allowing the slave trade to continue for another twenty years:

> How is it possible we could do it consistent with our ideas of government [or] consistent with the principles and documents we endeavor to inculcate upon others?... Where is the man, who under the influence of sober dispassionate reasoning, and not void of natural affection, can lay

his hand upon his heart and say, I am willing my sons and my daughters should be torn from me and doomed to perpetual slavery? We presume that man is not to be found amongst us: And yet we think the consequence is fairly drawn, that this is what every man ought to be able to say, who voted for this constitution....[89]

The most reasonable interpretation of these tensions is that the Founders were torn between sticking to philosophical principle and satisfying the economic considerations of a few. Many historians argue that they compromised not only for military reasons (in the case of the Revolution) and political stability reasons (in the case of the Constitution), but also because slavery really was on the decline at the time, and should the cotton gin never have been invented and manumission never been made illegal, the peculiar institution might have died a natural death. This account requires some nuance but seems to make the best sense of the facts on the ground and has general support among historians.

In contrast, the opening essay of the 1619 Project departs from this account, claiming that the Revolutionary War, for instance, was fought to protect the institution of slavery.[90] Its author, Nikole Hannah-Jones, refers to two episodes that seem to indicate that slavery was at stake in the revolutionaries' battle with the English and claims that the English were verging on abolition themselves. Historians of all stripes, however, have argued that a collection of all the evidence weighs heavily against this as a significant motivation for revolution. Instead, they say, there is nothing to indicate that England had any intention of ending slavery itself or ending it in the colonies, nor did the revolutionaries believe they did or mention fear of this as a motivation for the Declaration. Hannah-Jones refers to the Dunmore Proclamation, in which the royal governor of the British Colony of Virginia promised freedom to slaves that joined the Crown's cause, as well as the 1772 Somerset decision in England, which claimed that slavery was not supported by the common law. While these two events certainly made a few American slaveholders nervous, there is little evidence that these were major factors in the American colonists' decision to go to war with England.[91] (Hannah-Jones later softened the claim in response to widespread criticism.)

In the case of the Somerset decision, for instance, it was hardly even covered in the Southern newspapers. As distinguished historian of the American Revolution and man of the left Gordon Wood argues, it's in America, not England, where serious abolitionism is gathering strength:

> The first anti-slavery meeting in the history of the world takes place in Philadelphia in 1775. That coincidence I think is important. I would have liked to have asked Hannah-Jones, how would she explain the fact that in 1791 in Virginia at the College of William and Mary, the Board of Visitors, the board of trustees, who were big slaveholding planters, awarded an honorary degree to Granville Sharp, who was the leading British abolitionist of the day. That's the kind of question that should provoke historical curiosity. You ask yourself what were these slaveholding planters thinking? It's the kind of question, the kind of seeming anomaly, that should provoke a historian into research.[92]

Wood not only disagrees that these two events were great motivations to the revolutionaries, but also takes issue with Hannah-Jones's claim that the Founders didn't really believe what they were saying. If that were true, why say it so often?

At the Constitutional Convention, Gouverneur Morris called slavery "a nefarious institution" that had "the curse of heaven...

where it prevailed." James Madison purposefully left the term out of the Constitution to avoid any admission of "the idea that there could be property in men." John Adams opposed slavery throughout his life, and Benjamin Franklin became the president of the Abolition Society in 1787. Thomas Jefferson called it a "moral depravity" and "a hideous blot" on the country. Furthermore, Jefferson and other Founders were critically aware that slavery could very well be the undoing of the nation. Jefferson likened it to holding a wolf by the ears, such that neither keeping it nor letting it go seemed like a viable option. When he heard of the Missouri Compromise of 1820, he assumed it was the beginning of the end of the union. The failure of these men to carry out their values, some of them in their own households but all of them in and for their country, is and will remain one of the most bitter incongruities of American history. But that is no evidence that they did not really believe what they wrote, stated in speeches, and for which they organized and lobbied. One might think that historians are simply being defensive of an America that they don't want to see maligned as complicit with evil, and there may indeed be historians like this. But the ones we refer to here are trying to get the facts straight for a much better reason: the legacy of Black America itself.

The very reason that slavery in America stood out as a scar on our reputation, a taunt from our enemies, and a cause of deep sectional fear and distrust is *because* the Founders really believed what they said. No one is accusing Brazil, which imported ten times the number of Africans as America did, of being hypocritical. That's because Brazil never claimed that all men are created equal and endowed by their Creator with certain unalienable rights. It was America's founding documents that made this audacious claim, a declaration that resounded across the world.[93] And the tradition of Black liberation in America has consistently pointed to the painful tension between America's founding values and its practices as the source of the progress we've made. There was a rash of voluntary manumissions following the Revolution,[94] as well as the establishment of societies dedicated to increasing manumission and supporting the recently freed. Wood argues that the Declaration made Southerners more ashamed of the institution of slavery, thus forcing them to root around for some justification for it, which they found in a revival of the "natural slavery" argument of Aristotle.

THE BLACK AMERICAN PRO-CONSTITUTIONAL TRADITION

Phillis Wheatley was the first American Black woman to publish a book and only the second American woman of any race to do so. Here she praises George Washington (prior to his victory!):

> Proceed, great chief, with virtue on thy side,
> Thy ev'ry action let the goddess guide.
> A crown, a mansion, and a throne that shine,
> With gold unfading, WASHINGTON!
> be thine.

At the same time, she passionately denounces slavery. Here in poetry:

> But how presumptuous shall we hope to find
> Divine acceptance with the Almighty mind
> While yet o deed ungenerous they disgrace
> And hold in bondage Afric: blameless race
> Let virtue reign and then accord our prayers
> Be victory ours and generous freedom theirs.

And here in prose:

> Otherwise, perhaps, the Israelites had been less solicitous for their Freedom from Egyptian Slavery: I don't say they would have been contented without it, by no Means, for in every human Breast, God has implanted a Principle, which we call Love of freedom; it is impatient of Oppression, and pants for Deliverance; and by the Leave of our modern Egyptians I will assert that the same Principle lives in us.[95]

In 1774, a group of enslaved people sent a petition to the governor of Massachusetts, arguing that "we have in common with other men a natural right to our freedoms without being deprived of them by our fellowman.... There is a great number of us sencear...members of the Church of Christ.... Bear ye onenothers Bordens How can the master be said to Beare my Borden when he Beares me down with the Have [heavy] chanes of slavery and operson [oppression] against my will...how can the slave perform the duties of a husband to a wife or parent to his child."[96]

For his part, Frederick Douglass initially agreed with his mentor William Lloyd Garrison that the Constitution was a failure because of its compromise with slavery. Garrison greatly admired the Declaration of Independence but bought Supreme Court Justice Taney's argument that the original intent of the framers could never have been equality among the races. Eventually, though, Frederick Douglass decided in favor of Lysander Spooner's suggestion that we ought to be bound by the actual terms of the contract as worded, as we would under contract law normally. Breaking with his mentor, then, Douglass called the Constitution a "glorious liberty document," grounding his famous and fiery abolitionist speech, "What to a Slave is the Fourth of July?" in the very text of the Constitution itself.[97] Through his appeal to the great American principles of individual freedom and equality before the law, Douglass could credibly shame his white audience for their failure in allowing slavery to persist.

Political scientist Lucas Morel contrasts Hannah-Jones's approach to that of Ralph Ellison, author of *The Invisible Man*: "... her argument is reminiscent of one by Ralph Ellison, who wrote in a 1970 *Time* magazine essay that 'it is the Black American who puts pressure upon the nation to live up to its ideals.' But Ellison, though aware of the early republic's shortcomings, still called the Declaration of Independence, Constitution, and Bill of Rights 'sacred documents.'"[98]

Likewise, in 1963, Martin Luther King Jr. argued that:

> In a sense, we have come to our nation's capital to cash a check. When the architects of our republic wrote the magnificent words of the Constitution and the Declaration of Independence, they were signing a promissory note to which every American was to fall heir.
>
> This note was a promise that all men, yes, Black men as well as white men, would be guaranteed the inalienable rights of life, liberty, and the pursuit of happiness.
>
> It is obvious today that America has defaulted on this promissory note insofar as her citizens of color are concerned. Instead of honoring this sacred obligation, America has given the Negro people a bad check, a check which has come back marked "insufficient funds." But we refuse to believe that the bank of justice is bankrupt. We refuse to believe that there are insufficient funds in the great vaults of opportunity of this nation. So we have come to cash this check—a

check that will give us upon demand the riches
of freedom and the security of justice.[99]

King was quite progressive in his politics, but he still acknowledged the moral leverage that the statements in the founding documents offered Black Americans. Consider that departing from
the complex account of the American Founders—bearing with it
all the tensions of disappointed conscience—means that we must
eschew sound historical analysis as well as the legacy of so many
great Black writers and heroes of freedom. It's not worth it.

DOTH WE PROTEST TOO MUCH?
THE PROBLEM OF ONE-THING-ISM

We return to the concern that white Americans are resisting the
message of the 1619 Project and other similar efforts among
the progressive left because they don't want to be decentered
in American history. Perhaps this is the case for some who have
taken up the pen against the project. On the other hand, we argue
that others (many of whom are Black and range from Marxist to
"cranky liberal" to conservative),[100] who have been more careful in
their differentiation between praiseworthy elements of the project and questionable parts of it, are pressing a pivotal matter, not
just for American history, but for our functioning as a deeply pluralistic society that still retains some shared ideals. They stand in
solidarity with heroes of the abolitionist and civil rights eras who
understood that it was the true and good claims of the Founders
and America's founding documents that made America's treatment of Black Americans stand out as rank hypocrisy whose confrontation it would be impossible to avoid. This approach not
only stands on more accurate historical grounds but also allows
Black and white Americans to share in addressing both the proud
and the shameful elements of our history together. Furthermore
this same story of high ideals alongside practical failure to live up

to them provides meaning for the countless other Americans who came later, seeking freedom but often experiencing terrible treatment: Irish Catholics, Chinese railroad workers, the Japanese of World War II's internment camps, and many others. While this requires a more complicated narrative, it grants a more substantive foundation for all Americans to share together.

In rejecting the total re-centering of American history on the Black experience, we fully reject the past re-centering on only the European settlers' experience as well. In fact, we reject any flat, two-dimensional, monomaniacal narrative of an American history rich with many cultures, contradictions, and complications. Americans are not so simple that we cannot tell a nuanced story about ourselves. Jonah Goldberg has coined the pithy term "one-thing-ism" for a tendency in modern academic culture to act as though the newest lens with which one can productively view a phenomenon must now become the only lens through which all things are viewed. This tendency is apparent on both sides of this argument over American history, whether one holds that the ideal of America is a false pipe dream or an untouchable sacred artifact. The frustrating thing about this oversimplifying tendency is that many of these lenses are useful and interesting ways to tell deeper and richer stories, to include more forgotten people in our account, and to inculcate into ourselves and our children a better and more sophisticated moral language. But the tendency to favor one lens over all others and overplay its insights has in many cases caused an overcompensation, not in the direction of embracing different and complementary lenses, but only in the embrace of some new, other one-note perspective that must then, through academic combat, oust the first entirely. We hope in the following pages, if it's possible to do so briefly and concisely, to do justice to the interesting and complicated ways that philosophical ideals, social institutions, economic realities, and cultural and religious commitments interact together to weave a story of ourselves that is heartbreaking yet hopeful.

Chapter 3

Liberation Through the Freedom to Move: The Struggle for Black Property

"If I was free, massa; if I was free, I would go to work
for a year, and get some money for myself,—den—
den—den—den, massa, dis is what I do—I buy me,
fus place, a little house, and little lot of land."
—a Louisiana slave to Frederick Law
Olmstead just before the war

"What's the use of being free if you don't own land enough
to be buried in? Might juss as well stay slave all yo' days."
—an old man to Whitelaw Reid in 1865 [101]

Many Americans are not aware that the category of "slave" was not immediately a racial category in American history. Even as slavery or indentured servitude of any kind became increasingly a Black phenomenon in America, the justifications for this morphed from an appeal to regrettable economic necessity in the late eighteenth century to a framing of paternalistic care of inferior people in the early nineteenth century. This hardening and mythologizing of race relations adds a complicating twist to the usual experience of defeudalizing an economy, since the underclass was divided among themselves: poor whites, free Blacks, and enslaved Blacks. Post–Civil War, rich whites successfully deputized poor whites to deny Blacks—whether they had been free or were newly emancipated—the protection of the law as it was enjoyed by most whites. Post–Civil War Southern white elites conspired to retain their feudal privileges and deny Black people the opportunity to gain economic power in a wide variety of ways: cultural humiliation, the attempt to form cartels, legislation prohibiting freedom of employment, legislation prohibiting property ownership, vigilantism, re-enslavement through false imprisonment, and discrimination in education.

But Black Americans fought back with vigor. They taught themselves to read, registered official complaints to the Freedmen's Bureau, ditched farms where they were being trapped in debt, armed themselves against lynch mobs, and created Black-only economies and self-help societies. As Frederick Douglass declared a mere fifteen years after the war: "We have only to reflect a moment upon the situation in which these people found themselves when liberated. Consider their ignorance, their poverty, their destitution, and their absolute dependence upon the very class by which they had been held in bondage for centuries, a class whose every sentiment was averse to their freedom, and we shall be prepared to marvel that they have, under the circumstances, done so well."

Lessons in Classical Liberalism #6: Feudalism Versus the Open Economy

A free market economy is a "defeudalized" economy; that is, free market economies strive to remove all special privileges from economic life. They dismantle the price-fixing and barriers to entry of the medieval guild. The merchant—a person with no special name or history but who creates wealth by getting things from where they're in high supply to where they're in low supply—inevitably busts up the old class system of aristocratic landowner and serf-peasant. Slowly but surely, the society jettisons the cultural prejudice against trade as an occupation as most citizens learn to value the innovations of the entrepreneur and all the benefits that redound to them because of his herculean efforts. Finally, they reject the tariff protections for a nation's own industries, opening up to international trade. At the base of this defeudalizing process is liberty: the liberty to live where one chooses, do the work that one voluntarily agrees to do, charge the prices that one sets oneself, own what one earns, purchase what one values, marry whomever one pleases, and, perhaps most of all, to leave when one deems that a better opportunity has arisen.

The rule of law looms in the background of any market economy. After all, the liberty we have just described will not be popular with the established powers. Aristocrats will fight tenaciously against their loss of status to those upstart merchants; artisans, their loss of control in the face of open competition; and capitalists, their loss of profits when new businesses challenge their market hegemony.[102] What must a liberal system of law do?[103] It must reliably defend the rights of each individual to her bodily integrity and her property, and it must hold those who make contracts with her to their end of the deal. Should any class or group of people be excluded from these protections, the system will have violated one of the main tenets of the natural law: that all true law is applied generally to the whole population without favoritism.[104] Such injustices also have terrible economic consequences; those who are excluded from the protection of the law will have far fewer opportunities to develop economically, while the entire economy loses out on their potential contributions. This is the basic insight of development economics, which by necessity focuses heavily on building strong legal institutions of property and contract and eliminating political corruption.[105] Much of the prosperity described in Chapter 1 arose from the marriage of liberal legal infrastructure with improving attitudes toward business as a respectable vocation. In the eighteenth century, attitudes toward trade changed as more and more people began to realize that it allows for creative cooperative endeavors whose productivity increases redound to all through higher incomes and new, cheaper, or higher-quality products acquired through peaceful exchange.

Members of the Southern planter class self-consciously positioned themselves as the nobility within a feudal economy.[106] Nested in an emerging global economy based on liberal law, Southern planters did what they had to do to keep the plantation going, but often chose to forego more profitable options that would have undermined their vision of themselves as a kind of paternalistic aristocracy. In that sense, they set up a pre-capitalist, anti-bourgeois culture ripe for the defeudalization that was already proceeding apace in Europe and in the North. This process has never been an easy one, but the post–Civil War South added another complicating factor to what other Western cultures had already endured, or were simultaneously enduring. In the early eighteenth century, as the population of Black enslaved people grew to a threatening size, white planters generated a clever workaround against the possibility that poor whites might rise up in solidarity with their fellow Black workers. They racialized slavery.

THE BLACK WORK ETHIC

The desire of Black Americans to acquire their own property developed early on. Anthropologist Sidney Mintz describes the reaction of enslaved Black Americans to the bizarre mash-up of markets and slavery in their own experience this way: "[t]orn from societies that had not yet entered into the capitalistic world, and thrust into settings that were profoundly capitalistic in character on the one hand, yet rooted in the need for unfree labor on the other, the slaves saw liquid capital not only as a means to secure freedom, but also as a means to attach their paternity—and hence, their identity as persons—to something even their masters would have to respect."[107] Enslaved people were often allowed to have a small plot of their own, and many endeavored to sell the produce, either in the open marketplace or to their own slaveholders. Exhausted from the day's labor for their slaveholder, they would sleep for a few hours, then get up with the moon in order to work their own tract of land.[108]

Enslaved people with skills in the trades were also sometimes allowed to "rent themselves out" in town, leading in some cases to a kind of virtual freedom in the sense that the enslaved rarely had contact with his slaveholder. Even though most of one's wages had to be turned over to the slaveholder, the chance to keep some cash and to experience some independence in one's day-to-day living was a huge draw to this kind of work. The creation of significant Black trading networks (skilled work in the upper South and sale of agricultural products in the lower South) were financially beneficial to both the enslaved and slaveholders as individuals.

Unsurprisingly, some whites complained of the "independence, self-esteem, and arrogance" that such entrepreneurial endeavors encouraged, and they pursued multiple legislative attempts to limit these endeavors all the way up to the Civil War. South Carolina, for instance, passed laws against enslaved people selling products in the marketplace in 1741, 1779, 1787, and 1788.[109] A group of Tennessee slaveholders argued against allowing masters to let their slaves self-hire, since it "lessened the dependence of a slave on his master" and had "dangerous consequences."[110] In a certain way these slaveholders were correct. Frederick Douglass reported that the freedom to make agreements for his own labor and collect his wages "armed my love of liberty with a lash and a driver, far more efficient than any I had before known."[111] In another case, plantation owner John Liddell, in Louisiana, was furious to find that four of the men he'd enslaved had been renting out their own labor secretly at night for years! In the year prior to his discovery of their clandestine business, they had made $500 entirely without his knowledge. Liddell went on to lobby the state legislature for a law "prohibiting the employing and hiring of slaves without consent of the owners under heavy penalty."[112] The eagerness of enslaved Black Americans to work hard for themselves and their own families presented a conundrum to whites, both slaveholders and the working class. On the one hand, their products and skills were highly valued in the marketplace; on the other, the sense of independence and confidence such work imparted clashed with the cultural requirements of the slave system.

There are thousands of cases of enslaved Black Americans working overtime to win their own or another's freedom. Manumission, whether bought or freely granted, became a threat to the overarching system, such that many states made it illegal or required court approval and removal from the state for manumitted slaves.[113] Most Black "slave owners" nominally owned their own family members, whom they had purchased from their white owners but could not legally free. In one case, a Methodist bishop inherited two slaves, one of whom was too young to be sent away and another who did not wish to be removed to a faraway state in order to be freed, as Georgia law required. When confronted by his denomination for participating in slavery, he pleaded that he was an "unwilling trustee" of the two people, trapped by the legal system with no way out.[114] Of course, some of these stories of incredibly hard work and longing for freedom end in only more heartbreak. Fanny Smith of Virginia, after making payments on herself (an absurd phrase if ever there was one) and her two children for ten years, was sold shortly before her final payment.[115]

Her slaveholder kept detailed records of her payments that we retain to this day, but it goes without saying that the court did not exist that would defend her against his treacherous betrayal of their agreement.

In stark contrast to the overwhelming evidence of the entrepreneurial spirit in the Black population, including the need to limit such efforts by repeated legislative action, the attitude of former slaveholders regarding the Black work ethic after the Civil War seems either to be a put-on or willful self-deception. Stupidly, former slaveholders assumed (or pretended) that since Black enslaved laborers often found ways to shirk their unpaid work under the old regime, they would not respond to normal market incentives after emancipation.[116] They claimed that Blacks would die out without the motivation of the whip, rather than work voluntarily. As we will see in the chapter on eugenics, updated versions of this Black extinction theory persisted into the twentieth century. Of course, like any rational beings, enslaved people were not motivated to expend more labor than necessary in the service of their slaveholders![117] But their efforts in their own gardens and in instances of self-hire were so well-known that some planters even published new systems of plantation management suggesting that in-kind or cash incentives ought to be tried.[118]

The claim that the Black population would rather fade away than work gets even more absurd, if that's possible, when we consider the employment data from the 1890 census (the first one with racial categories). Black males were employed at 79 percent, in comparison to white males at 77 percent, and Black females at 36 percent, in comparison to white females at 14 percent. Clearly Black Americans wanted to provide for their families just like anyone else and were willing to do so. In fact, Black and white employment rates remained neck and neck until the 1940s.[119] It cannot be denied that Blacks after the Civil War preferred more leisure time for themselves, and especially for their wives and tiny children, than they had on the plantation. It's bizarre that the tendency of newly emancipated Blacks to work at similar ages and for similar hours as white workers, rather than follow the grueling schedule of the plantation, was attributed to laziness rather than freedom.

LAND

Immediately after the Civil War, the greatest desire of most emancipated formerly enslaved people was clear. They wanted to own their own farms. Union General Rufus Saxton reported that "[t]heir love of the soil and desire to own farms amounts to a passion—it appears to be the dearest hope of their lives."[120] In fact, Black desire for land was not new at all, as is clear from multiple attempts to crush it. In 1796, St. George Tucker, a lawyer and future district court judge, suggested a system in which no Black person, free or slave, be allowed to own any lands or buildings, so that the Black "seeds of ambition would be buried too deep, ever to germinate."[121] Many states had, prior to the Civil War, prohibited property ownership for Blacks, including in Georgia, where an 1818 law was upheld as late as 1878 in the *Swoll v. Oliver* ruling.[122] In the 1853 *Bryan v. Walton* case, the precedent was upheld as well, stating that "the intent of the 1818 Act was to '...divest free persons of color of the property held by them at the time of its passage.'"[123] Florida disallowed ownership without the consent of a white guardian, and Louisiana tried to incorporate such a prohibition in its 1852 constitutional convention but failed.[124] What couldn't be legislated often became de facto law, as many white landowners refused to sell to Black people and shunned those who did.

Millions of acres of land became available for homesteading after the passage of the Homestead Act of 1862, although Black people would not be eligible until their citizenship was established in 1866. There were even efforts to ensure that the act did not exclude Black citizens, passed in 1876, but ultimately, the act did little to secure land for Black people. Many of the available tracts that weren't useless swampland were out west, a costly journey from their southern homes, and sometimes in states like New Mexico and Oregon, where Black people weren't allowed to live anyway.[125] Homesteads also required extensive capital to set up, more than even many white people could muster. Out of 1.6 million individual homesteaders (as opposed to speculators, railroads, and other businesses that found ways to claim the land), over the course of forty years, only a few thousand were Black.

Alternatively, the Southern Homestead Act of 1866 offered lands in the South itself. Unfortunately, much of the land was timbered, which in addition to the price of the land, made it difficult for poor whites and newly emancipated Blacks to secure the capital necessary to clear the land and make it usable. Initially, the effort by Radical Republicans to make these lands available was motivated by the desire to reward loyal whites, give freedmen a fighting chance, and punish and dismantle the planter aristocracy. As we've seen, however, it didn't actually help the freedmen get land, and the inability to set up large endeavors like lumber mills may have inadvertently harmed them by slowing growth for the already devastated Southern economy even further. Anyway, in 1876 the act was repealed, largely in an effort to get those larger industrial lumber efforts up and running.[126]

WHAT EVER HAPPENED TO FORTY ACRES AND A MULE?

The origin of the famous "forty acres and a mule" dream of Black ownership hearkens back to a program launched by Union General William T. Sherman, with the advice of twenty Black leaders who recommended land ownership as the best way forward for the freedmen. Sherman distributed forty thousand acres of coastal land in Georgia and South Carolina to one thousand former slave families. The mule was not an official part of the deal, but the

Union Army had confiscated thousands of cattle on Sherman's infamous March to the Sea, and many of these families received a mule along with their land. This was the "greatest land redistribution program ever benefitting African-Americans in this country's history."[127] The recipients didn't receive certificates of ownership, however, but rather certificates of "possession." Then a bill was passed that gave the Freedmen's Bureau permission to lease land that had been abandoned by Confederates, although it was only a tiny amount, and they weren't allowed to transfer the title. Once President Johnson granted amnesty to former Confederates, many Black families were actively dispossessed of land they'd been working on their own, as vast tracts of land were returned to their former owners. Thus, the dream of forty acres and a mule, which had spread like wildfire among the freedmen, only lasted in reality for about nine months, from Sherman's program (Circular #13) beginning in January 1865, through the Freedmen's Bureau's bill in March of that year, and finally ending with President Johnson's Circular #15 in September, declaring that the freedmen's land would be returned to the previous owners.

By 1876, the percentage of Black Americans owning their own land did not exceed 6 percent of the Black population, although those numbers would balloon over the next forty years to 25 percent.[128] It's true that even forty acres per household was not in and of itself much, financially speaking, and without tools and training in land management it's not clear how many farms would have been viable. But historian Robert Higgs argues that an overemphasis on the small cash value of such an asset misses the larger point about what private ownership does for a community.[129] Black Americans who owned their own land and lived on it could have retained the money or goods that they spent on rent, sold the land to someone else for a profit, or cooperated with Black neighbors to combine their farming efforts for greater efficiency. Such savings might have resulted in expansion of their land holdings and purchases of better tools or more animals for farming.

Running their own establishments, Black Americans would have avoided the disputes over cheating that were so common with white owners, many of which involved violence and intimidation. And perhaps most importantly, the skills-building and independence of the family farm might have changed the trajectory of the Black experience profoundly, particularly when compared to the continued dependency of the tenant-farmer. To be clear, private ownership is no economic panacea, but it's also not just a matter of money. It's a matter of the inculcation of the habits of a commercial society. These skills have a quiet but profound ripple effect on financial viability and stability that passes down through the generations.

While the failure of various attempts to get land for Black farmers fills us with regret, we must also frankly admit that there is no precedent in this historical period for a formerly enslaved people to receive any compensation for their unpaid labor. On the contrary, the most successful, peaceful instances of emancipation at the time involved compensation, not to those who had been enslaved, but to their slaveholders. These funds compensated owners for the loss of their initial investment while the practice of slavery was still legal. Even today, those who find it useful to entertain counterfactuals argue that ultimately, compensated emancipation would have cost far less than the cost of the Civil War itself, though they admit that it was in no way a politically viable option in 1860.[130] Torturous questions around justice versus political expedience plagued the issue of slave emancipation from the beginning.

MOBILITY AND THE FAILURE OF THE CARTELS

This brief flash of hope for real land ownership was followed by the rise of sharecropping. In Robert Higgs's *Competition and Coercion: Blacks in the American Economy 1865–1914*, he argues that sharecropping and the associated crop liens at the country store are often misunderstood.[131] It's true that freedmen were systemically barred from getting land for themselves and therefore had to resort to sharecropping. But Black people, and many poor whites as well, actually preferred sharecropping to wage labor, though clearly they would have preferred ownership to both of these options. Frankly, gang labor for the plantation owner still felt a lot like their former situation—with overseers monitoring them constantly and brandishing whips and pistols. Oftentimes owners would make excuses to pay less or demand extra work for no extra pay. Workers began to demand "shares," flexible contracts in which workers received some percentage of the actual crops, rather than cash payments.[132]

Given what little legal leverage the freedmen had after the war, one might question why their demands meant anything at all to white planters. They now had one weapon they hadn't had before—the ability to leave. Higgs calls the newfound freedom of movement the formerly enslaved people's "most precious jewel of emancipation."[133] Planters were now desperate for labor to keep their farms going, and the competition for Black labor among the planters made up for some, though not even close to all, of what Blacks lacked in real contract rights. In fact, poor whites followed suit and participated in the sharecropping system in huge numbers.

It worked. Shares went up from as little as one-tenth of the crop initially to one-half by the 1870s. Contracts also shifted from shared rent to fixed rent, especially for skillful tenants.[134] In a fixed-rent system, laborers paid a set amount, either of cash or the crop, to the owner and kept the rest. This not only constituted a much greater incentive to work efficiently but also decreased to near zero the extent of day-to-day oversight of work. The sense of independence and being one's own boss was a change deeply valued by these workers, most of whom had so recently been enslaved and forced to work in gangs under the overseer's lash.[135]

These shifts in the types of contracts plantation laborers were willing to make with their owners often benefitted the owners as well, who wanted efficient work and to mitigate their own risk. But the best situation for the owners was one in which the competition that was driving up laborer's shares was gone altogether. There were efforts all across the South to form cartels among owners so that none would offer higher shares than another and therefore remove any incentive for workers to leave and go to their neighbor's farm instead of staying put. These schemes carried on for decades and even included outright laws that made it illegal to change employers without permission. But "such was the demand for negro laborers," one Freedmen's Bureau official recalled, "that any combination to abridge their freedom in seeking and changing homes, or to control the price of labor, failed utterly."[136]

It's not hard at all to track the efforts of the planters to combine forces and limit competition for labor: they published them in their local newspapers! They argued that if they could just cooperate with one another, then the freedmen would have to "consent or starve." But they went on to describe their own failure. We're "each outbidding the other" one planter lamented, and "the negro in the meantime feeling like a maiden with a dozen suitors at her feet—entire master of the situation."[137] The ability of Black laborers to move, even from one farm to another in the same county, created a jarring situation for the planters, one in which their former hostages had real economic leverage.

Lessons in Classical Liberalism #7: Cartels and the Power of Voting with Your Feet

The situation described above is a perfect example of a basic economic insight: the inherent instability of cartels. Adam Smith observed that if businessmen gather in a room together for more than a few minutes, they'll conspire against the public (in this case, their employees).[138] Cartels—the collusion of businessmen together to fix prices, wages, or innovation—are famously unstable. Why? Since fixed prices are highly unlikely to reflect the realities of supply and demand, market pressures will arise that tempt individual members of the cartel to defect from the agreement in order to capture greater profits. That is exactly why planters attempted to use laws, such as those that made it illegal to change employers without permission, to stop their fellow farmers from destroying the power of the cartel from the inside out. State enforcement is generally the only way to uphold such agreements for any length of time.

Note that the real source of the threat to the planters' power over their labor force was *other* white planters. However, the real root of the threat was the ability of laborers to leave an employer or even a county or region if they so wished. The willingness and ability to change employers allowed Black laborers to bid their shares up by pitting the white planters against one another. This example provides a picture of the more general observation about a competitive system: as much as business owners would love to pay their employees less and sell their goods at a higher price, the ability to work for someone else or buy from someone else undermines such schemes organically. Unlike laws that fix prices or wages or break companies, the competitive system operates organically, adjusting constantly to changing circumstances before attempts at cartelization or monopolization have a chance to succeed.

For those courageous enough to make the journey, they could often do even better by leaving the deep South altogether. Between 1870 and 1910, 535,000 Blacks left the South, moving mostly to the northeast and north central regions of the United

States (particularly New York, Philadelphia, and Chicago). They were searching for jobs in service industries that paid better than farm work. That 90 percent of the Black population remained in the South during this period, however, obscures the amount of migration that was occurring within the South, as many moved out of Virginia, the Carolinas, Georgia, Kentucky, Tennessee, Alabama, and Mississippi, and headed for Arkansas, Texas, and Oklahoma. They perceived that ownership or sharecropping opportunities might be better in the latter regions, and indeed, land ownership expanded in Appalachia where whites were more likely to help their Black neighbors get lands and jobs. (The hostile legal environment made it difficult to operate without a white advocate.)[139]

Even more significant was the shift from rural to urban dwelling within the South that doubled the proportion of Blacks living in cities. Black migration to cities paralleled white patterns of movement, resulting in huge gains in material welfare: better schools and housing, as well as a greater variety of food, medicine, and social institutions from which to choose.[140] The concentration of Black communities in cities allowed for the emergence of Black business centers, including merchants, craftsmen, and professionals. Wages were higher in the cities, Blacks were freer from oppression, and in time it would be from the cities that Du Bois's "talented tenth" emerged.

Yet again, however, white legislators used the power of the state to limit the power that Black citizens were gaining through their ability to move. Long-distance moves could be quite intimidating, requiring information, debt retirement, and other forms of assistance. Those who moved out of state were often recruited by an "emigrant agent" who would help them successfully to leave, choose a destination, and make the journey. These agents worked for out-of-state endeavors in need of more laborers. This free market in labor, however, threatened the labor supply in the deep South or, at the very least, forced land owners to make better contracts with their workers for fear of losing them. Therefore, they employed their political power to "discourage or effectively ban" emigrant agents, thus setting up yet another legal obstacle to Black economic freedom.[141]

Starting with nothing, rising up from a situation in which they were purposefully kept as ignorant as possible, and surrounded by those determined to keep them in their place, Black Americans were able to make serious material gains by the turn of the century. These gains should not be minimized. It's true that they remained in relative poverty, with absolute incomes consistently lower than even poor whites. But the Black economy grew at a rate faster than the white economy, improving the average income by more than double and, possibly, triple of what it was in the late 1860s. Even poorer Black Americans were able, by the turn of the century, to set aside portions of their incomes for something more than mere necessity. As we will see in future chapters, they invested in "churches, lodges, consumer durables, travel, amusement, and savings."[142] Their diets improved, and many came to live in improved housing—all due to their ability to move and to work for their own, rather than another's, gain.

Economic historian Robert Higgs demonstrates that, despite a deeply hostile culture and discriminatory laws of every kind, Southern farm wage rates, rental contracts, and merchant credit terms did not differ significantly between whites and Blacks.[143] This arose neither from Black power nor white benevolence, he argues, but from simple competition. White planters in the marketplace had to choose between their preference for wealth and their preference for discrimination. Those who chose discrimination found themselves without any laborers for that year's crops. Indeed, market forces forced whites to turn to the political realm to maintain supremacy. The legislative measures that emerged from their efforts indubitably harmed Blacks and negatively affected Black economic opportunities. Southern state governments removed funding from Black schools and refused to provide legal and police protections to Black citizens.[144] Solidarity among whites in their attempts at discrimination were successful in these cases because "legal sanctions...could be brought to bear against mavericks within the group."[145] Options with economic consequences—such as the choice to move, to invest, or to build one's human capital—were painstakingly blocked by white political action at every turn. In the face of these efforts to stop Black liberation through the marketplace, Black Americans tripled their per capita income by 1914. Higgs concludes that "[s]uch salvation as the Black man found, he found in the private sector."[146]

EXCEPTIONAL CASES: BLACK VIRGINIAN PROPERTY AND THE FREEDMEN'S TOWNS

Many have noted with some puzzlement that Black Virginians exceeded all other Black Americans in average wealth, not just today, but clearly in both the 1920 and the 1940 census. Some have suggested that a disproportionate number of free Black people, originally transported as indentured servants from Congo through Angola, may be the explanation.[147] It's true that the descendants of free Black people were far more likely to have inherited some property or family business, for obvious reasons. Furthermore, Fort Monroe became the corridor for tens of thousands of fleeing slaves, so that many who settled in the area had already self-selected for courage and determination.

Central to the story of Virginia's success stands the Hampton Institute. Free Black Mary Peake worked tirelessly to educate the children of formerly enslaved people. After Mary's untimely death in 1862, missionary groups carried on her efforts, and Hampton Institute launched in 1867. It churned out one thousand teachers over the next quarter century. Hampton Institute would shape the literacy movement across the Black community in the South that resulted in an almost completely unlettered population reaching a literate majority by 1910. Higgs calls the achievement of so much in such a short amount of time (and with so few resources) an accomplishment "seldom witnessed in human history."[148] The "Black elite" that arose from this movement in Hampton, Virginia, were so sophisticated and cosmopolitan that it made little sense to their white neighbors that such a people should be subjugated. Due to the influence of Hampton, many Black leaders fought hard toward the specific goal of obtaining property in order to run successful businesses and become economically independent. By the end of the nineteenth century, Virginia property holdings by Black Americans far exceeded the average for Black people throughout the country.[149] As leaders like Booker T. Washington spread out to other great Black institutions like the Tuskegee Institute, they took this philosophy of economic freedom with them, forming a Black elite who became the most prominent drivers of movements for equal rights and economic uplift.

The same can be said for the freedmen's towns such as Mound Bayou, the home of the great T. R. M. Howard (you'll hear more about him in Chapter 6). These were all-Black "freedom colonies" set up by freedmen to achieve the dream of landownership on their own.[150] The incredible growth in Black landownership by 1900 was in a great part driven by these families. The number and success of the towns is astonishing: over seventy-five officially established freedmen's towns popped up across the South and Midwest, including thirty in Texas and Oklahoma alone. However, those numbers do not capture the true movement, which included hundreds of communities connected by church, school, and a shared sense of place, even if their existence was "unofficial" in terms of legal incorporation.[151] Although many of the towns faded over time as residents migrated north, some retained their distinction as thriving Black communities until the mid-twentieth century, when the federal highway system and urban renewal destroyed them. This includes Houston's once-famous Fourth Ward.

In their landmark work on the subject, historians Thad Sitton and James Conrad writing on freedmen's towns sound a lot like Higgs's or Schweninger's writing on Black property ownership and economic development (the two main authors we've drawn upon so far in this chapter). They complain that historians pass over these exceptional cases too quickly, largely because they didn't proliferate through most of Black America. Instead, they argue, we ought to be struck with curiosity as to how these illiterate, penniless, formerly enslaved people managed to get land for themselves and spawn a burgeoning Black elite. There may be many reasons that they are easily overlooked, including their scattered, rural existence and an inevitable lack of records. These internal settlers purposefully went to out-of-the-way places where whites wouldn't bother them. They settled on swampy or otherwise difficult tracts of land for the same reason. Nevertheless, a stubborn pride in the land and in their habits of frugality and deep family ties developed and persisted through the ravages of the Depression and World Wars. They were so stubborn, in fact, that these self-segregated Blacks even fought school integration efforts that they saw as a threat to their own community schools.

Perhaps the most difficult part of recounting their history is squaring it with the terror of Jim Crow. These communities stand out as sparks of Black empowerment that simply sidestepped some of that painful history by keeping away from the oppressors altogether. Havens of Black family tradition and pride, the freedmen's towns demonstrate the power of personal freedom and property ownership for the flourishing of exceptional communities. The story of Black asset accumulation and the whites who undermined or destroyed this economic development continues in the twentieth century.

Lessons in Classical Liberalism #8: The Economics of Discrimination

The most famous classical liberal work on discrimination comes from economist Gary Becker, a leader in the Chicago school of economics of which Milton Friedman was also a part. He has been called by some the "greatest social scientist" in the latter half of the twentieth century. In his 1957 book, *The Economics of Discrimination*, Becker casts racism in the cold language of an economist, as a "preference for discrimination."[152] He then analyzes how much it costs people to fulfill such a preference. If Black workers are excluded from a particular work force, for instance, the constriction of the labor supply to a smaller group pushes the price of labor up, increasing costs for employers. If sellers restrict the group of people to whom they're willing to sell, they restrict their own possibilities for profit. If a transportation company has to provide two separate cars for two different groups when one would have sufficed for both, they're going to have to pass the cost of that extra car on to the consumer. In other words, discrimination is expensive. If people want to indulge in discrimination, they're going to have to pay for it, which makes the willingness to let go of discrimination financially rewarding. Indeed, we see many employers and companies lobbying against Jim Crow laws because they did not want to lose business or pay higher labor costs. The temptation to simply surrender one's preference for discrimination in order to do better economically can undermine racist practices in trade. And the more competitive the market is, the more expensive it is to indulge one's preference for discrimination. The freer the market, the greater the incentive to include anyone who could make a good employee, customer, or supplier. William Hutt, a South African economist and classical liberal, made similar points in his 1964 book, *The Economics of the Colour Bar*.[153] He attributed much of the apartheid system, not simply to racism, but also to the desire among the unionists to gin up as much pro-discrimination sentiment as possible in order to restrict the supply of labor and extract higher wages.[154]

Sometimes Becker's argument has been caricatured, as though he's saying that the free market will magically fix racism. Of course it can't. Racism is a highly complex phenomenon that requires individual, cultural, and moral transformation as well as institutional transformation to overcome. Becker's argument actually supports the insight that addressing racism involves institutional change. Racists in power are fully aware that allowing freedom of contract between everyone will tempt racists away from indulging their preference for discrimination by making it profitable to be nondiscriminatory. That's why they scrambled to impose a plethora of municipal, state, and federal laws in order to increase the cost of nondiscrimination by making it illegal (or they made it functionally illegal by refusing to enforce just laws, as with the lynching of whites who defended Black victims).

Becker helps us see that, once again, a classical liberal analysis recognizes the institutional nature of racism, since racists felt that they had to insert coercive intervention into people's voluntary interactions with one another in order to keep them separate.

Chapter 4

No Liberation without the Equal Protection of the Law: Black Resistance in the Face of Atrocities

"The way to right wrongs is to turn the
light of truth upon them."
—Ida B. Wells, 1892

The 2019 HBO series *Watchmen* acts as a sequel to the famous graphic novel of the same name, a kind of superhero dystopia. While the story lines are based on an alternate reality, many viewers were shocked to discover that the depiction in episode one of the 1921 Tulsa massacre of Black Wall Street was all too real. Blacks and whites, many highly educated, expressed dismay that they could have been unaware that a sort of Beverly Hills of the Black community existed at such a time in our history, much less that white neighbors and police destroyed a thriving town of ten thousand people, dispossessed its citizens, and murdered hundreds in a frenzy of envy and rage.

While conservatives are correct that any society needs a hopeful and unifying concept of itself, it cannot be correct that achieving this requires denial and self-deception. This is particularly true when that hopeful and unifying concept is the Constitution—the guarantor of the rights of the minority against majority oppression. In this chapter, we will review just a few of the most egregious cases of rights violations, failure of the state to provide police protections, and failure of the state to ensure legal protections for citizens in its jurisdiction. These protections are among the most basic that any political order must provide to its citizens, and the failure to do so constitutes a straightforward injustice.

We must warn our readers in advance that we describe in this chapter acts of violence that are deeply disturbing, both in terms of their shocking cruelty and in terms of the sheer number of people affected. It is difficult to read.

THE COLFAX MASSACRE

Although Radical Republicans in Congress and President Grant, to a lesser extent, attempted to secure African Americans' civil rights, their experiment in Reconstruction ultimately failed.[155] From 1870 to 1877 (in some Southern states) Republican governments, supported by federal troops, were able to guarantee Black civil rights including their participation in government. By 1877, however, federal troops had been withdrawn from all Southern states, and Black Americans were left at the mercy of racist whites. Democratic "Redeemers" took over the state governments and quickly disenfranchised Blacks, established Black codes, and enacted systematic discrimination that amounted to "slavery by another name" in many areas of the South.

Even while federal troops had occupied sections of the South, it was extremely hard for them to protect Blacks' civil liberties, and each election in which Blacks participated led to further frustration and resentment by the dominant white population. The Ku Klux Klan, the White League, and the Knights of the White Camellia terrorized Blacks, especially in rural areas where the federal presence was less visible. Violence erupted across the South. The number of injustices committed against Blacks during this time is difficult to quantify. The most glaring example of the conflict between Democrats and Republicans, whites and Blacks, took place in Colfax, Louisiana.

On Easter Sunday, April 13, 1873, over one hundred Black citizens were killed in what came to be known as the Colfax Massacre.[156] The massacre occurred in the aftermath of the hotly contested 1872 gubernatorial contest in Louisiana. Both the Republicans and a fusionist party made up of racially conservative Republicans and Democrats claimed victory. The election was full of fraud and intimidation, and ultimately it took federal intervention to establish Republican government in Louisiana.[157] In the wake of the Republican success, Grant Parish Black Republicans seized the courthouse in Colfax (about 150 miles north of Baton Rouge), hoping to ensure that Democrats did not take over the parish government.[158]

Almost immediately, word spread that a Black militia had taken the courthouse. In a short amount of time, a mob of around 150 former Confederates and members of the Ku Klux Klan travelled to Colfax to take back the courthouse.[159] By the beginning of April, their numbers swelled to around 400, but they were unable to force the Republicans from Colfax. As such, they sent out the call "for 'reinforcements,' and formed a 'veritable army' of vigilantes" from the surrounding area "to suppress negro domination."[160] In the meantime, small skirmishes broke out, and atrocities were committed. On April 5, Jesse M. Kinney, a Black man, was shot in the head while peacefully building a fence. The Blacks in control of the courthouse prepared earthworks on April 12, and on Easter morning, April 13, they prepared for an assault.[161]

What happened next is detailed by the House of Representatives "Report on the South":

> Easter Sunday, April 13, a large body of whites rode into the town, and demanded of the colored men that they should give up their arms and yield possession of the courthouse. This demand not being yielded to, thirty minutes were given them to remove their women and children. The Negroes took refuge behind their earthwork, from which they were driven by an enfilading fire from a cannon which the whites had. Part of them fled for refuge to the courthouse, which was a one-story brick building, which had formerly been a stable. The rest, leaving their arms, fled down the river to a strip of woods, where they were pursued, and many of them were overtaken and shot to death. About sixty or seventy got into the courthouse. After some ineffectual firing on each side, the roof of the building was set fire to. When the roof was burning over their heads the Negroes held out the sleeve of a shirt and the leaf of a book as flags of truce. They were ordered to drop their arms. A number of them rushed unarmed from the blazing building, but were all captured. The number taken prisoner was bout thirty-seven. They were kept till dark when they were led out two by two, each two with a rank of mounted whites behind them, being told that they were to be taken a short distance and set at liberty. When all the ranks had been formed the word was given, and the Negroes were all shot. A few who were wounded, but not mortally, escaped by feigning

death. The bodies remained unburied till the next Tuesday, when they were buried by a deputy marshal from New Orleans. Fifty-nine dead bodies were found. They showed pistol-shot wounds, the great majority of them in the head, and most in the back of the head.[162]

When all was said and done, more than one hundred Blacks were dead—many of them murdered in cold blood.

The Colfax Massacre was "the bloodiest single instance of racial carnage in the Reconstruction Era," but it was representative of the thousands of other incidents across the South where racist whites terrorized, killed, and ultimately stripped Blacks of their dignity and their rights.[163] From 1866 to 1875, *in Louisiana alone*, over 2,100 people were killed for their political opinions—many of them Black.[164]

If the massacre of over one hundred Black Americans wasn't enough, Colfax was also a turning point in the history of Reconstruction. After the massacre, Republicans took back the parish, and federal authorities indicted ninety-eight of the whites who had assailed Colfax.[165] These men were indicted for violating the Enforcement Acts rather than for murder at the state level, mainly because the lawyers for the victims thought that the largely Democratic state courts would not administer justice equally.[166] Of those indicted, "only nine were arrested and brought to trial in New Orleans, and by the summer of 1874 most them had been acquitted."[167] The case ultimately made its way to the Supreme Court in 1876, where the court ruled that "the Enforcement Acts applied only to actions by the state, not by individuals."[168] As such, the ruling removed the mechanisms by which the federal government could protect the individual liberty of Blacks in the South.

For almost fifty years, Colfax was largely forgotten—at least by whites. But in the 1920s, local officials put up a monument that glorified the three white attackers who died in the assault on the courthouse. The monument still stands today. It reads: "Erected to the memory of the heroes Stephen Decatur Parish, James West Hadnot, Sidney Harris, Who fell in the Colfax Riot fighting for White Supremacy / April 13, 1873." In 1950, a state historical marker was erected on the highway near Colfax. To this day it reads: "COLFAX RIOT: On this site occurred the Colfax Riot in which three white men and 150 negroes were slain. This event on April 13, 1873 marked the end of carpetbag misrule in the South."[169]

After an initial attempt, the federal government failed to protect the life, liberty, and property of Blacks across the South. What's more, whites in both the North and South reimagined the Civil War as an honorable war in which both had fought with honor to protect their way of life. The construction of this narrative may have been important for bringing whites in both sections together under one flag, but it came at a terrible cost to Blacks, who despite being free would have to fight and struggle to maintain any semblance of dignity and respect during the Jim Crow era.[170]

CONVICT LEASING

"Turke finally told the older white man that he and his son would have to do whatever they chose—kill him or imprison him—but that he would not plead guilty to a crime dreamt up by others. 'Kill me or do what you please,' Turke said. 'I propose to do what is right.'"[171]

Immediately upon taking back power, white Democrat "Redeemer" governments began to find ways to reestablish white supremacy and dominance in the South. Local and state officials had to be strategic, using creative new laws to ensure Black Southerners remained in an inferior social and economic condition. Some of the measures adopted included vagrancy laws, pig laws, and even laws banning Black men from switching employment. The pig laws, which were passed in Alabama, Georgia,

Florida, and Mississippi, converted previous misdemeanor offenses into felony offenses. For example, stealing a pig worth one dollar could result in a felony charge and five years in prison. Tennessee's laws were so harsh that if someone stole an eight-cent fence post, they could find themselves sentenced to hard labor.[172] Vagrancy laws were the most common, and they were purposefully vague. The result was that "virtually any freed slave not under the protection of a white man could be arrested for the crime."[173] White law enforcement would routinely stop and ask Black men (and a few Black women) for proof of employment. If the person being questioned could not prove employment, they would be arrested and become a criminal.

Once these Black men were convicted, state and local governments had to figure out what to do with them. The widespread criminalization of Black life meant that caring for these "criminals" could quickly burden the state and local authorities. By 1877, all the Southern states, with the exception of Virginia, adopted a system of leasing convicts to private entities as a way to profit from the convicts' labor without being forced to care for them.[174]

How was this possible? After all, the Thirteenth Amendment had guaranteed an end for slavery. But the amendment came with a qualifier: "Neither slavery nor involuntary servitude, *except as punishment for crime whereof the party shall have been duly convicted* [emphasis added], shall exist within the United States, or any place subject to their jurisdiction." So local and state officials made Black men (and some poor whites) criminals by making new laws and selectively enforcing them against the people they wanted to forcibly control. The term "convict leasing" makes it seem like this episode in our history is simply about making imprisoned criminals work. But this gravely misunderstands what happened in the years after the Civil War and even as late as the 1950s. The leasing of men for labor on farms and in industry was only nominally the leasing of convicts. That's because a significant number, quite possibly the bulk of the men arrested, charged, and sent to work, were not criminals at all.

In Douglas Blackmon's *Slavery by Another Name: The Re-Enslavement of Black Americans from the Civil War to World War II*, he explains how perfectly innocent people were caught up in a web of what we can only properly refer to as an underground slave market. This market served some large farms but also the burgeoning Southern industries of coal and steel. The states realized that they could improve their budgets by collecting on any convicts they delivered as laborers, and a group of conspirators in many small towns, including a justice of the peace and a few of his trusted friends, realized that they could personally enrich themselves by doing so as well. In a legal environment in which Black men were close to completely helpless, these supposed lawmen arrested them for the following reasons: carrying a weapon (almost all men did so at the time, but it was only illegal for Blacks), riding on empty freight train cars, speaking loudly in front of a white woman, "vagrancy" (having no job or appearing to have no job), changing employers without permission, voting illegally, using obscene language, selling whiskey, selling cotton after sunset, and performing other either trivial or innocent activities.[175] When the demand for laborers went up, these already trivial accusations could simply be made spuriously against any Black man at hand, with the help of a white "witness" who was paid for his services. In a survey of the scant records we retain, many prisoners simply have the phrase "not listed" in the column where the charges should go. In one 1898 board report, the "not listed" group was in the majority.[176]

The "trial" was often conducted in a matter of a few minutes, with exorbitant court fees added to the fine that the justice of the peace meted out. This was the real trick. Once the "criminal" owed some amount surpassing several months wages, a white man could pay his fine for him, with the understanding that the Black man could pay off his debt by working at the farm or in the mines for no less than a year. While there, the man would be charged for supplies or medical treatment and forced to stay longer to pay his newly acquired debts.

One of the terrible ironies of this practice is that overseers ran the work gangs with the attitude of slavers, but no one legally owned these workers. These men believed that "African-Americans under the lash were the key to building an industrial sector in the South."[177] That meant that the "convicts" were treated far, far worse than anything they had endured on the plantation, where at the very least, their owners limited their own cruelty to protect their investment. Sheriffs were allowed to keep any extra money from the food allotment, creating a perverse incentive to feed the laborers as little as possible. Working from 3 a.m. to 8 p.m., they rarely saw the light of day. The men were whipped mercilessly; water tortured; kept in filthy, vermin-infested, unventilated quarters; and left for dead when waves of sickness swept through the camps.[178]

Without any personal incentive to take care of the men, and with fresh laborers easily available, overseers treated these unjustly imprisoned Black men as entirely expendable.[179] The death rates increased at such an alarming rate that the head of the 1906 Board of Inspectors of Convicts argued that "[i]f the state wishes to kill its convicts it should do it directly and not indirectly."[180] In Alabama the leasing program began in 1875. By 1877, 20 percent of the prisoners had died in custody; by 1878, 35 percent; by 1879, 40 percent. Some of the prisoners were teenagers, and even children as young as seven are listed on the records.

The scale at which the leasing programs operated cannot be exaggerated. Hundreds of thousands of Black men were ultimately victims of convict leasing. To their credit, a few white men of conscience poured themselves into the project of investigating and rooting out the practice, at great cost to themselves. Due to their vigilance, the system was eventually dissolved—or perhaps transformed—but not before hundreds of thousands of lives had been irrevocably ruined. It's hard to approximate the damage done to individuals, their families, and their communities. One of the most pernicious changes that resulted from criminalizing Blackness was the shift in the ways that Black men were perceived by whites. Before vagrancy laws, Blacks were generally viewed as hard working, loyal, and trustworthy. By the end of the nineteenth century, however, whites viewed Black men as dangerous and criminal. This perception of Black masculinity would have devastating consequences in the twentieth century.[181]

Was this system of exploitation profitable? Yes, it was—at least for the state government and the white business owners who were exploiting the convicts' labor. But was this system a product of free markets? The answer to this is emphatically no! The system of convict leasing in the South was a result of cronyism, racism, and unjust imprisonment combined with the desire of a few to exploit the many for financial gain. Arrangements such as this have been with humanity since the beginning of civilization. But this system cannot reasonably be called a product of a free enterprise system—far from it. Setting up the system of convict leasing required that state governments ignore their citizens' individual liberty and also that they engage in corporatist practices of partnering with select businessmen offering them cheap labor at the expense of any competitors in the market. The infrastructure of a free market is the rule of law—the protection of one's property in oneself and in one's possessions, as well as the right to due process of law when accused. In a truly liberal society, where government protects the rights of all citizens through the equal application of justice, such abuses would not be possible.

THE FIGHT AGAINST WHITE LYNCH MOBS

The criminalization of Black life by white Democrat "Redeemer" governments was coupled with laws designed to disenfranchise Black men and keep them from enjoying their civil rights. After

1874, most Blacks in the South lived under the rule of governments that had no intention of protecting their individual liberty, but those who lived in the cities had some respite. However, during the 1880s there were significant attempts to segregate the cities. Blacks were disenfranchised through "the use of poll taxes, constitutional literacy tests, election fraud, and voter intimidation." In addition to assaulting Black political rights, these governments also "passed laws forcing the separation of the races in schools, on streetcars, and elsewhere in society."[182] From 1882 to 1968, white mobs terrorized countless Black families and lynched 3,446 Black Americans. An additional 1,297 whites were also lynched, often for helping Blacks.[183]

Although the number of Blacks who died from lynchings was less than the number who perished from the system of convict leasing, the psychological effect of lynching cannot be overstated.[184] Lynchings usually targeted young Black men who were new to an area. These men were usually accused of murder, property damage, or theft. The lynchings themselves were "highly choreographed and ritualized," and they served as public events for the white populations. They were always held in public, and participants had little fear of punishment.[185] Indeed, sometimes lynchings even served as an occasion for a family picnic, and historians have examples of photographs for the lynchings being converted into postcards. According to historian Steven Hahn, lynchings fed "on a deep culture of social and political violence" and "lynch mobs sought to reestablish the boundaries that they believed were being traversed."[186]

These public assassinations horrified and terrorized Blacks across the United States. In May 1918, a plantation owner in Georgia was killed. Hampton Smith, who was known to be abusive, had been shot, and Hayes Turner (a Black man) was accused of pulling the trigger. Mr. Turner was hunted down and killed. His widow, Mary Turner, denounced the mob for murdering her husband. On May 19, the mob turned on Mrs. Turner. Several hundred people descended on her. They "tied her ankles, hung her upside down from a tree, doused her in gasoline and motor oil and set her on fire." Killing Mrs. Turner was not enough for the angry white mob. While she was still alive, "a member of the mob split her abdomen open with a knife and her unborn child fell on the ground" where it was promptly "stomped and crushed." When Mary Turner's body was ultimately found it was also "riddled with hundreds of bullets."[187]

Most of the time, it was Black men who suffered lynching. In May 1918, Jesse McIlherron, a Black man who carried a gun and "resented the slights and insults of white men," got into an altercation with three white men. The men insulted and threatened one another, and McIlherron "fired six shots, killing two of the men." McIlherron fled but was ultimately captured, and planning promptly began for him to be lynched. The call went out, and families from as far away as fifty miles travelled to Estill Springs (the spot selected for the occasion) to watch him burn. Here is how Walter White, the assistant secretary of the NAACP, and an investigator of lynchings described what happened next:

> McIlherron was chained to a hickory tree while the mob howled about him. A fire was built a few feet away and the torture began. Bars of iron were heated and the mob amused itself by putting them close to the victim, at first without touching him. One bar he grasped as it was jerked from his grasp all the inside of his hand came with it. Then the real torture began, lasting twenty minutes. During that time, while his flesh was slowly roasting, the Negro never lost nerve. He cursed those who tortured him and almost to the last breath derided the attempts of the mob to break his spirit.[188]

While lynch mobs undoubtedly terrified Black Americans, Black Americans also used their voices to denounce lynching and formed voluntary associations to prevent such terrorism. Ida B. Wells became the most prominent anti-lynching voice in 1892 after witnessing three Black men be lynched in Memphis, Tennessee. Their deaths set Wells on a crusade against lynching and in the pursuit of justice that would take her all the way to Britain.

Like many lynchings, the altercation in Memphis began with something seemingly trivial: a group of white boys and a group of Black boys who had been playing marbles with one another got into a fight over the results. Cornelius Hurst, the father of one of the white boys, whipped one of the Black boys (who had gotten the better of the tussle). The fathers of the Black boys decided to confront Hurst at his home. These frustrated dads were quickly labeled a mob, and the police were called, although they determined there was nothing to report.[189]

Whites' anger and resentment, however, ran far deeper than a disagreement over a game of marbles. W. H. Barrett, a local white grocer, was immensely frustrated that Black residents banded together to create the joint-stock People's Grocery Company. The Black-owned grocery had been opened in 1889 in the same mixed neighborhood as Barrett's store. After three years, the People's Grocery was doing well, and Barrett did not like the competition.[190]

When word got out that a Black "mob" was marching on Hurst's home, Barrett took it upon himself to look for the now dispersed mob in the People's Grocery store. He entered the store and accused the Black clerk, Calvin McDowell, of hiding members of the Black mob. What happened next is disputed. Barrett "claimed that he came to the aid of Hurst and was assaulted with a pistol and a mallet." The white man declared: "My head was badly bruised, and my face covered in blood." In contrast, McDowell claimed that Barrett struck him with a pistol and that in the ensuing fight, he got the best of the white man: "Being the stronger, I got the best of that scrimmage."[191]

McDowell may have gotten the best of Barrett in the scrum, but Barrett knew how to turn the situation to his advantage. He and Hurst went to a Shelby County judge who issued a warrant for the grocery clerk. McDowell was arrested but quickly released on bail. Barrett though was not done. He convinced a grand jury to indict his competitors for "maintaining a public nuisance." That is when things cascaded for the People's Grocery. Although they got the grand jury charges dismissed with only small fines, the Black community decided to hold a meeting in the People's Grocery to discuss the situation. Some of the participants at that meeting were understandably angry and frustrated with the treatment they were being forced to endure. There was some heated rhetoric, and someone recommended "dynamite as a remedy for the 'damn white trash.'" Barrett got word of the threat and once again convinced the judge that there was "a conspiracy against whites"—warrants were issued for two Blacks who frequented the Black-owned grocery store.[192]

Barrett knew that the police would look for the Black men at the People's Grocery, so he spread a rumor that a white mob was going to march on the store. In response to those rumors, Blacks stationed armed guards at the store (as was their right per the local laws). When nine armed white men wearing civilian clothes approached the store, the two Black guards fired: three white police officers were injured. The two guards fled when the white authorities began rounding up Black men. The white press published headlines such as: "A Bloody Riot." At the same time many white men were being deputized to deal with the Black threat. The People's Grocery was looted, and around $1,800 of merchandise was stolen. The newly minted "deputies" broke into hundreds of homes and ultimately arrested some thirty Black men as conspirators. Thomas Moss, the president of the joint-stock company that owned the store, was among those arrested. The Black state militia guarded the jail to ensure that no harm came to those who had been arrested, but they were soon stripped of their right to bear arms. The same Shelby County judge "issued an order to disarm all the city's Black citizens" including the Black state militia (which was subsequently disbanded).[193]

Three of those arrested, Thomas Moss, Calvin McDowell, and Will Stewart, were seized by a group of whites demanding justice. None of the men had any priors on their record, and all claimed they were innocent. What they all had in common was that they held prominent positions in the People's Grocery. Despite their claims of innocence, the three men were taken about a mile outside of town and were shot to death. McDowell, who had resisted, had his eyes gouged out.[194] With his dying breath, Moss was reported to have said, "Tell my people to go West, there is no justice for them here."[195]

This incident demonstrates that when Black Americans participated in the marketplace and civil society to build a prosperous business and community it outraged whites. Black economic success often fueled violence against them and without protection of their individual liberty from the local, state, and federal government, much of the economic success achieved by Black Americans was ephemeral. The lynching of Moss, McDowell, and Stewart was an abrogation of justice, as was the looting of the People's Grocery, the confiscation of Blacks' weapons, the breaking into their homes, and the arbitrary arrests of Black men. Far from protecting their rights, government—at the behest of white supremacists—had curtailed their freedom of speech, their right to bear arms, and their right to peaceful assembly, and had failed to protect Black citizens' right to life, liberty, and property. In short, this incident was a complete failure of the justice system.

These murders outraged Black Memphians, the eastern press, and Ida B. Wells, who co-owned and operated the *Free Speech* in Memphis. Wells described the "shock" of Memphis's Black citizens as "beyond description" and set about writing an editorial denouncing lynching. Wells wrote:

> The City of Memphis has demonstrated that neither character nor standing avails the Negro if he dares to protect himself against the white man or become his rival. There is nothing we can do about the lynching now, as we are outnumbered and without arms. The white mob could help itself to ammunition without pay, but the order was rigidly enforced against the selling of guns to Negroes. There is therefore only one thing left that we can do; save our money and leave a town which will neither protect our lives and property, nor give us a fair trial in the courts, but takes us out and murders us in cold blood when accused by white persons.[196]

Blacks responded to Wells's call—thousands of them left for the Oklahoma Territory.[197] The efforts of Blacks to vote with their feet—by leaving the city—was enabled through donations by Black businessmen, Black churches, and emigration societies that raised and distributed funds to aid those who wanted to leave Memphis.[198] Wells estimated that around six thousand Blacks had left Memphis by early May, and she was happy that the loss of Black consumers was being noticed by white Memphians.[199] Among those Black Memphians who would ultimately end up in Oklahoma, and Tulsa specifically, was Captain Townsend D. Jackson, who had served as policeman and president of the local Republican club in Memphis before travelling west with his family in 1889.[200] But more on Black community in Tulsa's story to come.

Wells also embraced Blacks using their economic power to draw attention to the injustices being committed against them.

Wells praised and encouraged Blacks who stopped riding the electric trolleys in Memphis. Her voice was thought to be so influential that the superintendent and treasurer granted her a meeting. In a conversation with the two men, Wells decried respectable whites' compliance with the injustices perpetuated against Moss, McDowell, and others. No one had been held accountable for their lynchings, and Wells exclaimed to the two white men: "The Colored people feel that every white man in Memphis who consented to his death is as guilty as those who fired the guns which took his life, and they want to get away from this town."[201] The boycotting of the trolley lines in Memphis—and especially at around the same time in Indianapolis—foreshadowed the effectiveness of Black boycotts during the Civil Rights Movement in the late 1950s and 1960s.

The deaths of Moss, McDowell, and Stewart led Wells to embark on an anti-lynching crusade in the pages of the *Free Speech*. Prior to the incident, Wells believed that most lynchings were the result of white women being violated by Black men and that there had to be a kernel of cause even if the punishment was inhumane. The lynchings in Memphis, however, led her to recognize the economic and social reasons behind the barbaric practice. In her autobiography, Wells recounted the three had been lynched "with just as much brutality as other victims of the mob; and they had committed no crime against white women. This is what opened my eyes to what lynching really was. An excuse to get rid of Negroes who were acquiring wealth and property and thus keep the race terrorized and 'keep the nigger down.'"[202]

Frederick Douglass came to the same conclusion. In July he penned an article titled "Lynch Law in the South" in which he denounced lynchings as "an effort to neutralize one poison by the employment of another." He condemned the "howling mob" that rendered its verdict "without judge or jury" as the real "crime." Douglass suggested that the horrors of lynching would be stopped by one of two scenarios. The first was for good Southerners and the justice system to stop the atrocities. The other potentiality was that Blacks might respond in kind to white violence. Given the entirety of his writings, it is likely that Douglass would have preferred that liberal institutions address the inhumane injustices being committed against Blacks. But Douglass also realized that "oppression can make a wise man mad" and had advocated the use of violence to secure and defend one's liberty.[203]

Wells penned another article on lynching and explicitly addressed the justification for white terrorism: rape. She pointed out that many of the recent lynchings across the South had nothing to do with the protection of white womanhood. Instead, they were murders driven by political and economic motives. She exclaimed that "nobody in this section of the country believes the old thread-bear lie that Negro men rape white women." She warned that "if Southern white men are not careful, they will over-reach themselves and public sentiment will have a reaction; a conclusion will then be reached which will be very damaging to the moral reputation of their women."[204]

The response to Wells's article was vehement. Luckily for her, she was out of town on a preplanned trip to the Northeast. While Wells was touring New York and Philadelphia, the white press in Memphis was denouncing her article—although they misattributed it to J. L. Fleming, Wells's co-owner of the *Free Speech*. The *Memphis Chronicle* insisted to readers that "[t]he fact that a Black scoundrel is allowed to live and utter such loathsome and repulsive calumnies is a volume of evidence as to the wonderful patience of Southern whites."[205] The *Memphis Scimitar* went further, explicitly threatening Fleming: "If the negroes themselves do not apply the remedy without delay it will be the duty of those he has attacked to tie the wretch who utters these calumnies to a stake at the intersection of Main and Madison Sts., brand him on the forehead with a hot iron and perform upon him a surgical operation with a pair of tailor's shears."[206]

Fleming, fearing for his life, left town, but that did not spare the *Free Speech*. While in New York, Wells read about the ransacking of her paper back in Memphis. The most dramatic account asserted that "a mob had descended on the offices of the *Free Speech*, destroyed its furnishings, and posted a death threat to anyone attempting to publish the paper again."[207] Wells considered returning to Memphis but was warned against it by her lawyer and others who informed her through telegrams that whites were watching her house and were waiting for her. Some believed there was a real possibility that Wells would be lynched if she returned. In her autobiography, Wells wrote that "whites had declared they would bleed my face and hang me in front of the Court House."[208] Wells prudently decided not to go back to Memphis. Years later, she reflected that whites had it out for the *Free Press* prior to her article. Wells summed up the events in Memphis as follows:

> For the first time in their lives the white people of Memphis had seen earnest united action by Negroes which upset economic and business conditions...In casting about for the cause of all this restlessness and dissatisfaction the leaders concluded that the *Free Speech* was the disturbing factor. They were right.[209]

Although she was forced to leave Memphis, Wells did not stop writing about the horrors of lynching. Indeed, her exile led her on the path to become one of the most influential voices in the country against injustice. In June 1892, Wells published "The Truth about Lynching" in the *New York Age*, which Wells signed "Exiled."[210] It was clear that she wouldn't be silenced. Later in the year, she published her pamphlet *Southern Horrors* that documented the ways in which whites used lynching as an economic and social tool to keep Blacks down and to preserve their own status and power. She followed it up three years later with a more detailed pamphlet titled *The Red Record*.

Wells's insistence on justice caught the eye of Frederick Douglass, whom she met in 1892. Wells viewed Douglass with awe, and he was equally impressed with her. Douglass exclaimed in a public letter: "Brave woman! You have done your people and mine a service.... If American conscience were only half alive, if the church and the clergy were only half Christianized, if American moral sensibility were not hardened...a scream of horror, shame, and indignation would rise to Heaven wherever your pamphlet shall be read."[211] Two of Douglass's friends invited Wells to speak in England and Scotland. Douglass himself was too old to go, but he encouraged Wells to do so. Douglass told Wells, "You go my child, you are the one to go, for you have the story to tell."[212] With Douglass's strong support, Wells embarked on a speaking tour in England and Scotland in 1893 and 1894.[213] Wells ultimately married in 1895 and settled down in Chicago. She would spend the remainder of her life writing, speaking, and organizing for the civil rights of Black Americans. When Douglass died in 1895, Wells was "too overcome with grief" to write a fitting tribute. She explained that the day she heard of Douglass's passing, it "was the saddest since she had received the notice that she had been orphaned."[214]

The horrors of lynching and Black Americans' response to it in the 1890s gave rise to many of the strategies and tactics that Blacks would use in the twentieth century to combat injustice. The reality, however, was that the promise of participation in a liberal society was broken for Blacks in Memphis. When they engaged in commerce and competed with whites, they became targets of violence. When they used their First Amendment right to denounce the violence, they were threatened, harassed, and shut down. The only remaining option to many Black Memphians was to vote with their feet. Many did just that: they stopped frequenting white trolleys, saved their money, and ultimately purchased tickets out west to places like Oklahoma where they hoped to establish communities and cities where their life, liberty, and property would be secure and protected.

WHITE RACIAL VIOLENCE AND THE TULSA MASSACRE

To many Blacks—used to state-mandated segregation, discrimination, lynching, and other abuses—Oklahoma promised to be a fresh chance to start anew. Prior to Oklahoma becoming a state in 1907 there was no formal law mandating segregation. Some Blacks claimed land in the new territory, and many others travelled to this "land of opportunity and freedom."[215] Black towns emerged across the state and even where whites and Blacks mixed, such as the town of Guthrie in which "the new arrivals of both races were too caught up in the promise of instant wealth, too distracted by the thrills of the raucous boomtown, to give bigotry much heed."[216] This isn't to say that the people in Oklahoma were racially egalitarian—they weren't—but without formal laws enforcing segregation, individuals of both races were free to hire, trade, and interact with whomever they wished.[217]

Things were still far from ideal in Oklahoma. Racism was very much still alive, but for a time the West looked like a place where Blacks could secure a better life. In Guthrie, Blacks secured important positions in the local government. Captain Townsend D. Jackson, who had fled Memphis in 1889, was a jailor and also served as a justice of the peace. In time, Jackson would serve on the police force in Guthrie and formed the Oklahoma Territory's first Black militia. Jackson watched as his children grew up and prospered. His daughter married a prominent young Black lawyer, and his son travelled to Nashville, where he attended Meharry Medical College. For a while Blacks prospered in Guthrie.[218] Unfortunately, by the late 1890s, the territory's government made laws to separate Black and white children in school. As racial mixing declined, Blacks focused on creating their own schools.

The question of race relations was central when delegates met in Guthrie at the Oklahoma Constitutional Convention to prepare the territory for statehood. By that time, a mixture of law and custom had resulted in the separation of Blacks and whites. This was not enough, however, for the Democratic Party, which sent the most delegates to Guthrie. Faced with President Theodore Roosevelt's threat to veto statehood if the Constitution included segregation language, the delegates had to wait for statehood and rely on their legislature to enact the measures.[219] Future governor and first speaker of the house, William H. Murray, aided the passage of Jim Crow legislation during the state's first legislative session. Murray argued that Oklahoma "should adopt a provision prohibiting the mixed marriages of negroes and other races in this State, and provide for separate schools and give the Legislature power to separate them in waiting rooms and on passenger coaches, and all other institutions in the state." Like many other whites, Murray longed for the "good old days" of the submissive Black man. He claimed that "as a rule they are failures as lawyers, doctors and in other professions" and concluded that he appreciated "the old-time ex-slave, the old darky—and they are the salt of their race—who comes to me talking softly in that humble spirit which should characterize their actions and dealings with the white man."[220]

Murray's arguments won the day, and the state legislature passed laws mandating segregation in 1907. For Blacks like Captain Jackson this meant a curtailing of their authority and ability to influence politics in Guthrie. In 1912, the mayor asked Jackson to only police Black areas of Guthrie. He promptly resigned. Jackson decided to move his family to Tulsa—one hundred miles east. According to journalist Tim Madigan, "Jackson had heard that Negro prosperity without precedent was taking root there" and believed that "industrious Blacks in Greenwood [the Black section of Tulsa] had finally succeeded in placing themselves beyond the reach of white malice."[221]

But Jackson and the Blacks of Greenwood only met dashed hopes. From 1890 to 1908 Blacks were almost completely disenfranchised across the South, and the number of atrocities committed by whites did not abate. In Wilmington, North Carolina, the legitimately elected government was overthrown in the only coup d'état in United States history. White supremacist Democrats suppressed Black voter turnout in the state elections but were unable to take the city government away from the Republicans (many of whom were Black). In response, they gathered and drafted a "White Declaration of Independence" that exclaimed that "we will no longer be ruled, and will never again be ruled by men of African origin." On November 10, 1898, an organized a mob of some two thousand armed white supremacists overthrew the local government—killing sixty people in the process.[222] In 1898, Wilmington had been described as "the freest town for a negro in the country." Black businesses prospered, Blacks held political office, Black banks loaned money to entrepreneurs, and Blacks and whites lived side by side.[223] By the end of the year, however, all that was gone, and Blacks began fleeing Wilmington by the thousands. Two years later, the state of North Carolina passed Jim Crow laws disenfranchising Blacks.[224]

Despite the atrocities in Memphis and Wilmington, in Springfield (1908) and Slocum (1910) Captain Jackson was still optimistic that Blacks could improve their lot.[225] Addressing community leaders in Greenwood upon his arrival, Jackson declared that "with money and property comes the means of knowledge and power." Channeling the message of Booker T. Washington, Jackson exclaimed:

> A poverty-stricken class or race will be an ignorant and despised class and no amount of sentiment can make it otherwise. If the time shall

ever come when we possess in the colored people of this country a class of men noted for enterprise, industry, economy and success, we shall no longer have any trouble in the matter of civil and political rights; the battle against the popular prejudice shall have been fought.

Jackson held his son up as an example. Dr. Andrew Jackson was admired by Blacks and whites alike and was considered one of the best Black surgeons in the country.[226]

For the time being, Greenwood flourished. John Williams was the finest mechanic in Tulsa, white or Black, and managed his own garage, where Tulsa's leading citizens brought their vehicles to be worked on. Williams also owned the confectionery in Greenwood, which was the "headquarters for sweets, candies, nuts, fruits in season, ice cream, cold drinks, cigars, tobacco, and fresh butter every day." The confectionary quickly became the most likely place for young Black men to propose to their sweethearts. Williams also owned the Black movie theater, where young and old alike gathered to view the latest silent films.[227]

While Williams may have been Greenwood's greatest entrepreneur, he wasn't alone. Indeed, Greenwood sported a wide range of professionals and those who provided services to the community. Their consumers often worked across the tracks in white Tulsa where they found jobs as chauffeurs, maids, nannies, gardeners, laundresses, shoeshine boys, bellhops, and doormen. These laborers brought "their money home to Greenwood to spend on haircuts, barbeque, booze, prostitutes, groceries, jewelry, movie tickets, bootleg liquor, visits to Black doctors when they were ill, and on Black dentists when their teeth hurt" (perhaps from too many sweets at Williams's Confectionary). All in all, life was good in Greenwood, and the prosperity of its citizens earned it the label of Black Wall Street.[228]

As World War I came to an end, racial unrest across the United States exploded. There were over twenty race riots in 1919—the most prominent being in Atlanta, Chicago, Houston, and Washington, DC.[229] The racial violence that broke out across the country might have served as a warning to Greenwood. Although many Blacks had achieved economic success, and some even garnered respect from Tulsa's whites, all it would take was a spark to ignite racial hatred and resentment. In an instant their homes, schools, jobs, and even lives could be taken from them. This was the precarious reality of Black existence in 1920 America.

On June 1, 1921, that spark unleashed a firestorm of white violence that left Greenwood in ashes. The burning of Greenwood began with an altercation between a Black man and a white woman. Dick Rowland, a local Black man, was accused of assaulting Sarah Page, a white woman, in an elevator. Both worked in the Drexel Building. Page operated the elevator, and Rowland shined shoes. To use the Black-only restroom, Rowland used Page's elevator a couple times a day. The two developed a friendship and may have had a consensual relationship—but this is unclear. On May 30, 1921, when Rowland was on his way back to his shoeshine stand, he stepped into the elevator and either fell into Sarah or intentionally assaulted her—accounts vary. Page smacked Rowland with her purse, and when the elevator stopped on the ground floor, she screamed, "I've been assaulted!" Rowland took off running to his mother's home, where he spent the night. The next day he was arrested and taken to the local jail. The sheriff, Willard McCullough, made Dick's mother feel a little better the next day by letting her know that the investigators were skeptical of Page's story. McCullough assured her that they were holding Dick for his own safety.[230]

Unfortunately, justice was not allowed to run its course. The publisher of the *Tulsa Tribune*, Richard Lloyd Jones, published the headline, "Nab Negro for Attacking Girl in Elevator" in which they claimed that Rowland had "attacked" Page, "scratching her hands and face and tearing her clothes." If Jones's editorial itself wasn't bad enough, the paperboys hawked the paper by exclaiming: "Extra! Extra! To Lynch Negro Tonight! Read All About It!" Minutes after the afternoon edition hit the streets, a white mob began to form: "The paper had cast a match to the dry kindling of race in Tulsa."[231]

Sheriff McCullough transferred Rowland that afternoon to the county lockup that provided his prisoner with better security and protection. It was a good thing, too, because within hours crowds formed around the facility. In response to the formation of a white mob, Blacks in Greenwood grabbed their guns and made their way to the courthouse.[232] McCullough spoke with Black leaders and promised them that if they could keep their people from engaging the mob, he would protect Rowland. But both whites and Blacks continued to gather. Finally, at 10:15 p.m. tensions boiled over. An older white man confronted O. B. Mann—a respected Black veteran—shouting, "Nigger, what are you going to do with that pistol?" Mann responded that he was "going to use it" if he "needed to." The white man insisted that Mann give him the weapon, to which Mann responded, "Like hell I will." The old man lunged at Mann, and the pistol discharged. In the next minute hundreds of shots could be heard, and chaos ensued. As the crowds dispersed and Blacks made their way back to Greenwood, twenty or so people, Black and white, were either dead or wounded.[233]

On the fateful morning of June 1, 1921, things were quiet in Greenwood—at least initially. At 5:08, however, a loud whistle broke the peace. It was a signal and, "[a] lusty cheer welled up among the thousands of whites poised at various locations on the edge of Greenwood."[234] The white mob moved through Greenwood taking hostages, burning buildings, looting, and killing those who resisted. Whites deployed a Gatling gun and a biplane in the assault. Whites from all sections of the Tulsan society joined the mob as did members of the national guard and local police. Captain Jackson's son surrendered to the whites who came to his house, but two young white boys raised their guns at him and shot him twice in the chest.[235] Blacks resisted, but the results were devastating. Around three hundred died, and over eight thousand Blacks were homeless as Black Wall Street lay in ruins. To add insult to injury, the atrocities were swept under the rug, and generations of Tulsans never heard about the Tulsa massacre.[236]

So, what to do with these stories of atrocities committed against Black Americans? First of all, we must recognize that real injustices have taken place, and to the extent that we can, we should make efforts to make such injustices right, as the Tulsa Race Massacre Centennial Commission aims at doing.[237] These stories also demonstrate, however, that Black Americans were extremely successful in creating prosperous communities through the marketplace. It was often white resentment that fueled lynchings—as in Memphis. Ultimately, the lesson of this chapter is that markets can't function without the rule of law and therefore cannot by themselves ensure Black betterment. Governments—at all levels—failed to protect Blacks' right to life, liberty, property, freedom of contract, right to trial by jury, and more. The market didn't fail Black people. Indeed, Blacks prospered as entrepreneurs, professionals, and laborers within the free enterprise system. It was America's political institutions that failed them.

LOOKING FOR SOLUTIONS: TRANSITIONAL JUSTICE

In international settings a process of transitional justice has been implemented after a period of human rights abuses, such as in Argentina in the aftermath of a dictatorial regime, in South Africa following apartheid, and in Eastern and Central Europe after the fall of communism. Transitional justice acknowledges that there have been justice violations on a massive scale, partially because the corruption of the legal authorities meant that such actions were tolerated, and it was impossible to get justice in the normal way. It also acknowledges that there is a need for peacemaking between two deeply alienated communities in order to function together well moving forward.

Anthony Bradley lays out the Chicago Principles of Post-Conflict Justice and their possible application for our context in his article, "Finally Healing the Wounds of Jim Crow."[238] Briefly, the seven principles include prosecution of human rights violations; formal investigation of crimes by truth commissions; the acknowledgment of victims in the form of access to justice, remedies, and reparations; implementation of vetting and sanctions against violators (such as corrupt authorities); official programs to create institutional memory and to memorialize victims in particular; respect for traditional religious and cultural approaches; and institutional reforms to support the rule of law and reestablish trust in the system.

Bradley observes how unrealistic it was to think that we could simply change the laws without acknowledging the harms that had been committed, expecting the very same people to enforce the new laws—whether in the courts or in the streets—who had been creating and enforcing the old laws (whether de facto or de jure) the day before. Human beings simply do not turn on a dime in this way. How much social confusion could have been avoided if we had charged assailants with their crimes, spent resources on investigating the stories of victims and made them widely available, dealt with corruption in the legal system, and empowered the Black church in its role as a cultural healer such that telling the truth could have led to reconciliation? He also argues that it's not too late.

The fascinating thing for our anti-tribal project of ideological unbundling is that none of the principles above are principles of "social justice." They're principles of plain old justice, applied to recovery from a massive social conflict. Bradley explicitly contrasts social justice with transitional justice, as transitional justice focuses on specific crimes with clear victims, and he's not the only one. Greensboro, North Carolina, already went through the process of a truth and reconciliation commission to deal with the murders of communist protesters by a group of KKK and Nazi Party members in 1979.[239] The mayor of Tulsa Oklahoma—a white Republican—launched an archaeological investigation into the remains of the Tulsa Massacre.[240] The question of reparations for Jim Crow has reentered the Overton window of worthy topics in political ethics; we deal with this complicated question in our epilogue on "All the Controversial Stuff."

As a theologian, Bradley is particularly interested in the role of white evangelicals in telling the truth about their churches' historical involvement in racial oppression. The point here is not to make some blanket statement about complicity but to do real investigatory work, hold particular individuals accountable, and make tangible amends. Reparations to those Japanese families who were interned during WWII, and official acknowledgment that the internment ought to have been illegal, is a good example of a case in which the United States has undertaken such a project in the past. Another more wide-ranging example is the restoration of art pieces stolen from Jewish families by the Nazis. In spite of the fact that museums sometimes paid a lot of money to acquire these paintings, it is understood as a matter of justice that they must be returned and are often done so in formal events acknowledging the history of Nazi theft.[241] This approach to justice is, in a sense, inherently conservative, as it appeals to specific violations of bodily integrity and property rights and sees the legal rectification of such violations as legitimate because of the inalienable nature of human rights.

Conservatives should fully embrace the legal rectification of specific past harms in their local states, towns, churches, and other social institutions, as well as the proper cultural memorialization of victims. If conservatives and libertarians champion property rights, the right to due process of law, and support for these in our institutional memory and symbolism as they say they do, this should be straightforward for them. In fact, they can bring a measure of integrity to such proceedings that it may lack without their presence. Sadly, third-wave anti-racism can drown the straightforward harms and the witness of Jim Crow survivors in a grab-bag of far more controversial complaints about ill-defined "systems"—capitalism, imperialism, whiteness, heteronormativity, and what have you—and their effects on a wide range of apparent victims. Truth and reconciliation commissions, on the other hand, have a singleness of purpose; they are part of a legal approach already established in international law to redress concrete crimes and focus on the local communities in which the crimes occurred.

Certainly, conservatives may object that all this lament works against a functioning society's "founding myth"—the positive conception of itself upon which its patriotism and unity are founded. And yet a large portion of the conservative movement is deeply religious in the Judeo-Christian tradition, in which the people of God are known especially for getting called out by prophets for idolatry and oppression of the weak, repenting, asking God for mercy, and then writing the whole sordid episode down for all of posterity. This both-sinner-and-saint tension ought to be perfectly familiar to conservatives. Surely, the great thing about America is not just its excellent political principles but also its efforts to make its reality conform to its ideals. Transitional justice is a fundamental element of this process.

Lessons in Classical Liberalism #9: The Commercial Society and the Vice of Envy

Deirdre McCloskey, economic historian and all-around polymath, is famous for her sheer astonishment at the economic growth that the bourgeois revolution has ushered in, measuring it as amounting to a factor of thirty (meaning that our economic situation is about 30,000 percent better off than it was three hundred years ago). Her philosophical and literary insights help to curb some of the excesses of cold and calculating economists, with their vision of one-dimensional, utility-maximizing human beings. Instead, she insists that all seven medieval virtues—Love, Hope, Faith, Wisdom, Justice, Courage, and Temperance—are part of the good human life and even of the good human economic calculation. She also notes how the famous seven vices—the seven deadly sins—are just as deadly as they ever were, contra popular but silly claims that market activity is essentially about greed. In particular, she hearkens back to the burgeoning markets of the Dutch. One can still see in the Magistrate's Court the figure representing Justice trampling the sins of Greed and Envy. Why is this so important? Because these are the vices that, if not crushed by Justice, will undermine the entire market order. Greed and Envy are compulsive, and they are willing to destroy. Envy is especially destructive because it focuses on status. A status good is the kind of thing that is only valuable to a person if they have it and others do not, like a collector's item. In a commercial society, most goods are not of this kind. I want a nice car or delicious food so that I can enjoy these things, not so that I claim a higher status than you. When others do well, we may even feel that it benefits us. Their having a nicer house or opening a new shop is a "positive externality"—something that affects me positively even though I wasn't any part of it. Maybe your nice house raises my property value, or your cool shop brings more business to my restaurant next door. In general, we want to increase the number of ways in which we are experiencing win-win scenarios with our fellow citizens, not only because these are mutually beneficial but also because it helps us to see one another as loci of cooperation. The vice of envy destroys all this by making what could be a win-win scenario into a win-lose scenario, simply because of the adoption of a different attitude. If I see your nicer house or cool new shop as putting you above me in some sense that I feel I cannot abide, I am now incentivized to tear you down in any way I can. This then moves us from a win-lose scenario to a lose-lose scenario in which neither you nor I am able to enjoy the positive ripple effects generated by your success because I have destroyed them.

For this reason, the vice of envy is especially incompatible with commercial societies, where part of the social contract is the willingness to let whoever succeeds or fails in the market do so without government interference. All citizens understand that while the rise of a competitor can place painful pressure on particular businesses, the overarching system of competition makes all our businesses more efficient in serving customers, creating better products and lower prices. If the need to destroy those who do well overrides this commitment to the social contract, we will not only miss out on the goods and services they have to offer, but we run the risk of undermining the entire system of justice, which only makes everyone in the society poorer and the constant threat of violent conflict greater. In this chapter, we see how white envy of Black success led to egregious violations of justice that impoverished both Black and white neighbors. In Dante's *Divine Comedy*, envy is countered by the virtue of love and a strong sense of interdependence—all too appropriate for those in the same community who stand to gain from economic interaction if they can set aside obsession with status. Creating a culture that celebrates one another's successes and sees them as beneficial to all is paramount for a well-functioning commercial society.

Chapter 5

Liberation Through Civil Society: The Black Church

"The Black Church has no challenger as the
cultural womb of the Black community."
—C. Eric Lincoln and Lawrence Mamiya in
The Black Church in the African American Experience

A common mistake in social analysis involves dividing our social world into two major arenas: the government and the market. Either we're holding certain goods in common and distributing them as a whole society through the government or we're holding things privately and trading them voluntarily through the market. This is a false dichotomy, as it elides over the arena of life perhaps most dear to us: civil society.

Lessons in Classical Liberalism #10: Civil Society

Civil society includes all those voluntary efforts that comprise our cultural life but are fundamentally noncommercial: families, neighborhoods, churches, charities, sports leagues, and book clubs. Of course, all three of the categories mentioned above—government, market, and civil society—overlap with one another at times, but the conceptual distinction between them is not difficult to grasp. I may pay a fee to enter a bowling league, but I'm not there to consume a good or service, primarily. I'm there to indulge in a hobby and to be a part of a community of people I will see every week, invite to my Christmas party, and network with when one or another of us needs a job or a recommendation for a new doctor or hairstylist. I see my fee as a way of buying the bowling alley's time and paying for the matching shirts we all wear—but I can't buy the friendships, camaraderie, and sheer enjoyment that I'll experience. There is no Bureau of Friendship in the government, and no Friendship Store at the mall, nor could there be. Friendship is, in its very nature, an organic, voluntary, and noncommercial good.

Recent scholarship (like Robert Putnam's famous *Bowling Alone*) has also shown that the role of civil society plays a much larger part in our well-being than we notice. It's easy to overlook participation in civil society institutions because they are a scattered collection of activities that we rarely consciously group together. It might not occur to a person, for instance, who is a member of Alcoholics Anonymous, sits on the board of a local charity, participates in a church small group, exchanges advice on a parents' Facebook group, and meets with neighbors on Saturday mornings to weed the community garden, that all those activities can fall under the one heading of civil society, but they do. None of these activities are primarily matters of commerce nor are they the proper purview of the state. Some things just can't be bought, nor can they be forced. In his work, *Alienated America: Why Some Places Thrive While Others Collapse*, Tim Carney digs deep into the data to show that an analysis of social interconnection does a far better job of predicting strong social outcomes (such as high employment, low crime, good physical health, and low addiction rates) than an analysis of mere economic status in terms of wealth or income.

In the late nineteenth and early twentieth centuries, relatively poor Blacks in America built some of the most robust social institutions in the country, including the Black family, the Black church, Black social organizations and schools, and Black mutual aid societies. The strength of these institutions then enabled the growth of local Black economies and the Black political movement for civil rights. The bandwidth that allowed for these developments came not from extra money or time, which very few Blacks had, but rather from extra community. Blacks were able to create and sustain thick social institutions because their communal life was already so strong, primarily as a result of overwhelming participation in the Black church.

The plain truth is that many of the great achievements that we celebrate during Black History Month have the Black church to thank, even if the achievements themselves were political or commercial in nature. And this demonstrates the power of civil society: the prevalence of healthy social institutions determines both economic growth and political stability. When those institutions go, much of the goodness for which they provided a foundation goes too. Black civil society is a triumph of our American story, but as we'll see in later chapters, the partial destruction of these institutions also goes far to explain the contemporary frustrations of struggling Black communities. On the other hand, their remaining strength, and the possibility of their renewal, is a source of great hope.

BLACK FOLKS' RELIGION

In contrast to the majority of the ten million Africans trans-ported to the New World through the transatlantic slave trade, those four hundred thousand who were brought to the American colonies retained less distinctively African cultural practice than those in the Caribbean and South America, though many African elements did remain. The sad truth for most of the victims of the transatlantic slave trade, particularly in South America, is that the labor of these Africans—mostly men—expended in the sugar fields and diamond mines of Brazil, for instance (where 40 percent of all imported Africans ended up), simply killed them. Between the transatlantic journey itself and the harrowing death rates associated with their forced labor, it is no exaggeration to describe the slave trade with the New World as a genocide against West Africans. In places like Cuba, Trinidad, and even New Orleans, Africans working in large groups without as much con-tact with their slaveholders incorporated elements of their native religion into new pan-African conglomerate religious practices, such as Haitian vodou. For most Africans in the American colo-nies, however, a flourishing population and little contact with the African homeland after the first generation led to the creation of a distinctively Black practice of Christianity.[242]

The development of such robust Christian faith among those cruelly enslaved by other Christians has often been a source of puzzlement and even pain in the formation of Black American identity. After all, why should a people so cruelly oppressed val-ue the "white man's religion"? First, Southern slaveholders did not initially evangelize their slaves, and their practice of religion was not the source of Black conversion to Christianity; second, Black believers picked up on elements of the faith from Hebrew and Christian scripture that were downplayed in white theology; and third, Black Christians were shut out of white Christian in-stitutions in such a way that their own faith practices developed independently and freely, becoming a center for all Black communal life.

BLACK CHRISTIANITY IN HISTORICAL PERSPECTIVE

It's worth recalling that Christianity is indigenous to Africa, as the early church was deeply anchored there. The first gentile (non-Jewish) convert to Christianity was a Black African[243] eunuch (Acts 8:26–40). Church fathers Tertullian, Origen, Cyprian, Athanasius, and Augustine were all African. The Ethiopians were the most eager and anchored converts in the history of the world, defending Eastern Christianity from oppression throughout the medieval period. Indeed, 62 percent of Ethiopians are either Eastern Orthodox or Protestant Christians today. Much of North Africa, especially Egypt, was majority Christian through the tenth century, when massive Arab immigration changed its demographics.[244] In fact, the only state to successfully resist political takeover by Islam was the prosperous and deeply Christian Nubia, persisting in their faith into the 1400s. In contrast, Black people in North America hailed from West Africa, where either Islam or various forms of local religion were more common. (The Kongo is an exception here; it appears that the Stono Rebellion of 1739 in South Carolina was actually an effort of Black, Portuguese-speaking Catholics from that region.)[245] This obscured for many white and Black people in America the extent to which Africa was a Christian continent up to and including the medieval period.

Although the Christian population in Africa dipped for a few hundred years as Islam progressed rapidly, Black Christianity is back in full force in the twentieth and twenty-first centuries. Africa is now home to 26 percent of the world's Christians (that's 650 million people, half of Africa's total population), while another 39 percent hail from South America and Asia. Christianity was never a "white" religion, as we have shown, but even if the Europeans dominated the faith from the seventeenth to the nineteenth centuries, Europeans and North Americans now make up only 34 percent of the Christian faith, and many of those people are not white anyway.[246]

Black Christians remain the most solidly Christian demographic in America. Depending on the study, somewhere between 80 percent and 83 percent of the African American population self-identifies as Christian and claims to be completely certain about the existence of God.[247] Black millennials are significantly more likely to believe in God, pray, and attend religious services than other members of their generation.[248] As we will see in this section, the Black church became the central social institution of African American life, acting as a hub of economic and political life as well as religious devotion.[249]

The paradox of Black strength through the "white man's religion" unravels when we understand the way that Black Americans first became Christians: not generally through the influence of their masters but rather through conversion by evangelical revivalists and fellow slaves. It unravels further when we see how Black Christians adopted the theology of creation in Genesis, the theology of liberation in Exodus, and the theology of the Holy Spirit in the New Testament, transforming the docile faith of the plantation missionaries into a source of religious, economic, and political empowerment.

THE INSTRUCTIVE CASE OF FREDERICK DOUGLASS

In *My Bondage and My Freedom*, Frederick Douglass goes into great detail about his own conversion at the age of thirteen, describing his orthodox faith in his own sinfulness and salvation through "faith in Jesus Christ, as the Redeemer, Friend, and Savior of those who diligently seek Him." Douglass continues to describe the profound experience of conversion: "I saw the world in a new light. I seemed to live in a new world, surrounded by new objects, and to be animated by new hopes and desires. I loved all mankind—slaveholders not excepted; though I abhorred slavery more than ever. My great concern was, now, to have the whole world converted." He described his discipleship under "Father Lawson," a "good old colored man...[a] more devout man than he, I never saw." They sang, prayed, read scripture, and glorified God, spending every Sunday together, as well as attending mid-week prayer meetings.

Douglass explicitly distinguished between the tutelage of the white clergy member, Bishop Waugh, whom he could hear instructing his mistress, and that of Father Lawson. "I am careful to state these facts," he pronounced diplomatically, "that the reader may be able to form an idea of the precise influences which had to do with shaping and directing my mind." In contrast to the exhortations and prayer that he hears from Waugh, Douglass insists that "my chief instructor, in matters of religion, was Uncle Lawson. He was my spiritual father; and I loved him intensely, and was at his house every chance I got." Master Auld threatened to whip him for spending time with Lawson, which made him feel "persecuted by a wicked man," but the threats could not put him off his religious training with Lawson, since both he and his teacher believed that the "Lord had a great work for me to do."[250] Lawson and Douglass prayed together for Douglass's liberty, believing that the Lord would accomplish it. We now know that Douglass did successfully escape, became a deacon and licensed lay preacher in the African Methodist Episcopal Zion Church (his church gave him the use of their basement to publish his abolitionist newspaper, the *North Star*), and became one of the greatest American writers and orators of all time.

This account, however, appears in 1855, in a work published ten years after his *Narrative of the Life of Frederick Douglass*. In Douglass's original account of his life, he says less about his own conversion but has plenty to say about the hypocritical Christianity of the slave masters. His critique was so harsh that some readers supposed him to be "an opponent of all religion." In order to counter this view he added an appendix. No account could with more righteous anger rain down judgment on *"the slaveholding religion,"* which Douglass refuses to even associate with "Christianity proper": "Indeed, I can see no reason, but the most deceitful one, for calling the religion of this land Christianity. I look upon it as the climax of all misnomers, the boldest of all frauds, and the grossest of all libels." He weaves the words of Christ, the warnings of the Old Testament prophets, and the apocalyptic vengeance of the eschaton together to wholeheartedly condemn the association of Christianity with slavery. There is no way to accurately summarize Douglass's prophetic testimony against the slaveholders' religion; I can only recommend to our readers to read these few pages of noble rage for themselves.[251]

Douglass's account of himself represents a particularly clear example of the general picture we are painting of Black Christianity as it developed under slavery: evangelical conversion, discipleship by other enslaved Christians, persecution for one's faith by slave masters, and a deep and abiding distinction between the true Christian faith and the "corrupt, slaveholding, women-whipping, cradle-plundering, partial and hypocritical Christianity of this land."[252]

THE FAITH OF THE REVIVALISTS AND THE FAITH OF THE SLAVEHOLDERS

In the early 1700s, half of the parishes in Virginia had no clergy at all, and half of the white South Carolinian population were "living regardless of any religion, there being only one Church (at Charleston)."[253] A missionary described the people of Georgia as having "very little more knowledge of a Saviour than the aboriginal natives" since they had "no opportunity of being instructed in the principles of Christianity or even in the being of a God."[254] On the other hand, Lauren Winner, scholar and episcopal priest, describes a warm, if less audaciously expressed, faith among the Anglicans of the South, and many dissenting groups coexisted with their Anglican neighbors in places like South Carolina.[255] More than irreligiosity, failure to evangelize enslaved people probably arose from slaveholders' fears that conversion could lead to freedom.[256] In a striking passage in the book of Jeremiah, the Hebrews are directly commanded by God to free all Hebrew slaves. They initially do so but then back out of the agreement they made and re-enslave those recently emancipated. They are recompensed for this decision by subjection to "sword, plague, and famine" followed by the "dead bodies" of the leaders becoming "food for the birds and the wild animals." Since the Hebrews of the Old Testament were forbidden from enslaving their own brethren, it only stood to reason that Blacks who became Christians might appeal to scripture and history for their own freedom. The slaveholders' fear was not entirely unfounded, as many slaves later made exactly this argument.[257]

Therefore, Blacks enslaved in the South were even more unchurched than their masters. The first wave of substantial embrace of Christianity among the enslaved population came with the First and Second Great Awakenings of the mid- and late 1700s. The term "evangelical" originates in these revival movements. The term carries some connotations in contemporary America that do not align with its history or its use in the broader global evangelical movement, which embraces over six hundred million people, or 25 percent of all Christians, according to the World Evangelical Alliance. We use the term here in its historical, and now global, sense: based on *evangelion*, meaning "good news," it focuses on "a fervent Christianity marked by an emphasis on converting outsiders." It is often broken down into four main attributes: 1) a high regard for the Bible, 2) a focus on Jesus's crucifixion and its saving effects, 3) a belief that humans need to be converted, and 4) the belief that faith should influence one's public life.[258] While these waves of religious revival included Protestants of all sorts, the main groups involved in the South were Methodists and Baptists, while Anglican leaders disapproved (although many laymen did not follow their lead). Both Albert Raboteau and Nathan Hatch, scholars of Black American religion, describe how the revivalist Methodists and Baptists approached matters of faith in a way that particularly attracted Blacks:

1. Methodist circuit preachers and other travelling evangelists came to the people rather than waiting for the people to come to a church. Churches were too far away for many people in the South anyway, and often Blacks were not allowed to attend or, having never been exposed to the faith by their slaveholders, saw no reason to give up their one day off to do so.

2. The emphasis on a personal conversion experience and "plain doctrine" made Christianity a possibility for enslaved Blacks who almost certainly would not be allowed to complete the kind of lengthy catechization process typical in Anglicanism.[259]

3. The evangelicalism of the movement had an egalitarian effect: Christ died for each individual person, we ought to preach to everyone regardless of their external circumstances, and any person might be called to become a preacher and exhorter himself (or even *her*self, in some cases![260]). White preachers "earned the right to be heard" by welcoming Black brothers and sisters into full communion.[261]

4. The fervor of the Great Awakening and the decentralized nature of Baptist congregations overcame some social barriers, allowing for biracial churches, ordained Black ministers, and independent Black churches. The

ordination of Black preachers and exhorters meant that Black leadership was officially recognized, a great source of pride for Black Christians.

5. Revivalism allowed for religious expressions that integrated African folkways: "The powerful emotionalism, ecstatic behavior, and congregational response of the revival were amenable [to them]...forms of African dance and song remained in the shout and spirituals of Afro-American converts to evangelical Protestantism."[262] The revivalists appreciated Black forms of ecstatic worship, while others, such as Presbyterians, tended to discourage "sounds, chants, catches, or hallelujahs."[263]

While Americans often think of the slaves as accepting the religion of their masters, this wasn't at all the experience of Black Christians during the Great Awakenings. Enslaved Blacks were converted—right along with many whites—either by a different set of white people bringing a very different kind of Christian faith or by other Black people who had already been converted through revival and were filled with missionary zeal for the members of their own race.

The egalitarianism of the evangelical revivalists posed a serious threat to slaveholders, who often directly disapproved of them. Methodists, after all, stated explicitly and on several official occasions throughout the 1780s that slavery was a great evil and a violation of Jesus's law of love for one's neighbor. The father of Methodism, John Wesley, was consistent on this point throughout his life and even made church membership dependent on a commitment to emancipate one's slaves.[264] Wesley's influence, however, was largely limited to England. Wesley's follower Bishop Thomas Coke followed suit in America, though. While spreading the Methodist message, Coke was threatened by a mob, charged in two counties for preaching against slavery and forced to run from a bounty on his head.[265]

Many Presbyterians and Baptists also opposed the institution initially. The Baptist General Committee in the Virginia Assembly officially opposed slavery in 1785 and 1790, declaring it to be against God's law and "inconsistent with republican government."[266] Backlash from slave owners, however, led to a dismissal of the issue from the committee, which declared it a civil question. Although Quakers were not deeply affected by the Awakenings, they were a zealous community already and also famously anti-slavery, based on the same religious grounds of equality before God, love of one's neighbor, and doing to others as one would have done to oneself. What's more, the slave insurrection in 1800 called Gabriel's Rebellion was led by a group that included a famous preacher and was grounded on identification with the oppressed Israelites and the hope of overcoming great odds in battle like the prophets of the Hebrew scriptures. It didn't help the revivalists' case when it was found out that the men had agreed to kill everyone except Quakers, Methodists, and Frenchmen on account of their friendliness to the liberty of Black people.[267] Another slave rebellion arose directly out of an African Methodist Church and its leadership in 1822, and of course, Nat Turner's revolt of 1831 was also inspired by his conviction as a preacher and prophet that God had directed him to rebel.[268]

Nevertheless, Black preachers and churches continued to multiply everywhere and, when suppressed, met in secret. Their faithfulness sometimes embarrassed the nonevangelical whites who tried to stop Blacks from preaching or worshipping. When Black evangelist Andrew Bryan, his brother, and fifty others were imprisoned and severely whipped for gathering to worship, a cut and bleeding Andrew cried out like an apostle from the book of Acts, saying that he rejoiced at his persecution for Christ's name and that he "would freely suffer death for the cause of Jesus Christ."[269] (He later became the pastor of one of the oldest Black Baptist churches in America in Savannah, Georgia.)

THE DOCILE RELIGION OF THE PLANTATION MISSIONARIES

The legal backlash from slaveholders that followed slave rebellions created a troubling situation. If Methodists, Quakers, or another group of egalitarian revivalists didn't want to be barred from preaching to enslaved Blacks by their slaveholders, they could not appear to be undermining the institution of slavery or encouraging arrogance or rebellion among slaves. The planters were passing laws to forbid Black preachers and Black participation in worship, although they had to walk some of those laws back under pressure from religious societies. Nevertheless, evangelicals found themselves compromising their anti-slavery fervor and Christian egalitarianism in order to maintain access to their own church members as well as to future converts. As Raboteau describes, "[t]he egalitarian trend in evangelicalism which drove some Methodists, Baptists, and Presbyterians to condemn slavery foundered on the intransigency of that institution in the South."[270] Instead, church leaders, both Black and white, began to reassure slaveholders by arguing that the newfound faith of their slaves would make them better and more obedient laborers.

Under the plantation mission system of the 1830s and 1840s, missionaries, chaplains, Bible distribution, pamphlets, Sabbath schools, and all the other mechanisms of the Evangelical United Front would be used to develop the spiritual lives of enslaved Black people. In fact, evangelicals hoped to have a salutary spiritual effect on the slaveholders as well, as they called them to support these efforts on behalf of those they enslaved.[271] But unlike the national nature of these efforts elsewhere, those in the South had to be local. The rise of abolitionism and the sectional tensions over slavery made the Southerners suspicious of all efforts centralized at a national level.[272] In many cases abolitionist efforts in the North so terrified the planter class that schools, societies, and church meetings on the plantation had to be shut down, at least temporarily. The plantation missionaries chose to shore up the spiritual inroads being made in the eyes of the slaveholders by arguing that the evangelization and spiritual nurture of the slaves was a major plank in the Southerners' innovative "positive good" defense of the institution of slavery.[273]

NECESSARY EVIL VS. POSITIVE GOOD

Note that both the positive good argument for slavery and the inclusion of evangelical concerns in its justification triumph rather late in the career of American slavery. Although the political thinkers of the colonial period sometimes laid out positive aspects of slavery that they thought might outweigh the clear negative ones, the Revolutionary generation engaged in an existential struggle with the schizophrenia of their claims to liberty and the idea of property in people. They hoped for, and even assumed, eventual abolition. But just as St. Augustine once prayed, "Lord, make me chaste, just not right now," they put it off indefinitely.[274] With no idea of how the two races could coexist as equals, they trusted some future generation to untangle the problem.

In the 1820s and 1830s, however, the abolitionism that the Awakenings inspired was making such inroads that Southern planters began to develop moral defenses of slavery. Aristotle, in a revolutionary move for the system of war enslavement under which the Greeks lived, had argued that only a natural inferiority could justify one human ruling another. If both people involved were fully rational and capable of virtue, such a relation would be totally absurd. But if one person is akin to our rational capabilities (intellect), while the other is akin to our irrational ones (physical ability) then it would make sense for one to rule the other just as our reason ought to rule our bodily desires.[275] By adopting an increasingly intense racism, one that claimed the total incapacity of Black people to run their own lives successfully, the planter class attempted to justify slave subjection as paternalistic care. They then believed they could righteously compare themselves as slave-holders to Northern factory owners, whose workers, they claimed, were far worse off than enslaved Black people. As the plantation missionaries ingratiated themselves to slaveholders with promises of obedient Christian slaves, the slaveholders easily incorporated their willingness to provide Christian instruction to the slaves as part of the positive good of bondage.[276] The term "positive good" is recorded for the first time in 1829, when Stephen Miller, the governor of South Carolina, used it in a speech. The state of Virginia's General Assembly was furiously debating compensated emancipation (freeing slaves and compensating owners for the loss of their investment). Apparently Miller's logic won out, as the measure failed in the legislature in 1832.[277]

Those slaveholders who claimed sincere conversion to Christianity immediately felt the contradiction between their faith and the institution of slavery. Slaveholders who evangelized their slaves testified that the converts became presumptuous. If they needed to "correct" them in their labors, they stopped attending services.[278] Some planters begged for some other preacher to come and instruct those they enslaved since it was unworkable for them to do it themselves: the "relationship between *Master* and *slave* made void the best efforts of the most pious owners in Christianizing them."[279] Others became sanctimonious and cruel taskmasters, over whom slaves preferred an unconverted lush for a master, who might simply leave them alone. Even supposedly evangelical Christian slaveholders often objected to the further religious instruction of their slaves on the grounds that it had an equalizing effect and could lead to insurrection.[280] "Labor as they might, the missionaries could not yoke together the goals of slave instruction and slave control into a stable and permanent union. Inherent in the recognition of the slave's claim to humanity and even more in the assertion of his *right* to Christian instruction was...an implicit threat, even though muted, to the practice of slave control and management."[281]

The institutional church also struggled with the tension between the gospel and slavery. As "brothers and sisters," slaves could charge whites with serious sins that could bring them under church discipline, even though Black testimony was held as meaningless in a secular court of law. Questions also arose about the validity of second marriages of enslaved people who were separated from their first spouse by sale. Some churches commanded members to do everything within their power to keep the marriages of the enslaved together on pain of church discipline.[282]

There were other contradictions and difficult questions as well. Should *Sola Scriptura* Protestants teach slaves to read and give them access to the whole Bible? Should evangelicals who ascribe to the priesthood of all believers ordain Black people to preach? Can masters pledging allegiance to the love-one's-neighbor-as-oneself Messiah come under church discipline for cruelty to slaves? Performative contradictions between claims of spiritual equality and the realities of earthly oppression played out in multiple ways, embarrassing church members and councils, who were sometimes completely befuddled by the bizarre ethical questions the contradictions created.[283]

Enslaved Black people resented the teaching of plantation missionaries in the 1830s and 1840s and refused to be catechized by them; it was *this* experience to which they referred when using the term "white man's religion," not Christianity in general.[284] They realized that some missionaries were peddling a form of slave Christianity that only discussed obedience and compliance to the master's will.[285] When masters allowed slaves to attend church, they ensured that the main themes were always obedience to one's master, causing slaves to make a distinction between "the hypocritical religion of their masters and the true Christianity," rejecting the "slaveholder's gospel of obedience to master and mistress."[286] And Black acceptance of "true Christianity" cannot be explained by ignorance either. Missionaries recorded the intellectual sophistication of the theological questions they received from enslaved Blacks: "deism, skepticism, universalism...all the strong objections against the truth of God; objections which he may perhaps have considered peculiar only to the cultivated minds... of *critics* and *philosophers!*"[287] We know from later accounts that many of the enslaved people who were catechized by the plantation missionaries secretly reasoned out for themselves that their masters' power over them fell far short of the standards of Christ.

Meanwhile, free Blacks in the South were running their own congregations despite white restrictions. By the time of emancipation, many established Black congregations had already been in place for half a century and in some cases even longer. A few towns in the South had a Black Baptist church prior to a white one.[288] Free and enslaved Blacks worshiped together, despite intense class distinctions between them in some cases. One of the missions of such institutions was to further the Black self-help philosophy by answering the petitions of enslaved Blacks who needed financial assistance to purchase themselves.[289]

While biracial churches existed for a time after the Awakenings, most had split into white and Black congregations by the time of emancipation. Blacks technically submitted to white insistence on governance of Black churches but created such clever agreements with them that for all practical purposes, the Black churches often governed themselves.[290] In some exceptional cases, powerful white pastors petitioned against white oversight of Black preachers and churches, citing the religious liberty of both themselves and Black Christians. For instance, a statute disallowing Black ordination violated "the sacred rights of the black to preach, exhort or pray, if God called and commanded him to do either." White Baptists might want to ordain a Black man, in which case such laws violated "the dictates of our own consciences.... Our religion is a matter between us and God, with which no power on earth has a right to interfere. Soul-liberty is the rightful heritage of all God's moral creatures. Not over the religion of the slave has civil authority any power, nor yet has it over that of the citizen." This statute was especially offensive because it "trespasses...on the rights of God. It dictates to the Almighty on what color his preachers shall be." It constituted "heaven-daring impiety" put forward by a "self-exalted and heaven-defying tribunal."[291] The statute was repealed. Baptists and Methodists frequently licensed Black preachers.[292]

We might be shocked that early Southern planters, ostensibly Anglican Christians themselves, delayed evangelizing their slaves to avoid having to free them. But we see the hypocrisy of Baptists, Methodists, and even many Quakers also, who compromised their views on slavery as an institution. One way of understanding this is to note that while both the morality of slavery and of the evangelization of slaves might seem like they should be paramount in the mind of a Christian, that wasn't always the case. Anglicans put less emphasis on evangelism than revivalists, though they had active missionary efforts. Some revivalists opposed slavery out of hand, but others thought it might just be part of an imperfect and fallen world. Nor should a condemnation of Southern religious compromise distract us from the real hypocrisy and failures of many other groups as well. Northern Puritanism could be overly scrupulous and tyrannical. Quakers were often as upset by card playing and drinking as they were by slavery. Evangelical revivalism has been criticized as overly emotional and lacking in depth and staying power. Despite the spiritual egalitarianism described above, the vast majority of whites, north or south—even abolitionists—were thoroughgoing racists, in the sense that they believed Blacks to be intellectually inferior to whites.

If one focuses on the worldwide phenomenon of slavery, the moral pressure brought to bear against the institution in America ought to astonish us with its idealism. If one focuses on the standard of human equality in America's founding documents and the moral perfection commanded by Christ and many of his followers, the institution's persistence ought to scandalize us with its hypocrisy. Upon reflection, what Raboteau discovered in his study isn't, after all, so surprising. While it's easy enough to complain about hypocrisy, the plain truth is that it takes a certain kind of fanatical radicalism to follow through on principles that require the upending of a central institution of one's social system. The radicals will be branded as dangerous fools by all those who stand to lose in the bargain, and it will take courage and the willingness to be socially ostracized to stick to one's principles. It's important to remember as well that many radical movements for equality have been deeply dangerous and foolish; without the benefit of hindsight it's not always easy to tell which ones are realistic or how to go about it wisely. It's paramount to take up a broad perspective, both global and historical, as opposed to a utopianism that skews our perception of what's possible. From that larger perspective, the egalitarian achievements of the evangelicals ought to astound us. From the perspective of their own religious precepts, however, they fell far short.

BLACK CHRISTIANITY IN SECRET

Planters' fears that their converted slaves would interpret Christianity as implying their own equality and freedom were well-founded. While we've described the development of an institutional Black church prior to emancipation, Raboteau famously describes the Black church as "the invisible institution" because the heart of Black Christian spirituality had to develop in secret. No matter how independent the Black church, open meetings were always subject to white scrutiny. Many masters disallowed Black believers from going to church at all; some were disallowed from prayer itself. Those who were allowed to go were subject to "the rule of gospel order" in every sermon, meaning that preachers only talked to them about obedience to masters and prohibitions on stealing or lying. One interviewed former slave complained that "[n]othing about Jesus, was ever said and the overseer stood there to see the preacher talked as he wanted him to talk." Instead, slaves met at secretly appointed times and places, called "hush harbors," hiding their prayers, preaching, and singing in various ways, such as gathering on their knees in a circle over a pot full of water to drown out the sound.[293] And they absolutely prayed just as the masters feared: they prayed for deliverance from bondage, and with assurance, that they, too, like "the chillun of Is'ael" would someday be free.[294] Many suffered terribly for their insistence on this corporate worship, flogged and beaten if they were found out. The reality of this invisible institution is borne out by the numbers: Frederick Douglass reported 468,000 official Black church members in 1859; forty-five years later, that number had jumped to 2.7 million. Those who came south to evangelize the ex-slaves found many of them already deeply engaged in the faith and even the finer points of doctrine and Christian practice.[295]

It's fair to criticize the political implications of the revivalist theology as an underemphasis on the alleviation of earthly suffering and unjust institutions, and an overemphasis on the afterlife as an escape from this "vale of tears." Nevertheless, the effect of an enthusiastic evangelical Christianity on white abolitionists and Black slaves alike gives the lie to Marx's claim that religion is nothing but the "opiate of the masses." Judeo-Christian religion fits badly into the model of religion as social control. The Old Testament prophets more often than not spent their time confronting the Israelite kings for idolatry (or in the famous confrontation of King David by Nathan, adultery, lying, and murder)[296] and calling out injustice against the poor, widows, orphans, and strangers.[297] Jesus's early followers enraged the Roman rulers by claiming that Jesus was the true King and that they were subjects of another kingdom entirely.

The traditions of prophetic confrontation and kingdom of God theology were not lost on Black Christians and were obvious enough to white slaveholders that some of them (though not all) suppressed Christian conversion and practice among slaves through violence, some even jailing slaves for preaching and for singing spirituals about freedom.[298] A man called Praying Jacob told his own slaveholder to go ahead and shoot him since he would not stop the practice of pausing to pray three times a day (the slaveholder was too ashamed to do it). Thomas Jones was whipped for attending prayer meetings and Methodist class meetings. Eli Johnson refused to stop holding prayer meetings, declaring, "I'll suffer the flesh to be dragged off my bones...for the sake of my blessed Redeemer." One enslaved preacher, James Smith, was tied to a chair by his master all day on Sunday so that he could not preach but continued to evangelize throughout the week. Another enslaved man whose name was not recorded reported that his slaveholder "was determined to whip the Spirit out of me, but could never do it."[299] In some cases, slaveholders were cowed and embarrassed by the holiness of those they enslaved and relented. Many, many reports have been recorded claiming that cruel enslavers became terrified on their deathbeds, calling the slaves in to beg for their forgiveness. The intense conversion experiences and holy living of enslaved Christians created "a sense of individual value and a personal vocation" that encouraged them to stand up to their slaveholders. Historian Donald Mathews claims that while whites were "broken down" by preaching, due to their sense of conviction about sin, Blacks were "lifted up" because they were "enabled to celebrate themselves as persons because of the direct and awful contact with divinity which healed their battered self-esteem."[300] Undeniably, this interior moral training was indispensable for their efforts to escape slavery and create a way of life after emancipation.[301]

Raboteau compellingly argues that "the extent to which the Christianity of American slaves was hindered, proscribed, and persecuted justifies applying the title 'confessor' and 'martyr' to those slaves who, like their ancient Christian predecessors, bore witness to the Christian gospel despite the threat of punishment and even death at the hand not of 'pagans,' but of fellow Christians."[302] To those Christian faithful among the slaves, the contradiction of a slaveholding Christianity was not simply a lamentable circumstance for themselves but also nothing short of heresy. Since the slaves converted under and maintained a radical evangelical Christianity distinct from the religion of their slaveholders, they often stood in judgment of their slaveholders' gospel as false and of their faith as heretical. They saw themselves as true followers of the faith. They even believed that God had "selected them for some mysterious purpose...to demonstrate in one people the full maturation of Christianity."[303]

CONTRIBUTIONS OF BLACK THEOLOGY

The distinction between the American Black Church and white evangelicalism seems to have crystallized over the years, particularly when it comes to politics. White evangelicals struggle to articulate why there was active opposition to the civil rights movement among their churches (and in contrast to at least some mainline white Christian churches such as the Episcopalians). Today, they are often seen as deeply uninterested in racial justice, even at the level of their theology. In contrast, several of the most puzzling distinctions and apparent contradictions in American Christianity seem to be reconciled in Black theology as it is grounded historically in the spirituality of the slaves and even of free but oppressed Blacks in the institutionalized church.[304] First, Black theology sees the whole world as "crammed with heaven," so to speak;[305] there is no significant secular/sacred distinction. Second, Blacks' visceral identification with the children of Israel informs their sense of historical identity. Finally, these two theological priors allow the Black church to sidestep many of the most contentious religious debates waged in the white church community in the late nineteenth and early twentieth centuries, such as concerns over the "social gospel," the maintenance of historic orthodoxy, and the relationship of faith to science. The Black church avoids the tenacious Gnosticism (a discounting of the material world as unspiritual) that dogs much of Western Christianity, allowing it to naturally evolve as the institutional hub of the Black economy and the fight for civil rights. Meanwhile, its independent development, so powerful for the Black community, has made it a kind of nonentity for white evangelicals.[306] A deeper appreciation of the theological contributions of the Black church could go far in healing this divide. Given that conservatism in America is so deeply entangled with white evangelicalism, conservatives who want to engage with the Black community need to appreciate the Black church and its contributions.

THE SECULAR AND THE SACRED

Today, 80 percent of all Black Christians in America (and therefore 64 percent of all Black Americans) belong to one of just a few "independent, historic, and totally black-controlled" denominations: the African Methodist Episcopal (AME); the African Methodist Episcopal Zion Church (AMEZ); the Christian Methodist Episcopal Church (CME), the National Baptist Convention, USA, Incorporated (NBC); the National Baptist Convention of America, Unincorporated (NBCA); the Progressive National Baptist Convention (PNBC); and the Church of God in Christ (COGIC). That is, Black American Christians tend to be Baptist, Methodist, or Pentecostal.

Given the emphasis of the evangelical revivalists on a personal experience of conversion, great weight was put on the experience of repentance for one's sin. Thus, "giving the gospel" often begins, in this tradition, with the idea of sin against a holy God. But Black experiences of oppression shaped their approach differently, and whether coincidentally or not, it led to a theology more in line with the larger Christian tradition in which the first reality to address when telling the story of salvation is not sin but, rather, creation. In creation, God creates all things from nothing and declares his handiwork to be good. He makes humans in his own image, and all people come from the same set of parents, Adam and Eve. Therefore, we are all the children of God—brothers and sisters—and God is our Father. Every person is made in the image of God, a doctrine that granted Black Americans a deep sense of self-worth under circumstances that constantly devalued them. W. E. B. Du Bois claimed that organizing churches was itself the "first form of economic cooperation among Black people."[307] Economic and political efforts were channeled through separate organizations such as mutual aid societies and the NAACP, but their beginnings were in the church. In fact, one might argue that the more intense the repression of Black people in the larger society, the more of a haven the church became. Lincoln and Mamiya call the Black churches between 1890 and 1910 the "sole place of sanctuary," where organizations such as the National Baptist Convention, USA, "spoke out against racial violence and waged campaigns against segregation in public accommodations and discrimination in the armed service, education, and employment."[308] While Blacks in the South were uniformly shut out of voting and all forms of political participation, large Baptist conventions were merging, and the number of Baptist pastors tripled.[309] In describing his Southern rural parents to Kenneth Clark, James Baldwin said that their "relationship to the church was very direct because it was the only means they had of expressing their pain and their despair."[310] In Clark's description of Martin Luther King Jr., he notes this deep coalescence of the inner life of faith and the outer life of action: "...Martin Luther King's philosophy of love for the oppressor is a genuine aspect of his being. He personally does not differentiate between this philosophy and the effectiveness of the non-violent direct-action approach to the attainment of racial justice, which he personifies and leads. For him, the philosophy is not just a strategy; it is a truth."[311] In Baldwin's interview with Clark, Baldwin calls King a "real Christian. He really believes in non-violence."[312] Social analysts used to a strong divide between the secular and the sacred often have trouble properly understanding Black culture, which for both theological and practical reasons could indulge in no such luxury.[313] Instead, the deep and abiding commitment to certain Christian orthodoxies served as the foundation for Black political claims.

THE CHILDREN OF ISRAEL

Enslaved Black Christians were deeply biblical in their orientation, weaving the stories of Bible heroes through all their preaching, singing, and praying. Limited by their slaveholders from learning to read, however, they proceeded by oral tradition, committing long passages to memory, developing a powerful tradition of preaching, and incorporating the stories into their most treasured religious ritual, the singing of spirituals. Famously, these songs were often meditations on the themes of bondage and freedom, which for the slaves were both spiritual and practical in application.

While many of the stories of the Bible are relevant to these themes, surely the most famous is the story of Passover, in which God commanded Moses to lead the Hebrew people out of their slavery in Egypt and into the promised land of Canaan. Surely, this is one reason why the entire book of Exodus (excepting the Ten Commandments) was excluded from the infamous Slave Bible, a version of the Bible created for slaves that edited out all references to liberation. One Union Army chaplain complained that "[t]here is no part of the Bible with which they are so familiar as the story of the deliverance of the children of Israel."[314] One of the most famous spirituals captures this identification with Israel's slavery in Egypt: "When Israel was in Egypt's land/Let my people go/Oppressed so hard they could not stand/Let my people go/ Go down, Moses, way down in Egypt's land/Tell old Pharaoh: Let my people go." Frederick Douglass explains how the phrase "I am bound for the land of Canaan" in a corporately sung spiritual meant *both* that the singers will reach heaven and that they will make a "speedy pilgrimage to a free state, and deliverance from all the evils and dangers of slavery." Booker T. Washington confirms this double meaning in the spirituals when he relates how the singing in the slave quarters increased in both quantity and quality as they anticipated political emancipation: "...they had been careful to explain that the 'freedom' in these songs referred to the next world, and had no connection to life in this world. Now they gradually threw off the mask; and were not afraid to let it be known that the 'freedom' in their songs meant freedom of the body in this world."[315] Prayers also emphasized God as divine deliverer when His people committed civil disobedience in the face of oppressive earthly authority: "O sweet Jesus, ain't you de Daniel God? Didn't you deliber de tree chill'un from de firy furnis?"[316] A pagan king threw Daniel to lions for praying to God, if you recall from the biblical text, but God shut the lions' mouths; Daniel's friends Shadrach, Meshach, and Abednego[317] were forced into a fiery furnace for refusing to worship another pagan king, but a mysterious fourth figure appeared in the furnace with them, and they did not burn.[318]

Between their reliance on oral tradition and, therefore, stories, and their relation to the story of Moses, the Black church developed a deep knowledge of the Old Testament. Anthony Bradley argues that the Black tradition comes to Jesus through Moses, the white through Paul. He claims that "the Mosaic starting point is free to articulate why God cares about personal salvation, economics, business, education.... Therefore the black church tradition, had an easier time making a case for why God cared about slavery, Jim Crow, civil rights, etc."[319] These contrasting emphases led to very different attitudes about the translation of one's religious life to politics.

The spirituals also affirmed the biblical principles that undergirded the slaves' refusal to accept their situation as a good or just social arrangement, as the whites claimed. In their sweet contemplation of heaven, the enslaved looked forward to the

Judgment, when the proverbial "sheep and goats" would be divided, as Christ had foretold[320]: "And de Lord will say to de sheep. For to go to Him right hand; But de goats must go to de left." The theme of the poor and the righteous "crying out for justice" is ubiquitous throughout the Hebrew scriptures. The slaves were not at all terrified by the idea of God as a judge, since a good judge decides rightly by punishing oppressors and extending grace to true believers whose sins had been paid for through the death of Jesus Christ. The Day of Judgment, then, would be a great day in which sins against the poor, widow, orphan, and stranger are finally avenged. One white observer recounted, "I never saw a negro a Universalist; for they all believe in a future retribution for their masters, from the hand of a just God."[321]

THE BLACK CHURCH AND THE WHITE CHURCH

To non-Christians, some of the doctrinal details we're covering may sound obscure, but we underestimate the role of specific religious beliefs in our cultural and political life to our own peril. Just as understanding the history of the Black church is necessary for understanding the civil rights movement and formation of Black American culture more broadly, understanding the tensions between the white and Black church today may hold the key to the future of racial reconciliation.

Lincoln and Mamiya argue that the Black church has been the "most conservative" and the "most radical" institution *at the same time*: "The complexities of black churches as social institutions require a more dynamic and interactional theoretical perspective because they have played more complex roles and assumed more comprehensive burdens in their communities than is true of most white and ethnic churches."[322] These roles include "their school, their forum, their political arena, their social club, their art gallery, their conservatory of music. [The black church] was lyceum and gymnasium as well as sanctum sanctorum. Their religion was the peculiar sustaining force that gave them that strength to endure when endurance gave no promise, and the courage to be creative in the face of their own dehumanization."[323]

Debates among white Christians were (and still often are) answering questions that Black Christians simply weren't asking. In *Doctrine and Race*, Mary Beth Swetnam Mathews read thousands of Black church publications to get a sense of how Blacks were thinking about doctrine during the famous modernist-fundamentalist debates that are often taken as a defining moment in twentieth-century American Christianity. Much of the commentary coming out of the Black churches saw both fundamentalists and modernists as innovators.[324] Black Christian writers often saw these debates and the denominational splits they caused as evidence of disunity among white Christians who were suffering from a lack of practical holiness. Black Christians affirmed the "old time religion" or "conservative religion": the inerrancy of the Bible, the Virgin Birth, the divinity of Christ, the need for holy living, and Jesus's eventual return.[325] Black Christians were happy to include fundamentalists as brothers and sisters in Christ, and to agree with them on the traditional aspects of the faith to which both groups adhered, but their demands that all Christians must adhere to their fringe views on literalist biblical interpretation and premillenial eschatology (the rapture view of the end-times) were "theologically suspect."[326] As AMEZ bishop G. C. Clement argued, the "bitter strife" between white fundamentalists and white modernists led to "the confusion of the unchurched and to the amusement of the believing, and to the disruption and retardation of the Kingdom." Instead, the AMEZ church "felt little of this eruption...the Bible remains the only standard of faith and doctrine required for membership in our fold and much latitude is allowed in its interpretation."[327]

While writers in the Black denominational publications severely critiqued the modernists, their reasons for doing so did not entirely overlap with white fundamentalists either. Two of the hottest topics for fundamentalists were evolution and the social gospel. While writers in the Black church affirmed God as creator of the world and the accounts of Genesis 1 and 2 as true, they shied away from absolute pronouncements on scientific debate. Part of this hesitance involved the deep theology of creation that has always been a marker of Black American Christianity. As one writer put it, "The question of how we came here is of minor importance; of major significance is why we are here. The Bible practically passes over the first and concerns itself almost exclusively with the second."[328] Black preachers and editorialists insisted that science and religion were not at odds and that the church needed to resist a "medieval" sort of limitation on the freedom of thought and education.[329]

While both fundamentalists and Black Christians were grieved by the modernists' departure from orthodox belief in Christian doctrine, the modernist's embrace of Christian social ethics was not part of the problem from the Black church perspective. In the nineteenth century, the rise of the social gospel emphasized the role of the church in ushering in God's kingdom through various sorts of social, economic, and political change to assist the poor and oppressed. Social gospel theologians complained that traditional Christianity dealt only with individual sinfulness but failed to correct institutional injustices. [330] For Black Christians, there was nothing new about the notions that one's faith gave one a special duty to the marginalized or that unjust institutions should constitute a Christian concern along with sinful individuals. Problems with the social gospel arise, they claimed, when its adherents believe that *only* institutions need to be redeemed, or if they hold that human effort *alone* could heal the world. Fundamentalists rejected the social gospel outright, but for Blacks, the fundamentalists had created a false dichotomy between "conversion and social justice." Instead, the church should "embody both the evangelism duties and the social justice calling."[331] A concern for just institutions and the proper treatment of those most easily brushed aside in a society arose from a "literal reading of the words of the prophets."[332] AME *Christian Recorder* editorialist Richard Wright criticized fundamentalists for what he saw as a kind of Gnosticism: a "religion so entirely 'spiritual,' and ethereal, that the white man had no pressure from the outside to stir him to think in terms of social obligation."[333] A dichotomy between one's love for a sinner's soul and the care for her material circumstances was simply nonsensical from the perspective of the Black church.[334] The promise of God's deliverance was always something holistic: deliverance from both hell and the power of sin, in one's body, soul, and spirit, for the individual, the family, and community.

In the meantime, the relationship between the white and Black church in America has remained contentious. Pentecostalism's auspicious beginning as a biracial movement crumbled within two decades, dividing between the Black Church of God in Christ and the white Assemblies of God. Martin Luther King Jr. famously referred to Sunday morning as the most segregated hour of the week and complained bitterly against white clergy in his "Letter from Birmingham Jail." In books like *God's Long Summer* (by Charles Marsh) and *The Color of Compromise* (by Jemar Tisby), historians record how the white church (with a few exceptions) was not only complicit in racism and racial oppression but oftentimes the source of it. One of the most famous cases having to do with antidiscrimination law was Bob Jones University, which lost its tussle with the IRS over whether an institution with racially discriminatory policies could have 501(c)(3) status (ironically, their policy actually arose from a lawsuit by an Asian family who objected to their child meeting and marrying a white student while at school there). While BJU admitted Black students starting in 1971, it maintained its ban on interracial dating till 2000, when a furor arose over the policy because George W. Bush spoke there.

There are bright spots. Cardinal Ritter integrated the St. Louis parochial system in 1947 on pain of excommunication. The Greek Orthodox Archbishop marched in Selma with Martin Luther King Jr. and was, in fact, the only other church leader to do so. Many individual white Episcopalians marched as well, and seminarian Jonathan Daniels was killed in 1965 for his work to integrate juries. The Pentecostal leader Oral Roberts has a particularly striking history of racial reconciliation efforts going back as far as the 1950s and made Oral Roberts University's interracial character central to its mission when it began in 1963. Surely, many more individual cases exist, and racial reconciliation efforts have led to a flurry of denominational statements across the American Christian scene over the last forty years, repenting for racism in the church and committing to a better future.

Today, some theologically orthodox Black Christians complain that their church traditions and theologies are ignored or even denigrated among white theological conservatives who champion slaveholders like Jonathan Edwards and George Whitefield instead (Whitefield was initially an abolitionist but ended up campaigning to institute slavery in Georgia to support his orphanage). They claim that the Black church tradition has unique insights gleaned from its high view of scripture and persistence through suffering, insights that could enrich the spiritual lives of their brothers and sisters of all races.[335] Currently, efforts toward racial reconciliation and multiethnic congregations have been frustrated by the polarizing rancor that infected the entire political scene in the 2010s.

LIBERATION AND ECONOMIC FREEDOM

As a result of these massive social and theological divides between Black and white Christians in America, current religious discussions that draw on the heritage of the Black church's emphasis on liberation—spiritual, political, and social—are sometimes criticized by white Christians as a flirtation with Marxist liberation theology, such as that touted by Catholic priests working in Latin America in the mid- and late twentieth century. In the view of liberation theology, a commitment to social justice for the poor includes an assumption that capitalist systems of economic organization are exploitative of the peasant class and that a completely revolutionary reorganization of social power is the only solution.[336] To conflate Black American theology and Latin American liberation theology, however, is a grave mistake.

First and most importantly, it's ahistorical to do so. The Black theological identification of their own liberation with the liberation of the Hebrews from Egypt is two hundred years older than liberation theology, which developed in Latin America in the 1960s and 1970s. The Black church tradition of liberation developed in the eighteenth century. It involves a sense of God's anger and impatience with oppressors and a faith that His divine help is not far off. Those who oppress are greedy and power-hungry and have been in every age. Therefore, the message of a holistic liberation is both timely and timeless; it involves no particular theory of history beyond the general Christian belief in God's kingdom as both coming now but also not fully here yet. It critiques the institution of slavery but does not critique the market system itself. In fact, it demands as a part of justice the protection of property and exchange—an unavoidable conclusion for those steeped in the Old Testament, where dozens of passages assume, defend, and punish the violators of the institution of private property.[337]

What did freedom from oppression mean for these enslaved men and women? It meant neither being enslaved nor subject to mere second-class citizenship. It meant being able to move, to work for wages and keep them, to buy land and work it, to go to school and learn, and to participate in republican government through voting and running for office. It meant having one's bodily integrity, property, and contracts just as well-defended by the justice system as anyone else's. Black Americans were asking for the same legal privileges enjoyed by white American citizens. Like the American revolutionaries demanding the rights of Englishmen, Black people demanded the rights of Americans.

The emphasis on both earthly and spiritual liberation, then, is part and parcel of the Black church tradition. It can be contrasted with the influence of people like Southern theologian James Henry Thornwell and his doctrine of the "spirituality of the church," which released the white church from responsibility for political injustice.[338] While the focus on liberation in the Black church tradition has sometimes given rise to more radical forms of Marxist liberation theology in the academy, it's important that in our efforts to listen to Black voices, we listen to the voices of regular Black people and not just to those authors whose radicalism comports well with trends in academia. Listening to Black and brown voices, then, means listening to the voices of that majority of Black Americans who so defy our social and political categories with their mixture of traditional religious commitment, socially conservative views on the family, entrepreneurial enthusiasm, and deep concern for the poor and oppressed.

Chapter 6

Liberation Through Business: Black Self-Help and Empowerment

"But I am not tragically colored.... No, I do not weep at
the world—I am too busy sharpening my oyster knife."
—Zora Neale Hurston[339]

"[Those students who engaged in nonviolent protest] were
really standing up for the best in the American dream,
and taking the whole nation back to those great wells of
democracy which were dug deep by the Founding Fathers in
the Declaration of Independence and the Constitution."
—Martin Luther King Jr. April 3, 1968[340]

The National Civil Rights Museum in Memphis offers an
inspiring experience about the ability of a people to achieve
liberty in the face of racism and state-sanctioned oppression. To
see the hotel room where Dr. Martin Luther King Jr. slept the
night before he was murdered is especially powerful. The whole
museum demonstrates the resilience of Black Americans from

1880 to 1954. Those years were, in many ways, some of the darkest days for Black Americans, and yet they didn't back down. In the face of lynch mobs, white riots, systematic disenfranchisement, and the advent of separate but equal Black Americans held on to their enterprising spirit and built a foundation from which they advanced their own liberation.

The museum opens with a quotation from W. E. B. Du Bois, "There is in this world no such force as the force of a man determined to rise. The human soul cannot be permanently chained." The exhibit declares, "This is the story of a people, of hopes and dreams, of challenge and change. It is an American story. This story and struggle that started many centuries ago, continues today—with you."[341] The museum is correct; it is essential that we not forget—and indeed learn from—the amazing achievements of the nineteenth century and early twentieth century.

While many guests are drawn to exhibits about Rosa Parks and King, the museum does an excellent job of emphasizing that the civil rights movement did not begin in 1954 in Montgomery. Indeed, the museum takes visitors through the hard work and toil that had to be performed by thousands of Black Americans to provide the foundation that enabled the success of civil rights advocates of the 1950s and 1960s.

That is the story of this chapter. It is a story of Black uplift. It is the story of how Black Americans banded together to create robust educational institutions, mutual aid societies, and flourishing industries to cater to both Black and white customers. It is the story of how all these manifestations of Black economic progress came together to help form various political organizations, such as the NAACP, which would ultimately make the push for true equality. We should celebrate the successes that were the result of activism and protest in the 1950s and 1960s. Nonviolent direct action led to amazing victories for Black Americans and created a United States that better lived up to its founding principles that all men are created equal. But we shouldn't forget why those protests were able to succeed—the protesters were standing on the shoulders of giants who laid the foundation for Black equality. This chapter is about Black self-help. It is about the multitude of voluntary associations and organizations that Blacks formed to improve their lives. Often facing impediments put into place by the state and federal government, Blacks had to form their own civil society. They formed schools, churches, fraternal lodges, life insurance societies, antilynching societies, civil rights organizations, and associations to promote Black businesses. As the museum puts it: "African Americans formed national associations that tackled racism on a variety of fronts. These organizations, philosophies, and strategies laid the foundation for social and political movements to come."[342] Combined, they created a thick Black civil society that helped Blacks overcome the hardships imposed on them by state-sanctioned segregation, the stripping of their civil rights, lynching, the reemergence of the Ku Klux Klan, and almost complete exile from American politics.

THE EDUCATION OF BOOKER T. WASHINGTON

While the National Civil Rights Museum gets much correct, it mischaracterizes Booker T. Washington when it calls him an "accommodationist." In this, the museum is undoubtedly drawing on many histories that present a binary of accommodation vs. protest as the two strategies for addressing white racism. In these narratives—which often quote his Atlanta Exposition Speech where he told Blacks to "cast down your buckets where you are"—Booker T. Washington is labeled as an accommodationist who gave up on Black political rights to promote industrial education and Black economic uplift. In contrast, these narratives generally praise W. E. B. Du Bois for opposing accommodation and demanding equality through protest.[343] In reality, Black economic improvement provided a firm foundation of donors, participants, and supporters for future civil rights activism.

As historian Robert Norrell demonstrates, this binary is an unfair and simplistic portrayal of the struggle for Black equality from 1890 to Washington's death in 1915. It is a narrative that draws extensively from Du Bois's own interpretation, an interpretation he constructed to make himself look better and make Washington look worse. In doing so, Du Bois seems to have been driven by personal animus. In reality, Washington's and Du Bois's strategies were more similar than many imagine, and Washington actually engaged in political activism throughout his time as "leader of the race"—but had to be as clandestine as possible given his Southern surroundings, as Du Bois well knew.[344] Both men deserve credit for their promotion of Black education and for their organization efforts. Indeed, it is difficult to imagine that the civil rights movement would have been possible without their efforts.

Born into slavery in 1856, Booker T. Washington was eventually educated at the Hampton Institute in Virginia. During his nine years of enslavement, Washington came to value education. As he later recalled, "From the moment that it was made clear to me that I was not to go to school, that it was dangerous for me to learn to read, from that moment I resolved that I should never be satisfied until I learned what this dangerous practice was like."[345]

Leaving Appomattox, Washington and his family moved to West Virginia to be with family. He went to work in the local coal mine, but he longed to be educated. In this he joined most Black Americans after 1865. As Washington explained, "It was a whole race trying to go to school, few were too young, and none too old, to make the attempt to learn."[346] As we've already mentioned, Black Americans engaged in what has to be the most rapid and most successful literacy campaign in world history from 1865 to 1910.

After a struggle with his stepfather, who enjoyed the income young Booker brought into the family working in the coal mine, they worked out a deal whereby the boy could do both. Washington worked from four in the morning until nine and then attended school. It was at school that he adopted Washington as his surname and became Booker T. Washington. His time in school combined with his employment with Viola Ruffner, the wife of the owner of the coal mines, fed his appetite for knowledge. In Ruffner's service, Washington developed an appreciation for "Yankee values." He was "disciplined, careful, efficient, and intensely acquisitive," and "he learned to account meticulously for every peach sold and every penny collected and to appreciate capitalist enterprise." Washington developed a serious work ethic, and in time he acquired the ability to communicate effectively in both speech and writing. His time in Mrs. Ruffner's service also trained him in the way in which white people thought and behaved. He came to understand them on a more personal level—a skill that would serve him well later in life both in fundraising for Tuskegee and also in navigating Southern white prejudice.[347]

While serving the Ruffners, Washington also learned a lesson that would stick with him for his entire life. In 1869 a scuffle broke out between a white and Black miner. The local chapter of the KKK threatened the Black man. In response, local Blacks armed themselves and came to his defense. The two sides erupted in violence near the Ruffners' home, and Washington witnessed the shootout. General Ruffner (the owner of the mine) convinced Blacks to stand down (he was able to do so because he was the most prominent Republican in town, and they viewed him as an ally). As a reward for deescalating the situation, General Ruffner was hit in the head with a brick and knocked unconscious—which caused permanent injuries. Enraged whites didn't give up on enacting vengeance on the Blacks who had challenged them. They formed groups of night riders and attempted to drive every last Black person out of town.[348] Washington understood what was going on. Prosperous Blacks and Republicans who would enable them to practice their civil rights were the targets of Klan violence. At that moment Washington recognized that the purpose of white terrorism was "to crush out the political aspirations of the negroes, but they did not confine themselves to this, because school-houses as well as churches were burned by them, and many innocent persons were made to suffer."[349]

Historian Robert Norrell explains that Washington realized in this moment that "racial conflict was so clearly destructive to the interests of Black people that it made little sense to engage in it, especially when one saw that the town's most prominent white man could be struck down, apparently without consequence to the attackers, when he tried to thwart other whites who treated blacks as their enemy."[350] It was a powerful lesson, and it would be one that Washington would deploy as "leader of the race" and as leader of the Tuskegee Institute. It was also a lesson that would, in time, lead to many Northern Black leaders (who were less likely to experience white vigilante violence) to condemn Washington as an accommodationist who refused to stand and fight for what he believed in.[351]

Washington continued his education at the Hampton Institute, whose emphasis was on providing the equivalent of a middle school education today. Their program focused on developing students' industrial skills and encouraging economic independence. This education was deemed satisfactory for training Black teachers to teach in the emerging Black primary schools. Washington was instructed in "spelling, grammar, composition, rhetoric, elocution, and vocal training." All of this, especially the courses on rhetoric, served him well. While at Hampton, Washington studied the lives of successful Black politicians and activists including Frederick Douglass and those active during Radical Reconstruction, as well as agricultural science.[352]

When Booker T. Washington graduated in 1875, he and his Hampton classmates faced a rather difficult task. In the previous ten years, hundreds of the newly established Black schools had been burned to the ground and "dozens of teachers terrorized and killed." The education at Hampton had prepared these young men and women to go out into a country in which their vision and their skill set were often unwelcome by the majority white population. Upon leaving Hampton, Washington's task was to drive an additional "fore-post of civilization on the old ground of barbarism." While he understood that many whites would stand against him, Washington had also learned that some whites, such as the Ruffners and the white educators and 175 supporters of the Hampton Institute, would help him in his struggle.[353] The next forty years would require courage, tenacity, and no small amount of shrewd strategizing.

TUSKEGEE: THE MODEL COMMUNITY IN THE HEART OF HATRED

After a short spell teaching back in his hometown and a short time attending seminary, Washington returned to Hampton as a teacher. In addition to his classes, Washington served as an understudy to the financial manager of the college, learning how to run such an institution. In hindsight, it appears that the president of Hampton had already decided that Washington would make a fine educational administrator.[354]

In 1881, Washington was asked if he would be willing to move to Tuskegee, Alabama, to organize and run the new educational institution there. Alabama would present him with unique challenges. He had already learned that politics were "an uncompromising, indeed dangerous, place for an ambitious young black man to focus his energy." Washington focused instead on education which in "the almost unanimous opinion of all of Booker's white friends in the 1870s was the best avenue to black progress." As such, Washington travelled back to the South, where his race would define his existence, where danger was constantly present, and where the challenges of Black Alabamians were tremendous. Over the next twenty years, white resentment of Black progress would threaten to remove Blacks not only from politics but from education as well.[355]

Building Tuskegee wasn't easy, but Washington set about creating a pristine institution to serve students and the surrounding communities of color. Washington ensured that the school owned the land and not the state of Alabama (which was run by a large number of white nationalists). Furthermore, it was "crucially important" to him "that the land was owned and the crops and livestock produced, by black people."[356]

The campus that Washington was given needed to be developed, and Washington and the students literally had to build the campus from the ground up. The first building project consisted of erecting an assembly hall, classrooms, a library, a dining hall, and dormitories. The first building to be completed was Porter Hall. Once it was completed, Washington invited Blacks from the surrounding area to tour the building. Washington later recalled how they reacted: "They would take hold of the door knobs, put their hands on the glass of the window panes, feel the blackboards, and then stop and gaze wonderingly again at the plastered walls, the desks and furniture. It seemed impossible to them that all this could have been brought into existence for the benefit of Negroes."[357] Perhaps even more impressive to local Blacks was the powerful message that Washington was sending about their ability to produce for themselves.

Later, Washington determined that the buildings should be made of brick, but there was no brickmaker in the area. So, the students set about producing bricks themselves. After several failed attempts they succeeded.[358] When the buildings were complete, Washington reflected that the ordeal had taught the students the lesson of perseverance, benefitted the school, and would demonstrate "to hostile whites that schooling made blacks valuable, not worthless."[359]

Indeed, Tuskegee continued to make bricks and sell them to whites in the surrounding area. The construction of Tuskegee by Blacks demonstrated that they were just as capable as whites at improving themselves. Likewise, by selling bricks to whites,

Washington was pushing back against white nationalist notions that an improvement in Black Alabamians' condition would harm the material well-being of whites. Instead, Washington pointed out, "We had something they wanted; they had something we wanted," and as a result economic interdependency through trade left both white and Black better off.[360]

In the long run, Washington hoped racial interdependence would result in better race relations and contribute to the material condition of Blacks. Or as he put it, "The individual who can do something that the world wants done will, in the end, make his way regardless of race." At his core, Washington believed "that there is something in human nature which always makes an individual recognize and reward merit, no matter under what colour of skin merit is found...it is the visible, the tangible that goes a long way in softening prejudices." As Norrell points out, however, while he was "correct in his overall psychological theory... throughout his career Booker Washington would ignore the fact that in practice the visible evidence of black achievement often hardened white prejudices and resentment."[361]

Nonetheless, Tuskegee grew quickly and from its beginning benefitted Black people across the region. The school produced teachers and placed them in rural schools, it supervised those schools' curricula, helped solve problems that arose, and secured funding and other resources. In its early days, almost all of Tuskegee's graduates became schoolteachers in rural areas, and many of them created the schools they taught in.[362]

In Tuskegee, just as in the example of his own life, Washington demonstrated by doing that Black self-help, uplift, and improvement were possible. At a time when white nationalists claimed that the Black population was declining and that they were on their way to extinction, Booker T. Washington was demonstrating that to be patently false. In fact, the Black population was growing, Blacks were dramatically increasing their standard of living, and they were becoming literate. They were building a foundation for future success.

The Tuskegee Institute, through its success, refuted the claims of white nationalists. By 1895, the Institute had almost eight hundred students, which meant it had the largest enrollment in the state of Alabama—even more than the state's flagship university in Tuscaloosa. Students continued to graduate and populate the southeastern United States. Furthermore, the institute itself continued to grow as Washington purchased more land. The success and expansion of Tuskegee "represented black achievement and independence" at a time when many Southern whites were looking for ways to limit Black social mobility.[363]

Washington's efforts in Alabama were not limited to building Tuskegee. In 1882, he organized the Alabama State Teachers Association (ASTA). The ASTA was the first professional organization for teachers in the state, and it offered Black educators—who were struggling to educate their students while also overcoming a lack of funding and oftentimes white antagonism—a place where they could come together in fellowship. They could discuss their areas of need, and the organization provided them with a support network. Most importantly, they were reminded that they were not alone in the cause to educate Black Alabamians. These teachers were dedicated to their pupils, and they were, in Washington's words, "teachers, not only in the school-house, but on the farm, in the flower-garden, and in the house, and we have a central light whose rays will soon penetrate the house of every family in the community." These teachers were the rock "the race can stand securely thereon till it has served the great ends of our creator."[364]

In addition to the ASTA, Washington created the Tuskegee Negro Conference in 1892. The purpose was "to bring together for a quiet conference, not the politicians and those usually termed the 'leading colored people,' but representatives of the masses—the bone and sinew of the race—the common, hard working farmers with a few of the best ministers and teachers." Although only seventy-five farmers were invited, over four hundred ultimately attended. There they "agreed on a set of self-improvement measures: to buy land and raise their own food, to learn a trade, to demand that ministers and teachers instruct people in domestic economy and morality, to build their own school buildings and extend school terms." The conference also discussed the ideas, popular among some, that Black people should move back to Africa, but they rejected it outright, explaining they intended to be "prosperous, intelligent, and independent where we are."[365] The Tuskegee Negro Conference was held annually, and by 1898 more than two thousand people attended.[366]

Students of Washington did the same—creating mutual aid societies and self-help organizations wherever they moved. Slowly but surely, Booker T. Washington was building the foundation for Black success in Alabama. For example, William James Edwards built Snow Hill Industrial Institute and founded the Black-Belt Improvement Society, which created cooperatives for Black farmers, instructed them in scientific farming, and encouraged "better domestic living."[367] Washington praised these efforts and established the Southern Improvement Company in 1901 that supplied graduates with credit and advice on how to succeed.[368]

At the same time that Washington was encouraging the creation of self-help organizations in Alabama, Black fraternal societies were springing up across the nation. In the face of exclusion, terrorism, and violence, Black Americans banded together. Along with Black churches, fraternal societies "were mainstays of self-organization for blacks during the difficult times of segregation, disenfranchisement, and threatening violence that prevailed from the 1880s to the mid-twentieth century."[369] As more and more Blacks were stripped of their ability to participate in the political process, fraternal orders and other self-help organizations "provided a virtual panorama of African American civil society."[370] These organizations, spurred on by the encouragement of Black leaders like Washington, were laying the foundation for Black economic improvement in the present and further Black success in the future.

LEADER OF THE RACE

Following the death of Frederick Douglass on February 20, 1895, Black Americans began searching for a new leader. They ultimately passed the mantle to Booker T. Washington. By the late nineteenth century, the task of combating white racism was more challenging than ever. Lynchings were on the rise, *Plessy v. Ferguson* made separate but equal the law of the land in 1896, and white nationalists were hellbent on stripping Black Americans of their right to vote. The goal of many whites in the South was to carry out the complete and utter alienation of Black Americans from the political process. These challenges would have bedeviled anyone who had been tasked with preserving Black political, civil, and economic rights. It would prove especially difficult for a man who lived in the South, where the threat of violence was always present.

In the 1890s, scientific racism guided mainstream public opinion. Most Americans were racist: they believed that white people were superior to Blacks. All the major publications, *Harper's Weekly*, *The Atlantic Monthly*, and *Century*, published stories and cartoons that "depicted blacks speaking outlandishly, acting crudely, and looking grotesque." As Norrell reminds us, "The authors and cartoonists, most of them northerners, referred to African Americans as 'niggers,' 'darkies,' and 'coons,' and regularly described them as savage, uncouth, bestial-looking, dishonest, and idle."[371] In short, public perception and sentiment—in both the North and the South—was that Black people were inferior to whites and were only fit for manual labor. According to this logic, no amount of education could improve "the negro"—he was intrinsically unfit for civilization. Racist whites even insisted that "crime among the Negroes increases with their education."[372]

It was in this context that Washington addressed the Cotton States Exposition in Atlanta. His speech would catapult him to national prominence, but its contents would provide fuel for his future Black critics. Speaking before the Atlanta conference was going to be difficult. As a white farmer reminded Washington on his departure: "You have spoken with success before Northern white audiences, and before Negroes in the south, but in Atlanta you will have to speak before Northern white people, Southern white people, and Negroes altogether. I fear they have got you in a pretty tight place."[373] The farmer wasn't wrong. Washington would have to find a way to please everyone while still promoting Black interests and delivering his narrative of Black improvement.

Washington's speech was an attempt to carve out a place for Black progress in the South, but in the process he conceded much of the Southern narrative about the folly of Black political involvement. Washington began by arguing that if the South was to succeed it needed to encourage Black uplift. As he put it, "No enterprise seeking the material, civil, or moral welfare of this section can disregard this element [Black Southerners] of our population and reach the highest success."[374] Washington then thanked the organizers of the exposition for allowing Black Americans to exhibit their achievements, and he emphasized his hope that the exhibit would encourage more Blacks to take up the task of industrial progress.

Washington's overarching goal, however, was to convince white Southerners that Black improvement would benefit them as well. He explained that while it had been natural for Black Americans to want political equality immediately after slavery, their experiment in government had been an example of putting the cart before the horse. What was needed now was for each Black man and woman to "cast down your buckets where you are." Washington called for racial reconciliation and harmony (albeit on white terms) and insisted that his fellows cast their bucket "down in agriculture, mechanics, in commerce, in domestic service, and in the professions." He insisted that "[n]o race can prosper till it learns that there is as much dignity in tilling a field as in writing a poem. It is at the bottom of life we must begin, and not at the top. Nor should we permit our grievances to overshadow our opportunities." It is subtle, but Washington was not saying that Black Southerners should forget the atrocities committed against them. Rather, he was asking them to put these past injustices in the back of their minds and focus instead on improving their material condition. It's hard to say when Washington envisioned, if ever, that whites would be required to recognize the wrongs that had been committed against Blacks. But in 1895, his message was clear: the focus should be on Black material progress.

Washington then called on Southern whites to recognize that Black Southerners could play a meaningful role in the modernization and improvement of the South. In doing so, he proposed a partnership between the races that allowed for economic interdependence but also for social separation. He called on Southern whites to:

> Cast down your bucket among my people, helping and encouraging them as you are doing on these grounds, and to education of head, hand, and heart, you will find that they will buy your surplus land, make blossom the waste places in your fields, and run your factories. While doing this, you can be sure in the future, as in the past, that you and your families will be surrounded by the most patient, faithful, law-abiding, and unresentful people that the world has seen. As we have proved our loyalty to you in the past, in nursing your children, watching by the sick bed of your mothers and fathers, and often following

them with tear-dimmed eyes to their graves, so in the future, in our humble way, we shall stand by you with a devotion that no foreigner can approach, ready to lay down our lives, if need be, in defense of yours, interlacing our industrial, commercial, civil, and religious life with yours in the way that shall make the interests of both races one.[375]

Washington concluded this appeal to reconciliation and cooperation with a statement that would be oft repeated in the years ahead by his opponents as an acceptance of Jim Crow: "In all things that are purely social we can be as separate as the fingers, yet one as the hand in all things essential to mutual progress."[376]

The goal of Washington's speech couldn't have been clearer; he wanted to convince whites to stop fighting Black education and economic progress. Washington pleaded that "if anywhere there are efforts tending to curtail the fullest growth of the Negro, let these efforts be turned into stimulating, encouraging, and making him the most useful and intelligent citizen."[377] In exchange for white cooperation in Black material improvement, he was willing to concede that "the wisest among my race understand that the agitation of questions of social equality is the extremist folly, and that progress in the enjoyment of all the privileges that will come to us must be the result of severe and constant struggle rather than of artificial forcing."[378]

In other words, Washington argued that Black people needed to demonstrate themselves capable of self-improvement and progress before they demanded their full political rights. Those had to be hard words to utter for a man who would do much work behind the scenes over the next two decades to ensure Black political rights. In his Atlanta speech, he strategically conceded "what was already lost—independent black political power—in order to reduce white hostility."[379] Caught in the cultural conundrum of being Black in the South, Washington realized that any outward hostility over political rights would lead to white backlash against Black education and material progress. Booker T. Washington decided to prioritize the latter. Furthermore, Washington's Atlanta Exposition Speech was the beginning of his long battle "to give whites a new way of viewing blacks"—one that would reframe Blacks as allies in the struggle to modernize the region rather than an enemy whose progress necessarily hurt whites.[380]

Washington's speech was well received across the country—by Northern whites, Southern whites, and by most Black Americans. A Black lawyer in Chicago exclaimed that "no word uttered by a colored man during the past 20 years will go farther and do more to set us right in public opinion." W. E. B. Du Bois, who would later become Washington's fiercest critic, praised the speech as "a word fitly spoken" and as "the basis of a real settlement between whites and blacks in the South."[381] Du Bois's comments demonstrate that he clearly understood, at least in 1895, the strategy of Washington's address in Atlanta. A co-founder of the Afro-American League (which organized Blacks to fight for their political and civil rights) and editor of the *New York Age*, Timothy Thomas Fortune exclaimed, "It looks as if you are our Douglass. You are the best equipped of the lot of us to be the single figure ahead of the procession." Fortune went further in an article titled, "Is He the Negro Moses?" declaring that Washington's Atlanta speech had debunked the claim that Black Americans were inferior to whites without the "mental rasp and development of the Anglo-Saxon."[382]

Following his Atlanta speech, Washington became recognized as the "leader of his race" by both Blacks and whites across the country. He would often be unfavorably compared to Frederick Douglass in the years ahead, but as Norrell points out, the two men had much in common: "They shared strong commitments to the Protestant ethic and the Republican Party, objections to emigration to Africa, suspicions of the labor movement, an emphasis on industrial education, and optimism about blacks' future in America."[383] The last two points were especially important in the face of an organized effort by white nationalists to deny Black Southerners access to education and economic opportunities. Washington would fiercely push back against such racist efforts to claim that Blacks had no future in American life.

Under Washington's leadership from 1895 to roughly his death in 1915, the strategy for improving the lot of Black Americans would be industrial education, the promotion of mutual aid societies, the creation of self-help organizations, and the encouragement of education. Despite his critics' claims, however, Washington did not relinquish "the black claim to equal rights. Indeed, he pursued all the rights due to blacks, though in his own way."[384] As it turns out, these years were pivotal. Large numbers of Black Americans became more economically independent, joined an array of civil society organizations, and laid the foundation that would enable them to take back their civil rights in the decades to come.

FIGHTING FOR BLACK POLITICAL RIGHTS AND AGAINST DISCRIMINATION

As we discussed in Chapter 3, the years from 1890 to 1920 were especially bad for Black political rights. Jim Crow spread across the South, and a flurry of new Southern constitutions stripped Black Southerners of their ability to participate in politics. Those who were outspoken in public against lynching and the rollback of Black political freedom were driven out of the South by violence or by the threat of violence—think back to how Ida B. Wells was forced to leave Memphis.

Some Blacks fought back, organizing boycotts of segregated streetcars from 1895 to 1906. Across the South, Washington's greatest supporters, Black businessmen and professionals, organized boycotts of trolleys. According to Norrell, Washington approved of these efforts "because the withdrawal of patronage and the lodging of complaints with traction companies represented businesslike, careful responses that he thought might yield benefits." After all, "a boycott was an exercise of economic power designed to elicit a specific change in future behavior, whereas protests against white violence came to be perceived as after-the-fact ranting."[385] Washington was convinced that Black economic power would win the day. He declared that whites would quickly recognize that "the Negro's nickel is necessary to keep the street railway corporation alive."[386] Despite his support, and the support of a growing Black professional class, the boycotts all ended in failure.[387]

We need to ask ourselves why these boycotts didn't succeed whereas in Montgomery, some fifty years later, Rosa Parks, Dr. Martin Luther King Jr., and the Montgomery Improvement Association would achieve a victory that would launch the modern civil rights movement. There are many reasons, but one of the most important has to be the foundation of support that the NAACP and Black activists had in the 1950s. That support came from an array of Black professionals, from an active network of churches and their congregations, and also from self-help organizations and Black fraternal orders. In short, the foundation wasn't there in 1905. Fifty years later it would be.

In addition to his support for the streetcar boycotts, Washington fought for Black political rights in other ways—often behind the scenes. He did his best to promote Blacks for political positions, especially at the federal level, believing that these appointments were of symbolic importance.[388] For instance, Washington worked tirelessly to get President Theodore Roosevelt to appoint William D. Crum as the collector of the Port of Charleston. While Crum's appointment was languishing, Washington secured another victory for his race when William H. Lewis was appointed assistant US attorney for Boston. This was the highest position any Black American had ever held in the federal government.[389] To try and get Crum across the finish line, Washington organized a nationwide lobbying campaign that contributed to his eventual appointment.[390]

Washington also engaged in what might be described as a public relations campaign to improve the image of Black Americans and to provide a counternarrative to white nationalists. He did so by writing countless newspaper articles, publishing multiple books, and using his influence with President Roosevelt to demonstrate the possibilities for Black achievement were endless.[391] A week after the appointment of Crum, Roosevelt invited further advice from Washington on federal appointments. The president invited him to dine with him in the White House. This decision was monumental—no Black person had ever dined in the White House before. Washington later wrote that the invitation represented "recognition of the race and no matter what personal condemnation it brought upon my shoulders I have no right to refuse or even hesitate."[392]

Washington dining with Roosevelt and his family—including his daughter—caused an uproar across the South and in truth endangered Washington's person. Ben Tillman, the Democratic firebrand senator from South Carolina, proclaimed that "[t]he action of President Roosevelt in entertaining that nigger will necessitate our killing a thousand niggers in the South before they will learn their place again." His fellow Southerner, James K. Vardaman, the governor of Mississippi, was also outraged: "President Roosevelt takes this nigger bastard into his home, introduces him to his family and entertains him on terms of absolute social equality."[393]

In contrast, Blacks praised Roosevelt and Washington for the symbolic importance of the dinner and for the courage both exhibited in the aftermath. Emmett Jay Scott, one of Washington's closest advisers, wrote to him, "It is splendid, magnificent! The world is moving forward." A minister from Chicago praised the dinner as "an omen of the coming of that day when we shall

neither be favored nor hindered because of the color of our skin."
A Birmingham minister likewise wrote to Washington, "We negroes feel that you are greatly honored, indeed, and that you have
done more to advance our interest in new territory than any living man." Norrell concludes that "the White House dinner represented an embrace of racial equality by the most powerful white
man and the most powerful black man in the United States."[394]
Southern whites understood the significance as well, and they
were outraged!

Threats were made against Tuskegee, and the sentiment across
the South was that Washington and Roosevelt had betrayed
them. The white press was universally outraged. The Memphis
Scimitar exclaimed that Roosevelt "having a nigger to dine at the
White House" was the "most damnable outrage which has ever
been perpetrated by any citizen of the United States." According
to the paper, the dinner would teach Blacks that "any Nigger who
happens to have a little more than the average amount of intelligence granted by the Creator of his race, and cash enough to pay
the tailor and the barber, and the perfumer for scents enough to
take away the nigger smell, has a perfect right to be received by the
daughter of the white man among the guests in the parlor of his
home." A populist paper in Alabama asserted, "Poor Roosevelt!
He might now just as well sleep with Booker Washington, for the
scent of that coon will follow him to the grave, as far as the South
is concerned."[395] As a result of this breach of Southern "etiquette,"
threatening letters poured into Tuskegee, and an assassin even
confessed to being hired to kill Washington.[396]

In 1902, Washington's loyalty to President Roosevelt paid
off, and he was asked to advise the president on federal appointments. Most significantly, he needed a replacement for the federal judge in Montgomery. Washington recommended Thomas
Goode Jones, whom he described as "a gold democrat, and is a
clean, pure man in every respect."[397] Despite the fact that Jones

had not supported the Republican ticket in 1900, Roosevelt took Washington's advice and appointed Jones to the bench.

This was one of the most influential actions that Washington took as leader of the race. Although Jones was white, he would be an important ally in the struggle to preserve Black liberty. In 1903, Jones "convened a federal grand jury to investigate peonage" in Alabama. What they found was exactly what we described in Chapter 3; Black men were often accused of a trivial crime, were found guilty, and then signed a contract to work on a plantation instead of being shipped off to Birmingham as a leased convict. Once that man was close to fulfilling his term, he was often convicted of another crime and was coerced to sign another labor contract. This peonage system was in clear violation of the Constitution, and Judge Jones intended to put an end to both peonage and convict leasing. Ultimately, "the grand jury indicted eighteen men on ninety-nine counts of enslavement. Along the way, Jones declared Alabama's contract labor law unconstitutional."[398] Washington's efforts in getting Jones appointed had paid off. This was a major victory.[399]

These early victories over convict leasing and peonage in Alabama were offset by a crushing loss. In 1902, Washington began financing a legal challenge to the newly enacted Alabama state constitution, which had stripped Black Alabamians of their political rights. A group of Black Montgomery professionals created the Colored Men's Suffrage Association, and Washington provided the money to bring the challenge to court. The lawyer on the case ultimately filed five lawsuits. According to Norrell, Washington's "goal in all the cases was to reach the U.S. Supreme Court to get a judgement on whether the new constitution violated the Fourteenth and Fifteenth Amendments."[400]

Washington's support of Judge Jones once again paid off as he helped one of the cases make it all the way to the Supreme Court. Pursuing a process that looked a lot like the NAACP's later strategy of achieving liberty through the courts, Washington insisted, "I believe there is a way to win, or at least put the Supreme Court in an awkward position. We must not give up our efforts." Unfortunately, a month later the Supreme Court dashed Washington's hopes by ruling "against disfranchised blacks in Virginia in two well-financed cases argued by two prominent white lawyers from Old Dominion." As Norrell concludes, "The highest tribunal simply would not be persuaded to protect black voting rights." A short time later, a challenge to Louisiana's constitution, which Washington had also supported, failed in state court.[401] Although Booker T. Washington was pursuing a strategy similar to the one that would ultimately result in watershed court victories in the 1950s, the reality was that there was only so much that could be achieved with respect to Black political rights in the early 1900s.

Washington consistently provided resources for court challenges behind the scenes while serving as leader of the race. He didn't advertise his efforts for the obvious reason that doing so would put him, and the Tuskegee Institute, in danger. Du Bois and other critics would later claim that he didn't care about Black political rights, but they were aware of his efforts. In fact, Washington even financed Du Bois's lawsuit against the Pullman Company. Washington had been trying for years to get Robert Lincoln, Abraham Lincoln's son and president of the Pullman Palace Car Company, to live up to his father's example. Washington consistently wrote Lincoln and appealed to his sense of responsibility. As Washington exclaimed in one letter: "It does seem to me that a rich and powerful corporation like yours could find some way to extend in some degree, protection to the weak."[402] Washington's moral challenges fell on deaf ears, but his critics were undoubtedly aware of his efforts to end discrimination and restore Black political rights.

Washington's efforts at protecting Black civil liberties may look minuscule when compared to the great achievements of Martin Luther King Jr. and the modern civil rights movement of the 1950s and 1960s, but in reality his efforts made a crucial difference. Washington's greatest effect, however, was in encouraging and empowering Black economic achievement.

BOOKER T. WASHINGTON AND BLACK ECONOMIC UPLIFT

In 1889, Emmett Jay Scott, Washington's private secretary and an entrepreneur in his own right, and Thomas Fortune, a prominent newspaper editor and Washington adviser, encouraged Washington to create an association of Black business leaders. Scott had gone to school in Houston and witnessed the "dynamic growth" in that region of Texas. He was especially impressed with two organizations that encouraged "economic community development: the Houston Commercial League and the Houston Business League." Scott believed in "Washington's idea that blacks demonstrate their individual and collective progress through building solid institutions and strong organizations within the African American community."[403] The result of their efforts was the National Negro Business League (NNBL).

The first conference of the NNBL was held in 1900. According to historian Maceo Crenshaw Dailey Jr., the purpose of the organization was to bring "black businessmen and women...from around the nation to share success stories, describe economic opportunities, establish partnerships, discuss strategies for increasing consumption, and promote the spirit of capitalism in the African American community." Membership in the organization grew rapidly, and by the time of Washington's death in 1915, hit forty thousand members over six hundred chapters.[404]

Members of the NNBL came from the North and South and from a large variety of sectors in the American economy. As the introduction to the records of the NNBL explain: "Some [members] were the owners of small businesses; some were professionals such as undertakers, doctors, etc.; many in the South were farmers;

and others were craftspeople who aspired to build organizations that extended beyond their personal resources."[405] During its history, the NNBL would have many prominent members. For example, Junius G. Groves, who was featured in Washington's 1907 book *The Negro in Business*,[406] was known as the "Potato King of the World" because he used growing methods that enabled him to grow "more bushels of potatoes per acre than anyone else in the world."[407] John S. Trower created a vibrant catering business in Philadelphia that would make him one of the wealthiest Black Americans at the time of his death (he was reported to be worth over a million dollars).[408] H. C. Haynes developed a "ready to use razor strop" that he produced and sold to Black and white barbers across the country.[409] Samuel R. Scottron was an impressive inventor who was best known for patenting the curtain rod and the "leather hand strap devices" used on trolley cars to stabilize people and keep them from falling.[410]

Perhaps the best-known member of the NNBL to Americans today is Madam C. J. Walker. White businesses often ignored Black consumers' unique needs, which created an opportunity for Black entrepreneurs like Walker. By creating "Madam Walker's Wonderful Hair Grower," she provided a product that hundreds of thousands of Black women demanded. Walker was a savvy advertiser, running ads in Black newspapers across the country. She eventually expanded her business and released an entire line of hair care products. Walker also invested in a factory to mass-produce her wares. Of course, this meant that she would need saleswomen. By 1910, she employed around twenty thousand "Walker Agents" who went door-to-door promoting Walker's products. Although her entrepreneurial talents led to her being extraordinarily wealthy, Walker was just as proud of empowering thousands of Black women to forge their own path to success. One of her brochures advertised the opportunities she offered them: "Open your own shop; secure prosperity and freedom." Walker emanated free enterprise and self-help. As she told her agents, "I had to make my own living and my own opportunity. Don't sit down and wait for the opportunities to come. Get up and make them." Walker and the other businessmen and women who came together to forge the NNBL demonstrated that even in a society where rights were not being fully protected, markets could serve as a liberating and empowering force.[411]

Although the National Negro Business League did not accomplish all its goals, it did provide a network for Black businessmen and women and connected them to other Black organizations such as the National Negro Press Association and the National Negro Bankers Association. Furthermore, in the midst of one of the darkest periods in Black history, it provided a "strategy for survival." Historian Kenneth Hamilton concluded that a significant purpose of the NNBL was to "provide a network of support for the small but developing business and professional classes and enable individuals to continue the fight for the right to individual freedom and dignity in the face of a virulent atmosphere of racism."[412] To Du Bois, however, this self-help through economic improvement strategy was lacking. As injustice and violence against Black Americans intensified, Washington's critics insisted that they needed to publicly demand political and social rights.

DIFFERENT PATHS TO THE SAME DESTINATION

In April 1903, W. E. B. Du Bois published *The Souls of Black Folk* in which he directly challenged Washington's vision of prioritizing Black material progress. Despite the fact that Washington was still funding Du Bois's lawsuit against the Pullman Company, he lambasted Washington for surrendering Black political and social rights when he delivered his speech in Atlanta in 1895—a speech that Du Bois labeled "The Atlanta Compromise." Du Bois asserted that Washington's strategy "practically accepts the alleged inferiority of the Negro races." Washington was "striving nobly to make Negro artisans business men and property-owners; but it is utterly impossible, under modern competitive methods, for the workingmen and property-owners to defend their rights and exist without the right to suffrage."[413] Du Bois concluded with a call to arms against Washington:

> So far as Mr. Washington preaches Thrift, Patience, and Industrial Training for the masses we must hold up his hands and strive with him, rejoicing in his honors and glorying in the strength of this Joshua called of God and of man. But so far as Mr. Washington apologizes for injustice, North and South, does not rightly value the privilege and duty of voting, belittles the emasculating effects of caste distinctions, and opposes the higher training and ambition of our brighter minds,—so far as he, the South or the Nation, does this,—we must unceasingly and firmly oppose them.[414]

Historian Robert Norrell labels Du Bois's criticisms in 1903 as opportunistic and full of "half-truths." After all, Du Bois had praised Washington's 1895 Atlanta speech at the time it was delivered, and Du Bois "knew that Booker had neither accepted inferiority nor relinquished political or civil rights, because he [Du Bois] had worked closely with Booker to challenge railroad discrimination and disfranchisement in Georgia." Likewise, Du Bois's claims that Washington did not appreciate higher education were false and he knew it. As Norrell points out, Du Bois "knew of Washington's support for Fisk University, his preference for hiring teachers from good liberal-arts schools, and his frequently stated position that an academic education was entirely appropriate for blacks who could put it to use." And finally, Du Bois was very much aware of the limitations that Washington faced in running a school in the heart of Dixie. Washington had to protect his students. As such, Washington avoided any public protest for political and social equality and preferred to pursue those goals discreetly.[415]

For all the half-truths in Du Bois's denunciations of Washington, he was correct that the fight for Black political and social equality needed a champion. Violence against Black Americans had not abated, and Black political rights were nonexistent in the South. As such, in 1905, Du Bois called Black men together at Niagara Falls to form an organization to promote "racial justice."[416] The Niagara Movement platform began by acknowledging the "progress in the last decade, particularly in increase of intelligence, the buying of property, the checking of crime, the uplift of home life, the advances in literature and arts, and the demonstration of constructive and executive ability in the conduct of great religious, economic, and educational institutions." It then shifted to what needed to be done beyond Washington's program. Specifically, it called for Black Americans to be given "every single right that belongs to a freeborn American—political, civil, and social" and declared that protest was a legitimate means to secure those rights: "The voice of protest of ten million Americans must never cease to assail the ears of their fellows, so long as America is unjust."[417] Although the Niagara Movement was short-lived, many in its movement viewed it as a precursor to the NAACP.[418]

Whereas Washington put the emphasis on Black economic uplift, the Niagara Movement insisted on agitating for political and social equality. This was a difference in strategy, but the end goal was the same. As Norrell explains, "The real purpose of [Washington's] strategy was equal economic status for blacks and eventually political and social equality."[419] Washington thought constant agitation would lead to unnecessary conflict with Whites and to violence. In contrast, the Niagara Movement declared: "Of the above grievances we do not hesitate to complain, and to complain loudly and insistently. To ignore, overlook, or apologize for these wrongs is to prove ourselves unworthy of freedom." They concluded that "[p]ersistent manly agitation is the way to liberty."[420] For both Washington and Du Bois, the ultimate goal was political and social equality.[421] The question was how best to get there.

THE NATIONAL ASSOCIATION FOR THE ADVANCEMENT OF COLORED PEOPLE

The outbreak of racial violence in Springfield, Illinois, in 1908 was the catalyst for the formation of a nationwide interracial civil rights organization to fight for Black equality. As more and more Black Americans moved north, tensions began to increase in Illinois. In August, two Black men were arrested in quick succession—one on charges of murder and the other for rape. A mob of angry whites assembled outside the Sangamon County Courthouse with the intention of lynching the accused. Unable to get their hands on those two men, "the mob turned its wrath on two other black men, Scott Burton and William Donegan, who were in the area. They were quickly lynched." But even that didn't satisfy the mob. They then decided to ransack Black-owned stores and neighborhoods. When over four thousand troops finally got whites to stop the rioting, eight Black people were dead, hundreds of thousands of dollars in property was destroyed, and over two thousand Blacks had been displaced. Although around 150 suspected mob participants were arrested, threats from other members of the mob resulted in most whites being unwilling to testify.[422]

The Springfield riot served as a warning for Northern white reformers who cared about Black equality. Historian Patricia Sullivan describes it as "the most harrowing incident of antiblack violence in the North since the New York City draft riots nearly a century earlier" and concludes that "suddenly, it seemed as if the violence and brutality that characterized southern race relations were spilling northward."[423] White reformers Mary White Ovington, Henry Moskowitz, William English Walling, Florence Kelley, Lillian Wald, and Oswald Garrison Villard (a longtime Washington ally) joined forces with Du Bois, two Black clergymen—Bishop Alexander Walters and Reverend William Henry Brooks—and Dr. W. H. Bulkley, who was a Black school principal. Together they issued "The Call" on the one-hundred-year anniversary of Abraham Lincoln's birth. It concluded by requesting that all "believers in democracy to join in a national conference for the discussion of the present evils, the voicing of protests, and the renewal of the struggle for civil and political liberty." Signees of "The Call" included "W.E.B. Du Bois, Ida B. Wells-Barnett, John Dewey, William Lloyd Garrison Jr., Bishop Alexander Walters, Rabbi Stephen Wise, Lincoln Steffens, Ray Stannard Baker, Jane Addams, William Dean Howells, and Mary Church Terrell."[424] This new coalition would include men and women, Black and white, but at its advent it was predominantly a Northern coalition—a fact that would soon change.

The following year, the group held the National Negro Conference. Around three hundred men and women—around half white and half Black—attended, and Du Bois described the event as "a visible bursting into action of long gathering thought and brooding."[425] At Villard's request, an invitation was sent to Washington (albeit at the last minute), but he had to decline because of a prior engagement. In his response, Washington acknowledged that if he attended it "would probably inhibit discussion" (several of the other Black attendees were vehement in their opposition to him and his program by 1909). Washington also graciously acknowledged that "there was work to be done that one in his position and probably no one living in the South could do" and added that "there is work which those of us who live here in the South can do, which persons who do not live in the South cannot do." Washington concluded that "if we recognize fairly and squarely this, then it seems to me we have gone a long ways."[426] Despite this promising statement, Washington and the NAACP would have a cool relationship until his death six years later.

After much debate, and after overcoming much distrust between the Black and white delegates, the National Negro Conference agreed to a set of resolutions. The resolutions of the conference "condemned all forms of racial discrimination and called for equal educational opportunities, equal expenditure of public school funds for white and Black students, and the strict enforcement of the Fourteenth and Fifteenth Amendments." One final resolution, adopted in the final session, pledged the delegates to create a new nationwide civil rights organization. At the second iteration of the conference, that organization became the National Association for the Advancement of Colored People.[427] Its primary strategy would be to seek equality through the courts. As Sullivan explains, "From the beginning, the NAACP focused on the law and the courts as a primary arena for exposing injustices, publicizing its cause, and obtaining the enforcement of basic legal and constitutional guarantees—a new and innovative strategy for a national reform organization."[428]

Like almost all advocates of Black civil rights, the NAACP called for the United States to live up to its ideals and to acknowledge and protect Black individual liberty. The problem wasn't the country's liberal institutions; the problem was that the promises laid out in the founding documents and the purpose of those institutions were being inhibited by racial discrimination. The NAACP was determined to change that. It would be a long journey, but eventually they would turn the tide.

FITS AND STARTS ON THE LONG ROAD TO EQUALITY

Following Washington's death in 1915 at the age of fifty-nine, the NAACP took up the mantle of promoting Black betterment.

They and Du Bois, who was the editor of the organization's magazine, *The Crisis*, quickly discovered how difficult achieving such progress could be.

From its founding in 1909 into the 1920s, the NAACP was faced with significant political and cultural challenges. During this time, they crafted the "machinery" that would be used in later decades to win monumental court decisions and protest injustice. During the vehemently racist administration of President Woodrow Wilson, they "confronted head-on the deepening segregation of the federal government." The NAACP used "publicity and protest, litigation and lobbying, community-based organizing and demands for national action."[429] In addition to a hostile president, the organization also had to contend with an array of white nationalist propaganda including the release of *The Birth of a Nation* in 1915. The film celebrated the Ku Klux Klan and depicted Black Americans (particularly Black men) as racially inferior, violent, and hypersexual.[430]

Additionally, increasing racial violence across the country marked the early years of the organization. During World War I, half a million Southern Blacks escaped Jim Crow and moved to the Northeast, Midwest, and West.[431] The influx of Black Americans into Northern cities such as New York, Chicago, Detroit, and Philadelphia—where they got jobs and helped with the war effort—resulted in racial tension across the country.[432] White on Black violence broke out in at least twenty-six different cities.

These acts of lawlessness occurred after many Black veterans returned from World War I, where they had been treated with more respect abroad than they received at home. Du Bois had called on these men to not just "return from fighting" but to "return fighting." When confronted with white mobs and violence, they heeded Du Bois's call. Unorganized whites made up the majority of the mobs that attacked Blacks across the US in 1919—although the second iteration of the Ku Klux Klan would claim millions of members by early 1920s. In Washington, DC, white mobs attacked Blacks indiscriminately, which led DC's Black community to band together and form their own militias. The result was chaos and violence resulting in President Wilson's call on troops to end the confrontation. In Chicago thirty-eight people were killed (twenty-three Black and fifteen white), over five hundred others were injured, and over a thousand Black families were homeless following the destruction of their neighborhoods.[433] The bloodiest single episode of white violence thus far occurred in Elaine, Arkansas, where around one hundred Black Arkansans were killed.[434] This violence was followed by a surge in KKK membership and more atrocities such as the Tulsa Massacre in 1921.[435]

To Black Americans, it must have felt like the worst of times. Those who became economically prosperous, as Booker T. Washington had encouraged, did not gain the respect and acceptance of their white brothers and sisters. Instead, they were the objects of their envy and resentment. Likewise, when Black Americans attempted to fight back against white violence, they often were slaughtered due to the fact that they were not as well armed as whites (partially a product of gun control measures to keep firearms out of the hands of Blacks), because they were always a minority and were outnumbered, and because the authorities often looked the other way or encouraged white violence outright.[436] In truth, no strategy seemed to be working.

Through it all, the NAACP continued its work, Black civil society continued to expand, and Black businessmen and women continued to accumulate wealth. According to Sullivan, "By the late 1920s, the NAACP could claim a string of legal victories striking down various discriminatory policies in housing, voting, education, and criminal justice." But even the organization itself admitted progress had been slow. Charles Houston, who served as the NAACP's litigation director, said that the organization's "greatest achievement" during its early days was to keep "the light burning on the lonely peak of absolute equality."[437]

The NAACP, Ida Wells, and other Black activists also did their best to support Republican efforts during the 1920s to pass a federal anti-lynching law. When Warren G. Harding became president, he brought Black citizens back into federal positions (Woodrow Wilson had all but purged them during his administration), implored Congress to pass an anti-lynching bill, and forthrightly denounced the Ku Klux Klan. Harding travelled to the heart of Dixie—Birmingham, Alabama—and proclaimed, "I would say let the black man vote when he is fit to vote; prohibit the white man voting when he is unfit to vote."[438] For its part, the NAACP threw "its full organizational strength behind" the anti-lynching bill. They mobilized public sentiment and pressured Republicans to bring it to the floor of the Senate for a vote.[439] In the end, despite the efforts of the NAACP and a cadre of Republican senators, Southern Democrats threatened to use the filibuster to kill the legislation calling the measure the "most daring and destructive invasion of states rights in history." Republican senators held out a week until they relented so other legislation could be considered. Harding didn't pressure them to hold firm either. He spoke out in favor of the legislation but only after it had already been tabled.[440]

Despite the amazing success of the Harlem Renaissance, in truth, the 1920s were full of disappointments in the struggle for Black political and social equality.[441] But it is also true that many of the efforts of the decade paid off later. For instance, A. Philip Randolph, in the face of a massive amount of postwar hostility toward labor movements, became the chief organizer of the Brotherhood of Sleeping Car Porters, which represented the many Black employees of the Pullman Car Company.[442] In 1925, he began a long battle with the Pullman Company, the American Federation of Labor, and many Blacks who frowned on Black unionization. It ultimately took ten years for him to get the AFL to recognize the Black union and another two to get a contract from the Pullman Company. This was a momentous moment; Black laborers had successfully forced a company to recognize their right to collectively bargain.[443] While unions are often thought of as outside the free market framework, in reality they play an important role through negotiations of determining wages and working conditions. It's only when government intervenes, either on the side of labor or capital, that the equilibrating forces of the free enterprise system are inhibited.

The onset of the Great Depression stymied Black economic gains. From emancipation to the death of Booker T. Washington, Blacks had tripled their per capita income.[444] Admittedly, they were beginning from a very low base, but the improvements were significant. With hundreds of thousands of Blacks moving into the cities and finding work in manufacturing, Black economic conditions continued to improve during World War I. The 1920s witnessed some improvements, especially for Black Americans who worked in white collar professions. But it is important to remember that only 4.6 percent of Blacks worked white collar jobs (that was almost double from what it had been in 1910, but it was still a very small portion of the overall population). Furthermore, the prosperity of the 1920s was not distributed equally. Black farmers, for instance, continued to languish along with their white counterparts, and almost 32 percent of Blacks in the workforce continued to work in "domestic and personal service."[445] It was also true that Blacks were often the first ones fired when the economy hit a rough patch as it did in the depression of 1920–1921, the recession of 1924, and the recession of 1927. As such, Black unemployment hovered above the national average throughout the decade.[446]

As uneven as the economic progress was in the 1920s, the Great Depression decimated Black Americans. According to historian David M. Kennedy, by 1940 Blacks "earned, on the average, 39 percent of what whites made" and "almost nine of ten black families eked out a living on incomes below the federal poverty threshold."[447] Their condition wasn't made any better by the fact that many of President Franklin Delano Roosevelt's New Deal programs didn't benefit them to the extent that they benefitted white Americans. For example, the Social Security Act and the National Labor Relations Act excluded farm workers and domestic workers, who were predominantly Black, from receiving benefits.[448]

On the eve of American entry into World War II, A. Philip Randolph—along with a group of Black leaders including the executive secretary of the NAACP—met with FDR to discuss the exclusion of Black workers from the defense effort and segregation in the military.[449] Roosevelt listened to them with his "customary charm," but a couple of weeks later his administration announced that "the policy of the War Department is not to intermingle colored and white enlisted personnel in the same regimented organizations." Randolph rightly felt betrayed and proposed a radical idea for the time: "I think we ought to get 10,000 Negroes to march on Washington in protest, march down Pennsylvania Avenue." Many Black leaders recoiled at the plan, and even the NAACP offered only "lukewarm support." But many rank and file Black Americans were intrigued by the idea that Randolph might be able to summon so many Black protestors.[450]

The prospect of such a demonstration rattled FDR, and in June 1941 he held a second meeting with Randolph. The result of the meeting was Executive Order 8802, which declared: "There shall be no discrimination in the employment of workers in defense industries or government because of race, creed, color, or national origin."[451] This was a turning point in the struggle for Black equality. One Black paper reported that the executive order "demonstrated to the Doubting Thomases among us that only mass action can pry open the doors that have been erected against America's black minority."[452]

During World War II Black Americans found their voice and called for double victory: victory over the racialized Nazi regime abroad and victory over racism and Jim Crow at home.

Double V, as the campaign was known, was very successful. Black Americans "embraced the idea that with the sacrifices of over one million Black men and women in various branches of the military during World War II and six million more working in defense plants, they would not allow Jim Crow to remain unchallenged either during or after the war." This was "the opening salvo" in the quest for equality and individual liberty that would define the civil rights movement following the war.[453]

THE FOUNDATION OF THE MODERN CIVIL RIGHTS MOVEMENT

During World War II the membership of the NAACP skyrocketed. It grew by more than ten times its prewar levels to around five hundred thousand members.[454] Many of these members belonged to Black fraternal societies. Often left out of the narrative on civil rights, these societies emerged quickly after emancipation and experienced tremendous growth in the early twentieth century. During Jim Crow, when Southern Blacks were prevented from civic engagement, fraternal lodges "allowed their members to work together, engage in mutual aid, and assert a public presence."[455] An editorial in the *American Independent*, a popular Black newspaper, explained the importance of Black fraternal societies: "We have nothing left us for civic and moral development except our secret orders. We have been successfully eliminated from the politics of the south and we have nothing left to help us develop a useful and helpful citizenship except the church and secret societies."[456] In short, these lodges trained Black Americans in politics and organization, and they enabled them—along with churches—to create a robust civil society, the core ingredient in any group's success.

Black fraternal societies quickly became one of the pillars of Black social life. In addition to giving "ordinary African American men and women virtually the only chances they might have to get elected to offices, to run organizations, and to learn and exercise organizational skills," these orders also provided social insurance for the community.[457] They provided economic security for members by offering life insurance and sick leave for those who paid their dues. Historian Carter G. Woodson declared that Black fraternal societies were "more prosperous than any other large enterprises among Negroes." In fact, by the early years of the 1920s, these organizations had around "2.2 million members and owned $20 million worth of property, including grand headquarters buildings, banks, and hospitals and social welfare institutions" in cities across the country.[458] Given that there were about twelve million Black Americans in 1920, that means that over 18 percent of the population was involved in a fraternal order. By the 1950s that percentage would be even greater.

Black fraternal societies also played a key role in the success of the NAACP by providing money, members, lawyers, and most importantly of all a vast network that could be drawn on when the need for racial solidarity was greatest. Throughout the struggle for civil rights, Black lodges helped raise money for the cause. In 1958, these societies raised so much money for the NAACP that Thurgood Marshall—the chief counsel for the NAACP Legal Defense and Educational Fund—"publicly declared that without Masonic financial assistance, many of the NAACP's victories before the Supreme Court would not have been possible."[459] One of the most prominent Black lodges, the Improved Benevolent and Protective Order of Elks of the World—or for short the Black Elks—pledged "the full weight of our membership, our money and our property in the fight to keep the NAACP's banner flying." The Black Elks also encouraged their members to join the NAACP. In an editorial in their national newspaper, they insisted "every local Lodge and Temple" to go "on record with a Life Membership." The editorial explained that the NAACP needed all the help it could get to "fight the Southern protest in every court of law, whenever and wherever it is necessary."[460]

Finally, and perhaps most importantly, Black fraternal societies provided the NAACP with lawyers and an extensive network of support. Early in their history, Black lodges had to fight off legal challenges by white lodges that didn't want them to use their name. In the process of ultimately emerging victorious at the Supreme Court, the societies "facilitated the development of the oppositional traditions, organizational infrastructures, and leadership networks that kept resistance alive under Jim Crow and laid the building blocks for future political and civil rights–related work in the decades to come."[461] In the process of waging these legal battles, a large number of Black lawyers got essential experience coordinating "litigation in multiple states and across different levels of government."[462] Many of these fraternal lawyers later went on to work for the NAACP.[463]

The Black Elks and other Black fraternal societies also contributed to the cause for civil rights by educating their members and the community in activism. For instance, the Black Elks created an educational department whose purpose was to "teach all members about their constitutional rights and how to protect them." These societies often served as "schools of self-government" and often "promoted a worldview among members that encouraged them to champion campaigns for civil rights."[464] By the 1950s, fraternal orders were at the heart of the civil rights movement "as financial contributors, inter-organizational facilitators, and direct organizers and activists."[465] As sociologist Theda Skocpol concludes, Black fraternal societies "developed the collective and strategic capacity to mobilize human and financial resources on behalf of the widespread, popularly rooted protests that, in the 1950s and 1960s, finally broke the back of legal racial segregation in America."[466] Along with the Black church and the efforts of men like Booker T. Washington and W. E. B. Du Bois, Black fraternal societies provided the foundation for civil rights movement.

THE SPARK THAT IGNITED THE CIVIL RIGHTS MOVEMENT

Some members of these Black lodges also became civil rights leaders themselves. T. R. M. Howard was a member of the International Order of the Knights of Tabor but later broke off to form the United Order of Friendship of America.[467] In addition to founding a new Black fraternal society and creating a hospital for its members—in which he served as one of the doctors— Howard also "became a Mississippi legend in civil rights" when he helped organize and found the Regional Council of Negro Leadership (RCNL). The RCNL brought together Black fraternal leaders, Black businessmen and women, and Black educators. It "promoted voting registration campaigns, equal treatment by law enforcement, self-help, and entrepreneurship" and "included two future heads of the [Mississippi] NAACP."[468] In addition to his organizational efforts, Howard mentored many prominent civil rights leaders including Medgar Evers, Charles Evers, Fannie Lou Hamer, Amzie Moore, Aaron Henry, and Jesse Jackson.

Unlike some others who flirted with communism, T. R. M. Howard was an avid supporter of American capitalism, free enterprise, gun rights, and individualism.[469] Howard recognized that the United States hadn't lived up to the promises of the Declaration of Independence, but like Frederick Douglass before him and Martin Luther King Jr. after him,[470] he insisted that the core promise of America was worth fighting for and shouldn't be jettisoned.[471] Howard merged Washington's belief in Black entrepreneurship and self-help with Du Bois's insistence on civil and political rights. The combination would provide the foundation for the struggle for civil rights in Mississippi and would place Howard at the heart of the spark that ignited the civil rights movement.

In 1954, the NAACP recorded a massive victory in their struggle for racial equality in *Brown v. Board of Education*. On May 17, the Supreme Court unanimously ruled to overturn school segregation. Chief Justice Earl Warren drove a stake through *Plessy v. Ferguson* when he concluded in the majority opinion "that in the field of public education the doctrine of 'separate but equal' has no place. Separate facilities are inherently unequal."[472] After over forty-five years of the NAACP insisting that the United States live up to its liberal values, the courts finally delivered.

Brown was a crushing blow against segregation. It encouraged and empowered Black Americans and also led to a massive backlash against equality from whites. In Mississippi, Howard insisted that Blacks reject the now forthcoming proposals from white politicians to provide equal funding for segregated Black schools.[473] Almost immediately, whites formed "Citizens' Councils" to terrorize and intimidate Blacks and to ensure that integration of schools would never happen.[474] Specifically, Citizens' Councils mobilized white politicians, sheriffs, and businessmen to harass Blacks who supported integration in Mississippi. In some instances, they even had banks call in loans of Blacks advocating for civil rights, refused credit to them, and threatened their lives.[475] The momentum and encouragement from the *Brown* decision were dissipating.

In response, T. R. M. Howard called a meeting of the RCNL at Mound Bayou. The city of Mound Bayou was all Black and ensured that the members would be able to conduct their meeting in peace. In many ways, the city was a testament to what Black Americans could achieve when their right to life, liberty, and property was respected. At the RCNL meeting Howard announced what amounted to a "counter offensive against the Citizens' Councils." He planned to reduce Black dependence on white businesses by starting "the biggest mail order boom in the history of the South." Most importantly, Howard found a way around the Citizens' Councils' attempts to deny Blacks access to credit. Howard "proposed a plan for black businesses, voluntary associations, unions, and churches to go deposit their accounts in

Tri-State Bank in Nashville (which was black owned)." Historians David and Linda Beito call this "a stroke of genius" that ultimately enabled "the bank to advance loans to civil rights activists who were otherwise unable to get them."[476] With the NAACP's stamp of approval, the plan was put into place. The effects were dramatic. By February 1955 white bankers had largely ended their attempts to freeze the credit of Black activists.[477] The success of Howard's plan was a powerful message about the possibility of using Black economic power to support and promote Black civil rights.

Later that year, in August 1955, the murder of a fourteen-year-old boy who was visiting his family from Chicago would provide the spark that ignited the civil rights movement—his name was Emmett Till. Till was accused of flirting with a twenty-one-year-old white woman, Carolyn Bryant, in a convenience store. His offense was allegedly not addressing her as ma'am and then letting out a "wolf whistle" while leaving the store (in a 2008 interview with historian Timothy Tyson, Carolyn Bryant admitted that she lied about Till's actions during her testimony).[478] Early the next morning, around two o'clock, Roy Bryant and John William Milam knocked on the door of the house that Till was staying in. When the door opened, they forced themselves inside and kidnapped the boy. Three days later, his body was found badly mutilated in the Tallahatchie River.[479]

Till's body was sent back to Mamie Bradley, Till's mother, in Chicago, where she made the decision to have an open casket at his funeral. It was a decision that would ignite Black resistance that would become the civil rights movement. Prior to the funeral, Bradley reached out to John H. Johnson, the founder and editor of *Ebony* and *Jet* magazines, to ask him to run images of Till's body in the casket in *Jet*. Bradley's goal was for "the world to see what they did to my boy." Johnson described his decision to print the images as one of the most difficult decisions he had to make, but he ultimately decided to print them. Reflecting on his decision years later, Johnson remarked, "I was afraid to do it" but it ultimately "let the world experience man's inhumanity to man."[480]

When the images were published in *Jet*, they had a profound effect on the nation and especially on Black Americans. Beito and Beito describe Till's body as such: "The combined effects of a gunshot to the head, a severe beating, and exposure to the elements had horribly disfigured his body. The top of his skull was missing, the head had a one-inch bullet hole, the tongue protruded grotesquely, the skin was badly decayed, and an ear, an eye, and a tooth were missing."[481] Blacks cried out for justice to be served, but the men who murdered Till were ultimately found not guilty by an all-white jury (protected from double jeopardy, the two men admitted a year later in an interview with *Look* magazine that they had killed young Emmett Till—they were paid $3,000 for their story, which is equivalent to $30,400 today).[482]

Howard, as well as Black Americans across the country, was outraged. He had played a key role during the trial. Howard housed the witnesses and Till's mother at his estate in Mound Bayou (which was safely guarded by a large number of guards with a small arsenal of guns and ammunition at their disposal) and even rounded up witnesses for the defense.[483] After the trial Howard refused to let the murderers go. He gave interviews and wrote comments that "appeared frequently in *Jet*, the *Chicago Defender*, the *Pittsburgh Courier*, the *Afro-American*, and the *California Eagle*." Indeed, "the Till case propelled Howard into the national Black media and civil rights spotlight as never before."[484] Howard travelled the country, condemned the FBI, and delivered speeches that encouraged Black activism in the face of injustice.[485] Howard was so outraged, that he revitalized A. Philip Randolph's proposal for organizing "1,000,000 red-blooded Americans to march on Washington in protest to the deaf ear" that federal officials had turned toward the atrocities being committed against Black people in Mississippi.[486]

Howard's first stop to promote his "Freedom March on Washington" was in Montgomery, Alabama, where he had been invited by a young reverend—Martin Luther King Jr. Speaking to a packed house, Howard "promoted the Freedom March," recounted the success of the Tri-State Bank in fighting the white's attempted credit freeze, and condemned the federal government's inability—or unwillingness—to address the Till murder.[487]

Rosa Parks, a seamstress and an official in the local chapter of the NAACP, was in attendance. Parks later recalled that Howard's speech was the "first mass meeting that we had in Montgomery" since Till's murder. Four days after Howard spoke at the Dexter Avenue Baptist Church, Parks was arrested for refusing to give up her seat to a white man on a city bus. Parks "later emphasized that Till's murder was central to her thinking at the time of her arrest."[488]

Parks's refusal to give up her seat on that city bus ultimately led to the Montgomery Bus Boycott in which the Montgomery Improvement Association, led by Martin Luther King Jr., carried out a successful yearlong boycott of the racial segregation of the Montgomery public transportation system. Their success launched the civil rights movement, but it is hard to imagine their success without the tremendous work that had come before. After all, previous attempts to use Black economic power to end segregation and discrimination had failed.

But in 1955 things were different. For one, there was a strong foundation, built over the preceding seven decades, of Black businesses, Black fraternal societies, and important organizations like the NAACP. Furthermore, new technologies such as television would play a key role in showing white, middle America the atrocities being committed against Blacks (especially in places like Birmingham). There was also the significant pressure on American politicians to end its system of apartheid in the midst of the Cold War. As more and more African and Asian nations declared independence from the colonial masters, they correctly asked (and were prodded by the Soviet Union to ask) why they should align themselves with the United States when people who looked like them were not guaranteed equal citizenship in the "land of the free."[489] Most importantly, however, leaders like Martin Luther King Jr. were able to motivate and organize millions of Black Americans into a movement that ultimately forced the country to move closer to the promise made in the Declaration of Independence: "We hold these truths to be self-evident, that all men are created equal, that they are endowed by their Creator with certain unalienable Rights, that among these are Life, Liberty, and the pursuit of Happiness."[490]

Lessons in Classical Liberalism #11: Dispersed Benefits

Social scientists, and especially economists, often talk about concentrated benefits and dispersed costs. This concept arises in cases where a particular policy clearly benefits some observable group, such as when corn farmers benefit from corn subsidies. But the cost of the policy may actually outweigh the benefits to the particular group, though it's harder to track because those costs are dispersed. So for instance, making ethanol out of corn (an inefficient choice, according to environmental scientists) and putting corn syrup in all our food (also a product of protectionism in the sugar industry) may have all sorts of costs that are difficult to calculate. This has the dangerous effect of making those costs hard to see, to think about, and to take into account when we do a cost-benefit analysis of a new policy. What's worse, the group that benefits is incentivized to lobby hard, while the groups that bear the cost may not even be able to identify the cause of their problems, much less organize to defend themselves.

On a more positive note, there is also such a thing as dispersed benefits. The fact that Black people in America, despite their continuing obstacles, had freedom of religion and the freedom to assemble, move, and become educated allowed them to form a complex web of thick social institutions. These institutions created a sense of community, purpose, and economic hope. It was all these accomplishments taken together—strength through the theology and community of the church, wise and courageous leaders, business successes, and fraternal organizations—that led to the ability to fight back against the political domination of white supremacy. But just as dispersed costs are hard to track, dispersed benefits can be too. It's important to painstakingly lay out the various elements of this history in order to grasp the full picture of the evolutionary progress of Black America.

It's an awful paradox of American life that these dispersed Black cultural benefits came about as the result of a very identifiable concentrated cost—Black oppression. Like many things in life, something good and beautiful arose out of morally repugnant circumstances. It is our task to untangle this paradoxical history.

Chapter 7

No Liberation without Freedom of Contract: Eugenics, the Minimum Wage, and Labor Unions

The intervention of the federal government during Reconstruction and later during the fight for civil rights upheld Black rights when state and municipal governments sought to suppress them. This has often led to the assumption that central control tends to be less biased than local control or that those invested in the federalism of the American tradition aren't very sensitive to racism. If this were true Americans would be in the enviable position of having a fairly straightforward solution to issues of injustice—just centralize! Unfortunately, an examination of various forms of social engineering undertaken by the progressives, starting in the late nineteenth century and still underway today, demonstrates that the centralization of power can often mean the uniform imposition of an unjust system instead of a merely balkanized one. We'll address the drug war and mass incarceration in later chapters, but three that were imposed in the first half of the twentieth century shaped Black American destiny, possibly to an even greater extent than violations of noneconomic civil rights did: the campaign for workers' rights, the policies of the Federal Housing Administration, and the building of the federal highway system.

WHO IN THE WORLD IS WOODROW WILSON?

Woodrow Wilson was America's famously progressive twenty-eighth president, presiding over the country during World War I. He was the son of a Presbyterian clergyman and professor of theology and was married to the daughter of a Presbyterian clergyman. He studied German political science in graduate school at Johns Hopkins, a new university explicitly modeled after the German style. He studied with Richard T. Ely, social gospeler and founder of the American Economics Association, and Herbert Baxter Adams, Anglo-Saxonist and founder of the American Historical Association. Wilson later became the president of Princeton University, the governor of New Jersey, and a leader in the establishment of the League of Nations. As governor he signed New Jersey's forcible sterilization legislation, in order to eliminate the possibility of reproduction for "the hopelessly defective and criminal classes."[491] As an academic, he declared that the Constitution's "radical defect" was its separation of powers, since no organism—and society is an organism, he insisted—could thrive in a state of inner conflict. American government lacked a fourth branch of a purely disinterested administrative nature, which could "decide at once with conclusive authority what must be done."[492] He advocated against child labor and dangerous work for women, for the regulation of various forms of measurement, and for the centralization of charity in the state. He teamed up with future Supreme Court Justice Louis Brandeis to form his presidential platform, which aimed to break up trusts and lower tariffs. He selected William Jennings Bryan as his secretary of state, and together they formed a presidential cabinet stocked with a veritable who's who of progressive thought, including Franklin D. Roosevelt as assistant secretary of the Navy. He established the Federal Reserve System, the Federal Trade Commission, federal limitations on working hours, and federal subsidies for farming and railroads.

As a war president, Wilson created the first propaganda office (the Committee on Public Information), and passed the Espionage Act and the Sedition Act, inspiring the founding of the American Civil Liberties Union in response. In Wilson's book *The State*, he argues that democratic government is a uniquely English inheritance, arising from the natural instincts of the race. It only follows logically, then, that he later published in *Atlantic Monthly* his approval for Jim Crow and the total loss of voting rights for Black men, since he believed Blacks to be incapable of self-government. He called them "insolent and aggressive, sick of work, [and] covetous of pleasure," which made them a "danger to themselves" and others if truly free.[493] When he became president, the formerly integrated federal government was re-segregated, and he screened his Johns Hopkins classmate's tour de force, *Birth of a Nation*, at the White House, which quotes Wilson himself in explicit praise of the Ku Klux Klan.[494]

Perhaps to our ears these few paragraphs of description sound like an almost random collection of facts about the man. Is he just another complex figure with positions and actions difficult to reconcile? No. Wilson represents the essence of progressivism: holding a liberal, "social gospel" theology of societal rather than individual salvation, influenced by the Hegelian holism and Bismarckian administrative state of Germany, derisive of the Constitutional tradition of limited powers, a lover of central power wielded by a new class of experts like himself, and a deeply reflective and thorough-going racist and eugenicist. These attributes are not in contradiction with one another at all but, rather, could be attributed to any number of academics, politicians, and bureaucrats in the Progressive Era.[495] They represent the hope that a new, efficient, and scientific approach to human governance would replace the messy, unplanned world of free social and economic interactions.

PROGRESSIVISM AND THE EUGENICS MOVEMENT

In the late nineteenth century, the upper echelon of American society residing in the northeast often sent the scions of their families to Germany to study. In Germany, Otto von Bismarck was busy uniting all the old princedoms into one centralized state while appeasing workers stirred up by socialist movements through his "state socialism" or "social liberalism." Bismarck's administrative state taught the progressives of England and America three central lessons: 1) liberal individualism was selfish and atomistic; we must think, rather, in terms of the collective and its good; 2) industrial capitalism is unscientific and wasteful; we must empower disinterested experts to engineer greater efficiency in all aspects of life; and 3) colossus economic organizations, including firms and trusts, were ruining the working class through their monopoly power; we must fight the exploitation of labor and the corruption of politics by business interests.[496]

The rage for a more "scientific" way of managing society didn't stop there either. Darwin's evolutionary theory was on the ascent, except that his concept of natural selection was still controversial until the 1940s. Many progressives accepted Darwin's views about common ancestry but questioned whether the aimlessness of natural selection couldn't be replaced with a purposeful and more efficient social selection. Ascribing to a "survival of the fittest" model might encourage the survival of the undesirable since the jungle-like environment of the Gilded Age encouraged vicious traits. Instead, progressives ascribed to a kind of human husbandry: a model of centralized control of human interaction that drew from the wisdom of thousands of years of human imposition on nature through animal breeding. Furthermore, this more "scientific" approach to human society also appealed to evolutionary theory, phrenology, and crude intelligence testing to rank the racial groups, with Anglo-Saxons or Teutonic peoples inevitably ranked highest and Africans lowest.[497] Not only would we eliminate "dysgenic" matches and behaviors, but we would do so along explicitly racist lines.

It cannot be overstated just how academically acceptable, and indeed popular, eugenics was in America during the first three decades of the twentieth century. Only when Hitler's earthshaking attempt at Aryan mastery arose did the American and English rage for eugenics even begin to subside. The main players in the various eugenics organizations of the day included American presidents, members of their cabinet, and heads of various governmental agencies. They were prominent university presidents and economic advisors to heads of state. They were world-famous novelists, playwrights, and poets. As Thomas C. Leonard states in his short but brilliant *Illiberal Reformers*, "[i]n the first three decades of the twentieth century, eugenic ideas were politically influential, culturally fashionable, and scientifically mainstream."[498]

Some statements were bold, as when Harvard's Frank Taussig, in a widely used economics textbook, no less, grieved that society has not yet reached a level of scientific sophistication such that we could "proceed to chloroform" undesirables "once and for all," and so must use other forms of legal and economic suppression for the time being.[499] Supreme Court Justice Oliver Wendell Holmes famously declared that the surgical sterilization of women is within appropriate state power, since "three generations of imbeciles is enough." His fellows on the court William Howard Taft and Louis Brandeis joined in the opinion.[500] The state imposition of eugenicist goals would reform the world. Tens of thousands of Americans were forcibly sterilized.

Others were more circumspect. The most famous economist of the twentieth century, Lord John Maynard Keynes, held honorifics in several eugenics organizations and spoke broadly about population control. In more private correspondences he spoke more straightforwardly of England's next task of controlling the "quality" of future generations since birth control had allowed them to address the quantity problem. But he also attached his utopian vision of our wealthy and pleasant future to the eugenics plans laid out in a novel by H. G. Wells, the review of which he published in the same "Future" section of his self-edited collection as his now-famous essay, "Economic Possibilities for our Grandchildren."[501] The life of leisure and the death of greed and vice, it seemed to Keynes, depended on culling the population not just to the right number of people but also to the right kind of people.[502] Years later Keynes made his views entirely explicit in an exchange with Margaret Sanger, the founder of Planned Parenthood: "In most countries we have now passed definitely out of the phase of increasing population into that of declining population, and I feel that the emphasis on policy should be considerably changed—much more with the emphasis on eugenics and much less on restriction [of population growth] as such."[503] Additionally, just two months before his death in 1946, Keynes declared eugenics to be "the most important, significant and, I would add, genuine branch of sociology which exists...."[504]

What exactly did the progressive eugenicists propose to do? First, the disabled must be removed from the gene pool. Those deemed mentally defective, the physically disabled, and epileptics were to be sterilized or kept celibate in asylums. Second, the race must be kept pure. Immigration (particularly from Asia and Eastern/Southern Europe) should be severely limited and intermarriage or even social mixing between Blacks and whites forbidden. Even American women who married foreigners had their US citizenship revoked. Third, many progressives still held a Lamarckian view of evolution at this time, which meant that certain behaviors like drinking, gambling, and prostitution must be crushed so as not to be passed on to the next generation. Finally, concern for the worker meant concern for the able-bodied and sober Anglo-Saxon male head of household. Therefore, women, children, Blacks, immigrants, and the disabled must be kept out of the workforce in order to protect a family wage for such men and to properly maintain their homes, thus strengthening the race and the nation.[505]

Politicians pursued the first goal in two ways: immigration restrictions and forced sterilization. The Immigration Act of 1882, famous for ending one hundred years of open borders and for targeting the Chinese in particular, also targeted any "lunatic, idiot, or any person unable to take care of himself or herself without becoming a public charge." Such pronouncements broadened in 1907 to include "imbeciles," "feeble-minded persons," and those with "any mental abnormality whatever." Finally, in 1917, the list became truly exhaustive, adding "arthritis, asthma, deafness, deformities, heart disease, poor eyesight, poor physical development and spinal curvature" to the list of unacceptable attributes. As to those Americans born with the offending characteristics, President Theodore Roosevelt wished "very much that the wrong people could be prevented entirely from breeding; and when the evil nature of these people is sufficiently flagrant, this should be done. Criminals should be sterilised and feeble-minded persons forbidden to leave offspring behind them." American industrialists Andrew Carnegie, W. K. Kellogg, and many other highly respected leaders directly funded the sterilization efforts, so that "[b]y 1938, 33 American states permitted the forced sterilisation of women with learning disabilities and 29 American states had passed compulsory sterilisation laws covering people who were thought to have genetic conditions. Laws in America also restricted the right of certain disabled people to marry. More than 36,000 Americans underwent compulsory sterilisation before this legislation was eventually repealed in the 1940s."[506]

In hindsight, perhaps the most sickeningly ironic part of this story is that Nazi propaganda for their 1933 Law for the Prevention of Progeny with Hereditary Disease cited American efforts as a justification. After the terrible slaughter of the Holocaust was discovered, the Allies were in the odd position of having no credible grounds with which to charge Nazi slaughter of the disabled as war crimes or as deserving of reparations, since the Allies had similar laws (or had them quite recently) themselves.

At the same time legislation was being passed, academic eugenicists instituted almost four hundred courses on eugenics across the country's most prestigious universities in order to popularize the ideas, and Americans dominated the worldwide conferences on the subject. The American State Department undertook to send out the invitations to the International Eugenics Conference itself.[507] In short, far from being a minority position among white American progressives, eugenics was central to their worldview.

The second goal, which included the exclusion of Asians and Southern and Eastern Europeans, was of course also accomplished by the new rush to restrict immigration in the late nineteenth and early twentieth centuries. Prior to this, the country was absorbing 750,000 new immigrants a year, but these laws were so restrictive that the number plummeted to a tiny 50,000. Leonard gives his readers a taste of the sort of language that the eugenicists employed in their fight for these policy changes. Here is Leonard's collection of comments from Edward A. Ross, highly respected sociologist at Stanford, Cornell, and the University of Wisconsin:

> immigrant peoples...[were] pictured with "sugar-loaf heads, moon faces, slit mouths, lantern-jaws and goose-bill noses".... He maligned the new arrivals as "cheap, stucco manikins from Southeastern Europe", "masses of fecund but beaten humanity from the hovels of far Lombardy and Galicia," and "the slime at the

bottom of our foreignized cities," the "Slavs immune to certain kinds of dirt," who brought to America a "rancid bit of the Old World," the "hirsute, low-browed, big-faced persons" who clearly "belong in skins, in wattled huts at the close of the Great Ice Age," the childish, frivolous, and "cheaply gotten up *manana* races," the "stupid and inert peoples" poaching on "the preserve of the bright and industrious," "the dullard races... last to abandon the blind fecundity which characterizes the animal," and the "transients with their pigsty mode of life."[508]

As to Blacks, the "Negro Problem" was another great excuse to exclude immigrants; after all, according to the logic of the eugenicists, if America already had to deal with its Blacks, why should it also have to deal with other inferior races? The progressives employed several tactics, some aimed at both immigrants and Blacks, others at Blacks alone. Widespread support of exclusion from voting through literacy and wealth tests excluded both communities. Jim Crow legislation created a whole new level of separation of whites from Blacks in everyday life never before known in Southern society. Eugenicists displayed great concern that birth control and abortion be eugenic rather than dysgenic; that is, they wanted to make sure that Blacks and immigrants were encouraged to use contraception while Aryan or Nordic types reproduced more liberally.[509] Today, there's a debate between pro-lifers and pro-choicers about the relationship between racism and abortion, but it's not necessary to delve into that to acknowledge the plain history. Placed in historical context, Margaret Sanger's eugenicist ideas weren't unusual, nor was she alone in her fight to concentrate contraception and abortion efforts in communities perceived to be a threat to the white race.[510]

But there was one more tool in the eugenicists' toolbox to address the threat of both Blacks and immigrants. While the eugenics movement was popular among political and social scientists in general, it had a special hold on the economists. Many economists saw immediately how they could manipulate wages to support the healthy, white, male head of household and undercut those who might otherwise overtake him demographically. Thus, the birth of the modern minimum wage, the "holy grail of American progressive labor reform."[511]

THE MINIMUM WAGE

Just as many do today, progressives in the early twentieth century believed the minimum wage to be a support for the dignity and well-being of workers. More unfamiliar to us, though, is their praise for its effects on unemployment. While today free marketers argue *against* the minimum wage because it makes it illegal (or an act of charity) to hire people who are not very productive, these earlier progressives actually argued *for* the minimum wage on the exact same grounds.

Lessons in Classical Liberalism #12: A Wage Is a Price

One source of confusion that often arises with regard to minimum wage debates involves the mixing of descriptive and prescriptive ideas about prices. Taken from the viewpoint of economics as a social science, a price is not something an economist recommends; it's something he tries to understand. From the neoclassical perspective of modern economics, most prices reflect an equilibrium between supply and demand for the good in question. In turn, prices serve an indispensable function in the economy: they act as little pieces of information about supply and demand that help regular people calculate how to spend. Did the price of the wood I was going to use to panel my basement go up? Then either it has become more highly demanded and therefore scarcer, or something has interrupted the supply of it, making it scarcer. As a consumer, I don't actually need to know what happened; I see the higher price and consider building with an alternative instead. Thus, the scarcer type of wood is conserved, and I can still keep my costs low. This is what we call economic calculation, and every day, in many ways, we make these cost-benefit evaluations based on the prices of things. When a good that is demanded becomes scarcer, the higher price attracts new producers into the market, bringing the supply up, and which in turn lowers the price back down again, to the benefit of the consumer. When the price of something drops because people are no longer interested in it, this signals to the producers that their time would be better spent elsewhere. Thus, these little pieces of information—prices— allow us to coordinate with one another in a highly complex web of economic interactions without needing to know a lot of background information to which we couldn't possibly have access (or have the time to access). Furthermore, this decentralized system of constantly adapting prices allows for far more complexity and flexibility than any "command" economic system in which some central planner determines what is made, how much, and where it goes. That benighted planner could have no possible idea about all the local information that is packed into that simple little measurement, the price.

Nevertheless, many prices may seem offensive to us, as when the price of water bottles or toilet paper goes up in an emergency, or when someone pays some ridiculous amount of money for a celebrity's used toothbrush. And if the prices of certain objects can give offense, how much more can the price of a person's labor? It's easy to confuse the idea of economic value, which always reflects the simple facts of supply and demand, with metaphysical or objective value. Objectively, the task of the elementary school teacher is precious to me, particularly when my children are in school! But economically, there may be many people willing to become elementary school teachers, and the training itself may present few obstacles to completion, such that the supply of teachers is high enough to keep the wage in the middling range. If the teacher himself values his work by what he is paid, he may feel insulted. But if he values his work according to its value to those he serves, he will feel pride. In fact, although we may genuinely feel that teachers deserve to make $1 million per year, it would be a terrible outcome for us if this were the case. Very high wages would make the cost of education prohibitively expensive.

So from the perspective of simply trying to understand why something costs what it does, the economist sees a wage in much the same way as she sees any other price, as a reflection of supply of and demand for that labor. But at the turn of the twentieth century, when progressive thought was blossoming, the neoclassical turn had not yet quite won out. Many economists were still operating on the classical labor theory of value, in which the price of something ought to be determined by the labor that goes into it, regardless of supply and demand. Thus, many progressive economists labeled businessowners' profits as necessarily exploitative, since they skimmed from the workers what value the workers' labor itself had endowed to their goods. Others accepted the neoclassical, subjective theory of value but still felt that wages were a unique kind of price, since people relied on them for their livelihoods. The notion of a living wage emerged at this time, helped along by the writings of Leo XIII in his encyclical *Rerum Novarum* (Of New Things). To Pope Leo, a living wage was an important reflection of a human person's dignity and value.[512] Now that the world was shifting away from more feudal ways of organizing labor and moving in the direction of market participation, he wanted to ensure that workers were treated as human beings and not just as cogs in the new industrial machine.

Hopefully, you can already see the tension between the descriptive and prescriptive approach to a price, including a wage. If prices are pieces of information about supply and demand, and that information is what allows the market ecosystem to adapt to constantly changing circumstances, then wages must reflect the actual situation concerning the supply of whatever type of labor is under discussion and the demand for that labor. If the price is prescriptive on the other hand, and we set minimum wages by law in order to sustain, say, a four-person family, we simultaneously send a different signal out into that complex web of economic interactions. What we communicate to employers is that the price of labor has gone up, so that employers will necessarily try to conserve the amount of labor they use. In other words, we create unemployment. Inevitably, the class of employee that will be first to go are those individuals who are hardest to employ. People with little human capital—low on experience, education, or special training—are also the least productive. Since it only makes sense for an employer to hire someone at a rate equal to or below the amount of value their productivity can generate, relatively unproductive people will be cut from the ranks. But there may also be cultural factors that make someone hard to hire. Perhaps his race, gender, or language offends the other employees or the employer himself. Perhaps she has a criminal background. To keep the peace, an employer will often avoid hiring such a person. But at a low enough price, they may be tempted to tell their employees that they'll just have to deal with it. Or if the supply of laborers suddenly drops due to war or strike, or the demand suddenly spikes due to innovation, employers may be willing to put up with the complaints of prejudiced co-workers, as well as their own.[513]

The willingness of owners to hire whoever was cheapest is just the situation that the progressive economists wanted to avoid by instituting a minimum wage. Immigrants and Blacks in the new urban centers, already used to a lower standard of living than many (though certainly not all) of their fellow job-seekers, could "under-live" whites, and therefore drag down the wages of employees in any profession they entered. Immigrants could be kept out unless they were high earners. Paul Kellogg, the cereal magnate, suggested a two dollar and fifty cent per day minimum—a wage "50% higher than what the average low-skilled worker earned in 1910"—basically excluding the (Black) migration or (foreign) immigration of unskilled workers completely.[514]

Leonard explains the logic this way: "If the capitalist paid workers a living wage, he could not compete with unscrupulous rivals, who hired low-standard women, children, immigrants, blacks, and the feeble-minded." The concern of the progressives was that to allow such goings-on amounted to "race suicide."[515] Instead, the minimum wage could detect inferior workers by making them unemployable, and then forced sterilization or isolation through celibate institutionalization would deal with such persons scientifically. As Woodrow Wilson's commissioner of labor, Royal Meeker, put it, better that the state should "support the inefficient wholly and prevent the multiplication of the breed than to subsidize incompetence and unthrift, enabling them to bring forth after their own kind."[516]

UNEQUAL OUTCOMES OF MINIMUM WAGE POLICY

To bring this conversation up to date, many economists argue that the minimum wage has been a major source of economic inequality between Blacks and whites. Milton Friedman called it "the most anti-Negro law on the books," and his predictions about its effects appear to have been borne out in reality.[517] Here he is in an interview with *Playboy* in 1973. Teenage employment is particularly significant for the working class, for whom it often constitutes the "bottom rung" of their ladder to social mobility:

> In 1956, I think, the minimum was raised from seventy-five cents to a dollar—a very substantial rise. In the early Fifties, the unemployment rate among male teenagers was about the same for blacks as for whites. Both were about eight percent when the over-all unemployment rate was about four percent. In the late Fifties, after the minimum-wage rate was raised from seventy-five cents to a dollar, the unemployment rate of black teenagers shot up from eight percent to something like 20 to 25 percent. For white teenagers, it shot up to something like 13 percent. From that day to this, the rates for both black and white teenagers have been higher than before 1956. When they start to decline, a new rise in the minimum-wage rate comes along and pushes them up again. The black teenage rate has been very much higher than the white teenage rate, for reasons that are highly regrettable and that we ought to be doing something about: blacks get less schooling and are less skilled than whites. Therefore, the minimum-wage rate hits them particularly hard. I've often said the minimum-wage rate is the most anti-Negro law on the books.

In 2018, the US Bureau of Labor Statistics found that the majority of minimum wage workers are young, single, part-time workers who live in a middle- or upper-income household.[518] So even if the hope of the minimum or living wage advocate is to lift up those who are trying to support a four-person family on a minimum wage hourly job, the minimum wage policy is an extremely sloppy way to do so. It advantages well-off and well-connected teenagers while cutting out those who desperately need on-the-job training that they can acquire in no other way. Democratic theorist Elizabeth Anderson admits as much when she acknowledges the minimum wage's unemployment problem.[519] But like so many before her, she relies on yet another government program to make up for the problems caused by this government program—job training to raise the productivity of those who cannot get hired at the minimum wage. Anderson fails to understand the way job markets work: often through the skills-building, networking, and connections created in one's initial job, which is often itself found through organic networks in a community. There is no way to avoid the fact that people like to work with known entities. This reduces risk and solves an information problem. Better to get young teens into a low-paying job from which they can work their way up than to try and engineer their skill set from above.[520]

Even where a rise in the minimum wage does not appear to create a decline in employment, as in the one famous paper challenging the economic consensus on minimum wages,[521] it does lead to a reduction in future job growth as businesses raise their prices in order to cover the costs.[522] It should also be noted that this one paper is most definitely an outlier in the minimum wage literature. Most peer-reviewed articles on the subject demonstrate a decline in employment.[523]

This might be a good moment to stop and remind ourselves that a lack of employment isn't just about a lack of money. Giving someone money so that they can live without work will allow them to survive but rarely to thrive. Work is a major source of structure, self-esteem, and identity. People want to contribute something to their families, communities, and society, and when they don't, outcomes include depression, anger, and health problems.[524] Neighborhoods with high levels of unemployment are destabilized as helpful networks break down, and a sense of aimlessness and purposelessness takes over. Merely providing supplementary income does nothing to address these secondary effects of chronic unemployment.

BLACKS VS. THE UNIONS

Apparent also is the application of workers' rights arguments to exclude the American Black community in particular from employment. The labor union movement formed an important plank in the progressive platform. The president of the American Federation of Labor, Samuel Gompers, claimed that "Caucasians" would refuse to "let their standard of living be destroyed by Negroes, Chinamen, Japs, or any other." In fact, the efforts of the early unions to keep Blacks out of the trades, both through explicit charter and artificially high wages, was so notorious that Frederick Douglass, Booker T. Washington, and W. E. B. Du Bois all condemned the organizations. Douglass commiserated on the "folly, tyranny, and wickedness of labor unions." Washington was more interested in the South as a place for Blacks to prosper economically because he associated the North with hostile labor unions. Once Blacks started working in factories, he argued, the "trade union soon follows, and the Negro is crowded to the wall." Du Bois wavered in his views throughout his life but went through periods of intense resentment against labor unions: "... union labor strategy seems to be to form a union in a given plant, strike to obtain the right to bargain with the employer as the sole representative of labor, and then to close the union to Black workers, effectively cutting them off from employment."[525] Du Bois's ambivalent relationship with socialism may be believably chalked up to his experiences of white working class oppression of blacks, over and against, in many cases, the general indifference about race and nationality expressed by capitalist managers.

While the Republican party of the time had no problem with workers organizing to negotiate terms as a group, they also felt no compunction to legally forbid or require anything of employers or strike-breaking employees who were dealing with the unions. To do so, in fact, would have controverted their commitment to the liberal idea of free labor: that each person is free to work for whomever they choose and quit whenever they want, and that employers have the same freedom to hire and fire at will.

Perhaps the Black tradesmen of the time can be forgiven for thinking that free labor sounded like a good deal, all things considered. Not only were Blacks pursuing work as free economic agents, most of them for the first time, but their experiences during the Civil War had by no means created a sense of solidarity with the white working class. White butchers in Chicago called for a strike of any employer who hired Blacks in 1862. In the same year, Cincinnati workers drove out Blacks from waterfront work, and New Orleans dockworkers lobbied against Black workers as well. Race riots involving Irish longshoremen in New York broke out when shipping companies employed Blacks to break a strike in 1863. The unionists successfully purged all Black workers.[526]

In *Black Americans and Organized Labor: A New History*, Paul Moreno addresses Gary Becker's famous argument about the economics of discrimination. Becker observed that employers who prefer their own racial prejudices over finding the most productive worker at the lowest cost will certainly pay for that prejudice.[527] Martin Luther King Jr. expressed a similar sentiment, declaring that increasing industrialization and economic growth in the South would cause the "folkways of white supremacy" to "necessarily pass away," since "southerners are becoming good businessmen, and as such realize that bigotry is costly and bad for business."[528] Becker shows that prejudice leads to a net loss for the economy in general, and that at least in some cases, the desire to maximize profits could incentivize racial integration.[529] *Plessy v. Ferguson*, after all, was a lawsuit planned in cooperation with railway companies who wanted out of various states' requirements for separate cars, which alienated customers and increased costs. According to Gail Heriot, "The East Louisiana Railway had opposed the law prior to its passage, and there is some evidence that the railroads helped finance the case."[530]

Many other cases of management fighting segregation efforts exist. Economist Jennifer Roback uncovered the efforts of streetcar companies throughout the South to actively refuse and resist the segregation demands of their municipalities.[531] In the famous case of Branch Rickey hiring Jackie Robinson, Rickey claims to have acted from his deeply held Methodism, but the fact remains that, from what we can tell from accounts in the press, white baseball lovers wanted Black players, and Black players benefitted the teams. In lockstep with much of the story we're about to explore, white workers themselves were most often the source of segregation efforts: it was the white players who had insisted on segregating in the 1880s, and the same group comprised most of the opposition for Rickey as well.

Moreno agrees with Becker's insight about employers but points out that the same logic does not apply to unions. For them, exclusion of the disfavored race was a straightforward benefit (at least, in the short term), as it saved them from lower wages due to a larger labor supply.[532] Breaking from the current mainstream historical understanding of Blacks and unions, Moreno rejects convoluted accounts of management using racial animus to divide and conquer, undermining class solidarity.[533] Not only does this account lack historical evidence, it also overlooks a much simpler and more straightforward explanation: the traditional neoclassical economic analysis. In this approach, everyone behaves about as an economist would expect. Management tries to lower costs and raise productivity, while white workers limit the labor supply to drive up their own wages. White workers excluded Blacks by explicitly keeping them out of the union and then fighting to make the union the only available source of employees. They also did so by generating high wages for themselves through union negotiation, which in turn caused unemployment among more marginalized workers. When these tactics didn't work, white workers sometimes accepted Blacks into the union in a qualified way, thus nullifying Blacks' role as strikebreakers while granting them second-class membership that guaranteed little to no representation of Black interests as a group.

The upshot of Moreno's analysis is that the sordid history of the labor union movement and Black Americans is not simply an account of yet another arena in which the ugliness of American racism left its stain. It's more accurate to say that America's racial history created the division between Black and white workers, but an ideology of economic conflict motivated the labor union movement and its constant tendency to exclude Blacks. Class solidarity remains an elusive goal because the only way to get above-market wages for one group of workers (without the addition of new capital) is to limit the labor supply by excluding another group of workers. Politically powerless, Blacks made a good target, but so did immigrants and women.

Union exclusion of Blacks started as early as the 1810s when Pennsylvania mechanics lobbied to keep Black mechanics out. Again in 1830s Pennsylvania, those who dared to employ Blacks were boycotted. In contrast, the abolitionists championed the liberal view of "free labor" as one's right to buy and sell labor freely as a self-owning individual.[534] This created an odd tension, from today's perspective, between classical liberal abolitionists and labor reformers who saw Northern white workers as wage slaves. The labor reformers sometimes characterized abolitionism as a coordinated attempt to depress white wages.[535] Abolitionists, on the other hand, saw reformers' comparisons of wage-work to slavery as absurd and offensive, considering that the laborer was neither physically compelled to work nor lacking in legal protections from harm, luxuries that Black enslaved people did not enjoy.

Frederick Douglass thought that much of the white labor unions' efforts flowed from economic ignorance as much as racism itself. Douglass explicitly condemns the labor movement's "narrow notion of political economy" as a conflict-based zero-sum game. Their idea that "every piece of bread that goes into the mouth of one man, is so much bread taken out of the mouth of another" was not "villainy" but rather merely "honest stupidity."[536] He sincerely worried that many labor reformers were "more or less adherents of communism" who refused to acknowledge a man's rights to the fruits of his labor the minute he hired someone else, as though the division between capital and labor was so clear-cut and meaningful. Instead, the liberal view of political economy sees employers and employees as engaging in mutually beneficial exchange. A greater supply of labor may certainly affect wages for a time but can also be funneled into new and creative economic efforts.

Moreno divides the relationship of Blacks to labor unions into four main periods: 1) Reconstruction to World War I, in which the vast majority of labor unions explicitly barred Black membership, 2) the interwar New Deal period, in which unions gained the support of the administrative state but made little progress at inclusion, 3) World War II and through the civil rights era, as Blacks began to have some hope that the labor movement would truly include them but made greater gains through direct appeal to the federal government, and 4) the present era, in which the deep Black-union alliance that we think of today is almost exclusively on the side of unions in the public, not the private, sector. Moreno demonstrates that Blacks pursued work in a nonideological way. If anything, the Black community was mostly pro-free labor and felt that they had the best chance of stable income by working with employers. If a certain strategy to find and keep their jobs was working, they pursued it. In contrast, the labor union movement had progressive elements as well as straightforwardly communist elements. The more extreme communist elements made efforts with Blacks but were never going to be a good fit for them. Black workers were deeply uncomfortable with the violent eruptions surrounding various labor strikes as well as the deep-seated atheism of the communist element. Black workers were certainly open to the less radical notion of unions as a collective bargaining effort that could secure them good jobs, wages, and benefits. But they also understood that it would never really be in whites' interests to include them, and despite a brief period in which a few Black organizations endorsed the American Federation of Labor, Black relations with private sector unions were consistently sour.[537]

A CLASSICAL LIBERAL THOUGHT EXPERIMENT

Much contemporary political historiography paints the classical liberal approach as entirely untenable on matters of race and civil rights. What we needed, after all, was more federal intervention in order to rein in racist and oppressive state and local governments and racist employers and businesses. A political philosophy dedicated to individual rights, small government, and free markets would only perpetuate, it seems, the crushing social and economic inequality that hundreds of years of Black oppression and exclusion had generated. We might even see the whole scheme of apparently "neutral" liberal law as totally ineffective when it comes to addressing systemic racism, or even worse, as a mere fig leaf, a cover for the powers-that-be to justify their position. This is the argument made by most critical race theorists with regard to liberal law, and as classical liberals interpret the role of law and the importance of its neutrality in the strictest way, they become the target of the most wrath.

Barry Goldwater, longtime senator from Arizona and 1964 presidential candidate, provides the most challenging test case in this regard. His unwillingness to vote for the 1964 Civil Rights Act and his status as the inspiration for the conservative movement thereafter casts him as a pivotal villain of American racism in the minds of many historians. But the details of his story present a much more complicated picture. Goldwater was a conservative (he became more heavily libertarian-leaning as time went on), with a principled dedication to the Constitution. Back home in Arizona, he was in the NAACP and supported desegregation in his hometown of Phoenix. In DC, he voted for the 1957 Civil Rights Act, for the Twenty-Fourth Amendment (restricting poll taxes for voting), and he integrated the Senate cafeteria so that his Black administrative assistant would have a place to eat. He explained that he wanted badly to vote for the 1964 Civil Rights Act as well but was certain that two of the sections were unconstitutional. In fact, he conferred with then lawyer and future Supreme Court justice William Rehnquist on the matter, who assured him they were unconstitutional. Unlike Lyndon Johnson, Goldwater was good friends with John F. Kennedy, who after finding out that Goldwater would be running against him as the Republican presidential nominee, apparently said to him jokingly, "Are you sure you want this f***ing job?" After Kennedy's death, most of the nation voted for his successor in the greatest presidential landslide in American history. The only states Goldwater won were in the deep South and as states that had been historically Democrat. This marked the beginning of the reorientation of the South toward the Republican Party, a reorientation that must have been motivated by racial issues on the part of the voters, even if that wasn't the motivation of Goldwater himself. It's uncontroversial today to claim that without Goldwater there would have been no Ronald Reagan.

Isn't this story just a confirmation of the concerns of critical race theorists and others about the limitations of the American constitution and its system of liberal law? Even as a serious anti-racist himself, Goldwater's constitutional principle stopped him from voting for the most pivotal piece of anti-racist legislation in American history. The commitment of the American system to the property rights of individuals made it impossible for him to imagine limiting those rights—even in the service of such a noble cause as finally fully including Black Americans in social and economic life.

On the other hand, these very same theorists often express deep dissatisfaction with the way the actual civil rights strategy panned out, even as they stand in solidarity with the movement as a whole. School integration was hard on the Black community where it happened—with most Black teachers losing their jobs and Black kids absorbing racial hatred at school—and it took decades to actually be implemented fully anyway. The 1964 act oddly seemed to create civil unrest rather than quell it, and even with the addition of the later act in '67 and other important legislation and Supreme Court cases, the socioeconomic status of Black Americans has remained stubbornly unequal to that of whites. Critical race theorists would attribute all this to the deep-seated and tenaciously ingrained racism of the American system. Instead, we offer here a kind of classically liberal alternative time line. Classical liberals are split on whether this alternative reflects correct constitutional scholarship on the correct application of the Fourteenth Amendment; some prominent scholars defend it (such as Randy Barnett); others demur (such as Kurt Lash). It's a provocative idea, but it's important to see how a different legal grounding for civil rights might have been far more effective than the route that—largely due to historical accident—was taken.

BERNSTEIN'S *REHABILITATING LOCHNER*

To imagine this hypothetical thought experiment, we have to go all the way back to the late nineteenth century, as various arguments arose over the regulation of labor in the burgeoning industrial scene. The usual historical approach to this period sets up big business against the ill-treated worker. In a new age of industrial life and fast-paced economic change, it's fairly understandable that people would resort to regulation of business, dealing with health and safety laws, wage and hour laws, and anti-trust legislation. But such laws depart from the natural rights tradition of individual liberty, which affirms the right of every person to contract with any other person as he or she sees fit. These arguments, though they'd proven so valuable in the fight for abolition just a few decades earlier, began to be seen as hopelessly out of touch with the times. In fact, argued the progressives, the complexity of this modern world requires a complete jettisoning of such talk and a new commitment to the rule of technocratic experts who could help the blinkered individual navigate this brave new world.

From our perspective, it might look like these progressives were standing up for the little guy against an onslaught of powerful corporate monopolies. But it's important to understand the facts on the ground at the time, facts that present a far more complex picture. As we've already shown, the progressives of this era were overwhelmingly racist and eugenicist, and their love of state oversight of the individual only became less popular after the fascisms of Europe caused a predictable backlash in the twentieth century. Their labor laws were inevitably tied up with those commitments; women, Black people, and immigrants must be excluded from the workforce in whatever way possible. This could include overregulation of immigrant businesses, as in the famous Chinese laundry case, *Yick Wo v. Hopkins*. In this case, San Francisco's Board of Supervisors required permits for laundries but refused to permit any Chinese-owned laundries, despite their being far and away the majority laundry providers in the city. When Chinese launders were fined for operating without a license, they took the city to court. Since the law appeared to be neutral, the lower courts ruled against Wo, but the Supreme Court argued that the biased enforcement of the law violated the Fourteenth Amendment. Other cases dealt with limitations on the freedom of contract to work long hours, which more desperate populations were often willing to do, as in *Lochner v. New*

York and *Muller v. Oregon.* These cases challenged laws that limited working hours, the first for bakers and the second for women. The court argued that such laws defied due process by interfering unreasonably with the "right and liberty of the individual to contract." Other cases dealt with limitations on private schools that kept ethnic and religious sensibilities alive, as in *Meyer v. State of Nebraska* and *Pierce v. Society of Sisters*, and so on. The courts blocked at every turn the centrally organized, standardized, and socially engineered world that the progressives dreamed of during the period that is now referred to as the Lochner era (1890–1937). Though it was sometimes accused of being unduly influenced by laissez-faire economics, the Lochner court argued that they were simply upholding the older tradition of individual rights against what it interpreted as unconstitutional government overreach into people's personal choices.

These cases can also be confusing when it comes to arguments over the proper interpretation of the Fourteenth Amendment. The amendment was arranged to address the ways in which each branch of government could deny equal protection of the law. The first part, which states, "No State shall make or enforce any law which shall abridge the privileges or immunities of citizens of the United States" was clearly meant to limit the state legislatures from violating individual rights. But in the 1870s, a case arose in which Louisiana had granted a certain company a monopoly over the slaughterhouse business. When butchers sued, the Supreme Court decided that the state-granted monopoly had *not* violated the Fourteenth Amendment, since the purpose of the amendment was specifically to protect Black Americans. It quickly became clear that such an interpretation was gravely mistaken, but in order to align with precedent, the Lochner court used the language of the other parts of the Fourteenth Amendment— due process (which limited discrimination by the courts) and equal protection (which limited discrimination by the executive branch). The upshot is that the Lochner court was simply trying to apply the bit about "privileges and immunities" to these cases of state interference into economic life, but they had to use other language to do so.

The important point to note here is that Black Americans and other economically marginalized groups were consistently excluded because of these kinds of laws, and the Lochner court, however personally racist the individual judges might have been, appealed to their interpretation of constitutional principle to side with the marginalized groups and against those groups of established white European workers who wanted to eliminate their competition in the job market. The Lochner courts simply made no distinction between civil and economic liberty. As time wore on, however, the approach of the Lochner court was rejected and eventually bizarrely reinterpreted to refer only to civil liberties (as in *Griswold v. Connecticut*).

BLACK REPUBLICANS AND THE NEW DEAL

So had the classical liberal approach, which values both civil and economic liberties, disappeared completely? Not in the slightest. Franklin Delano Roosevelt remains one of the most popular presidents in American history. However, that legacy relies on a presentation of both the economic history and the history of civil liberties that has been pretty thoroughly debunked. We now know, for instance, that FDR's efforts to bring relief during the Depression actually made it far worse than it otherwise would have been and certainly extended its length by many years unnecessarily; America didn't recover economically until 1948.[538] We also know that the internment of the Japanese was not a terrible, exceptional case in an otherwise good presidential tenure, but just a severe example of FDR's generally blasé attitude to the civil rights of American citizens. Many instances have been brought into the popular imagination more recently, as attention to the specifics of systemic anti-Black racism has spiked: the

National Recovery Administration officially preferred whites over Blacks for jobs and created unequal pay scales by race; the Federal Housing Administration's redlining of Black and integrated neighborhoods (see Chapter 8); the Social Security Administration excluded traditionally Black occupations; and the Agricultural Adjustment Act left over one hundred thousand Black Americans jobless and homeless when it paid the owners of sharecropping lands to stop production.

In the following episode, we see why white and Black Republicans opposed the New Deal and what happened to them when they spoke up. J. B. Martin was a Black entrepreneur in Memphis who ran one of the largest Black-owned drug stores in the South and became president of several Negro baseball leagues. His mentor Robert Church was another financially prosperous Black Republican, and they were both very active in Shelby County Republican politics. Edward H. Crump, known as "Boss Crump," ran a corrupt political machine in Memphis. As long as Crump had to rely on the Black and Tans (the Republicans who favored integration, as opposed to the Lily-Whites), the Black community got to benefit somewhat. But as soon as Crump became deeply allied with Roosevelt, he abandoned the tenuous bargain he'd made between his political machine and the Black community.

Soon, segregation was further calcified by housing projects centered only in Black neighborhoods, razing Black-owned businesses and homes in the process. The overwhelmingly Black postal service in Memphis—the only city in America with a Black-run post office—was replaced with majority white employees. Meanwhile, Church was ascending quickly in the ranks of the Republican National Committee, becoming the first Black member in forty years. He and Martin argued against Roosevelt's regressive excise taxes on basic products that "had mainly served to 'fatten gluttonish politicians and high moguls in alphabet agencies, many of them filled to the gills with color prejudice.'"

Church argued that "the Negro is fundamentally a Republican because the Republican party is the party of rugged individualism and the Negro is an incipient capitalist."[539]

With Prohibition ending soon, Crump anticipated the loss of income from his bootlegging business. After years of unofficial tolerance, he suddenly decided it was a good time to crack down on Beale Street's bars and gambling houses, which only amounted to switching ownership into white hands. He even personally harassed Church by sending a constant stream of inspectors to his properties who seemed never to feel satisfied with them or their state of repair.

Church responded by working hard for the election of GOP presidential nominee Wendell Lewis Willkie, who, unlike FDR, argued for universal suffrage, integration in the entire federal government and the military, and anti-lynching legislation. What's more, he didn't have any corrupt bosses of city political machines on his donor books. With an ally like Willkie in the White House instead of FDR, the Black community of Memphis might get some relief. When Church led several rallies in support of Willkie, Crump was infuriated. He made threats and demands to stop the meetings. When Church did not relent, the harassment began. Police were dispatched in shifts to Martin's drug store, where they frisked every single person who came through the door. Other businesses owned by the Black Republican Elmer Atkinson got the same treatment. Letters were dispatched to journalists and others involved in the rallies threatening violence. Even after Willkie lost the election, Crump continued to send police to frisk all of Martin's customers, raided Beale Street on thin pretense and made dozens of arrests of Black men, and removed all Black Republicans from local committees. Martin's store was near ruin, but he couldn't find a lawyer willing to stand up to Crump's machine and take the case. Both Martin and Elmer Atkinson fled the city.

Crump set his sights on nineteen Black leaders in the city whom he accused of creating "race-hatred" by talking about "social equality." He stepped up raids and searches and began arresting men randomly for "loitering." Although there were efforts over the next several years to get the federal government's Civil Liberties Unit to intervene, nothing was ultimately done. Roosevelt had the war to think about, and he didn't want to alienate his good friend Crump or get involved in anything involving race. In spite of a clearly winnable case of civil rights violations, including of Fourth and Fourteenth Amendment rights, Martin, Church, and Atkinson were effectively exiled from Memphis. Their mantle would be taken up by someone with enough personal financial clout to withstand a thousand cuts: A. Philip Randolph.

Church and Martin maintained a broadly classical liberal approach to politics as Black Republicans and found serious allies on civil rights from within Republican ranks, just as Zora Neale Hurston and T. R. M. Howard would do after them. The dream lived on, but the persecution was intense. Instead of acting as a salve, Roosevelt and his New Deal simply became a powerful set of tools in the hands of corrupt city bosses like Crump to crush the Black community.

AN ALTERNATIVE TIME LINE

The assumption of the privileges and immunities clause in the Fourteenth Amendment is that citizens are free to do as they please unless the government can justify its intervention. If economic liberty is as fundamental as the liberty to speak or assemble or worship, for instance, then this would forbid municipal and state laws that require businesses to uphold segregation, that abuse zoning for social engineering purposes, that confiscate property unnecessarily, or that socially engineer neighborhoods through real estate law. *All these laws restrict economic liberty*. How ironic that the decision in the slaughterhouse cases specifically appealed to the Fourteenth Amendment's addition for the sake of Black Americans, only to justify economic interventions that could target Black people and other marginalized groups while appearing to be neutral.

In *Bolling v. Sharpe*, the Court ruled that the Constitution prohibits segregated public schools in Washington, DC. This case has only been confusing to scholars because Warren removed his references to the Lochner line of cases in his final draft as a favor to Supreme Court Justice Hugo Black. Once placed in that line of cases, though, the ruling makes perfect sense. Warren couldn't appeal to the Fourteenth Amendment since DC isn't a state, but he could appeal to the due process clause in the Fifth Amendment ("No person shall...be deprived of life, liberty, or property, without due process of law..."). He argued that the liberty of both Black and white families to pursue their children's education in association with whomever they choose is a fundamental liberty that government may not abridge. It's also quite suggestive, as we can imagine a slightly different reality in which the NAACP had enough money and enough lawyers earlier on to pursue more cases utilizing the logic of the Lochner court. The Lochner line of cases arose in the 1900s and 1910s, meaning that Jim Crow legislation had not yet calcified. If the segregation laws had been removed, if anti-miscegenation laws had been recognized as a violation of liberty, if once-integrated neighborhoods had been allowed to remain and flourish, if the FHA had not been allowed to ghettoize Black Americans, if the highways hadn't subsidized the vanilla suburbs, if the Black economic centers hadn't been razed, if property couldn't just be confiscated for so-called urban renewal, if there were no zoning laws pushing Black people out, if regulations couldn't be abused to crush Black business, if the drug war was handicapped because it violated the Fourth Amendment, what would America look like? Much individual discrimination would still have remained, surely, but could a more peaceful multiracial society have emerged organically, one whose general momentum was in the direction of natural integration, as opposed to the necessary violence of legally disrupting a calcified apartheid-like society that had been formed through thousands of laws and over the course of decades? Public accommodation laws have actually always been a part of the common law tradition anyway, but imagine the difference in imposing such a law on a population whose various levels of government had never been allowed to enforce legal segregation, since such force amounts to an unjustifiable violation of economic liberty.[540]

It is always hard to imagine a past and present so different from the status quo, and there are certainly scholars who disagree on this interpretation of the Fourteenth Amendment. This approach would certainly be far more limiting to American federalism, which has many advantages that are worth debating. Even if this interpretation is incorrect, however, the thought experiment helps us to see how respect for individual property and contract rights can lead to a far more healthy, integrated multiracial society than the sorts of antidiscrimination laws that arose in its stead. What might have been if we had avoided the long train of state abuses against Black Americans that we record in this work?

One thing is for sure: those opposed to economic liberty were flagrant in their opposition to the flourishing of Black people. They weren't on their side then, and we'd venture so far as to say that they aren't now either.

LOOKING FOR SOLUTIONS: ECONOMIC GROWTH

> "Some people say 'burn, baby, burn.' But I say 'build, baby, build' and 'learn, baby, learn' so you can 'earn, baby, earn.'"
> —Martin Luther King Jr.

As we've mentioned already on a couple of occasions, one of the toughest things about economics is keeping track of what is unseen: the businesses, jobs, and innovations that didn't happen because a particular policy created a disincentive to making it happen. In Michael Tanner's *The Inclusive Economy: How to Bring Wealth to America's Poor*, he makes many suggestions, which I'll outline here.[541] But he offers one overarching suggestion that confuses our tribal loyalties: if you want to help the poor, always favor policies that grow the economy. And yes, this will happen through the classic conservative means of reducing both taxes and spending (don't forget to reduce spending!) and by lowering regulations. Those on the margins are much more hurt by a recession, and much more helped by economic growth, than everyone else. Insofar as economic growth means low unemployment rates, better and cheaper consumer goods, and more expendable income, it could make all the difference for someone living paycheck to paycheck to have a job and be able to afford the basics for their family. The wealthy person may gain a disproportionate amount of money for his portfolio, but it will mean far less to his everyday life. While it's tempting to think that whenever the wealthy do much better, the poor must be doing much worse, most of the time the opposite is the case, although there are important exceptions to this rule, especially when cronyism is involved. The poor person tends to do better when the wealthy do better because the wealthy are her employers and customers. The only sense in which the caricature of class warfare becomes quite real is when the wealthy use their exalted position to gain political favors for themselves and entrench their businesses against healthy competition—whether we call that rent-seeking, privilege-seeking, or cronyism. This affects the poor negatively because established and politically well-connected businesses are able to thrive without being more inventive, or making anything more affordable or efficient. Instead, crony capitalists make bad profits by using the political system to discourage innovation, affordability, and quality. Cronyism, which often turns out to be welfare for the rich, ought to be opposed in no uncertain terms and utterly dismantled.

Tanner goes on to outline more particular policies: criminal justice reform and ending the War on Drugs; education choice; elimination of zoning and land-use regulation and reduction of property taxes to bring housing costs down; the removal of asset tests for public assistance, as well as of excessive banking regulations and barriers to nonbanks to encourage saving. We address the first two in other sections but want to draw attention here to his condemnation of NIMBYism and his suggestion that our incentive structures treat the poor as potential savers rather than as mere consumers.

NIMBYs are those who may talk the talk about caring for the poor, but in the end declare "Not in My Back Yard." They do this most often by abusing zoning laws to keep out new construction, particularly for affordable, multifamily ("high-density") structures. We saw the horribly racist and classist use of these laws in this chapter, but the tradition continues in a subtler form—subtler, but no less harmful. For instance, California's housing shortages are so bad and their housing prices so high that, in spite of their high incomes and progressive politics, taking cost of living into account makes California the state with the highest poverty rate in the entire nation. Poor people cannot afford to live there, because only rich people can afford to build new housing under the crushing weight of hundreds upon hundreds of building regulations. This is a very real, very straightforward example of how seemingly innocent and even well-intentioned regulations can create poverty. This bizarre overlap of progressive politics and NIMBYism repeats itself in other places, like Portland, Oregon, as well. A person can be very hip and cool in Portland, but if she's poor, she can't afford to live there. It may seem contradictory, but understanding economics, it makes perfect sense. People who want layer upon layer of (unnecessary) safety, environmental, and aesthetic regulations can't also create affordable housing for the poor, because these regulations are extremely costly to fulfill. Instead of believing that some far-off bureaucracy will solve our poverty problems, let us start a revolution in YIMBYism (Yes in My Back Yard) by repealing unnecessary obstacles and arguing for the property rights of high-density housing developers.

One of the "perverse incentives" we will discuss in our next chapter on the Great Society involves the way that government benefits are arranged to discourage just the sort of habits that allow one to emerge from poverty. One of these habits is saving, but most welfare benefits are set up to disallow any savings. The original intent of such arrangements—that the assistance go to only the truly desperate—has created the unintended consequence of discouraging saving altogether. It may seem odd to talk about saving among a class of people who require monthly assistance, but it really shouldn't be. To have a small savings account could be the difference between getting my car fixed and making it to work or losing my job. It could be the difference between remaining on assistance or saving up enough for two months' rent to a nonsubsidized apartment. It could be the difference between surviving from day to day or getting that certification I need to increase my income. It's insulting and shameful that the wealthy in our country are rewarded with tax breaks for their savings, but the poor are punished for theirs.[542] Instead of worrying about how desperate people ought to be before they can access government assistance, maybe we should worry about what incentive structures we've set up that trap them there. It's time to stop enabling survival mode and shift into thriving mode.

Chapter 8

No Liberation without Ownership: Housing and Highways

I n Richard Rothstein's masterful *The Color of Law*, he draws the readers' attention to the distinction between *de jure* and *de facto* segregation. Popularly, we think of segregation as something that people imposed culturally, as individuals or small communities. Whites didn't want to serve Blacks in their shops. Whites didn't want to live next to Blacks in their neighborhoods. Whites didn't want their sons and daughters to become romantically involved with Blacks. In response, Blacks developed their own separate social institutions and economy. While these stereotypes of whites were certainly true in many cases, Rothstein argues that this kind of de facto segregation does not even begin to adequately tell the story of how American cities and towns became as racially segregated (and unequal in outcomes) as they are today. Instead, he chronicles the multiple ways in which government at the municipal, state, and federal levels conspired to create a level of segregation that went far beyond what might have organically emerged if all citizens, Black and white, were subject to the same rule of law.

First, housing shortages caused by the world wars and the intervening depression made public housing a necessity for many families, not just impoverished ones. Government at all levels participated in these projects, and they were explicitly segregated.

Beginning in 1910, municipalities also attempted to use zoning to create purely white and purely Black neighborhoods. In 1917, during the Lochner era, the Supreme Court ruled that race-based zoning was unconstitutional. In response, many municipalities discovered zoning work-arounds. They relegated multifamily units—far more likely to be occupied by Blacks than single-family ones—to ghettoized areas near the industrial parts of town and far from the single-family homes more often occupied by whites.

Although these early efforts were explicitly motivated by concerns about race, many contemporary examples of zoning and housing regulation abuse are driven by class and even environmental concerns. Nevertheless, these efforts still have a disparate impact on Black Americans, who are overrepresented under the poverty line. As we just discussed, the NIMBYs must answer the YIMBY accusation that the former group is using government coercion to exclude people economically. Obstacles that limit the ability to create high-density housing are particularly harmful, as this is the only way that poorer folks are generally able to live near available jobs. But piling on layer after layer of aesthetic, environmental, and safety regulations can do just as much harm by making it unaffordable (and a logistical nightmare) to build anything new at all. This is the conundrum we're seeing in some of the most highly populated places in the US, such as Los Angeles and New York City. Sky-high housing costs are the direct result of a plethora of limitations on new construction. This keeps the poor out, or if they can get in, they're paying so much for rent that they can't save a dime. We're already seeing the spontaneous response to this in a great exodus out of California to more affordable cities. It should be noted that one of the most popular destinations for former Californians is Houston, which has no zoning laws whatsoever. Although this may sound absurd, Houston seems to be doing just fine.

The term "white flight" can also give the wrong impression, implying that whites moved to the suburbs to get away from Black people who were moving into the cities. Although it is true that many whites did not want to have Black neighbors, the reality is that the creation of suburbs was socially engineered by the central government. It created the federal highway system that subsidized the transportation costs to and from work, and financed and insured homes in the exact spots its bureaucrats wanted whites to move. Planners made it illegal for Black people to live there and impossible for them to buy there due to denial by the Federal Housing Administration and the Veterans Association. We'll see how they made it extremely difficult for Black people to buy in many places, even in all-Black neighborhoods or in rougher parts of town, so that Black home ownership rates have consistently lagged about 20 percent behind whites.[543]

The federal government carried out a plan to get more and more white citizens into their own homes. Assuming both that Blacks and whites would live more peacefully if kept separate and that white neighborhoods would retain property values better, the Federal Housing Administration refused to insure integrated neighborhoods. They also refused to insure any homes in all-Black neighborhoods, also deeming them a bad risk, even though residents were in many cases just as reliably employed as whites. Remember that into the 1950s, Blacks were employed at much higher rates than whites. Black men worked, on average, a bit more than white men, and Black women worked a lot more than white women. With Black marriage rates nearly equivalent to whites at this time, the combined income of a Black husband and wife may not have been huge, but many were perfectly steady, working-class households that should have been good bets for banks.

Unfortunately, that wasn't the case. In 1941, a real estate developer working on an all-Black, middle-income neighborhood saw his plans crushed when both local banks and the Prudential Life Insurance Company were told by the Federal Housing Administration that they would not approve the mortgages. The banks explicitly agreed to the project, only contingent on FHA approval. It might be impossible to calculate how many financial institutions would have overlooked their own prejudices to finance such creditworthy projects had they not known that FHA disapproval was inevitable.[544]

SHELLEY V. KRAEMER AND THE PROBLEM OF RESTRICTIVE COVENANTS

The case of restrictive covenants is more complicated. Since these were contracts made between one property owner and the next, it wasn't immediately clear that property owners were violating the rule of law by restricting future ownership by nonwhites. As private actions, perhaps it seems that restrictive covenants need not enter into a conversation about de jure segregation, which implies government interference. For a contract to be meaningful, however, it must be enforceable, and local and state governments chose to enforce these contracts. On the other hand, restrictive deeds were pretty difficult to enforce anyway, since any violation of them could only harm the original owner. If no one has standing to bring the case—meaning they were harmed by the action—then the court won't even hear said case. So when homeowners ran into this difficulty, they turned to various versions of a housing, or neighborhood, association. These are also contracts, but one in which all members of the neighborhood could claim to have legal standing as being harmed by the possibility of Black neighbors. Both strategies, individual restrictive covenants/deeds and group ones, bring up the sticky problem of private but deeply discriminatory contracts that the state is asked to step in and enforce as neutral arbiter. We argue that race-based restrictive covenants are objectionable from a classical liberal perspective, thus making state enforcement of such covenants objectionable as well.

Lessons in Classical Liberalism #13: Nuances in Property Rights and Contract Law

The classical liberal tradition has always acknowledged some boundaries around what is and is not an acceptable contract, as well as various nuances to add to the notion of a property right as an exclusive claim. To appeal to the most obvious examples, classical liberal polities will not defend contracts to enslave oneself,[545] for instance, or to agree to meet up so that one person can kill and eat the other person (this case really happened in Germany!).[546] Less obvious but just as valid are cases in which there is no way to avoid cultural factors in influencing how we handle property rights. There are a wide variety of views on how to handle marriage contracts, for instance, among classical liberals. But even if marriage was removed from state oversight and replaced with mere common property contracts between the said parties, that would not resolve questions about custody of children or property allocation when someone without a will dies. The common law tradition allows for "easements, covenants, nuisance laws, zoning laws, regulatory statutes" and other ways of dealing with the externalities problems that inevitably arise among neighbors.[547] In other words, liberal neutrality is something we maintain as well as we can in order to accommodate as many as possible in a pluralistic society, but it is not a panacea. Many questions will be determined by custom, imaginative association, precedent, and with an eye to the concrete context. The United States, for instance, has a history of generosity toward debtors, who can declare bankruptcy and have much of what they owe to creditors forgiven. This isn't really a question of commutative justice. Rather, we don't like the idea of debtor's prisons, and we do like the idea of risk-taking entrepreneurs. Texas purposefully built up its population by making their rules especially lenient, attracting business ventures. So we see that both contract law and property law can have many nuances that make them more robust in their role as fundamental institutions that enable productive social interaction.

There are a few interesting twists and turns to the way the courts handled cases that had to do with race-based restrictive covenants. In at least one case, an appeal to a race-based restrictive covenant was rejected because the homeowners could not, in fact, show that Black home ownership would reduce property values in the area. Oddly, the very fact of extremely limited housing options for Blacks made middle- and upper-class Blacks willing to pay well above market prices for housing in higher-value neighborhoods. (Actually, all Blacks paid more for housing than whites, because the supply was kept artificially low by such a wide array of restrictions.) Not only that, but generally those who attempted to break the race barrier in a neighborhood were professionals— Black men and women whose social standing often exceeded that of their white neighbors, including, in many cases, their income and creditworthiness. This means that the initial movement of Black people into a white neighborhood *improved* the average home values there because a home bought by a Black professional was certainly sold for a higher than market price. It was only the fear that their property values would decline because of prejudice that led so many whites to move out, making the eventual decline of the neighborhood a self-fulfilling prophecy. Setting the cultural tensions aside, had whites simply stayed in the neighborhood and touted their improved home values to buyers, they could have maintained those values. [548]

Nevertheless, in a free market we accept the role of happenstance in our financial endeavors. No one owes us a return on our investments; we accept that any owner is taking a risk. While on the whole, this system of playing the probabilities works out pretty well for our homes, retirement funds, and businesses, we know that losses are as much a part of the system as gains. Losses alert the entrepreneur to the realities of demand. So free marketers reject efforts to legally shield oneself from the vagaries of the market through regulatory capture, the formation of cartels, or any other manipulation of the legal and political system that entrenches the established at the expense of the innovators. Free marketers see these sorts of efforts as cronyism.

However, when whites protected their own property values and their prejudices by excluding nonwhites and those of Jewish descent from their neighborhoods, they also seemed to be exercising their constitutional right to associate and disassociate as they pleased. Such behavior seemed to be legal, if not moral.[549] In 1948, the Supreme Court ruled in *Shelley v. Kraemer* that the state could not participate in defending racist restrictive covenants, appealing to the Fourteenth Amendment's promise of equal protection under the law. But the reasoning in the case seems dubious at first: Justice Vinson argues that the state cannot defend a private contract that appeals to distinctions that the state itself could not make in, say, a piece of legislation. But this is patently absurd, as the state defends many wills and bequests that make all sorts of distinctions that the state itself could not make and continues to do so to this day. Legal expert David Bernstein gives the example of disinheritance if one marries a Catholic.[550] So what should a classical liberal think of the *Shelley* decision?

Bernstein persuasively argues that while the decision itself is not a gem of judicial clarity, there are two perfectly reasonable arguments in it that ought to be compelling to classical liberals:

First, the "state action" in question was actually more than just enforcement of a contract. Neither the Shelleys nor the seller had any interest in enforcing the restrictive covenant. It was a third party—a neighbor who wasn't any kind of party to the contract—who brought the case. That consideration makes room for the idea that the court's involvement does amount to a "public policy" consideration. Second, racial covenants always went in one direction: restriction of minorities by whites. If lots of different groups were establishing their own exclusive communities, then perhaps we could argue that state enforcement of said contracts is "racially neutral." But the facts on the ground don't hold for the actual history of racial covenants in the United States. And to drive this second point home, Bernstein points out that states often "refused to enforce all sorts of other, more minor, restrictions on alienability of property." If the state then insisted on enforcing this particular restriction, it starts to look like *discriminatory* state action. Because the states themselves enforced policies whose main aim was segregation, it's impossible to consider them only in the abstract, theoretical understanding of their role as neutral contract enforcers.[551]

Philosopher David Schmidtz makes the classical liberal case for *Shelley* even clearer. It's one thing, he says, for two people to make a racist agreement with each other. But it's something else entirely to bind all future owners by essentially making your racist agreement a part of the deed to the house (something like an easement). That turns what initially appears to be a matter of contract law into a matter of property law. Since police powers are far more expansive with regard to property law, enforcement really is a matter of state action, amounting to public policy. And there was nothing neutral about it: the state was being asked to defend the covenants against Black buyers, merely because they were Black (and many others were targeted by these covenants as well, including Asians and Jews). This violates the Fourteenth Amendment guarantee of equal protection under the law. Rothstein isn't wrong to remind us that the Fourteenth Amendment in its historical context dealt specifically with the concern that Blacks were not experiencing the benefits of the rule of law.

Why does it matter to dig a little into the legalities when it comes to restrictive covenants? It's because we don't want to eliminate all restrictive covenants (including neighborhood associations). When Rachel's mother-in-law bought into a community that required that 95 percent of the home sales go to people aged fifty-five and over, she discriminated against the young. But such an agreement does not violate the Fourteenth Amendment because there is no widespread pattern of youth-exclusionary policies and practices.

Let us consider an objection. One of the great strengths of reflective conservatism is its anti-utopianism. No person, and therefore no society, they claim, is without sin. We can't solve all the problems, nor should we try. Perhaps a conservative could object to our complaints about de jure imposition of segregation by pointing out that people are naturally more comfortable with those like themselves. There's a sort of organic sorting that happens simply as a result of an almost instinctual resonance we have with those of a similar cultural inheritance. Nor is this always a bad thing! "The Hill" is the famous Italian section of St. Louis, known for its delightful national character and delicious food. In order to avoid the loss of heritage, homeowners there sell directly to Italian friends and family members rather than go through real estate agents who are not even legally allowed to call this "the Italian part of town." What's the harm in this? Perhaps nothing at all. It might even encourage healthy integration by drawing community members from all parts of St. Louis and all walks of life into the city for a dinner out.

But the development of America's inner-city Black ghettos do not follow this organic, localized pattern. Time and time again, Rothstein presents examples of stable, integrated neighborhoods purposefully broken up by social engineers determined to create a segregated society. Factories attracted many Black and immigrant workers who lived peacefully near one another in order to be close to work. He describes "mostly black and white blocks... interspersed in central city" Atlanta prior to World War I.[552] The deeply segregated Atlanta apparent by the time of the civil rights movement was engineered through the manipulation of school site locations. At the turn of the century, Houston's neighborhoods were largely integrated as well, with "substantial numbers of African American and white children...in each of the city's six wards." In these types of cases, small schools were generally built, one for whites and one for Blacks, sometimes on the very same street. But in the '20s and '30s, city planners undertook a long-term vision to segregate the Blacks into the south side by building new Black schools and a Black hospital there. That way, any family that wanted to have realistic access to these resources had to move into (what quickly became) an all-Black neighborhood.

In other cases, various groups attempted integrated housing, or even just construction of equally nice segregated housing for Blacks, but these attempts were shut down by the Federal Housing Administration. In Palo Alto, writer and Stanford professor Wallace Stegner helped create a co-op with other professionals with the goal of building a four-hundred-home neighborhood. But when the FHA refused to insure any project that included Black members, the banks refused to make the loans. The co-op wouldn't throw over their Black members, so they had to sell the land they had acquired. The all-white building project (which the FHA *required* to include racial housing covenants)[553] that followed became the Ladera neighborhood that adjoins Stanford's campus today.[554] Other projects for intentionally mixed neighborhoods were blocked through creative rezoning or abuse of nitpicky local regulations, such as the Swarthmore Property Owners Association's attempts in 1954. A similar project in Deerfield, Illinois, proceeded apace until neighbors discovered it would be integrated. They marched on the town board meeting and vandalized the partially built homes. Police did not intervene.[555] In another abuse of zoning, the residents of Black Jack, Missouri, blocked a Methodist project to build an integrated neighborhood by requiring that new construction be limited to three houses per acre. Since the whole point of the project was to create higher-density housing for working-class families, this made the project impossible. Blacks who had hoped to own there sued, citing that they could find no housing in the inner city and were shut out everywhere else. The courts eventually ruled that the zoning practice was unconstitutional since it was explicitly racist. But since the ruling took five years to come down, a mixture of changes in interest rates and persistent neighborhood hostility made it impossible for the Methodists to proceed.[556]

For Rachel, seeing the story of Charles Vatterott among Rothstein's examples was particularly sad. He built St. Ann (which neighbors Ferguson, Missouri) according to the FHA requirements, including the *requirement* that all housing deeds include racial covenants barring Blacks. But as a serious Catholic and member of the Knights of Columbus, he was committed to meeting the needs of Black St. Louisans as well. He built the De Porres neighborhood for them, but because of the lack of FHA backing, they could only rent there, and he wasn't able to include the same neighborhood amenities. He tried to set up a savings plan for the eventual purchase of rented homes, but there was no way to avoid the decades of lost equity for these Black families.[557] Rachel grew up with his great-granddaughters, and the Vatterott family continues to do good work in the St. Louis area today. His story goes to show that even with the conviction to love one's neighbors and the creativity to create work-arounds, a government that is just as determined to socially engineer us from above can block good efforts at every turn.

Instead, conservatives would do well to point out that progressives, with their utopian dreams of efficient, streamlined, racially pure neighborhoods, invented many of the various legal machinations required to get around issues of constitutionality in order to establish their vision of society. The scientistic mind tolerates none of this messiness, with different people working out their issues among themselves in whatever haphazard ways they creatively devise. Listening to progressives try to resolve both the direct harms and the disparate impact of this history can be frustrating. Many of them, Rothstein included, resort directly to the same sorts of government interference that caused the problem, with the hope that if we just change the direction of the bias, we can change the outcomes. Consistently, they stumble on the issue of the unintended consequences of their schemes. To pick the most prominent and controversial example we possibly can, let's talk about the 2008 financial crisis.

HOW GOOD INTENTIONS CAUSED THE HOUSING BUBBLE AND BUST

Let's be clear about one thing first. There's nothing inherently best about owning a home. In terms of general productivity, a homeowner does less to boost the economy by building a home than he would by investing that money into a business.[558] Assuming that we're talking about the usual case, for a homeowner simply living in her home rather than renting it out or flipping it, for instance, a house is only an investment in one thin sense: home ownership forces us to save money we wouldn't otherwise save as we build equity in a home. But that's about it, and even that assumes that we don't refinance frequently to make improvements. Essentially, a home is a consumption good (even though it's often seen as an investment good), and what's more, it's one that limits our mobility. In the analysis that we've given above of the unjust practices of the government around home ownership, we are far more interested in the ways that these policies violated the equal protection of the law, encouraged segregation, concentrated poverty, and led to job loss and neighborhood destabilization than we are about home ownership itself as some hallowed goal. To the extent that the policies discussed here contributed to the inequality of white and Black asset accumulation, only a small part can be chalked up to home value itself. It's so important to understand the full ripple effects, or we'll focus our efforts on useless "solutions."

One useless solution to concerns about inequality is to lower lending standards in order to get more people into a home. This is just what Barney Frank did when, in 2003, he recommended that Fannie Mae and Freddie Mac "roll the dice a little bit more in this situation towards subsidized housing...."[559] Recall, as we walk through what happened, that it's all set against the background of the Federal Reserve's bizarrely low interest rates throughout the 2000s.[560] Artificially low interest rates tend to encourage more home-buying as well as more and more borrowing by banks. The point is that people and institutions make riskier decisions than they otherwise would, because the signal for risk—the interest rate—is pushed down. The result of poor monetary policy is often economic devastation such as the Great Depression and the Great Recession.[561]

For the uninitiated, Fannie Mae and Freddie Mac are quasi-governmental entities that allow shareholders to make profits from the finance activities undertaken, but with the implicit assumption of a bailout from government should these efforts go wrong. Fannie and Freddie owed an incredible one thousand times their net worth, a situation that no free market would ever allow, given the risks. Government removal of the risk of failure created the perverse incentive to take on riskier and riskier investments such as subprime mortgages (loans to people with poor credit scores). Any bank that did so knew that it could turn around and sell risky holdings to Fannie and Freddie anyway, so the old practices of strict underwriting became quickly passé. One of the most stunning facts of this history is that after Frank's pronouncement in Congress, the share of subprime mortgages shot up by 10 percent within the year. Of Fannie and Freddie's holdings, three-quarters were subprime mortgages by 2008. There are a lot of other factors here, too, such as governmental entities and rules that encouraged risky lending, favored housing-backed assets, and created a lack of accountability on the part of the ratings agencies by legally endorsing only the "big three." We don't mean to oversimplify here, but without getting into all the weeds, we hope that it's becoming clear that the hope of righting past wrongs in this kind of direct manner can trigger an avalanche of unintended consequences that actually worsen the position of those most harmed in the first place, and the chance of that happening is compounded by other wrongheaded state interventions into the free market.

Sadly, those consequences fell largely on the poor, who, trusting that banks wouldn't lend it if they couldn't afford it, were far more likely to be foreclosed on. But far more significant than that sort of direct outcome, the resulting economic downturn had the worst effect of all. In contrast to a fairly quick and robust recovery for upper income people, distressed communities experienced a far more extended recession, with continuing declines in employment and business development through at least 2015.[562] Of course they did. Already in a more tenuous social and financial position, poor families experienced painful hits to their income and their credit, killing any plans they might have had for further education and training, and even their ability to move to where the work was.

As we've mentioned before, one underlying theme of this book appeals to Adam Smith's condemnation of the "man of system" who "seems to imagine that he can arrange the different members of a great society with as much ease as the hand arranges the different pieces upon a chess-board."[563] While economically ignorant politicians and voters try to move people around like their pawns, it's the unseen conglomeration of individual choices, manifest in the culture and economy, that really determine what happens. Policies that promote general economic growth over targeted solutions like easier housing loans sound cold and mechanistic. Imagine, though, a poor man finally able to find work because there's a new business in town, or a desperately needed nonprofit able to raise enough funds from comfortable donors, or a teenager signing up for technical college because businesses desperate for his skills will employ him while he's in school and sometimes even pay for it, to boot. Many don't realize that those on the margins are the most affected by economic upturns and downturns. More savings in the bank for a wealthy person is nice for them, but not nearly as nice as a job when one didn't have one before or enough access to capital to start that small business. It's never "people versus the economy." People are the economy.

URBAN RENEWAL AND THE INTERSTATE HIGHWAY SYSTEM

The subsidization of all-white suburbs, along with the exclusion of Black and mixed neighborhoods from these subsidies, was intended to relieve the density of the cities and create idyllic "all-American" neighborhoods. In 1949, Congress passed the American Housing Act, which provided for even more FHA mortgage insurance funding, more public housing, and slum clearance. That last element was referred to as urban redevelopment and, later, urban renewal, although Black Americans referred to it as "negro removal." Planners deemed unattractive apartment buildings and ramshackle houses filled with minorities "slums," while many were in fact vital cultural and economic centers for poor but upwardly mobile working-class people. James Baldwin told this story in a 1963 interview that is worth quoting in full:

> A boy last week, he was 16 in San Francisco told me on television, thank God we got him to talk. Maybe somebody else ought to listen. He said,

"I got no country, I've got no flag." Man he's
only 16 years old. And I couldn't say you do. I
don't have any evidence to prove that he does.
They were tearing down his house because San
Francisco is engaging as all...most northern cities now are engaged in something called urban
renewal, which means moving the Negroes out.
It means negro removal; that is what it means.
And the federal government is accom- is, is, is an
accomplice to this fact. Now this, we're talking
about human beings: there's not such a thing as
a monolithic wall, or you know, some abstrac-
tion called a "Negro Problem." These are Negro
boys and girls who at 16 and 17 don't believe the
country means anything that it says and don't
feel they have any place here. On the basis of the
performance of the entire country...No, am I ex-
aggerating? [564]

By 1956, Eisenhower signed the Federal Highway Act into
law. Prior to LBJ's Great Society project, this act accounted for
the greatest (nonwar) expenditure of federal funds in American
history thus far. Since 90 percent of the funds for the highway
system came from the federal government, it was then open season for city planners to route the highway in order to complete
their social engineering goal of "vanilla suburbs." Now, whites
could commute to work in the city from their spacious suburban
homes, and even more "slums" could be cleared to make room for
the highway itself. This time, though, planners wouldn't be both-
ered with the legal responsibility to relocate the dispossessed—a
responsibility that had often been conveniently ignored in urban renewal programs anyway. Moreover, planners entrenched
the segregation between white and Black (or out west, Latino)

neighborhoods by running the highway in such a way as to permanently divide them.[565]

JANE JACOBS: THE HAYEK OF URBAN PLANNING

> "Respect—in the deepest sense—strips of chaos
> that have a weird wisdom of their own not yet
> encompassed in our concept of urban order."
> —Jane Jacobs

As these momentous feats of planning were undertaken, Jane Jacobs published *The Death and Life of Great American Cities* in 1961. In a scathing takedown of the aggressive urban planning craze, Jacobs developed a theory of the beautiful, life-giving emergent order of city street life that purposefully saw the world through the eyes of "very plain people, including the poor...the discriminated against...the uneducated...who tell with wisdom and eloquence about the things they know first hand from life."[566] Her nemesis was Robert Moses, who "[d]espite never winning a single election...reigned over a set of principalities that would rival a Hapsburg monarch."[567] Moses believed that the only way to adapt to the contemporary economy was to demolish much of the historic city as it was, and he hated Jacobs's book.[568] It's her book, however, and not Moses's architectural philosophy that became a classic, and Jacobs put her money where her mouth was too. She led protests against the routing of a four-lane road right through Washington Square Park, the centerpiece of Greenwich Village. Hilariously, the only time Jacobs ever physically set eyes on Moses was when he came to a community meeting against the roads to scream, "There is nobody against this—NOBODY, NOBODY, NOBODY, but a bunch of.... A bunch of MOTHERS!" He did not stay to hear their arguments. In her fight against the destruction of Little Italy and SoHo to run I-78 through them, she was arrested several times but escaped a jail sentence.

Since it's never a bad time to remind ourselves of the ever-present threat of cronyism, we ought to note that Moses's great strength was gathering together all the parties that would be interested in doing a lot of demolishing and new construction: "banks, labor unions, contractors, bond underwriters, insurance firms, the great retail stores, real estate manipulators...." Moses was an image of "political entrepreneurship" in the cronyistic sense; he had skill finding new ways to grease his wheels (and those of his friends) with taxpayer dollars. Jacobs, on the other hand, was a skilled community organizer, appealing both to the community members themselves and whichever high-level officials she could get to shore up her case. For her, it wasn't just a matter of preserving a historic park. Rather, Moses represented the "prevailing scientific rationalism" then ascendant in the planning and architectural communities. In contrast, Jacobs asked, "Why have cities not, long since, been identified, understood, and treated as problems of organised complexities?" In other words, why can't people see what would be obvious to any Hayekian thinker, that the more complex and advanced our economy becomes, the *less* we can successfully micromanage it? Rather, Jacobs studied with deep interest and real love the emergent patterns of urban life: the role of the corner store, the café where friends meet, or even the laundromat, the way a neighborhood can spring up around such things because people see one another and interact on the street. Although not at all ideological, Jacobs came to favor emergent order over regulation.

Jacobs had the bandwidth and voice to do what, sadly, so many Black and Latino Americans couldn't; she fought the system, rebutting designations of "blight" that would have led to "slum clearance" with her own documentation of the conditions, exploiting illegal meetings and designations by planners (through a spy at City Hall!) to delay and frustrate their plans, and outing their "secrecy and collusion" to an increasingly outraged populace. Part of what Jacobs understood was that the mixed-use architecture and the ethnic flavor of various neighborhoods constituted the functioning of life there. The idea that these people—collections of families, living near the factories or above the shops in which they worked, and attending the church on the corner—could just be removed and flung to the four winds without a great social fallout was as stupid as it was hubristic. She hated zoning, which flattened out the diversity of an organic city street—different kinds of people doing different kinds of things, but moving in and out easily, bumping into one another and sharing ideas.[569] The density of the city—what planners moved heaven and earth to avoid—is actually an important source of economic growth. The poor can afford to move where the jobs are, and natural networks arise that spur innovation. Fundamentally, the progressive obsession with central planning was also just plain anti-democratic. The people themselves understood best through their local knowledge what would work for them on their own streets.

EMINENT DOMAIN AND THE BRUTALISM OF THE CENTRAL PLANNERS

Sadly, although "Citizen Jane" won the intellectual war over urban planning and historic architecture, she appeared too late in the game to turn the tide. With FHA segregation in its fourth decade, her book came out twelve years into a national project of slum clearance that devastated minority neighborhoods in every major American city, and six years into the project of building the federal highway system that would change the face of the entire country.

In the Pixar film *Cars*, James Taylor sings about "Our Town" over a montage of happy cars pulling into friendly way-station towns.[570] Bonnie Hunt's character, Sally, explains to Lightning McQueen the difference between the straight, rational, scientistic lines of the interstate and the old two-lane state highway system: "Well, the road didn't cut through the land like that interstate," she recalls, "it moved with the land...it rose, it fell, it curved...cars didn't drive on it to make great time, they drove on it to have a great time." The montage proceeds to show how the small towns that dotted the old state highways became ghost towns as the highway bypassed them. In fact, the old Lincoln Highway and Route 66 not only connected towns across the country but formed the main streets of many of the towns they passed through. It's easy to dismiss such nostalgia; most would reflexively argue that the interstate highway system is, as economist Tyler Cowen puts it, "a high-return investment." It may have changed us socially and culturally in unforeseen ways, but it sure made us a lot richer, right?

Not so fast. As Clifford Winston has shown in his extensive research on the economic returns of the highway system as well as comparisons with alternatives, the system requires more wealth to maintain than what it creates. Indeed, funding the upkeep has become an infamous catalyst of pork barrel spending bills for cronies everywhere; and it's increased inequality by forcing taxpayers to subsidize the cross-country trucking of big corporations. In fact, there are plenty of workable alternatives that might have developed more in its absence—moving freight by train and ship[571] (look up the Jones Act), or even privately built and maintained roads—which would have kept costs internalized to the businesses that ought to bear them. Winston estimates that the system costs about $100 billion more, *per year*, than private alternatives would. The intervention of the government to provide this infrastructure also means that its routes and upkeep are determined by politics. Predictably, the politicized process means that funding isn't tied to the relevant measures of weight capacity and lane number, nor do cities adopt economists' suggestions about how to avoid congestion—wasting time, fuel, and clean air. Meanwhile, the crony oil and construction companies make sure it stays that way.[572]

Nevertheless, the behemoth project, which was finally completed in 1991 but requires constant upkeep, was wildly popular across America. The interstate highway seemed to be something we could all agree on, except by "we" we mean middle- and up-per-income Americans who benefitted from the jobs and the convenience but weren't being summarily dismissed from homes claimed through eminent domain. If the fact that the term *eminent domain* is derived from the Latin for supreme lordship doesn't sound bad enough, just wait till you hear how cruelly this legal mechanism has been wielded against poor and minority communities.

While the Constitution does allow for the taking (with restitution) of private property by the government for a public use, classical liberal scholar Ilya Somin argued before the United States Commission on Civil Rights that "the majority suffering from blight condemnations and economic development takings were racial and ethnic minorities, mostly poor African Americans or Hispanics"—those least able to lobby against the powers that be.[573] Furthermore, the government rarely covers their financial losses fully, leaving them even worse off than they already were from the loss of their communities and networks.

Odd Supreme Court couple Sandra Day O'Connor and Clarence Thomas made the exact same claim about eminent domain abuse when the infamous *Kelo v. New London* case was decided in favor of local governments taking private property only to hand it over to a different private owner. In their dissent, Thomas and O'Connor argued that:

> The consequences of today's decision are not dif-ficult to predict, and promise to be harmful. So-called "urban renewal" programs provide some compensation for the properties they take, but no compensation is possible for the subjective value of these lands to the individuals displaced and the indignity inflicted by uprooting them from their homes. Allowing the government to

take property solely for public purposes is bad enough, but extending the concept of public purpose to encompass any economically beneficial goal guarantees that these losses will fall disproportionately on poor communities. Those communities are not only systematically less likely to put their lands to the highest and best social use, but are also the least politically powerful. If ever there were justification for intrusive judicial review of constitutional provisions that protect "discrete and insular minorities," *United States* v. *Carolene Products Co.*, 304 U.S. 144, 152, n. 4 (1938), surely that principle would apply with great force to the powerless groups and individuals the Public Use Clause protects. The deferential standard this Court has adopted for the Public Use Clause is therefore deeply perverse. It encourages "those citizens with disproportionate influence and power in the political process, including large corporations and development firms" to victimize the weak.[574]

O'Connor and Thomas weren't alone in their dissent; the *Kelo* case excited so much outrage among the American public that forty-five states passed laws limiting eminent domain abuse.[575] While it's entirely legitimate to make a strong distinction between taking for genuine public use (like a highway) and taking for the far more controversial purpose of "economic development," it's not difficult to imagine that a gargantuan forty-seven thousand mile highway project and the thirty-five years of government takings it involved might have created a culture of dismissive nonchalance about appealing to blight, eminent domain, and the takings clause to get around legitimate property claims.

Lessons in Classical Liberalism #14: Public Choice Theory and the Farce of the "Economic Impact Study"

Defenders of eminent domain will argue that too much concern with minority property rights ignores the economic benefits of the city's redevelopment plans, and similar arguments have always been made in favor of the Highway Act as well. Therefore, it's worth stopping for a moment to talk about the problem of measuring economic impact. These sorts of takings will always be justified by their supporters by appeal to some improved economic outcome for the area once the blighted neighborhoods are replaced with the highway or the Walmart or whatever the city council has in mind to increase their tax revenues. But the economic impact studies that accompany such projects are smoke-and-mirrors level bunk. Here's a quick overview:

1. The first and most glaring problem with these studies is that they only ever measure the economic activity that will arise from the new project. They forget about the economic activity that will not occur because resources are being directed to this project instead of elsewhere. The acknowledgment of *opportunity costs* is one of the most fundamental insights of the economic way of thinking. It's not as though the taxpayer would have burned that money or hidden it in a mattress. Presumably, citizens would have spent their money, supporting businesses, or saved it at their local bank, which lends to businesses. But economic impact studies do not include the subtraction of the losses from the way that the money would have been spent if it hadn't been spent on this.[576] Therefore,

the studies *inevitably* claim that the project will be a net benefit.

2. The second issue arises from the dynamics of public choice. A private entrepreneur can succeed or fail at some project on her own dime, so she is highly motivated to predict correctly whether there really is the demand for her project and whether it really is financially sustainable over time. Public projects operate in quite the opposite direction. Politicians are motivated to do something—anything—to address constituent complaints and longings, but they will suffer nothing if the project ultimately fails. By the time the outcome becomes apparent, they'll probably be long gone to a higher political office. They are also motivated to "create jobs" by making government contracts available. Hearkening back to problem #1 above, politicians can always take the credit for giving out jobs, even if the recipients of those jobs would have been doing something elsewhere anyway. The whole operation creates a bundle of opportunities for corruption, as private companies vie for these easy, high-paid contracts that inevitably go over budget and over schedule. Understanding how the incentives in place for public projects differ from those for private ones helps to explain why public projects often take far longer and cost far more than the projected numbers in the impact study. This phenomenon is so pervasive that it has given rise to the phrase "government boondoggle," referring to wasteful spending for failed projects that continues to occur because entrenched interests drive political decision-making.[577]

3. Finally, problem #1 and problem #2 above combine to devastating effect. It's easy to laugh at the government wasting billions of dollars on projects no one needs, but it's not so easy when the project violates the prop-

erty rights of the poor, interrupts the organic development of centers of economic life, scatters community
members who relied heavily on their local connections,
and entrenches already established economic interests,
deepening corruption.

We've made a lot of claims about the effect of the highways
and urban renewal on Black and Latino Americans, and we've
explained a few economic concepts that predict poor outcomes.
Now let's see what actually happened.

In *The Folklore of the Freeway*, Eric Avila tracks the highways' march through several major cities. In Nashville, I-40 actually veers off its path to bisect the Black part of town.[578] In
Minneapolis-St. Paul, a hotspot of Black culture at the time,
planners rejected the northern route that would have taken the
highway near an industrial part of town and instead elected for
the central route. This route wiped out the historic Black Rondo
neighborhood, in spite of popular protests and even internal dispute over the question of why white and Black neighborhoods
were being destroyed when there was a perfectly serviceable alternative that could avoid that effect. Today, there's even a Rondo
Days festival that celebrates the old neighborhood every year. On
the festival page the mission reads: "Rondo Avenue, Inc. (RAI) is
dedicated to preserving, conserving and accurately interpreting
the contributions of the African-American community of Rondo
to the City of Saint Paul. This community was destroyed by the
construction of Interstate I-94 in the 1960's."[579]

Overtown in Miami was destroyed by I-95, in spite of the
fact that it was home to a healthy mix of low- and middle-income
Black and Afro-Caribbean families, as well as a thriving night-
life scene and a wide variety of well-functioning neighborhood

institutions. Overtown is now a wasteland, its people displaced to the "second ghetto" in outlying areas of Miami. Who can know what culture, what networks, what meaningful social associations were lost? Who can measure the differences in outcomes for these displaced families and their children? Would the shops, the churches, the schools, the charities be simply or easily reconstituted elsewhere? Of course not. The worst part of the Overtown story is that a perfectly good road could have been built elsewhere, preserving this thriving Black neighborhood and retaining the economic benefits. But a group of downtown businessowners and politicians pushed for the plan that was finally adopted.[580] And while we could discuss Robert Moses again here, with his evisceration of the old ethnic neighborhoods of Brooklyn, we won't. That's because Italians, Poles, Germans, Jews, and Irish could move out to the suburbs (though some restrictive covenants did target Jews), but Black Americans most decidedly could not.[581]

If anecdotal cases seem unconvincing, a libertarian scholar at the time compiled mountains of data on urban renewal for a dissertation that turned into a book. In 1964, economist Martin Anderson, who later served as one of President Ronald Reagan's closest economics advisors, released *The Federal Bulldozer*.[582] The *Boston College Law Review* harshly criticized the book at the time, claiming that it was too polemical and wrangling over interpretation of the data. In spite of this, the reviewer, Peter H. Nash, couldn't help but agree with the most relevant of his critiques of the urban renewal program. In fact, one of Nash's criticisms of Anderson is that he didn't apply all the same critiques of urban renewal to the highway program as well! After all, the highway program didn't even require the government to replace any housing or make relocation payments.

First, Nash agreed that, "[a]lthough regulations call for definite plans to relocate the dispossessed, the Urban Renewal Administration has not demanded compliance in most cities."[583] Second, he praises Anderson for "ably document[ing] the failure of the program to alleviate the shortage of decent housing for low and moderate income families." Nash goes on to describe this research:

> The author examined the progress reports of 326 renewal projects as of March 1961. These revealed that more than 126,000 dwelling units had been destroyed, as many as twenty percent of which were still sound. New construction on these sites amounted to 28,000 units, constituting less than one-quarter of those demolished. Of this total, only about 3,000 were low rent units within the financial reach of the displaced families. The average rent for the remaining units was $195 per month. In his analysis of the relocation program, Anderson makes a good point in indicating how urban renewal frequently hurts those it is supposed to help. Two-thirds of the persons who must be rehoused after the clearance of urban renewal sites are Negroes or Puerto Ricans, a fact that prompts civil rights leaders to call the program "Negro removal."[584]

Nash then goes on to describe how government reports work the numbers in order to underplay the problem (in much the same way they do with economic impact studies today):

> Private studies indicate that the displaced slum-dwellers generally move to other slums, for which they pay higher rents. In contrast, the federal government reports that eighty percent of 153,000 relocated families have moved into standard housing. Conflicting claims are brought about by the shifting definition of what

constitutes "standard" housing. Since local officials make the decision, a city may apply high standards to housing it wants to demolish for an urban renewal project, and then apply lower standards to other dwellings to justify quick relocation of the displaced persons. Thus the federal claim dissolves into semantic legerdemain. In addition, the Urban Renewal Administration opposes the Comptroller General's recent proposal to require a consistent criterion for judging "standard" housing.[585]

Today, the Congress for New Urbanism fights to convert badly placed or useless stretches of inner-city highway with walkable boulevards and surface streets. They complain about displacement, congestion, division, pollution, and sky-high accident rates. They've already completed these projects in Boston, Chattanooga, Milwaukee, New York City, Oakland, Portland, Rochester, Providence, Seattle, and San Francisco, as well as in a few places in other countries. The results? Citizens spend half as much on transportation. The revitalized sense of place that these spaces exude attracts businesses and residents. And the increase in density in a downtown business district increases tax revenues exponentially.[586]

There is a deep, sad irony in the fact that zoning laws, slum clearance, and highway projects that took shape with segregation and class loathing in mind are now all being painstakingly undone in an effort to bring back the diverse, mixed-use spaces that were already organically developing in the urban landscape of the early twentieth century.

LOOKING FOR SOLUTIONS:
NEIGHBORHOOD STABILIZATION

Any healthy community needs stable housing, enough to eat, employment networks, help for addiction and trauma, good education, and so many other things that are sadly lacking in our most struggling communities. While some think that such problems would be easily solved through mere policy changes, decades and decades of such attempts demonstrate the old classical liberal saw that central planning doesn't work nearly as well as we wish it would. Instead, we suggest that thinkers like John Perkins, Bob Woodson, Robert Lupton, and Brian Fikkert point us in a better direction. They present a vision of *shalom*—wholeness—for our struggling neighbors that incorporates their whole personhood into the healing process. Such an approach will require a revolution in our philanthropic models. Luckily, it's already underway.

One of the most astonishing facts of our time is that we have come to know so little about the way human life works that theoreticians on all sides offer solutions for our most struggling communities that are purely technical matters of government policy. Nothing could be more absurd. Communities whose sense of purpose, ownership, pride, and stability have been shredded over the course of decades must be rebuilt. There is much we can do by way of policy to make this process easier, but there is no policy that can generate—or even regenerate—the moral and cultural matrices necessary for family life and the social and economic networks that undergird flourishing. Nor should it! The greatest asset of any neighborhood is the people in it, and it ought to be *them*, not government or philanthropic planners, who determine and drive the rehabilitation of their own neighborhoods. The thinkers we mentioned above have instigated a paradigm shift in our philanthropic models along these lines. Some will lament that the strategies these thinkers recommend require wise, self-sacrificing people, deeply and personally embedded in the community for an eight-to-ten-year commitment per neighborhood block to see genuine stabilization emerge. Rather than persisting in the false belief that there is some faster, easier, simpler way, we ought to celebrate the fact that we have finally discovered an approach that really works. Neighborhood organizations all around the country are seeing lowered crime, high school graduation, jobs instead of jail, delayed child-bearing, and poverty alleviation through entrepreneurship. Shouldn't we be asking ourselves what they're doing? Shouldn't we become willing to completely revolutionize both our mindset and our charitable efforts to support what really works?

A. Charity Detox

Any of you who have stayed with us this far (or just flipped to the back of the book to find our solutions!) are looking for something eminently practical. In Robert Lupton's *Charity Detox* he lays out a step-by-step plan for how to make this shift for your organization. Starting with the Lupton Center's Oath for Helpers might be the best way to start to grasp how fundamentally our government and philanthropic approaches would have to change for us to see the sort of results he himself saw in the inner city of Atlanta:

THE OATH FOR COMPASSIONATE HELPERS

I will never do for others what they have the
capacity to do for themselves.
I will limit one-way giving to crises and seek
always to find ways for legitimate exchange.
I will seek ways to empower by hiring, lending,
and investing and offer gifts as incentives to
celebrate achievements.

I will put the interests of those experiencing
   poverty above my own even when it means
   setting aside my own agenda or the agenda
   of my organization.
I will listen carefully, even to what is not being
   said knowing that unspoken feelings
   may contain essential clues to healthy
   engagement.
And, above all, to the best of my ability,
I WILL DO NO HARM.

Brian Fikkert, author of *When Helping Hurts*, points out that chronic poverty is not just about a lack of material resources. It also includes a sense of aimlessness, unworthiness, and powerlessness. Simple provision of resources can *do harm* by reinforcing our neighbors' sense that they have nothing to offer. This is why the oath above emphasizes *exchange* instead of *gift*. Each person's dignity is upheld when he becomes a contributor to an exchange rather than a mere recipient.

B. John, Bob, and Lucas

John Perkins, founder of the Christian Community Development Association, was arrested and tortured in jail after participating in an economic boycott in Mississippi in 1970 (Perkins's father, a World War II vet, was murdered by a police officer). Perkins became convinced that whites as much as Blacks were held spiritually hostage by racism. His deep religious commitments led him to minister in the toughest neighborhoods. The organization he founded asks "practitioners" to commit to moving to an under-resourced neighborhood for at least ten years. To be clear, they are not arguing that anyone who wants to do anything for these neighborhoods needs to move there. Instead, they are saying that a few better-resourced and better-networked neighbors—supported by and networking with those outside the neighborhood—can empower those within to carry out their own visions for business, safety, and community. Practitioners break down the barriers of "us and them" by entering into the lives of their neighbors. Such people must be deeply in touch with their own brokenness and spiritual poverty if they are to avoid the temptation of becoming a "savior." This is what is meant by the idea in the oath of setting aside one's own agenda; our neighbors, not ourselves, must own their own process of rebuilding and recovery.

John Perkins identifies with, and his organization often uses, phrases like "social justice," by which they mean the special concern for the poor that is commanded in the Bible. In contrast, former civil rights leader Bob Woodson is a conservative and uses the language of the market to emphasize personal ownership. But John Perkins and Bob Woodson both understood the central insights of the oath long before it was written and proceeded to work with their neighbors effectively. By walking alongside their neighbors and teaching others to do so as well, they helped them manage their finances and become economically independent, own their homes and apartment buildings, and institute mentorships for the reduction of violence by gangs and in schools. It's not our buzzwords or our political affiliation that will determine our effectiveness at the level of the neighborhood, but rather our willingness to change our own approach in service to the truth. In fact, anyone who wants to be involved in such work should get used to hearing things that do not comport well with either of our traditional political ideologies. The acknowledgment of our history of systemic injustice against Black Americans does not imply that the solution to the problems this has created will be solved well in a centralized way. If the consequences have made their way all the way down to the institution of the family, then building back up will require real relational involvement in shattered lives, not just sending a check through the mail or building another set of projects.

One of Bob Woodson's central principles at the Center for Neighborhood Enterprise is to home in on the individuals and families he calls "social entrepreneurs." These neighbors have found ways to thrive in adverse circumstances and have been anchors on their block and in their schools. With more support, these grassroots leaders emerge as examples of what is possible for their neighbors as well. Similarly, Lucas Rouggly of St. Louis's LOVEtheLOU calls such neighbors "persons of peace." LOVEtheLOU has successfully stabilized the Enright neighborhood through personal presence, providing work through the community gardens and other enterprises, persevering with their neighbors through dangerous periods of violence, close and deeply relational work with the kids on the block, creating rent-to-own plans for refurbished homes, and providing connections with jobs. When a supporting church offered to fix up one of the beautiful but crumbling old houses on the block, Lucas made his neighbor Tawana an offer. Tawana has a strong positive presence and a servant's heart, and is known and trusted on Enright; she is a person of peace. If she would pay rent reliably for a period of years, the house would be hers, an asset to pass down to her children. In the meantime, the COVID pandemic hit, and many neighbors could no longer afford food or safely get to it even if they could afford it. Tawana's beautifully restored home morphed into a food pantry, with other neighbors helping to deliver food to 160 elderly and immune-compromised in the area. Which one is better? Lining up at a food pantry that's miles away from your home once a week to feed your children? Or walking to Tawana's house to help her make deliveries to the elderly and then taking some home to your children? Which one is more empowering? Which more dignifying?

People are not mere mechanisms. We can't treat education, housing, and income support like we would gasoline that we put in a car to make it run. People need to be loved, to know that they are worthy, to believe that something different is possible for them. People need *purpose and meaning*. We hope that this section acts as a reproof, both to conservatives and the toxic charity so typical of many churches and philanthropic efforts, and to progressives and the trap of perverse incentives built into our systems of government assistance. It's not enough that those who are struggling simply survive until tomorrow or next week. The hope of real emergence from a life of poverty must be made real. And it cannot be real unless there is a thriving local economy to enter, and thriving families and neighborhoods from which those laborers will arise.

Ask yourself one question before you close this book. What will you do next? What will you do to speak with intelligence and grace on our nation's history of excluding Black Americans from the rights of property, due process of law, and freedom of contract? What will you do, not just to criticize what doesn't work but to instantiate what does in your own community? Are you involved in charitable efforts that undermine the dignity of self-sufficiency for perfectly capable neighbors, and can you walk that organization through the process of shifting their mindset and strategies? Can you mentor a fatherless child, a parent who's willing but doesn't know where to begin, or an aspiring but poorly networked entrepreneur? Can you walk alongside someone who is reentering society after a period in prison? Are you aware of the organizations that are doing things the right way in your community? Are you learning from them?

Functional institutions are not built in a day, nor are they the work of one mind or one set of hands, but of many. Please, do not close this book without deciding on something. Read one of the books we recommended here. Reach out to Prison Fellowship to see what you can do. Call your ministry leaders and meet for coffee to look at the Chalmers Center website on effective philanthropy in your church. Look up the Christian Community Development

Association organizations in your city and ask how you can tutor a kid, mentor an entrepreneur, or a walk through life with a determined young parent.

As John Wesley once put it so succinctly, "Oh, just begin!"

Chapter 9

Two Steps Forward, One Step Back: The Crowding Out of Black America

"Social science is harder than physics!"
—Economist Glenn Loury

First, dear reader, stop a moment. Up until this chapter, we have dealt with policies that specifically targeted Black Americans (and sometimes others as well) and that did not fail to affect the majority of them. We now move on to issues—government dependency, family structure, the War on Drugs, and the criminal justice system—that often come up in discussions of Black America because, already occupying a socially and economically vulnerable position after Jim Crow, Black people are disproportionately affected by them. However, let us stop a moment and remember that these issues are not "Black issues" at all. Huge swaths of the American population, regardless of race, are affected by bad policies in these areas. At the same time, a growing Black middle and upper class emerges during this period that is thriving. While still dealing with the legacy of racism, these economically successful

Black Americans are not really the subject of these next two chapters. While we lament the story of those—still far too many—who have become economically trapped, we will also pause from time to time to celebrate that so many Black Americans no longer are. Now, let's discuss the Great Society.

Whether one's understanding of the effects of LBJ's Great Society is conservative or progressive can determine a whole lot else about one's attitude toward government intervention on behalf of the poor. We contrast three perspectives: conservatives' (including Black nationalists') argument that the perverse incentives arising from welfare programs destroyed the Black family; progressives' argument that it's the fault of departing manufacturing jobs and high levels of unemployment; and a third, more technical, explanation having to do with the way that the sexual revolution changed family structure. Ultimately, we think that both conservatives and progressives have some insight here but also badly overlook hypocrisy in their own movements. Before we do, though, we need to acknowledge that by the time the Great Society hits, Black Americans are starting to experience real economic flourishing, so that concerns about the least well off among us must shift from Black Americans to poor Americans, even if Blacks are still overrepresented below the poverty line. This matters, because it's unacceptable to perpetuate a stereotype that associates Blackness with poverty when most Blacks are middle-class and whites have always made up the majority of impoverished families.

BLACK ECONOMIC GROWTH

Before we delve into another round of dark reflections on failed social policy, let's talk about some good news. This chapter and the next will not really be about Black people, or at least, not the way that all our earlier chapters have been. Why? First, outstanding economic growth in the 1940s and '50s raised huge numbers of Americans out of poverty, including Black Americans, and this trend continued through the '60s as well. Second, the civil rights movement achieves several important things, not just the passing of the Civil Rights Act, but also a shift in the American ethos that increasingly marginalizes anti-Black attitudes and sees Black empowerment as a valid cultural goal.

A crushing 87 percent of Black Americans were living below the poverty line in 1940, but the drop to 41 percent by 1966 shows that the majority of the decline in poverty was already accomplished prior to LBJ's Great Society, due not only to general economic growth but also to the Second Great Migration from South to North and therefore from poorer rural circumstances to more opportunities in the cities, accompanied by gains in education as well. In fact, falls and short upticks in the poverty rates correspond quite well with the business cycle; periods of shock or recession correspond to a rise in poverty, while strong growth corresponds to a fall in poverty. The rate of Blacks below the poverty line continued to drop, hitting a low of 30 percent in 1974. However, it hovered there (the '70s was a notoriously bad decade for the economy) and actually climbed back up at times until the late '90s, when it finally began to go down again. Black poverty rates are now at a historic low of 20 percent, although they're still twice that of the white poverty rate (which has hovered between 7 and 11 percent for the entire period we just discussed).[587] Nevertheless, this is a huge gain for Black Americans, and furthermore, a full 23 percent of Black men aged eighteen to sixty-four have made it to the top third of the income bracket.[588] Today, with the majority of Black people describing themselves as middle class and living in the suburbs, it's absurd to equate "Black" with "poor" or even to equate urban culture with "Black culture"; concerns about grinding poverty are directed toward specific communities of poor people—many of which were always white (and now increasingly include Latinos as well), where high unemployment, low academic performance, and high crime rates also persist.

Recent years have seen a rise in concern about the state of poor (especially rural) whites, whose shocking rates of opioid overdose and suicide have now been lumped together as "deaths of despair." The term "white trash" has been a mainstay of American culture for hundreds of years, along with the hard-living cracker culture (yes, that's actually the proper scholarly term for Appalachian culture) derived from Scots-Irish ancestors of modern Appalachian whites.[589] What's harder to pinpoint is the cause of the crisis of addiction, imprisonment, and death that we've seen over the last decade. Increased economic hopelessness following the 2008 recession is a popular but not entirely compelling explanation.

Whatever the case, the issues of social pathology among poor rural whites and poor urban Blacks and Latinos are becoming mirror images of one another: crack and heroin in one, meth and opioids in the other; low marriage and employment rates, terrible health outcomes, and sky-high incarceration rates in both. In some cases, whites and Blacks are switching places, with fewer Blacks going to prison in the last few years and the decline proceeding at a much faster rate than for whites and Latinos.[590] At least one study showed the imprisonment rates for whites actually rising between 2006 and 2013, largely due to drug charges in rural areas.[591] For our purposes in this chapter, we need to keep in mind that while the issue of social policy in this period will have racialized effects, and although in some cases we have evidence of overt racism, we must shift focus now to the effect of state policy on *the poor*.[592] It's true that average Black *wealth* has remained stubbornly immobile, but most of the difference between Black and white wealth in America is concentrated at the very top; in other words, we don't have as many fabulously wealthy Black people as white people, but poor and middle-class Blacks and whites are fairly similar in their levels of wealth.[593] While in no way downplaying the frustrations and obstacles that Black tradespeople and professionals may still experience, we might say that at least insofar as their income goes, they have been liberated through the marketplace. As the conversation progresses, our focus on the least well-off will encourage awareness of the way class and race are (or are not) intersecting.

THE DIAGNOSIS: CONSERVATIVES AND BROKEN FAMILIES, PROGRESSIVES AND UNEMPLOYMENT, AND THE SEXUAL REVOLUTION

There is no way to avoid talking about family structure when we talk about poverty. As we'll see in a moment, the rise of single-parent households is absolutely central to understanding the poverty rate.

To sum up the data briefly, in 1960 67 percent of all Black children and 91 percent of all white children were born to married parents. In 1970, those numbers had moved to 59 percent and 90 percent respectively, then in 1980 to 42 percent and 83 percent, and in 1995 we seemed to hit some sort of equilibrium in the Black community, as the 33 percent in 1995 is now 36 percent.[594] Whites were at 76 percent in 1995, and are now at 74 percent.[595] (Latinos have now passed the halfway mark, with over 50 percent of children born out of wedlock.) While racial differences in marriage rates is important, class differences are as well. Marriage statistics expert Brad Wilcox points out that marriage receded first among the poor—both Black and white—and then among the working class as well. Today, the poorer one is, the less likely one is to be in a stable relationship or marriage.[596] While poverty has fallen precipitously, what remains is associated highly with single motherhood, and both poverty and single motherhood correlate with poor social outcomes for children. What's causing what is the more complicated question.

Conservatives and progressives have long differed on the most relevant causes of disparate Black outcomes in American life, with particular focus on the relation of single motherhood to poverty and associated problems. One of the most popular conservative arguments involves the insistence that government dependency created by the welfare state has been the major cause of disproportionately high poverty rates in the Black community. They argue that government dependency has disincentivized employment as well as marriage and fatherhood, leading to poorer homes and more destabilized communities. Any conservative worth her salt will be sure that the success of a healthy society depends on the stability of family life, and policies that undercut this fundamental institution will have effects that go far beyond the immediate. Plus, marriage is just cheaper and more efficient than single parenthood. Conservatives rail against poverty programs, not because of their costs (which are small in comparison to other programs like Social Security and Medicaid)[597] but because of their supposed effects. They argue that the welfare state has not only failed in its own stated goals of addressing social ills and reducing poverty but that it has also made the situation far worse.

Contemporary progressives balk at this explanation. The outcomes for LBJ's War on Poverty may not be thrilling, they say, but we've accomplished a lot more than conservatives would have you believe. Progressives consider the apparatus of the welfare state to be a necessary component of any compassionate democratic society. If anything, it should be far larger, along the lines of the Nordic countries' safety nets. Conservatives, they claim, are simply mistaken in their assessment, and what's more, their attitudes barely disguise their racism. Marriage rates went down as employment went down—not because of some social welfare policy but because of the exodus of manufacturing jobs that offered a stable job and income for Black men in the 1960s.[598] Suffering from the effects of overt systemic racism leading up to that point, Black men had very few employment options outside of the kind of manual labor that those jobs afforded. Conservatives, these progressives argue, associate welfare payments with their own stereotype of lazy but fertile Black teenage girls and their neglectful sexual partners. Dog whistles like the "welfare queen" and her "baby daddy," they say, are just ugly words that stigmatize poor Black Americans.

Finally, there's an economic and game theoretic argument about the network effects of changing mores that's less well-known and not particularly partisan, but possibly highly explanatory. In this account, the "contraception technology shock" of the '60s and '70s—first the pill and then abortion—broke down the social stigma for out-of-wedlock births. That might sound counterintuitive, since contraception, after all, is supposed to stop conception! The argument goes like this: In the old days, if a man got a girl pregnant, he married her. Everybody knew this, so very few women agreed to sex without a promise of marriage should pregnancy occur. There wasn't any use in a man trading in that sexual partner for a different one, since the new one would extract the exact same promise. So "shotgun marriages" reinforced marriage and partner fidelity. Once contraception became readily available, however, it was possible to have sex prior to marriage without the concern about pregnancy, which led to a rapid loosening of sexual mores. Women who didn't want to use contraception (or were unreliable in taking it) could no longer extract the promise of marriage if they got pregnant, since the man had plenty of other options for a sexual partner who would not make the same demand. So those women were under pressure to participate in the new sexual mores in the competition for a male partner but also likely to have a child out of wedlock.[599] We can add to all this the obvious social changes brought about by contraception, including higher female workforce participation and therefore less economic dependence on marriage. These strategic sorts of considerations can't explain on their own, though, the stark difference between Black and white rates of single motherhood. But it goes far to explain why marriage rates would take such a hit in the '60s and '70s, when, counter to the progressive story about unemployment, they took no hit at all during the Great Depression of the 1930s. (After an initial dip, marriage rates recovered quickly, and marriages made during the Great Depression were actually more stable in the long run.)[600]

While we've arranged this debate as though it's between conservatives, progressives, and no-nonsense social scientists, it doesn't actually line up that neatly. Some Black militants and purveyors of Garvey-ite Black independence, both at the time and today, have decried the welfare state as "welfare colonialism": a naked attempt of white society to engineer Blacks in the slums.[601] One central complaint of some in the Black power movement was the lack of Black capital: Harold Cruse wrote in "Behind the Black Power Slogan" that the main source of powerlessness for Black Americans is that there is no "black class of capitalist owners of institutions and economic tools."[602] Robert Blauner argued in 1969 that the greatest number of whites who would stand to lose by Black control of their own neighborhoods are the arbiters of welfare colonialism—"the social workers, the school teachers, the urban development people..."—an observation that tracks quite well with classical liberal class analysis, public choice theory, and the emphasis on cronyism.[603]

Some of these more militant or Black nationalist thinkers even spoke openly about the welfare state's effect on marriage and family life. Malcolm X directly blamed white welfare worker surveillance for his mother's breakdown and the breakup of their family in his autobiography.[604] Louis Farrakhan famously urges his followers in the Nation of Islam to reject government welfare and return to the traditional family. At a 2019 panel for debate between Black conservatives and progressives, rapper and Bernie Sanders supporter Killer Mike hushed the crowd's booing of Black right-wing pundit Candace Owens by reminding them that her complaints about the crumbling of the Black family aligned exactly with Louis Farrakhan's.[605]

So who's right? To repeat our opening quote of Black economist Glenn Loury, "Social science is harder than physics!" It's simply not that obvious how to disentangle the various explanations from one another, and most likely, the situation is what those in the social sciences call "overdetermined." That just means that there are lots of causes, and they are all probably contributing to the outcome together. In the next few sections we hope to show that all these stories have elements of truth and that it's often impossible to disentangle the causes from one another. We should always recall that the appropriate emphasis may very well depend on what region, state, or locale we're talking about. Progressives are right that unemployment plays a part, but often fail to blame the correct culprits for the job loss. Conservatives are right that the welfare trap plays a part but too often fail to apply the same logic when it comes to welfare for the rich (cronyism). They also underestimate how many nonmarried Black dads are deeply involved with their children. Both conservatives and progressives are talking about factors that simply overlap with the contraception technology shock and the demographic changes that followed. In a perfectly sincere response to Black nationalist concerns about white social engineering of poor Blacks, Great Society "community action agencies" were a genuine attempt to give Black communities real control of federal dollars. Trying to centrally plan local emergent orders, however, doesn't really work; either the dollars were taken over by entrenched establishment bureaucrats who raided the funds for their own purposes, or by radicals like Saul Alinsky who knew how to get paid to agitate against local governments but not how to help poor people build wealth.[606] What must we conclude? The only way to rebuild lost institutions of family, church, economic networks, and education is through decentralized, deeply personal and relational efforts that are holistic both in terms of a struggling person's whole life and also in terms of the life of a destabilized neighborhood. We must simply sacrifice our American desire for immediate gratification, because this one won't be solved by a push-button policy. We've got to be in the project of neighborhood stabilization—really in it—and for the long haul too. There are paradigm shifts in our philanthropic models that are already occurring and from which real hope and real change are already emerging.

THE WELFARE TRAP

> "Ghetto's got me trapped."
> —Master P

We acknowledge in the following section that rising unemployment played an important role in our plummeting marriage rates. A man who feels that he can't provide for his family, have a nice wedding, or even buy his girlfriend a nice engagement ring may very well delay marriage indefinitely, and a woman—even a woman in love—may feel that he's not good marriage material either. Conservatives argue that the rise of the welfare state also contributes to this phenomenon, and furthermore, they lay out why a plummeting marriage rate should matter to us—even to those who don't have a particularly traditional approach to social relations. This kind of thing is tough to talk about, because no one wants to return to the days when an out-of-wedlock pregnancy was so stigmatized it could ruin a woman's life. Instead of thinking entirely in terms of social stigma, we will respond to the conservative social critique by bringing the economic and institutional way of thinking to bear. What incentives are at play that draw people in one direction or another? How have we, as American citizens, set up a system that incentivizes middle- and upper-income people to set up their lives in one way, while encouraging lower-income citizens to set up their lives in a vastly different way? If that is in fact what we've done through the state apparatus, then it is we who ought to take responsibility for the current crisis.

The reflective conservative tradition (think Russell Kirk, William F. Buckley, or George Will) has always seen the family as fundamental. While classical liberals often have a more flexible view of what healthy family life might entail, both conservatives and classical liberals argue that families serve certain functions that could in no way be replaced by the state or even the proverbial village.[607] One need look no further than Aristotle's response to Plato's utopia, in which children were raised in state nurseries, divided up by their natural giftings.[608] It is better to be someone's actual cousin, Aristotle argued, than a son or a father in Plato's community. Why? Because natural affection inherently arises from privacy; the family members belong to that family especially and are loved as members of that family in particular. In Plato's community, the love is "watery" because to be everyone's son is to be no one's son. Family members are not one another's property, but there is an endearing sense of ownership: my dad, my sister, my husband, and so on. This insistence on the family is one of the main sources of tension between the realism of the classical liberal tradition and various utopian schemes. It is a mainstay of such schemes, from Plato to Marx, that the privacy of the family is seen as a competitor to solidarity with the state and is therefore dismantled. In contrast, classical liberals (along with Aristotle) see the family as the building block of the society, the most important context for the development of healthy citizens.

We need not leave the debate up to mere intuition, though. We have overwhelming evidence that the stability of the institution of marriage, having two parents in the home, and the involvement of extended family are highly correlated with positive social outcomes. Most broadly, marriage is correlated with a bunch of good outcomes for the marital partners themselves: they're happier in general;[609] have "better health, better earnings, higher levels of civic engagement, and better mental health";[610] they save and invest more; they drive more carefully and go to the doctor; and they feel significantly more stable in their marital relationship than couples who merely live together.[611] The correlation doesn't tell us how the causality works of course—perhaps more stable people are already more likely to get married. But it's no stretch to imagine that some of this causality runs the other way as well, that marriage actually brings about some of these good effects on average. The effects for their children are also significant, as being raised by a single mom correlates highly with lower education levels, lower income, and higher involvement in the criminal justice system. Once again, the causality might go the other way; women who are already more unstable might also be more likely to become single moms. But once again, we don't think it's a stretch at all to imagine that the exhaustion and overextension of being a single mom would be a major contributor to these outcomes. Our guess is that the causality runs in both directions for a kind of snowball effect of either positive or negative outcomes, depending on whether we're talking about marriage and an intact household for kids or single parenthood.

There is one outstanding study that can bring this point home without getting into every reason that social scientists worry about marriage rates.[612] In "Poverty in America: Trends and Explanations," three highly regarded economists—Hilary Hoynes, Marianne Page, and Ann Stevens—broke up the American population into household types: married with children, married without, single mother, single father, and, finally, single person, male, and female. From 1967 to 2003, every type of household experienced a lowering of the poverty rate in that group.[613] America was getting richer, no doubt. Real per capita GDP ("real" means adjusted for inflation) doubled between 1950 and 2000! But here's the really weird and counterintuitive part: the *overall* poverty rate still went up, from 10.7 percent to 12.7 percent by 2003. How is this possible? It is possible because the share of individuals raised by single moms went up so drastically (from 6 percent of the general population to 12 percent, from 1967 to 2003), and single mother households are the most likely to be in poverty.[614] *So even though there was a smaller percentage of single mothers in poverty along with every other household type, there were so many more single mothers in general, that it still drove the overall poverty rate up.*

This study drives the point home well, because it shows how family configuration can affect outcomes so strongly that even huge economic gains cannot eclipse it. Marriage is cheaper, it encourages more stable life choices, and it also just gives people the bandwidth to invest in their kids more, whether that be emotional, educational, spiritual, or otherwise. While there are many exceptions, it's a sad but unavoidable fact that, statistically speaking, kids born into a single-parent household are three to four times more likely to end up below the poverty line in their own adult life and are significantly more likely to be involved in the criminal justice system.

THE CROWD-OUT EFFECT

Economists are somewhat limited in being able to measure the effects that conservatives are concerned about because they can only address direct effects. It appears to them that there is no direct connection between a rise in the number of people on welfare and a rise in the poverty rate. But this isn't actually what concerns conservatives. Rather, conservatives are concerned about the nature of the poverty, particularly insofar as it is or is not *escapable*. To them, there's something really damning about the fact that the poverty rate has remained stubbornly around 12 percent since the mid-'70s, while we've spent about a trillion dollars a year on social programs. Why aren't a greater part of the population emerging from poverty when most everyone else in the society is doing better and better? And if they're not, is it because something is trapping them there? This is where the crowd-out effect comes in.

Crowd-out is a phenomenon in which the state (and toxic versions of private charity as well) ends up fulfilling the primary function of some important social role in such a way that the role itself disappears, taking its secondary effects with it. So for instance, if the primary function of the mutual aid society system was a kind of insurance, then Social Security took its place. In addition to yielding a very low return on one's investment, Social Security also unintentionally eliminated all the other functions that such societies served as a communal network: for employment, friendship, and moral education. An association of civil society such as the mutual aid society system serves as a sort of communal glue, helping people to know one another, help one another, stay connected to each other, and uplift one another economically. The material benefit of the insurance was like the tip of the iceberg that one sees poking out above the water, obscuring the massive glacier below. Once the institution is crowded-out by an external takeover of its most obvious function, all the rest of its benefits—many difficult to measure—are also lost.[615]

One of the most obvious functions of a father is to help support his family, but welfare benefits made it possible to do without this particular function. (Aid to Families with Dependent Children actually launched under the New Deal, but both benefits and the numbers on the welfare rolls exploded in the 1960s. Welfare Reform in '96 reined some of that in, but expansion of other programs, like disability, took their place.) In fact, while the requirements varied somewhat from state to state, it wasn't unusual for the law to require that there be no male parent present or that the income of fathers and stepfathers would count against one's benefits. The complaint that this would perversely incentivize fewer marriages arose immediately, although the causation isn't obvious from the data. Rather, we think that while the corresponding rise in unemployment is one cause of lower marriage rates among Black families, the availability of welfare had a negative effect—it reinforced less marriage by making it more convenient to go without.

We disagree with the accusation of William Julius Wilson, Larry Summers, and others that the welfare trap concept is unscientific because single motherhood continued to go up even when benefits leveled off or even fell in the mid-'70s.[616] The reason this argument doesn't disprove the crowd-out effect is that by the mid-'70s, the damage to the cohesion of certain cultural mores was already done; once social supports for the institution of marriage fell, the institution itself would inevitably suffer even further. We would concede, however, that our story of the initial rise in single motherhood due to unemployment, followed by the sustainability of single motherhood as a way of life due to generous welfare payments in the late '60s and early '70s, does not operate alone. Instead, the contraception shock of the early '60s and the ensuing sexual revolution made possible this profound shift in cultural practice. The point of including the crowd-out concept in our account is to draw attention to the way that cultural practices work. Once the state co-opts the role of the father then the sustainability of single motherhood under welfare serves to break down the system of social support for marriage. Promise, cultural expectation, and stigma recede, allowing the tendency to single motherhood to increase as children grow up in neighborhoods with very little marriage and suffer the effects of father absence.

Recently, Rachel spoke to a ministry leader in the inner city of St. Louis who said that marriage as a fundamental social institution had already disappeared by the time he started working in the neighborhood in the late '70s. Today, marriage is seen as a perhaps interesting but morally and socially indifferent option in impoverished communities, white and Black. As many Black Americans continued to emerge from poverty throughout this period, they took the previously established cultural norms of single motherhood with them, so that although only 20 percent of Blacks live below the poverty line today, over 70 percent of Black children are born to single mothers. Clearly then, single motherhood does not determine poverty. Nevertheless, it's an integral part of the story of persistent poverty and attendant negative social outcomes.

A FEW THINGS CONSERVATIVES MISS

Before we take account of the devastating effects of such a seismic cultural shift, we ought to acknowledge that doing so should not tempt us to make sweeping generalizations. The fact that mom and dad are not married does not mean that dad is not involved. In spite of the fact that so many Black children are born to single moms, 60 percent of Black dads live with their children. Assuming similar family sizes, that means that if 30 percent of Black fathers are married to the mothers of their children (or at least, were married to them and retain some custody), another 30 percent still live in the home, unmarried. Black fathers who do live with their children participate in the day-to-day of childcare, like changing diapers and playing.[617] Black fathers at home are more involved than white fathers in feeding their children, reading to them, bathing them, and dressing them, according to a CDC report on American fatherhood from 2006 to 2010. Unsurprisingly, fathers who do not live with their children are rarely involved with them in these day-to-day activities, although they often still have loving contact with their children also. This means that while those children who grow up with absent fathers will suffer in many ways that we are about to discuss, the majority of Black children are not in this situation.

Furthermore, in our discussion of father absence and its consequences, poor white and Latino children have joined the ranks in droves, although it took several more decades for the process to begin: 52 percent of Latino children are born to single moms and almost 30 percent of white children, with most of that growth occurring after 1980.[618]

Without such fathers in their lives children suffer in myriad ways. While contemporary people often feel uncomfortable talking about the differing roles of fathers and mothers as well as the importance of relationship commitment between parents, the data correlating father absence with negative social outcomes is so overwhelming that ignoring it is really inexcusable. Lacking a father in the home is highly correlated with juvenile delinquency, drug and alcohol abuse, suicide, teen pregnancy, poor academic performance, both childhood and adulthood impoverishment, future relationship failure, and future involvement in the criminal justice system. The psychological literature around father absence has become so sophisticated that the causal relationship between father absence and these negative outcomes can be traced.[619] This literature helps us avoid the concern that the correlation doesn't imply causation; of course, joblessness and involvement in the criminal justice system can also cause absence from one's paternal responsibilities but can clearly also be caused by the absence of one's own father.

While conservatives are comfortable emphasizing the role of father absence in adverse outcomes for the poor, they aren't always consistent. White evangelicals, who make up a core of the American conservative movement, are more likely to give of their money and time to voluntary efforts than any other group in America but rarely focus those efforts on mentoring fatherless children. Such efforts are more likely taken up by secular organizations like Big Brothers, Big Sisters. Further, nonprofit organizations that focus on Black urban centers often express frustration with the unwillingness of this crowd to help with job training and jobs for young Black fathers, even as they pour millions into other projects. We discuss the role of mentoring children and increasing employment more in our section on neighborhood stabilization. But just as we have asked progressives to take an honest look at the role of father absence in flourishing for the poor, we ask conservatives to beware of an attitude that says tut-tut but directs charitable efforts elsewhere.

If conservatives are getting at least part of the single motherhood story right when it comes to the government dependency that exploded after the mid-'60s, then they must also admit that government dependency creates similarly dysfunctional results among other social groups as well as institutions, both civil and commercial. Critics of racial stereotyping in the conservative emphasis on the problem of welfare dependency aren't wrong; the discourse has focused heavily on Black urban poverty. But the majority of welfare recipients have always been white, and the explosion of government dependency among poor rural whites has corresponded to a spate of joblessness, drug dependency, crime, and suicide in these communities. While a shifting economy can explain some of this, the persistent unwillingness to move for new employment opportunities, which would have reflected a venerable tradition of mobility in America, may certainly be a sign of the sort of dysfunction we're concerned about.[620] We can't gloss too quickly over the differences between concentrated and dispersed poverty though. This plays out in myriad ways, but just to take one example, think of education. While large rural districts will often encompass both wealthy and poor counties, high-population inner-city districts may have a contingency of 100 percent free lunch students.[621] If we think in terms of social networks, that means that the rural poor may still be exposed to examples of local employment, for instance, which the inner-city student may rarely stumble across as a matter of familiar experience, even if real opportunities for them do exist. The concentration of poverty in the urban situation will bring about some differing results from rural counterparts. Nevertheless, if one favors the welfare trap story, then it has to apply just as much to poor white people as it does to poor Black people.

WELFARE FOR THE RICH

Furthermore, if government dependency creates dysfunctional effects for the poor, then it necessarily does so for the rich as well. One institutional example of dysfunctional government dependency is the massive subsidization of college. The perverse incentives these subsidies created have led to high tuition rates, administrative bloat and waste, and a serious under-provision of laborers in the trades. While we've seen a rise in awareness about our lopsided labor market and more and more talk about the importance of the trades, as well as concern about the return on investment for college, we have rarely seen commentators treat the subsidization of college student loan debt as the source of perverse and distorting incentives in the same way that they've treated the welfare trap as the root of our inner city woes.

Moreover, corporate dependence on government protections, subsidies, loopholes, and contracts has caused massive economic distortions. For an exhaustive catalogue of such things, check out *Welfare for the Rich: How Your Tax Dollars End up in Millionaires' Pockets and What You Can Do About It* by Phil Harvey and Lisa Conyers.[622] We've already discussed the legacy of Fannie Mae and Freddie Mac in some detail. The famous Enron case works well too; many are unaware that Enron was an exceptional recipient of government largesse. Various federal agencies funded Enron's foreign investment projects to the tune of $3.7 billion. This skip-the-stockholder style of financing encouraged the company to make riskier and riskier overseas investments, since there would be no one to answer to if they failed. Such malinvestment creates massive economic distortions, sending false price signals down the chain that misdirect millions of other market actors. Research and budget analyst Tad DeHaven spoke with an employee:

> Bradley, a sixteen year employee of the now defunct Enron Corporation, demonstrates that the company was actually "a political colossus with a unique range of rent-seeking and subsidy-receiving operations." Manipulating the tax code, pushing for self-serving government regulations, and grabbing taxpayer handouts were all key components of Enron's energy empire. It's

not a stretch to suggest that in the absence of government, the Enron story never happens.[623]

Their manipulative and fraudulent bookkeeping practices arose from a culture of something-for-nothing-ism that their relationship to federal funding had already engendered. The fallout was devastating: $74 billion in losses to investors, the undermining of confidence in the entire energy sector (which delayed important projects), and a general fear that accounting practices couldn't be trusted.[624] What's worse, from a classical liberal perspective, is that the ordeal didn't engender a similar fear in schemes of corporate government subsidization.

There are myriad individuals, institutions, professional organizations, and corporations that we might have cited as examples here. Government intervention, though it may sometimes be necessary, can bring about massive unintended consequences, many of which the government itself can never undo. If conservatives want to be taken seriously concerning the welfare trap argument, then they need to be fighting just as hard against corporate welfare and other forms of dysfunctional government funding.

THE UNEMPLOYMENT STORY

Why does unemployment concern us so much? Because joblessness is so highly correlated with poverty and other bad social outcomes, like failing neighborhoods, poor health, and involvement in the criminal justice system. In spite of the popular stereotype of the working poor scraping by on minimum wage, 97.8 percent of people who are living below the poverty line have no full-time employment.[625] Widespread unemployment concentrated in a geographic area can gut a community economically, decrease the marriage rate, and lead to underground markets and other criminal activity. In other words, it's a recipe for disaster.

One of the most striking observations about the poverty rate is how well it tracks with the economy: periods of high unemployment correspond to a rise in poverty, and a booming economy with a fall in poverty.[626] In *Out of Work*, economists Richard Vedder and Lowell Gallaway discuss twentieth-century unemployment—really a new phenomenon arising from the shift from agricultural self-employment to wage labor in cities. [627] They explain that a huge part of this story involves the economic theories prevalent in various decades, and they make a good case that when bad theories won out, the interventions they recommended had deleterious effects. We really have to start earlier than the '60s to understand the economic circumstances that Black America found itself in during this period.

Surely racism and racially based discrimination was at its height in the period between 1890 and 1930, as we've discussed in previous chapters. We're also sure that for Black people, and even especially Black men, racial discrimination translated into extremely limited employment options during this period. And yet, Black employment levels at the beginning of the century were equal to or even higher than white employment levels. Black and white men worked at about the same rate (although for very different pay), while Black women were far more likely to work than white women. It should in no way be brushed aside that Blacks were often relegated to the toughest and least rewarding jobs, jobs they often had to do in order to fight to survive. We mention high levels of employment in this period because it's in such stark contrast to what happened midcentury. It's in the period from 1930 to 1950 that we see "the major increase in the nonwhite-white unemployment rate ratio, even allowing for adjustment for racial differentials in occupational and migration patterns."[628] So when economists adjust for other possible causes of unemployment, like moving from the South to the North where one might be disconnected from employment networks, we still see the largest divergence between Black and white employment in a period in which race relations were in many ways improving, and American manufacturing was still going strong. If neither discrimination nor a reduction in manufacturing jobs can explain the shift, what does?

Vedder and Gallaway show that policy makers during and after the New Deal unwittingly drove up Black unemployment by driving up wages. As we explained in Chapter 7, higher wages are wonderful for those who can get the job or keep the job, but higher wages also mean that the least well-off members of a society become impossible to hire because their labor becomes too expensive. Blacks were already disadvantaged in the job market by their historical relegation to only certain types of jobs, by racism from other white workers, and by the unfairness of the educational system. Climbing up from below, artificially high wages knock the bottom few rungs off the employment ladder, making it even harder to get started at all. There are five ways that this occurred in the relevant time period of 1930 to 1950—most of it a product of FDR's New Deal:

- The Davis-Bacon Act of 1931
- State legislation of "little Davis-Bacon laws"
- National Industrial Recovery Act of 1933
- The National Labor Relations Act of 1935
- The Fair Labor Standards Act of 1938

The Davis-Bacon Act appears to have been explicitly racist legislation. It required that all federal government projects pay a "prevailing wage," which was understood by all to mean a union-scale wage. George Will claims that "[i]t was enacted as domestic protectionism, largely to protect organized labor from competition by African Americans who often were excluded from union membership but who were successfully competing for jobs by being willing to work for lower wages." And he backs this claim up with evidence; here's Representative Robert Bacon arguing in 1927 for interventions to curtail Black and immigrant labor:

"Only by this method can that large proportion of our population which is descended from the colonists...have their proper racial representation." The congressional debate over the act was framed in terms of dealing with "competition with white labor throughout the country."[629]

The National Industrial Recovery Act kept wages high by insisting on very high minimum wages for any participating business. The floor of forty cents an hour, for instance, was "nearly 90 percent of the *average* hourly wage prevailing in mid-1933," meaning that it would exclude a huge portion of the workforce.[630] It's particularly odd that wages were being kept high at a time of such high unemployment. Letting wages go down would have allowed for the hiring of more workers. How can the market clear if prices aren't allowed to adjust? This strategy is one of the major reasons that the Great Depression persisted for such an unnecessarily long time, in contrast to similar market shocks, like the one in 1920–1921, that were followed by speedy recoveries.[631]

The Wagner Act of 1935 expanded unionization and entrenched union power among steel and autoworkers. By comparison, the Fair Labor Standards Act, with its minimum wage of twenty-five cents per hour, probably didn't distort wages much, even though it was more comprehensive in terms of the number of workers to which it applied. The section that required all employers to allow for union formation, however, certainly did lead to a rise in unions, particularly among garment workers and mine workers. If we recall that the unions both pushed wages up and often explicitly excluded Blacks, the effect of these two acts together on Black unemployment was unavoidable. Furthermore, these changes overlapped with the addition of national social insurance programs like Social Security and unemployment insurance, which raised costs for employers as well. As unionization became legally encouraged, the wage differential between union and nounion work rose from almost nothing in 1930 to 23 percent in 1941 and 33 percent by 1960.

Using statistical analysis, Gallaway and Vedder show that increased unionization was the main cause of rising unemployment, while the cost to the employer of social insurance benefits contributed to a further 2.2 percent rise in unemployment to the tune of 1.2 million extra people out of work. Combining rising unionization and social insurance, even the most conservative estimates place unemployment at 10 percent higher than it otherwise would have been. To bring this point home, think of it this way: if America had proceeded in a noninterventionist way following the 1929 shock, the Great Depression would have been over completely by 1936, if not earlier.[632] Increasingly, contemporary economists acknowledge this analysis of the New Deal reforms, but historians have not updated their own analysis, which means that there isn't much popular awareness of this version of the story.[633]

Who suffers the most during economic downturns? And particularly who suffers the most when the government response is to keep wages artificially high? You guessed it—the most marginalized groups bear the brunt. Whites leverage the power of the state to bid wages too high for immigrants, and immigrants use the power of the state to bid wages too high for Blacks.[634] People who have jobs do what they can to make them as cushy as possible, while those who can't get their foot in the door languish.

This is how a conflict theory approach to the economy will inevitably unfold, as each group sees others as their enemies: if you win, I lose. In contrast, the free market position holds that the free movement of goods and labor allows for creative exchange for mutual advantage. We can all win together. While dynamic markets often include painful transition periods as workers gain new skills, the freer the market, the more easily these adjustments can occur. Any legislation that makes it hard for workers to enter new occupations (like abusive occupational licensing laws) or to live within a reasonable distance of their work (like abusive zoning laws) will cause unemployment.[635] While short-term unemployment is probably a staple of any dynamic economy in which workers change positions more often, long-term unemployment need not be. It can also be stultifying, and widespread unemployment can create snowball effects for which there are few clear remedies. Strong institutions of civil society also play a huge role in successful transitions, as we saw in the way that the Black churches in the North helped to absorb Black workers coming up from the South during the Great Migrations. The loss of such institutions makes successful economic transition almost impossible.

As we've mentioned before, the artificial pumping up of wages is also a huge part of the story about the demise of American manufacturing. We don't mean to imply that the overarching economic story would have ultimately been different had we let wages adjust to economic circumstances: there's no doubt that a rise in global trade and a rise in automation would have eventually led to our current service and information-oriented economy one way or the other. Rather, the exclusion of Black Americans from the training and experience they could have built in these occupations meant that when the next economic transition came, some large portion of them were unfairly left behind. On top of that, the transition came too soon, as the union-driven high cost of American labor sped up the inevitable shift to outsourcing and automation. By the time the unions finally came around to serious talk of the integration of Blacks, the manufacturing jobs were already draining away. This is part of the "spatial mismatch" argument economists often make; as jobs moved out of the city, Black men who couldn't already afford to move were left with fewer options. So progressives are right that much of the story of cultural unraveling in the '60s and '70s has to do with unemployment, but they're strangely silent about how the centralizing ideas they champion were complicit in causing it.

THE LEAST WELL-OFF: BLACK WOMEN OR BLACK MEN?

Not just progressives but also conservatives and leftist intersectional theorists need to think deeply about the unemployment story. Specifically, Black sociologist Orlando Patterson asks us why Black women have outpaced Black men so thoroughly in education and professional attainment. Black women were considered less threatening to white employers, who were used to their familiar presence as domestic workers. This allowed them to enter the secretarial, nursing, and teaching worlds, and the knowledge of these opportunities in turn encouraged their parents to push them academically. At the same time, Black men were unlikely to have a chance in much besides manual labor, which in turn affected their own educational experiences. This might have been remedied if Black men had been invited into the trades, but we can't only blame the unions. We have a whole racist history of blocking Black male employment in any profession more lucrative or fulfilling than the menial. By the time real employment integration started in earnest, Black women were in a far better position to enter and compete with whites. They may have even benefitted from affirmative action programs at the expense of Black men, since an employer could check off two boxes, minority and female. As Black male unemployment went up, their marital chances went down, leading to the phenomenon of the Black female "rescuer" so ubiquitous today. While this role is terribly burdensome for many Black women, Patterson explains, they shoulder that burden through work, child-rearing, and participation in the church and neighborhood, all of which contribute to a sense of empowerment and meaning. He contrasts that with the experiences of poor Black men, who are also coping with their attempts to survive but whose outlets are often far less edifying. The result, Patterson concludes, is the toxic growth in the level of mistrust between men and women in the Black community that the psychology research has revealed. This adds yet another layer of difficulty to the healing of the family structure and community building.[636]

Conservatives, who are more liable to attend to the welfare trap story than to the unemployment story, can see from Patterson's narrative how much good jobs for poor Black men ought to occupy their voluntary efforts, particularly since a spate of welfare reform was already passed in the '90s. For their part, intersectional feminists need to address the greater negative social outcomes for certain Black people who are both *poor* and *male*, an outcome not well-predicted by their theory of overlapping oppressions.

EDUCATION IN THE ADVENT OF THE GREAT SOCIETY

We've talked about technological shifts like contraception, economic shifts like the availability of jobs, and cultural shifts like the importance of family structure. What about education? The desegregation of schools in the *Brown v. Board of Education* decision is considered one of the public launching pads of the civil rights movement. The "separate but equal" doctrine handed down by *Plessy v. Ferguson* not only enabled state and local governments to force businesses and institutions to segregate, but it failed utterly in its requirement that segregated services be funded equally. Local governments found many ways around the requirement, or they just flagrantly disobeyed. The NAACP litigated throughout the 1930s and 1940s to show that facilities for Blacks were either nonexistent or inferior to white facilities (including universities and train cars), not least because maintaining genuinely separate facilities that are equally funded is usually simply unaffordable.[637] Instead of requiring better funding, the courts generally responded to these NAACP cases by just requiring integration of the facilities. *Brown v. Board* was so sweeping in its implications and so disruptive to the educational order as it existed, particularly in the South, that it launched a decades-long conflict between school districts, states, and the federal government. Certainly we all can see in our minds' eyes the famous photos of Black children, some as young as six, surrounded by National Guard troops, running the gauntlet of angry whites with signs reading "Race Mixing Is Communism" and "Keep our White Schools White."

In a surprising turn, critics of the decision—or at least, of its wording and execution—have arisen in the unlikeliest of places: Linda Brown herself (the little girl whose family sued *in Brown v. Board*), as well as academics from the center-left to founders of critical race theory, like Derrick Bell.[638] While we can't go back and adjust the integration process to answer their critiques, we can think deeply about these critiques in a way that enlightens the current conversation around education reform.

The critiques fall along three lines: 1) the wording of the decision itself is actually demeaning to Black people because it assumes that Black children need the presence of white people in order to learn (Zora Neale Hurston argued this as well[639]); 2) the initial implementation was abusive because children were made to integrate a racist system first rather than the teachers, and the majority of Black teachers simply lost their careers; and 3) later efforts at managing the integration process, like busing, were mostly failures, leaving us with the system we have today. Our educational system remains deeply segregated and unequal because of the history of our housing and highway policies, as discussed in Chapter 8. Taking each in turn will help us see that the classical liberal solution would have been, and still can be, the best of all.

In one of Malcolm Gladwell's *Revisionist History* podcasts, he contrasts Leola Brown's motivations with the eventual court statement that emerged.[640] Brown insisted that her daughter Linda loved her Negro school and that the family was only suing as a matter of principle. But the court ruled that "[s]egregation of

White and Colored children in public schools has a detrimental effect upon the Colored children" and that "[s]egregation with the sanction of law has a tendency to retard the educational and mental development of Negro children." Instead of arguing that segregated schools are unequal because of unequal funding and facilities, the court seems to be saying that they are "inherently unequal" because Black children and teachers can't really accomplish a high-quality education on their own.[641] Contrary to this claim, however, we might contemplate schools like Dunbar in Washington, DC; P.S. 91 in Brooklyn, New York; or Frederick Douglass High in Baltimore, where working class Black children exceeded the white schools in academic performance up through the mid-'50s.[642] Apparently, learning well depended less on who kids sat next to in class and more on all the things we might expect: school quality and technique, school funding, and home background. Bell and others have argued that instead of appealing to the consistent failure of the law to create genuinely equal facilities, Justice Warren implied that poor Black children couldn't excel because they were only surrounded by others too much like themselves.

A Black teacher from the time period, Celestine Porter, argued that it was unconscionable that the children were sent in to integrate the schools in such a dangerous and hateful milieu. She insisted that the teachers should have integrated first and laments the fact that one of the first outcomes of integration implementation was the firing of Black teachers, who would no longer be needed now that Black children could attend formerly white-only schools. Even in cases in which the teachers' educational attainments far exceeded their white counterparts, they were fired. The count of Black teachers would eventually recover, but the experience of Black students left wounds. In *Acting White: The Ironic Legacy of Desegregation*, Stuart Buck argues that school integration put Black children into schools with teachers who did not understand them, like them, or believe in them (not to mention the behavior of the white students).[643] In the podcast episode we were discussing above, a former teacher from an all-Black school put it this way:

> Young people didn't have no business, didn't have no business being moved first to have borne the brunt of the segregation process. And it did something to the youngsters. It did something to them—it made them hate! It gave them a sense of nobody's here for me. And most of the students that they moved from the black schools into the white situation, we as teachers had been there to nurture them, to help them along, to recognize their difficulties, to work with them. When they moved into the white situation, teachers didn't know. They didn't know the teachers; the teachers were afraid of them.

It's tough to imagine Black children thriving in such an environment. And indeed, Buck argues, the negative experiences that Black children were having in integrated schools morphed into a dysfunctional association of educational attainment with whiteness.[644]

It's important to note that there just isn't any sign of this sort of attitude prior to integration; Black American culture valued education highly (as we saw in Chapter 3 with the communal push for literacy after emancipation), and those who excelled were universally praised and treated as exemplars. In "Graduation," Maya Angelou described the anticipation and pride, the wardrobe preparations and the refreshments, entertainments, and extravagant gifts leading up to her big graduation day. But the day itself was strange. The clueless white speaker, Mr. Donleavy, insulted everyone by mostly praising himself for the improvements he was making in the white schools, and then praising them only for the couple of successful athletes they'd graduated. His "dead words fell like bricks," and the mood in the room was grim; Donleavy rushed out. But Henry Reed, the valedictorian, gave a speech of deep intellectual and oratory power. He wove together his "tides of promise" and "waves of warning" with Hamlet's monologue, arguing with the poetry of his words that the Black students could determine their fate. Finally, Henry turns his back on the audience and faces the graduating students. He closed by singing "Lift Every Voice and Sing," and his audience joined him in the song. Many in the crowd were weeping openly. Henry restored the dignity and pride of the school by exemplifying its academic excellence in his stunning speech. His choice of the Black National Anthem paid homage to the obstacles that his classmates must constantly overcome, acknowledging the pain of Donleavy's ham-fisted slop, but rising above it with Black artistic accomplishment and soul power in the form of the song itself. We highly recommend that all our readers ruminate on Angelou's brief but poignant piece. Her brilliance exemplifies the Black American legacy in education.[645]

In one of the most interesting takes on the case, the father of critical race theory, Derrick Bell, argues that Black children might have been better off had the NAACP pursued a strategy that forced the court to actually equalize the funding and facilities rather than require integration.[646] This would have forced most schools to integrate anyway, since it would have been unaffordable to actually have two genuinely equal schools for each community. But even where it didn't, it would have given perfectly capable Black teachers a fighting chance at a more robust curriculum for their students. Bell defends his provocative position by quoting Du Bois: "Negro children needed neither segregated schools nor mixed schools. What they need is education."[647] Leola Brown wanted genuine choice and for her daughter not to be excluded based simply on race. The court wanted integration, assuming that Black children couldn't get a good education without it. And Bell and Du Bois wanted enough funding to give Black children a real chance for a great education. Choice, integration, and high-quality education are all good goals. But today, most children have no choice as to what public school they attend; that's decided by the school district boundaries. The "market" for public schooling is the real estate market. We already know that the housing market has been deeply distorted by our racist history, so basing our education system on it only perpetuates this injustice. Many schools remain segregated over sixty years after the *Brown v. Board* decision. Finally, many inner-city schools are notorious failures, both academically and in terms of safety and mental health.

What if there were a system that could provide choice, integration, and high-quality education to kids coming from tough neighborhoods? In fact, there is, but a mixture of privilege-seeking and ideology has obscured its role as the real solution. The classical liberal tradition provides nods to the concept of educational freedom in Adam Smith, Thomas Paine, and John Stuart Mill. Between the 1870s and the 1950s, the Netherlands, Vermont, and Maine all had some form of school choice. So when Milton Friedman wrote about it in 1955, he wasn't pulling the idea out of thin air.[648] Friedman, like a good economist, was primarily worried about the lack of competition in the system of government schools. Without choice, schools would inevitably be of lower quality (and higher cost) than they would if they had to compete for the funding that came with each student. He turned out to be quite right about this, as the worst performing government schools also spend the most per student, like Baltimore's outlandish $18,000 per student price tag. Washington, DC, has almost reached $22,000 per student, two to three times the amount spent in some of the most successful districts in the country. The assumption that such schools are dealing with a lack of funds is almost always wrong; it's not how much money they've got but how they're spending it.

Friedman was also perfectly well aware that the United States was in the middle of an epic battle over school integration in the

1950s. In a long footnote, he prioritizes integration over choice: if a voucher system increased segregation, then this was not the time to implement it. But he goes on to argue that it might not have that effect in the long run, by appealing to Becker's logic of the profitability of nondiscrimination.[649] You might remember Becker from earlier chapters; he was Friedman's student and wrote a book called *The Economics of Discrimination* in which he argued that given a preference for discrimination, some people may be willing to pay the price in order to indulge their prejudices. As a market becomes more competitive, it becomes more and more expensive to only hire, buy from, or sell to those of one's own race. This is why racists lobbied for Jim Crow laws; they were a way to create a government cartel that avoided the cost of their bigotry. So the chance of a better deal financially can sometimes pull people away from their preferences for discrimination because of the hit to their bottom line. This same logic could increase integration in schools if minority families are empowered through funding their children's education directly, creating a competitive market in which schools vie with one another to gain customers.

CONCLUSION: A PERFECT(LY AWFUL) STORM

This perfect storm of social circumstances first destabilized the marriages of poor Black families, then began to undermine the institution among the entire population of America. Poor white families followed in short order, then the working class of both races. The transition away from segregated schools was fumbled so badly that it soured some young Black Americans on education as a way up and out of poverty. The story of concentrated poverty among minority populations in inner cities cannot be told without reference to all four of these factors at once: changing ideas about marriage arising from the contraception revolution, rising unemployment due to racist and misguided policies, further deterioration of the family through the perverse incentives of the welfare state, and crumbling educational institutions. While poor whites were less vulnerable in some ways, that only meant that the process took a bit longer for them. The decline of marriage had less of an effect on whites who had always been wealthy, as opposed to the middle- and upper-class Blacks for whom the real chance at economic success only came after this seismic shift in social practice, leaving low marriage rates prevalent throughout Black America at all income levels. Poverty, family instability, and many of the attendant social outcomes such as addiction and incarceration now band together to undermine the success of poor and working class white, Latino, and Black Americans.

For many progressives the solution seems so clear, they become frustrated that conservatives continue to stymie their efforts. A greater social safety net will provide stable housing, guaranteed health care, a living wage, and decent schools. There's no reason, they argue, that the poor shouldn't have lives just as good and as dignified as everyone else, if only we had the political will to tax and spend to the extent necessary. This would be wonderful indeed, if it were true, but it is plainly false. While such programs are absolutely necessary for those who are truly unable to participate in the marketplace themselves, they have been equally destructive for those who can. Middle-class bureaucrats are among the special interests who siphon away the budget for themselves, while recipients' lives are micromanaged as they're strung along from month to month with little vision for a self-sufficient future. Individuals in destabilized neighborhoods have lost good employment networks and central social institutions that support healthy family life and hope for economic mobility. Failing schools, trauma from exposure to crime, and a high likelihood of incarceration have simply become normal. We must speak plainly: there is no clever policy, no cascade of legislation, no program or set of programs that could possibly repair the unspeakable damage that has been done. Instead, those very interventions have exacerbated what was already an uphill climb for poor Black

Americans. Sadly, philanthropic efforts have often simply aped government interventions in their style and substance, so that generation after generation of poor recipients of aid are taught to survive but rarely to thrive. This is utterly unacceptable. We must simply and squarely face the devastation in our poor communities and consider realistically what will actually be required to bring justice, healing, and prosperity.

The only possible solution to these problems must come from civil society, where individuals, churches, businesses, and neighborhood efforts can coalesce together to offer real, personalized, relational, decentralized partnership with struggling families in their neighborhoods. The rise of educational freedom has typified this kind of creative, local solution.

LOOKING FOR SOLUTIONS: EDUCATIONAL FREEDOM IS A JUSTICE ISSUE

We already know the story of segregated and unequal schools and the less-than-inspiring integration efforts that followed. Oddly, though, our chapter on housing and highways is probably more relevant for understanding our education issues today. Why? Because your school is determined by your neighborhood. The undermining of Black property rights, the (literal) ghettoization of Black Americans, and the racist slicing up of Black or Latino parts of town from the white parts of town with our highways—all these geographic factors add up to an education system that's perpetuating and increasing inequality far more often than it's solving it. Inner cities tend to have poorly performing government schools, so higher-income families rarely move there, keeping the area poor. Kids who go to bad schools don't find much success, locking them into poverty. And so the cycle continues.

Almost no issue defies our political tribalism more than this one. While "school choice" is associated with Republicans, groups that usually vote overwhelmingly for Democrats—Black and Latino Americans—also overwhelmingly favor school choice of some kind.[650] ("School choice" can refer to everything from highly regulated charters to educational savings accounts to full voucher systems for private schooling.) The issue is somewhat famous, in fact, for causing people to step across party lines in some surprising ways. The objections to educational freedom, some of which we'll review below, are largely coming from teachers' unions and their political bedfellows. But our education system isn't a jobs program for teachers. It's an education system for kids, and it's not okay when it fails as badly as it has been failing. Just how bad is it?

Our educational situation is fairly bleak in general, with the United States near the bottom in industrialized countries—especially in math. Those already struggling with poverty and crime in America's inner cities are in a state of complete crisis. Kids are falling several grade levels behind during middle school but are often shuffled through the system to graduate with elementary-school-level reading skills. Education ought to be at the center of any set of remedies for injustice, poverty, and inequality, since one's income and standard of living tend to go up with one's level of productivity. Sadly, going to school every autumn in America is associated with spikes in suicide, increasing mental health issues,[651] and shockingly disappointing academic outcomes.[652] Although most Black kids live in suburbs and do well in school, Black education statistics are dragged down by the poor outcomes in majority Black inner cities. But many inner-city schools demonstrate that—even with all the obstacles impoverished kids face—they do NOT have to have failing schools or poor academic performance. What's going on in these schools that isn't going on elsewhere?

Successful schools in impoverished areas stand out because they can control their school culture. They can hold high expectations for parents and strict boundaries for kids. They can fire poorly performing teachers and administrators. They can extend school hours and even meet on Saturdays! In *How the Other Half Learns*, Robert Pondiscio describes the Success Academy's rule requiring that the students have matching black socks for their uniforms. The point is not that it's so important for an impoverished student in the Bronx to have black socks. Rather, it establishes up front that the expectations in the school are strict, which enculturates the students and their families to a setting in which kids can really learn. It's important to recall that kids from especially chaotic and traumatic backgrounds can often benefit in an outsized way from a setting with extremely clear and consistent boundaries. Rather than feeling repressed, the structure at Success Academy makes the students feel safe. They can therefore enjoy learning, and their families can embrace a sense of relief that their children are safe and learning. This model won't work for everyone, but it's working incredibly well for these kids, whose test scores are through the roof in comparison to their peers: 99 percent of their students passed math and 90 percent reading.[653] Compare this to the dismal single-digit scores of comparably low-income students from the same neighborhoods. Many teachers there are young and nonunion, working insane hours. This causes a high turnover rate. While this is often brought up as an objection to the Success Academy model, it's not clear why. While this may not be ideal, a school like this is an excellent training ground for new teachers, requiring a high level of energy to educate populations from the most destabilized neighborhoods in our country, and it's impossible to deny the incredible outcomes.

It's true that not all charters achieve these amazing results, though they do have better or at least comparable results to schools serving similar populations. But perhaps even more important than the academics are the life outcomes. The sad fact is that many parents looking for better schools for their kids are just as worried about their kids being physically unsafe or getting involved in teen pregnancy, drugs, and crime as they are about academic achievement. We are now seeing data showing that charter school kids are far less likely to attempt suicide, be pregnant prior to graduation, or to end up in prison when compared with their peers in the same neighborhoods.[654] Any reader who is a parent (and I'm sure those who aren't as well) can imagine how precious this difference is. Being in a school culture in which learning is considered "cool" by one's peers or differences such as sexual orientation are accepted can make all the difference for a child.[655] Objections to the cultural differences in these schools often reflect the prejudices of the white middle class, who not only don't understand the stresses and needs of inner-city parents but who also badly underestimate what these parents are capable of when enculturated into the same sorts of expectations that suburban parents take for granted. Of course, one might object that these schools get such great outcomes by excluding families that won't reach their high expectations, and let's be honest: that's the point. To have a culture at all is to exclude certain behaviors and encourage others. Given the desperate and even hellish situation in our inner-city schools, we celebrate when those who are motivated to escape are given an escape hatch. Furthermore, there's plenty of data to show that those left behind in traditional public schools are not harmed—and are perhaps even helped—by the advent of educational freedom.[656] Don't let the perfect be the enemy of the good.

We can't address all the back and forth over educational freedom in such a small space, but since our argument is that educational freedom is particularly important for those "least well-off" populations that ought to concern us the most, we will address the claim that school choice is a holdover from segregation and is therefore racist. This argument arises from the history of massive resistance in the 1950s and '60s, in which a group of Virginians used a school voucher system to shut down the public schools and send white children to private schools (leaving no school at all for Black children!).[657] This is nefarious indeed. Nevertheless, other Virginians fought the voucher program on the grounds that it would have the actual effect of increasing integration once the courts forced the public school open again. Furthermore, educational freedom as a concept and as a practice long predates this episode, with philosophers Adam Smith, John Stuart Mill, and Thomas Paine sketching out the idea, and states like Maine instantiating it as early as 1873.[658] It's also a matter of course in the Norse countries so admired by progressives; Sweden, Norway, Denmark, and Finland all have school choice. The real question is what effect it has on integration today. Of course, the state of integration in the public schools today is very poor, since school assignment is based on geography, and the geography of where people live is often based on our history of racist housing and highway policy. While there's no reason to doubt that some people would use such programs to self-sort, the data coming out now shows that alternative schools have neither increased nor decreased the level of integration in schools.[659] Successes like the KIPP schools and Success Academy also show that Black and Latino kids do not need to be around white kids to succeed academically. The implication that they do has been a central complaint among civil rights activists about the wording of the *Brown v. Board* decision.[660] They objected to segregated schools on principle and because of unequal resources, not because schools with mostly Black students couldn't be good schools. These stunning success stories of alternative schools in Harlem, the Bronx, and other areas with failing government schools proves these activists right.

Finally, educational freedom is winning in the courts where, assuming the voucher or scholarship program is set up correctly, religious schools may not be discriminated against as recipients of funds for private education alternatives.[661] This opens up the possibility for Black churches of all denominations to take a lead role in providing schooling for inner-city children. Already a mainstay institution in many of these neighborhoods, properly resourced, the Black church could do for kids in tough neighborhoods what the Catholic church has done for many immigrant children. Actually, we should say that the Black church should *go back to* doing this for Black children, as the church was the central source of schooling throughout Reconstruction and in many other circumstances as well. The deep personal presence of the church in the neighborhood as well as the celebration of Black American life and history made possible by such schools would be life-changing for kids. We're perfectly well aware that such a turn of events would cause consternation among those who oppose public funding for religious education. We just want to remind those readers that their tax dollars already go to many religious institutions all over the country in the form of funding for pre-K schooling, Pell grants for college, and the funding of many social service provisions. There is simply no consistent basis on which to exclude K-12 schools, and the courts know it. For those who lament American educational outcomes in comparison to other developed economies, it ought to be noted that the Organisation for Economic Co-operation and Development (OECD) countries on average have 14 percent of their students in government-funded private schools, with some of the most prominent (such as Belgium and the Netherlands) over 65 percent.[662] The apparent apocalypse that will rain down on us if parents are allowed to choose religious schools does not appear to be forthcoming after all.

The upshot here is that the educational picture, so central for a child's success, is hopelessly bleak in our inner-city government schools. While the progress has been halting and there is no magic bullet, there is real hope in introducing other competitive models, particularly for kids who are dealing with malnourishment, destabilized neighborhoods, high crime, and personal trauma. This web of issues can be incredibly difficult to untangle, but it is simply unacceptable to continue promising that we will somehow fix government schools while maintaining the status quo.

Chapter 10

Prisons, Drugs, and Gun Laws: American Problems

In 1971, the US incarceration rate was about 150 for every one hundred thousand people. Today it stands at seven hundred out of every one hundred thousand. In fact, the United States imprisons its citizens at a higher rate than any other country whose incarceration numbers are on record. For the last ten to fifteen years, it's become more common to hear progressives, conservatives, and libertarians alike agreeing on the unacceptably high incarceration numbers in this country. While all three groups have disagreed on what got us here, a surprising overlap on possible solutions has emerged that has begun to make a real dent in the numbers. Some of the most aggressive approaches to decarceration have been led by Republican legislatures in red states like Texas, Kansas, Georgia, and Oklahoma.[663] There is also some disagreement among all three groups about the extent to which the disparate impact on Black (and Latino) Americans results from current or overt racism or whether a perverted system simply inevitably victimizes vulnerable groups, particularly if they're impoverished. Just as the social science on poverty can be hard to untangle so, too, can the data on prisons and policing. It turns out that none of our political tribes have a very good grasp on the causes of our mass incarceration crisis and therefore on how to shrink our prison population down to a number that actually comports with our current—generally plummeting—crime rates.[664]

We'll look at how each ideological group gets it wrong by blaming the things that fit with their political narrative rather than sticking to the data: the War on Drugs matters quite a bit but not as much as libertarians and many progressives think; contrary to popular progressive narratives, private prisons don't contribute much, but Black political officials have; and while it's a wonderful thing to find alternatives for nonviolent and "victimless" offenders as conservatives hope to do, they will also have to address sentencing for crimes categorized as "violent" if they really want to get our prison population down to a manageable size. In the end, adherents of all three of these political persuasions may be surprised to learn that it's our city and county prosecutors upon whom our current incarceration system hinges. The actions of these prosecutors are the main determinant of criminal justice outcomes but are deeply arbitrary, badly incentivized, and shrouded in a black box of noninformation. As we walk through these various points, related topics such as gun control and policing reform lead us to similarly counterintuitive conclusions.

Time to bust those bundles! If you've got a shred of tribalism left in you by this point in the book, say goodbye to it now.

THE TRUTH OF THE MATTER

To quote the first sentence of every book on mass incarceration, America's population accounts for 5 percent of world population, but 25 percent of the world's incarcerated population. It's jarring that in the land of the free the incarceration rate is the highest that's been recorded in the world, though we have no doubt that if North Korea reported its incarceration numbers, we'd at least trail theirs—a low bar indeed. The vast majority of prisoners are held in the state system, some 87 percent of the 1.5 million people in prison (the term "prisoners" excludes those in local jails). A particularly well-hidden population of incarcerated people are those sitting in county and city jails, many of them simply waiting to be charged, sometimes for months.[665] This number constantly fluctuates but hovers around seven hundred thousand. Remember, though, that this group of seven hundred thousand people are always different people, meaning that, though it's hard to pin down exact numbers, as many as twelve million Americans pass through our jails every year. That's a total of 2.2 million Americans incarcerated *at any given time*, with another five million under the surveillance of the criminal justice system through probation and parole. The United States boasts an overall incarceration rate of seven hundred per one hundred thousand citizens, while other developed countries cluster around the 100 to 150 per one hundred thousand rate. American society may deal with slightly higher rates of criminality than those societies, but certainly not five times higher today, as our crime rates have dropped back down to 1970 levels. No matter how tough on crime you may be, reader, surely there's something way, way off about these numbers.[666]

It hasn't always been like this. America's mass incarceration problems didn't start until the mid-1970s, and one might argue that they didn't really start till the mid-'90s. Why? Because crime really was going up beginning in the '60s and '70s, and at a terrifying rate. By 1991, violent crime had quadrupled its 1960s rate.[667] Even if we can look back now and say that we should have pursued alternative measures in many cases, we can hardly blame those who went before us for thinking that aggressive prosecution, more laws, mandatory minimums, three-strike rules, and other interventions into the system would work. Surely, they did contribute to the eventual decline of crime in the mid-'90s. Nevertheless, experts insist that we are very bad at actually grasping why crime rates go up and down (other suggestions include demographic changes in the number of young people, cultural shifts in family structure, economic despair, or environmental factors like lead in the water pipes), and so it's hard to know the extent to which all these efforts made a difference. The most damning statistic, however, shows that as crime rates dropped precipitously, imprisonment continued to climb, in some cases causing major overcrowding crises. This disconnect between actual crime rates and incarceration rates has stunned and confused the policy world, which became deeply engaged in the issue—from every part of the political spectrum—in the mid-2000s.

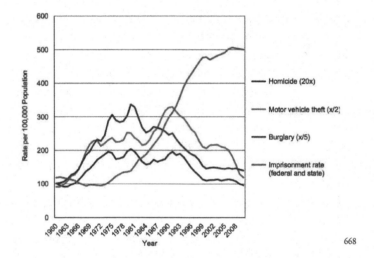

668

We do know some things for sure. First, young people, with their still-maturing frontal lobes, and young men especially, with their raging testosterone, commit crimes (sorry, young'uns, but it's true). Those in their thirties are far less likely to participate in drug crime than teens and twenty-somethings, and by forty years old violent crime recedes steeply as well. People tend to age out of crime. It doesn't make sense to think of people as "criminals" in terms of their identity. Instead, a person might be a criminal at one time in his life but is likely to be a fairly cooperative, law-abiding citizen later on.[669] The data for the "aging out" phenomenon is quite reliable, with studies dating back almost a century.

Relatedly, if we want deterrence, we need high arrest rates for real crimes, not long sentences. Future-oriented concerns don't motivate criminals, because they're young and aren't good at taking long-term consequences into account (remember that frontal lobe and all that testosterone?). What really does motivate is a strong possibility of being caught and punished quickly. Oddly, clearance rates—the rate at which police arrest and charge someone for a crime—are embarrassingly low: about 45 percent for violent crime and 17 percent for property crime.[670] We also know that these averages are dragged down by neighborhoods in which the clearance rate is almost zero, so that the sense among the young people who live there that they will suffer any immediate consequences for their behavior is, effectively, nil.

We really have to stop and let this sink in, particularly because there are decades of good, repeated, methodologically correct research on it:[671] *harsh sentencing does not deter crime*. Increasing punishment, whether by recategorizing crimes into more severe types and/or attaching harsher sentences, does nothing to make us safer. What could make us safer are higher clearance rates— swift and highly likely arrests with immediate, reliable consequences. The point bears repeating because it contradicts entirely the methods we've pursued so far, entangling ourselves in a system that is expensive, highly inefficient, and socially costly as well. Understanding this point up front allows us to entertain a wide variety of alternatives without being "soft on crime." It also points us to one of the most counterintuitive conclusions of our concluding chapter, particularly in light of the unrest during the summer of 2020. We need more (and better, and different) policing, not less police. More police on the beat brings down crime rates; this data is not controversial.[672] The injustice that infuriates so many is being driven by overcriminalization and mass incarceration. Policing needs to change, too, but not by being abolished. Also counter to what one might expect, this is both the conclusion of the experts and of the neighborhood, even smack in the middle of the contentious summer of 2020. In a Gallup poll conducted in late June and early July 2020, 81 percent of Black Americans and 83 percent of Latino Americans claimed that they want the same amount or even more policing in their neighborhoods than they have now (although Black Americans have a very low expectation of being well-treated by police).[673] Our critique of policing will be a matter of quality and focus, not quantity.

THE ROLE OF THE WAR ON DRUGS

Given the popularity and influence of Michelle Alexander's *The New Jim Crow: Mass Incarceration in the Age of Colorblindness*, it's imperative that we address the role of the War on Drugs up front. Alexander noticed the wildly disproportionate number of Black Americans in prison: one in three Black men will come into contact with the criminal justice system, but only one in seventeen white men will. There are about the same raw number of white men in prison as Black men, but white people outnumber Black people six to one in America.[674] She connected this to the development of the War on Drugs, which seems compelling since imprisonment rates went up around the same time that Drug War talk became central to politics. We have some evidence that the goal of these policies was control of Black men. Nixon's aide John Ehrlichman famously admitted that "[w]e knew we couldn't make it illegal to be either against the war or black, but by getting the public to associate the hippies with marijuana and blacks with heroin and then criminalizing both heavily, we could disrupt those communities. We could arrest their leaders, raid their homes, break up their meetings, and vilify them night after night on the evening news. Did we know we were lying about the drugs? Of course we did."[675] But we have other evidence that goes against that account. Nixon's tough talk didn't translate into very tough policies: his Comprehensive Drug Abuse Prevention and Control Act in 1970 "emphasized treatment and rehabilitation as well as *abolishing* federal mandatory minimum sentences for drug crimes."[676] Nor did imprisonment for drug offenses go up much under Nixon, or even years after his stint in the White House.

Perhaps the more damning point is that our system is decentralized, so federal policies aren't nearly as important as the local and state policies that changed, but many of those were run by newly elected Black leaders. Local policies in the inner cities that drove the rise of incarceration were created, in a high number of cases, by Black mayors, Black police chiefs, and other Black public officials. In James Forman's *Locking Up Our Own: Crime and Punishment in Black America*, Forman describes the rise of over-criminalization and harsh penalties under Black public officials in the Washington, DC, of the 1960s and 1970s. This book is heartbreaking because it describes in visceral terms the devastation of the heroin epidemic and the perfectly understandable panic it inspired in officials who saw their beloved city crumbling in front of their eyes. While libertarians have been at the forefront of calling out the failures of the War on Drugs, they can sometimes sound a bit too cavalier about "victimless crimes" and one's right to bodily autonomy. The facts on the ground for the leaders of 1970s Washington, DC, weren't so straightforward: death by overdose was becoming all too common, and poor heroin addicts had to commit approximately three hundred property crimes a year just to support their drug habit.[677] Forman records the stunning rise of addiction: from 1965 to 1969, the percentage of addicts in the city's jail jumped from a mere 3 percent to 45 percent. Heroin overdoses skyrocketed, and families were destroyed by their own desperately addicted relatives. In the end, the raw number of addicts in mid-1970s DC exceeded that in all of England.[678] The proudest and most militant of Black leaders were the ones most likely to become avid drug warriors, motivated to stem the tide of degradation for their fellow Black Americans.

The situation and rhetoric were quite similar in other cities like Detroit and Harlem, where Black leaders led an aggressive and punitive war against the rising tide of heroin. They saw treatment with methadone, which started out as a politically viable approach, as creating humiliating dependency. At the same time, they blamed the drug pushers for the terrible situation and so passed draconian punishments for distribution. Add all this up and you get a War on Drugs that was shaped and fought as much by Black local leaders with the best of intentions as it was by powerful, racist whites at the higher levels of government. While it is in vogue to say that Blacks with power are acting out their "internalized racism" against other Black people, the explanation that passes the Occam's razor test of simplicity is that Black and white leaders alike were legitimately horrified by the situation and ignorant of the consequences, so they implemented the policies that made the most sense to them at the time. It's okay to say that we screwed up and now we regret it.

And boy, do we regret it. The War on Drugs is such an embarrassing failure that the satirical newspaper *The Onion* declared "Drugs Win Drug War," a headline that now graces T-shirts and coffee mugs.[679] The war—new laws, new punishments, new police task forces, new equipment, new prisons—has little effect on use, as the demand for drugs is inelastic (it doesn't change much no matter the price), and drugs are readily available on the Black market. All these efforts cost hundreds of billions in enforcement, not to mention the intangible costs to families and communities. The effect on foreign policy is perhaps the most devastating of all, with violent, mafia-style drug cartels the de facto shadow government in many countries. After heroin came crack and cocaine, only to give way to opioids today. Very few argue with the claim that drug use can lead to addiction and terrible human costs. But it's now becoming thinkable to argue that approaching our drug epidemic as a criminal problem rather than a public health problem has failed utterly to avoid these costs. Furthermore, the power required to fight this war has become a source of deep corruption and constitutional compromise. The argument is not that hard drugs are not so bad, but that fighting them with laws and jails is. There has to be a better way.

While Alexander brought much-needed attention to this issue, and particularly to its disparate effect on Black Americans, she made a central blunder that has confused criminal justice reform efforts. Her narrative, what *Locked In* author John Pfaff refers to as "The Standard Story," makes the War on Drugs central to the meteoric rise in incarceration. But imprisonment for any sort of drug-related crime only explains 20 percent of our current prison population at any one time. It's true that more people cycle through on short drug sentences than on long sentences for violent offenses, and that means the War on Drugs accounts for a lot of people on parole as well. That's a huge number of people, amounting to hundreds of thousands, and ending the War on Drugs is of paramount importance. But even if we could snap our fingers and release every person guilty of a "victimless" crime today, our incarceration rates would still be multiples higher than what's necessary to properly address the amount of crime we're actually dealing with right now. The fact remains that we must rethink the appropriate punishment for crimes with clear, objective victims. That might make it sound like you're about to read a radical utopian treatise that recommends yoga for convicted burglars, but fear not—there are alternatives to prison that can do a much better job of meting out retribution and keeping us safe. And of course, prison will remain a perfectly appropriate punishment in the most dangerous cases.

THE CONSERVATIVE TURN

We'd expect a section on the conservative approach to the criminal justice system to start out by bashing their tough-on-crime mentality. While conservatives are well-known for their bluster in this regard, it's not really fair to assume that talk and action align. While Nixon talked tough but was quite moderate in his policies, progressives use compassionate terms but are just as likely to have favored—and even written—tough-on-crime legislation. Famously, Joe Biden is the actual architect of the infamous 1994 Crime Bill, which was then passed by Bill Clinton's administration, and we haven't forgotten Hillary Clinton's "super-predators" comment either. The more interesting thing about conservatives and crime is the mass conversion they've undergone in the last fifteen years, a conversion to the cause of criminal justice reform. David Dagan and Steven Teles lay out this fascinating story in *Prison Break: Why Conservatives Turned Against Mass Incarceration.*

Counter to the stereotypes, conservative thinkers and politicians have made a major about-face in their philosophy and policy of incarceration. Oddly enough, it started in the Nixon administration but not with Nixon. At the center of this surprising story is Nixon's special counsel, Chuck Colson, who went to federal prison for seven months for his involvement in the Watergate scandal. In the midst of his professional deconstruction, he became a Christian, writing his first book, *Born Again*, in 1976. But while in prison in 1974 he also discovered a deep well of compassion for the men he was in prison with, who he believed to be unjustly ignored by the Christian community. After all, weren't they persons made in the image of God, and didn't Christ say that if you visited one of them in prison, it's as if you'd visited Christ himself? Upon his release, Colson founded Prison Fellowship, an evangelical ministry to people in prison. As his work progressed, the buttoned-up churchgoers leading Bible study in prison began to discover just what Colson had: these men had done terrible things, but they were also hurting and lost. Many of them had heartbreaking backstories, and the experiences they were having in prison were not in general making them better, either, but worse. The issue was never whether or not they deserved punishment, but rather whether our system of incarceration was the best way to go about it.

As more and more evangelical Christians got involved with Colson's ministry or became aware of him through his Christian Worldview work, the otherwise deeply conservative group began to think more creatively about how these men could be handled by the criminal justice system. But it would have all fallen on deaf ears if it hadn't been for certain high-ranking conservative politicians going through their own personal conversions. Like Colson, Republican heavyweight Pat Nolan went to prison himself after being charged with accepting illegal campaign contributions. There, he experienced injustice and dehumanization that led him to fight against mandatory minimum sentencing. Conservative mega-donor Tim Dunn went into the prisons to visit and evangelize. There he, in his own words, "saw the fallout of over-incarceration" that inspired his financing of California's Prop 47, which reduced penalties for drug and minor property crimes. Michael Gerson, George W. Bush's speechwriter and *Washington Post* journalist, had worked for Colson immediately after his graduation from Wheaton College and felt that the experience shaped him deeply in his reform efforts. Nathan Deal, governor of Georgia and one of the most aggressive decarceration champions in the country, was moved to tears when his son, a judge, invited him to the graduation ceremony for successful second chances through the drug court he ran.

Dagan and Teles emphasize that such a break from the general tenor of conservative talk about criminal justice reform had to be led by people with real conservative bona fides. Pro-life, pro-traditional marriage, and fiscally conservative, this cadre of determined conservative leaders fit the bill. Soon, they brought along less faith-oriented Republicans like Newt Gingrich and Grover Norquist, men who had been avid crime warriors just a few years before but who changed their tack 180 degrees once they saw the numbers. The core group teamed up with Pew Research to provide detailed technical analysis and then helped to disseminate it through conservative groups like the American Legislative Exchange Council (ALEC), the Heritage Foundation, the Southern Baptist Convention, the Family Research Council, and the Evangelical Association.

Four factors played a huge role in the success of this surprising shift. First, conservatives' "law and order" instincts began to give way to their "minimal government" instincts when they saw firsthand that the system was expensive and ineffective. With a price tag of $80 billion and an 89 percent recidivism rate, they simply began to refuse to build any more prisons. It helped that philosophical libertarians like Charles and David Koch of Koch Industries and Senator Rand Paul of Kentucky were already deeply committed to the cause and thinking hard about solutions. Second, the sense of righteousness with which they approached the cause meant that they could give themselves permission to team up with unlikely bedfellows like the American Civil Liberties Union and the National Association of Criminal Defense Lawyers. Their coalition made ideological progress by emphasizing cases that would appeal to conservatives at places like the Heritage Foundation: civil asset forfeiture is an egregious abuse of property rights; the bureaucracies of the administrative state were generating new criminal law by the hour and undermining the fundamental principle of *mens rea* (a guilty mind, i.e., you have to be breaking the law on purpose); and the sheer cost of imprisoning or jailing 2.3 million people was reaching unacceptable levels. Third, prison overcrowding problems and state budgetary crises provided the perfect excuse to bring fiscally conservative Republicans on board with reform. Once their fellow state lawmakers were reeled in by the promise of savings in the state budget, they also became more deeply aware of how badly the incarceration numbers fit with crime rates. Finally, and perhaps most surprisingly, the fact that Texas and Georgia turned deep red politically meant that Rs and Ds were no longer in a fight to the death over who could be tougher on crime. With Democrats out of the way, no one would think a bunch of John Wayne types were being soft on crime.[680] Thus was born "smart on crime" and "right on crime."

In 2007, Texas passed its first serious reform bill, and since then, it has closed three prisons. With such a bona fide conservative state like Texas leading the way, Kansas soon followed, then Georgia and Oklahoma. Except for blue California, where the judicial branch forced the state to address overcrowding, all the leading state-level experiments in criminal justice reform have been from deeply conservative states and deep red state legislatures. Conservatives have abolished various mandatory minimums, allowed criminals to work off some of their time more easily, allowed tickets for misdemeanors rather than requiring arrest, recategorized some felonies as misdemeanors, passed the Prison Rape Elimination Act, defended prisoners' religious liberties, invested in reentry programs, cut probation, hired more officers, and piloted programs that provide creative alternatives to prison. If you'd asked anyone in the mid-'90s to predict our future and they'd said that Republicans in Texas, Kansas, Oklahoma, and Georgia would be the most avid criminal justice reformers in the nation, you'd have thought they weren't playing with a full deck. But here we are.

THE PROBLEM WITH OUR PERCEPTIONS

So some states have stopped prison growth and even reduced numbers a bit. Our prison numbers have shrunk slightly, and the Black-white gap in incarceration rates is closing as well. But we're nowhere near popping the champagne bottle to celebrate solving our mass incarceration crisis. The number of incarcerated citizens is still wildly out of step with what's required for safety and even for just retribution. Addressing this will take years, it will take an ongoing cultural shift, and it will take constant vigilance against our tendency to pay attention to anecdote over evidence. Unfortunately, our tendency to base our narrative on a few shocking events is incredibly difficult to resist, and with the rise of smartphones, the twenty-four-hour news cycle, and social media, it's getting worse instead of better.

Lessons in Classical Liberalism #15: Human Progress

We live, in fact, in the safest time and in one of the safest places in the history of the human race. Not only have we emerged from the regular-raids-between-villages phase of human civilization, we seem to have moved on from the deadly-warfare-between-modern-nation-states phase as well, straight through to the random-but-fairly-rare-terrorist-attacks (and hopefully we've left behind totalitarian-governments-slaughtering-millions-of-their-own-citizens too). Unlike some of the scholars who have become famous by pointing this out, namely Steven Pinker and his cadre of pro-Enlightenment rationalists, classical liberals don't believe that our future progress is inevitable. Human beings are pretty terrible to each other, and evolution doesn't work that fast. It could be that the threat of nuclear warfare is holding everyone at bay, or that we've all set aside our differences long enough to get rich off this new free trade thing.[681] None of that precludes the possibility that it will all explode again and turn back into the usual bloody nonsense eventually. Nevertheless, we are in an unusually peaceful moment just now, particularly in the developed, democratic countries, so we might as well enjoy it while it lasts.

But we won't, and there's the rub. Just like our visceral tribal instincts, that old fight-or-flight response moves us at a preconscious level, and the media-makers know it. The old saying went that "if it bleeds, it leads" and that's because we're wired to pay very close attention when we're in danger. We'll stay riveted to the screen as long as they stoke our fears and hatreds—contentment and benevolence, not so much. This is an absolute disaster for policy, which ought to be determined by good data and a sensible philosophy of governance. Instead, whole portions of the electorate will form their policy opinions on that one murderous immigrant, one attack by a felon on weekend release, one child abducted in a white van—whatever inspires an inflammatory headline and possibly a TV movie. The facts—that immigrants are far less likely to commit crime than American citizens or that the reforms we've implemented so far have caused no statistical rise in crime at all or that child kidnappings have never been rarer—will almost certainly get lost in the pounding of our amygdalas.[682] The truth is that your kid is more likely to die in a car accident because you drove them to the park than they are to get kidnapped because you let them walk.[683] Could someone inform all the suburban moms?

BLACK GUNS

When it comes to crime, drugs, and guns, these deeply human tendencies mean that we're very likely to constantly overreact to negative stimuli and underreact to positive. Our democratic system incentivizes politicians to play to those very impulses. Let's take guns as our central example here. We won't litigate America's gun control debate in these pages. Let's just say that there are lots of guns here. There are over four hundred million guns in America—more than one per person—and 40 percent of all American households have one.[684] We doubt very much that they'll be going anywhere anytime soon, even setting aside the entire debate over the Second Amendment to the Constitution. There's no denying that America has more of a gun culture than many other developed countries, and that means that violent crime tends to have more lethal effects.[685] There's probably a very interesting and complicated story about why that's the case (Rachel is Scots-Irish, and she's pretty sure it's her ancestors' fault, the quarrelsome bastards),[686] but for our purposes we simply take this fact of American life as a given. Just in case we needed convincing though, the contentious spring and summer of 2020 brought a massive spike in gun sales. By July, three million more firearms were sold than in a normal year, and Black Americans in particular saw a 58.2 percent increase in gun purchases in the first six months of the year.[687] The spike is the largest on record, and this doesn't bode well for those who were hoping that the United States would go the way of New Zealand on guns.

There have been so many guns in America, in fact, that there were never many legal restrictions on them, except when it came to Black people. Quite the opposite for whites, actually, who were legally required to own a gun for their participation in the militia in the Revolutionary period. There were dozens of total bans on Black gun ownership in every period prior to the Civil War, after which whites used the Black codes to justify bans, since the citizenship rights of newly freed Blacks were not initially legally acknowledged. We've already heard about the prevalence of gun ownership as a charge abused by the convict leasing programs of the later nineteenth century. By the twentieth century legislatures moved on to the abuse of gun regulations with racist intent. Famously, Governor Ronald Reagan passed the Mulford Act of 1967 in California, banning open carry in an effort quite specifically aimed at the Black Panthers, more officially known as The

Black Panther Party for Self-Defense. The Panthers had begun patrolling neighborhoods themselves in order to stem police brutality. Once they got wind of the legislation, they marched straight into the capitol, armed to the gills. The blowback was so bad, it not only led to a stricter law in California but probably also inspired the Gun Control Act of 1968. Ostensibly a response to the deaths of MLK and RFK, the act was openly touted by anti-gun journalist Robert Sherrill to have been passed "not to control guns but to control blacks." Legislators in the 1990s brought several attempts to outlaw cheap guns and ban guns in housing projects in what many saw as a covertly racist assault on the Second Amendment rights of Black Americans.[688]

Today, groups like the National Rifle Association, who supported the 1968 Gun Control Act but have been resistant to gun regulation in general, have been tellingly silent in famous cases such as the Philando Castile and the Breonna Taylor killings.[689] In both cases, Black licensed gun owners were shot at by police. In Castile's case, he informed the officer who pulled him over that he had a licensed gun in the car; when he reached for his wallet, he was shot seven times.[690] In Taylor's case, her boyfriend owned a licensed gun that he used to defend himself against what he assumed was a home invasion but turned out to be a no-knock raid by police. Taylor was killed in a hail of gunfire, sparking another round of outrage against police overreach. After investigation, it was discovered that the Louisville Police Department detective who applied for the raid lied about consulting the post office concerning "suspicious packages" delivered to Taylor's apartment; they turned out to be shoes and clothes from Amazon, and he'd never spoken to the post office.[691] The department responded by publishing pictures of Taylor holding her boyfriend's gun.[692] We now have data demonstrating that one's level of "warmth" toward a particular race affects the likelihood that one will judge a particular group's gun rights to have been violated by the government.[693]

One begins to get the feeling that the Second Amendment to the Constitution has never been applied in a very evenhanded way in the United States.

Even if gun control advocates are quite sincere in their goals of reducing violent gun death, though, they often fail to take into account the complicated relationship of guns and race in America. The success of the nonviolent civil rights movement depended on arsenals of guns. It's almost certain that there would have been many more massacres like the ones we described in Chapter 4 if Black Americans weren't so reliably armed; threats by the KKK were often thwarted by Black community members reminding law enforcement of their legal gun ownership rates;[694] attendees at early civil rights meetings were openly armed at all times to make sure they wouldn't be disturbed by their white neighbors;[695] T. R. M. Howard was armed to the hilt when he protected the family and witnesses of Emmett Till at his estate;[696] MLK Jr. kept guns in his house and was surrounded by voluntary armed body-guards everywhere he went after his home was bombed in 1956 (throughout his life, King maintained an ethical distinction between private self-defense and the massive acts of unarmed non-cooperation that comprised his struggle for civil rights).[697] What's more, if we're worried about the effects of overcriminalization on vulnerable communities, added gun control laws are one of the quickest ways to contribute to a racially disparate growth in our prison population. Black people are disproportionately represented (at 44 percent) in weapons charges, even though 10 to 15 percent *fewer* Black Americans own guns than whites.[698] Weapons charges are also even more overwhelmingly male than other types of crimes at a whopping 91.7 percent male.[699] Weapons charges are also popular for "charge-stacking" and parole violations, meaning that they constitute ways to increase punishment but are rarely the central legal issue. New gun control laws are destined to aggravate the overcriminalization of poor Black males.

IT'S MORE THAN JUST RACIAL DISPARITY

Conservatives may brush off such concerns by arguing that more Black people are involved in the criminal justice system because more Black people are committing crime. To a certain extent, there's truth to this. It would be unfair to the (also majority Black) victims of inner-city, urban crime if the system were to ignore their aggressors in a misguided attempt to make incarceration rates perfectly racially equal. But there's good evidence that, *even given differences in rates of criminal activity*, Blacks are over-policed, over-charged, over-convicted, and over-sentenced in comparison to their white counterparts who commit the same crimes.[700] The causes of this are more complicated than overt racism, though, which means the solutions may be counterintuitive. Let's take a look.

Contact with Police

- Strategies like New York City's stop-and-frisk overwhelmingly targeted minorities, and hundreds of thousands of people were stopped every year. Stopping and frisking with no probable cause for suspicion was discouraged after a 2012 lawsuit because of its unconstitutionality rather than its ineffectiveness. Nonetheless, crime rates continued to fall even after their demise. In fact, prior to the requirement for probable cause, nearly 90 percent of searches turned up nothing.[701]
- Black people are also twice as likely to be pulled over for "pretext stops," meaning that some extremely minor reason is used to pull someone over with the intent to pat them down and search their cars (and once pulled over, Blacks are again twice as likely to be searched). Police often word their requests in ways that lead uninformed citizens to believe they have no choice but to submit to these searches. It's important to note here that pretext

stops will always be more likely for those who are impoverished, as pretexts such as broken taillights or out of date tags lead to this kind of contact with police.

- It turns out that police are actually less likely to find contraband on Black drivers, and pretext stops in general are not a very efficient use of police resources, as they only result in finding contraband 12 percent of the time. Not only do such encounters gin up resentment between law enforcement and the community, but they also make violent encounters with police far more likely. Before his death, Philando Castile had been pulled over forty-nine times for minor infractions like failing to signal a lane change.[702]

- Since poverty and crime are highly correlated, it's no surprise that not just majority Black or Latino urban communities but also poor rural white communities have higher crime rates than the national average.[703] But it must also be taken into account that concentrated poverty and dispersed poverty have different effects, including the extent to which the poor are policed. In rural communities, people are spread out quite a bit and also tend to be geographically mixed with higher-income neighbors more often. Their illegal activities are more difficult to detect, and those committing illegal activities are not necessarily geographically grouped. Conversely, the extreme geographical concentration of poor urban communities, which tend to be populated by minorities, create stronger feedback loops for criminal activity while at the same time attracting more attention from the police, especially for low-level offenses like marijuana possession.

Arrests

- To the extent that we have data, studies show that Blacks and whites use and deal drugs at similar rates, and there are a few studies that show whites to be *more* likely to both do and deal drugs.[704] However, Blacks are four times as likely as whites to be arrested for marijuana possession, for instance. Meta-analyses of data have shown that disparities in arrest rates continue even after adjusting for "factors such as demeanor, offense severity, quantity of evidence at the scene, prior record of the suspect, and requests to arrest by victims."[705]

Charges and Convictions

- Setting aside prior disparities, Black people who are arrested are more likely to be charged than their white counterparts, all other things being equal. This is where the role of the prosecutor comes in, which is related to the prevalence of plea bargaining. Keep in mind the prosecutor is the fulcrum of the criminal justice system; although police make arrests, it's really up to prosecutors to decide what happens next. And prosecutors have an incredible amount of discretion. Furthermore, cases that are "pled out," meaning that the defendant agrees to plead guilty in exchange for a sentence lighter than the maximum allowed, always count as convictions. So prosecutors after a high conviction rate to please their voters will prefer plea bargaining, which is simple and quick for them.

- Coincidentally, by "stacking" charges that all have mandatory minimums, the maximum sentence allowed is sometimes absurdly high relative to the crime. If I purchase lobsters from Honduras that were packaged in plastic rather than cardboard, I can be charged not just with violating an administrative law but also with conspiracy (planning to buy them), smuggling (buying them), and money laundering (paying for them).[706] That means that the sentences that prosecutors can hold over defendant's head when plea bargaining can be incredibly intimidating, especially for those with only a low-paid and overworked public defender to assist them. The imbalance of power and resources between the public prosecutor and the public defender is a central issue for impoverished defendants.

- Because of a severe lack of transparency about what goes on in prosecutors' offices, we can only conjecture as to what's motivating the racial disparities. John Pfaff suggests that they might arise because prosecutors are more likely to be white themselves, but the fact that Black police officers are just as likely to rough up or kill Black suspects makes us wonder why the logic of this argument would be any different for prosecutors.[707] He also mentions the fact that prosecutors tend to be in a more comfortable socioeconomic position than those they prosecute; are white defendants less likely to be impoverished than Black defendants? The answer is yes. Even among those so poor that they could not "make bail," white defendants had an average annual income of $18,000 compared to Blacks at $11,000.[708] So although both Blacks and whites who are getting in trouble with the law are more likely to be poor, even out of the poorest of that group—those who couldn't make bail—whites were more well-off. The cultural assumptions that can accompany poverty could go far to explain why whites are more likely to have criminal charges dropped or to be offered less serious charges.[709]

Bail and Pre-trial Detainment

- In 2002, unconvicted people simply waiting for trial made up 29 percent of people in jail. By 2017, that number had jumped to 65 percent and had grown numerically from 182,000 people to 482,000 people. Across the country, Blacks are between 10 percent and 50 percent more likely to be detained pre-trial and are required to pay cash bail amounts that are twice as high.[710] These disparities remain even after adjusting for other factors that might explain them, like prior arrests or the seriousness of the charge.

Sentencing

- Even after adjusting for factors like education and prior criminal history, the sentences assigned to Black Americans who have been convicted of a crime are 20 percent longer than the sentences assigned to whites who have committed the exact same crime.[711]
- This disparity has been getting worse since a Supreme Court decision that allowed judges to stray from the United States Sentencing Commission's sentencing guidelines. However, while some of this effect arises from the judge having more leniency on white offenders than Black ones, it could also arise from the actions of the prosecutor. If the prosecutor chooses to charge with a crime that has a mandatory minimum, then the judge's hands are tied anyway. In fact, it looks like the prosecutor (and in tandem, the badly under-resourced public defender) is the central player in sentencing disparities, as Blacks are—all other things being equal—75 percent more likely to be charged with something that carries a mandatory minimum sentence.[712]

Time Served

- Finally, even if a Black person and a white person are charged with the same crime and sentenced in the same way, the Black person is more likely to serve out a longer portion of his or her sentence.[713]

While it is certain that some straightforward, personal racism is involved in many encounters between Black Americans and the criminal justice system, we see strong correlations with poverty as well, including in the white and Latino parts of the population. A significant part of the reason that Black Americans accused of crimes are experiencing some of these disparities is because they are overrepresented below the poverty line. In particular, Black poverty is far more likely to be concentrated in urban areas and to attract both over-policing of low-level crime (and thus longer criminal histories) and the stigma of the social pathology of the inner city. We also note how small racial disparities at each stage of involvement with the system can snowball into massive disparities by the time we get to the number of Black people in prisons and jails.

Aristotle once noticed that while well-being is clearly the purpose toward which our lives are aimed, we don't actually get well-being by pursuing well-being directly. Surprisingly, doing so can often make us deeply unhappy, as the happiness of this hour or this day often eludes us. Instead, if we pursue a life of balanced emotions and good actions, well-being arises as a natural and stable by-product. We can apply this insight here, where going at the problem of racial disparity straightforwardly not only fails but can even badly backfire. Addressing racism head-on, through implicit bias and anti-racism training, has proven totally ineffective in these contexts, as we saw in the previous chapter. For those who understand systemic injustice and its lasting consequences, this shouldn't be quite as counterintuitive as it first might seem. Just because disparate effects arise from systemic racism as a *non-prox-imate cause* (a cause that's a few steps back in the train of causes and effects) doesn't mean that anti-racism will do a good job of dealing with the *proximate causes* (the ones that are immediately relevant).

LOOKING FOR SOLUTIONS: CRIMINAL JUSTICE REFORM

Black Americans disproportionately suffer because of our mass incarceration crisis and the dysfunctions of our criminal justice system, so it comes as no surprise that the Black community would be a central source of activism in this area. But as all criminal jus-tice reformers know, there are really too many people in prison of all races, and too many poor without a decent defense, too many families and communities broken by unnecessary imprisonment, and too many people blocked from reintegrating into society after prison. The system of arrest, conviction, and incarceration is now running on its own bureaucratic logic, largely divorced from the needs of society for just retribution and safety. Some of us will cross our arms and ask why we should be giving lawbreakers any consideration. Please note that we're not asking for mercy in this section; we're asking for clear thinking and logic. A blanket condemnation of anyone who has broken the law will not get rid of tough neighborhoods with serious pressure to join in on gang activities, or hollowed-out rural towns hounded by devastating opioid dependency. It won't make our prison system any cheaper to maintain, any less corrupt, or any more sensibly aligned with our crime rates. It won't make prison an effective deterrence mechanism, and it won't reduce our sky-high recidivism rates. We beg the doubter to consider the possibility that we can make peo-ple pay for their violations of others in a much smarter way.

We recommend dealing with four major areas the reform of which could bring our prison population down to a reasonable level and heal the deep wound of over-incarceration and over-policing in poor, urban, Black communities and elsewhere:

A. Reducing overcriminalization: there are many things that simply do not need to be illegal at all or, if illegal, not criminally so

B. Rethinking incarceration: there are many charges for which incarceration is neither justified nor necessary, and alternatives are more effective

C. Reining in prosecutors and providing for a just defense; prosecutors wield an unacceptable amount of power with little accountability;

D. Refocusing policing: police need to be focused on detective work, and perverse incentives need to be removed; and

E. Creating diversion programs, improving the rehabilitative nature of prison, and dealing with reentering citizens; real creativity in our civil society institutions will be the only ultimate solution.

A. Reducing Overcriminalization

Many Americans are simply unaware of the growth in the sheer amount of law that has occurred over the last fifty or so years. In *Three Felonies a Day: How the Feds Target the Innocent*, Harvey Silverglate argues that many of us who think of ourselves as perfectly law-abiding citizens are actually committing felonies unawares. That's because the Code of Federal Regulations is full of vague, complicated, and highly technical rules that are both difficult to understand and impossible for one person to even know. In fact, no one actually knows how many laws are on the federal books, but after a two-year investigation, one group estimated them at about three thousand (you can follow "A Crime a Day" on Twitter to see just how absurd many of these laws are).[714]

The Federal Regulatory Code just passed one million restrictions, and more new ones are added every day.[715] While this might seem like a white-collar problem, it absolutely is not. Anyone trying to start even the smallest of businesses can run afoul of these types of rules. One of the gravest concerns around this explosion of administrative law is that the *mens rea* requirement in our common law tradition—the reasonable assumption that a person should have been aware of the criminality of their act—is being entirely undermined.[716] There is absolutely no way that we can be aware of this much law, and those with the least resources will be the most vulnerable to abuse that results from their ignorance. Congress ought to undertake the project of majorly simplifying the code and creating a committee that limits new additions.

State and local laws only add more layers onto this orgy of legislation (although administrative law is actually created by agencies that Congress created, not Congress itself). Occupational licensing has grown from one in twenty workers requiring a license to one in three, creating a firestorm of bipartisan backlash.[717] People want to be able to braid and shampoo hair without going to cosmetology school, be a barber without having to have a high school diploma, make pine box caskets without being a registered funeral home, arrange flowers or install home entertainment systems without going through a complicated and expensive licensing process. In 2010, a police SWAT team raided a barbershop, arresting thirty-four people for "barbering without a license."[718] Unnecessary licensing requirements play to established interests while crushing poor entrepreneurs. It's these unnecessary requirements that ought to be crushed. For necessary ones like nursing, teaching, and dentistry, consider Arizona's recently passed law accepting licenses from all other states. This makes it much easier for these workers to move to where the jobs are.

By far the most damaging set of laws for high arrest rates, over-incarceration, and negative relationships with the police, however, are drug laws. The comparison to alcohol, which is perfectly legal, is telling: those who die from excessive alcohol use add up to about ninety-five thousand people per year, with another ten thousand a year dying in drunk-driving accidents. Drug overdoses stand around sixty-seven thousand per year (and we're pretty sure not one of these was from marijuana). Nevertheless, we treat alcoholism as a medical issue but use punitive measures to address drug problems. This costs billions of dollars, erodes Fourth Amendment rights, gins up hatred and resentment between police and the community, feeds into police corruption, and disproportionately harms poor and minority users over citizens who are just as likely to use drugs—that is, wealthier white people. Given that the War on Drugs has had little effect on drug use (not to mention the devastating effects on foreign policy), there is absolutely no case for continuing it. The War on Drugs should end, full stop. Selling, buying, and using drugs ought to be a legal activity, and some of the resources once dedicated to the enforcement of drug laws can be funneled into effective treatment instead. If a total end to the war is too much to swallow, at least consider cooling the war by changing the seriousness of the offenses so that people are ticketed, for instance, rather than jailed.[719]

Many states have made real progress by reassessing the necessity of punitive measures. They've followed sentencing guidelines to avoid uselessly long sentences, downgraded some felonies to misdemeanors, reconsidered the thresholds for property crimes, and allowed misdemeanors to be dealt with by ticket instead of jail. Thinking creatively, we should take this kind of reassessment even further, as some crimes should just be torts. That is, some offenses, like theft, should be handled in civil courts instead of criminal courts, with monetary awards rather than prison as the punishment. That's because we are in many cases victimizing crime victims again; first, the thief steals their goods, and second, we make them (and all of us) pay for the thief's room and board! How much better would it be if such offenses were focused on making the victim whole by making thieves pay them back, with damages. Not only does this help rather than harm the victim, but the thief really does pay off his or her debt to that person and to society in a tangible, redemptive way that dignifies him. There are various ways this could be accomplished, such as with the use of oversight by ankle monitors for those offenders who go to work. For those who do not have a job, we should eliminate the practice of using near-zero wage labor for prison-made goods—a corrupt form of cronyism anyway. Instead, we should require that all are paid a market wage but garnish the wages to pay victims restitution. Those who committed crimes that we are suggesting ought to be torts could still live outside of prison, as they are no real danger to the rest of us, but will be provided with the job that allows them to pay restitution. This plan could apply to even violent crimes like assault since there are reasonable ways of knowing whether someone is a genuine danger to society or lashed out in a passion and is unlikely to do so again. When it comes to victimless crimes that we haven't already eradicated, we can be careful about perverse incentives by being as straightforward as possible. Damages rulings against drunk drivers and smugglers, for instance, can simply go back to the taxpayers in the form of a credit.

One perverse incentive that must be addressed is that the people sending an offender to prison aren't the people paying for him to be there. Usually, cities and counties arrest and convict, but states imprison. This means that cities and counties have no incentive to minimize the prison population. While it's probably impossible for cities and counties to pay for all their own citizens' incarceration (urban areas always generate more crime due to concentrated poverty), there are probably ways to align these incentives somewhat more by requiring that some percentage be paid by the locality of origin. But while we're talking about incentives, Chris Surprenant and Jason Brennan, authors of *Injustice for All*, suggest an even more straightforward solution. Make prisons compete to fill beds (and thus get the funding) by allowing prisoners to choose their prison. And even better than that, create bonuses for generating ex-offenders who do not recidivate within a set amount of time. Incentives matter, and they work. In no time, you'll be seeing prisons create better rehabilitation and reentry programs and crack down on corruption among guards.

B. Rethinking Incarceration

America is strangely focused on incarceration; it seems to be our one solution for practically everything. In fact, it ought to be a last resort, reserved for only the most dangerous criminals. This has been better understood in recent years, as states have experimented with diversion programs, alternative sentencing measures, and creative uses of probation and parole. First, for most crimes, the actual prison experience is genuinely cruel and unusual. Inmates are subject to separation from family and community, personal degradation, continued (or even novel) alcohol and drug addiction and abuse, their hopes of decent future employment dashed, their voting and gun rights gone forever, and subjection to violence and rape from truly dangerous inmates. Furthermore, it is now well known not only that the threat of prison fails to deter crime, but that prison often increases antisocial tendencies and hones criminal skills. Finally, many innocent bystanders are deeply traumatized as well—mothers, wives, children, and whole communities that are hollowed out physically, economically, and psychologically because many men are gone. The status quo is a powerful thing, but ask yourself: How does it make sense for us to spend billions of dollars to house and feed people while making both them and the communities they come from morally worse? It doesn't. In a somewhat tongue-in-cheek thought experiment, Suprenant and Brennan ask whether you'd prefer to be caned eight times or serve an eight-year sentence in prison. Everyone would prefer to be caned! And yet we consider caning a cruel and unusual punishment. The point of the thought experiment is to show that we all know prison is an inhumane punishment for many crimes. We just don't think about it because we're so used to it.

There are many hopeful alternatives to prison for those who are unlikely to be a danger to the community and that encourage offenders to rehabilitate themselves and their communal relationships. This leads to far more productive lives and more safety and peace for the rest of us. The wonderful thing is that the United States has a federal system, so many experiments at the local and state level can pave the way for other localities to follow. In *Ending Overcriminalization and Mass Incarceration: Hope from Civil Society*, theologian and criminal justice reform advocate Anthony Bradley runs through various experiments in several states. "Second Chance" laws allow first-time offenders to expunge their record, reducing the likelihood that they will recidivate by making it easier to get a job upon reentry.[720] Juvenile offenders have been successfully redirected to their family or community services rather than juvenile detention centers, bringing recidivism rates way down. Parole and probation reform can divert more people into alternatives for minor parole violations rather than sending them back to prison. Drug courts and veterans' courts can require strict adherence to a program of action while allowing offenders to live at home and work. These courts also have the advantage of increasing the sense of dignity of the offender by essentially saying, "Our standards are high, but we know that you will be able to do it," as Claude Steele suggests in his seminal work, *Whistling Vivaldi*. In contrast, simply passing time in a prison does not offer any sense of accomplishment by requiring something substantive. Those closer to the end of their sentences have been transferred to reentry programs as a kind of halfway house. There are also effective methods for separating offenders into categories of low, moderate, and high risk, which could help determine who should be funneled into such alternatives. Improved addiction treatment and expansion of educational opportunities have reduced populations by allowing for early release and shortened stints on parole. It's worth noting how changes in Texas affected the prison population: not only did it start to shrink, but the makeup of the population shifted, "with more dangerous offenders (those we fear) in custody and less of the 'knuckleheads' (that make us mad)."[721]

Oh, and end cash bail. There are hundreds of thousands of people sitting in jail right now who haven't even been charged with a crime. They just don't have the money to pay their bail, so they are waiting for their court date. That's just criminalizing poverty. End it.[722]

C. Rein in Prosecutors and Fund Criminal Defense Attorneys

The wide discretion of the prosecutor makes her the central figure in the drama of our criminal justice system. She has the most power, the most leeway, and the most influence on the outcomes for those involved in the system. We often hear the phrase "do the crime, do the time" but that is far from the reality of our system. Instead, conviction, sentencing, and time served fluctuate wildly between similar cases, undermining the confidence of the community in the justice of the system. Plea bargaining has practically done away with our system of trial by jury, and the prosecutor is terribly incentivized to get a high conviction rate no matter what.[723] There have been many suggestions about how to address this, from gathering more data on what goes on in the prosecutor's office, to appointing them rather than electing them, to dumping more funding into the woefully underpaid and understaffed criminal defense attorneys' efforts. Alternatively, Surprenant and Brennan suggest cutting through all of this mess of perverse incentives and failure to provide justice for the poor by a complete—but quite simple—reordering of our system: "Instead of having a pool of prosecutors, we have instead a pool of public attorneys, with equal pay and equal access to resources.

In any given case, a public attorney could be assigned to either a prosecutorial role or a defense role. Promotions might be based on winning, but in this case, any attorney up for promotion will want to garner 'wins' as defense, not just as prosecutor."[724] Or, they suggest, accomplish the same thing but just hand out cases to private attorneys according to a rationally devised fee schedule. Whatever we do, we cannot allow poor people to be treated with different standards than middle- and upper-income citizens are. Even in the narrowest sense of the word "justice," that ain't it.

D. Reforming Police

We know for sure that more police on the beat is one of the most effective ways to reduce crime in destabilized communities. But we also know that the relationship between police and the community has always been touchy at best but has been deteriorating badly in the last thirty years. And that's not just a random number; check out Radley Balko's *Rise of the Warrior Cop* to see how much policing has changed since the '90s. A new approach arose, characterized by the rise of SWAT in almost every department, grants to purchase military gear and equipment, and so-called "hot spot" and "broken windows" policing styles, which use harassment of community members to flush out real crime. People, especially marginalized people, want police in their neighborhoods[725]—just not like this.[726]

We already saw that many of the reforms people often discuss around policing are abject failures, including a whole lot of faddish new training programs, which creates a cottage industry for the trainers but makes no discernible difference in police conduct. When it comes to police, we maintain the same logic we've used on politicians, prosecutors, and citizens; they're not generally better or worse people than anybody else, but they are badly incentivized. Of course, much of the tension between police and community will go away when we reduce overcriminalization, especially the War on Drugs. On top of that, though, there are several reforms that are absolutely nonnegotiable, and others that we think are deeply interesting. As to the nonnegotiables:

1. We must end qualified immunity—a bizarre judge-made law that disallows civil lawsuits for violations of civil rights unless the case is exactly like some earlier case.[727] Instead, police can have malpractice insurance just like other professions do. Qualified immunity is not only legally nonsensical, it is deeply unjust, and creates a moral hazard by removing legal responsibility for police violations of civil rights. The legislature should abolish it.

2. We must find ways to reduce the power of or eliminate police unions. There's nothing wrong with government employees vying for decent benefits. But police unions have become deeply corrupt, massively powerful political lobbies, and they stack the entire deck against anyone who accuses a police officer, as the officer has the whole legal force of the union behind him. When Camden, New Jersey, disbanded their police department and joined the broader county's department instead, it freed them from their contract with the police union. Some of these changes were budgetary; the unions required a trained police officer to do work that could be done by a receptionist, for instance. But they also dealt with brutality and failure to stem crime: the officers had to reapply to work for the county and were subject to new psychological evaluation and training. The budgetary savings were then reinvested in more officers, and crime went down significantly.[728]

3. End taxation by citation and civil asset forfeiture, i.e., policing for profit. While traffic tickets create a lot of revenue, as a form of crime prevention they are a terrible waste of police officers' time; far fewer tickets are

necessary to truly keep people at safe speeds; they are a fount of unnecessarily negative contact with community members; and they set up poor community members for far deeper problems when unpaid tickets turn into arrest warrants, arrest warrants turn into a bail they can't afford, and stints in jail turn into lost employment. Many departments rely on traffic tickets in their budget, and if that's made illegal, they'll start ticketing you for having a basketball hoop in your front yard—just ask the people of Pagedale, Missouri.[729] So we really need to rethink how we finance our police departments entirely. Police themselves are not the ones emphasizing tickets; it's their city managers. In fact, police have consistently expressed discomfort with the pressure from above to write more tickets.

4. Civil asset forfeiture provides another deeply corrupt source of income for departments. In these cases, property that is even suspected of being involved with a crime can be confiscated, such as cars, large amounts of cash, or even entire homes. Not only is this practice legally outrageous—no one has to be convicted of a crime for the confiscation to occur, and it can be incredibly difficult and expensive to recover one's property, making it useless for the poor to even try—but the perverse incentives have also badly corrupted police tactics. In one story, police were targeting only one side of a highway because the cars coming in that direction might have cash gained from their drug deals in a nearby city. If they had targeted the other side of the highway heading toward the city, they might have found, you know, the drugs...but that wouldn't have been nearly as lucrative.[730] We ought to rein in taxation by citation and civil asset forfeiture while we work hard to fund police departments directly so that they can focus on effective police work rather

than on being forced to pay the bills by bilking our most vulnerable citizens.

5. Demilitarize the police. One of the greatest fears of anyone trying to maintain a republic is that the military will gain too much power and begin to function as a police force. In our case, we're accomplishing the same thing but in an indirect way. The change happened in many small steps: cops walking the beat turned into faceless squad cars;[731] new police management styles arose that created military style hierarchies;[732] politicians created a War on Drugs that meant massive increases in search and seizure, the invention of the no-knock raid, and SWAT teams in every town—jumping from three thousand SWAT raids a year in 1981 to eighty thousand by 2015;[733] the 1981 Military Cooperation with Civilian Law Enforcement Agencies Act was passed in order to fight the War on Drugs as a threat to national defense; and with the rise of antiterrorism efforts after 9/11, grants from the feds to local police departments funded military-grade vehicles and gear. What could go wrong? Well, a lot, actually. The sense of confidence and safety with police has plummeted, and studies have directly linked police in military gear with a decreasing willingness among citizens to cooperate with or trust them.[734] This whole trend needs to be turned back: cops are not soldiers, because following up on crimes is not a war. For the legal steps to rein in police militarization, check out Trevor Burrus's work in the *Handbook for Policy Makers* published by the Cato Institute. Christopher Coyne and Abigail Hall also explain the "boomerang effect" in their book *Tyranny Comes Home*, the phenomenon in which military techniques for international warfare become adopted for control of the domestic population.[735]

These reforms would go far to stem the tide of our bizarrely high rates of police killing and police brutality. For instance, Suprenant and Brennan take Germany's rate of police killings as a baseline, as an average representative of the generally safe, economically developed countries. Then they adjust for any differences in the crime rate and the higher likelihood that an American suspect would have a gun. They find that police *still* kill citizens at a rate four times greater than Germany would if they had our circumstances.[736] We're not suggesting that there are never appropriate instances for a police killing of a suspect; there most certainly are. Rather, as with prison populations, these numbers simply do not match our actual rates of crime.

Other interesting suggestions for reform include body camera requirements, national standards for police, third party review of police misconduct cases, and the creation of crisis assistance hotlines that deal with mentally ill citizens. Anything that (actually) raises the quality of our policing while allowing police to focus on their real job—detective work—will keep our communities safer by raising the clearance rate while simultaneously improving police-community relations. But it will also protect our police. We, the citizens of our cities, counties, and municipalities, are the ones asking police to enforce some truly ridiculous laws *and* deal with noncriminal disturbances while *also* being tasked with finding the money to pay their own salaries...oh, and do detective work. When things inevitably go wrong, we've removed most legal accountability but are shocked when that attracts and legitimizes bad actors. By restoring police to their proper task, paying them in an appropriate way, and holding them accountable, we restore integrity and dignity to the indispensable vocation of law enforcement.

E. The Role of Civil Society

As we've tried to emphasize throughout this work, life is not just politics or policies. Most of the goodness of our lives comes from our civil society institutions, and the healing of our communities and their relationship with the criminal justice system is no different. Not only do uninformed citizens need to grasp the seriousness of our situation and the deep danger of the trajectory we are on for the legitimacy of our republic, but they must also step in themselves to fill in gaps that policy never can. Anthony Bradley pulls together various examples of the vital role of civil society institutions in intervening and experimenting to create better outcomes for our criminal justice system.

Pre-incarceration interventions include a lot of creative work with juveniles. Just keeping young people out of detention is a huge step, as their experiences there often solidify their path to criminality. But it took a private foundation to promote coordination between courts, prosecutors, schools, and community organizations in order to redirect those teens who posed no danger elsewhere. This approach caught on and is now used in three hundred jurisdictions all across the country. There are community-driven mentorship programs for at-risk youth that have successfully reduced juvenile recidivism rates dramatically for its participants. An ex-General Mills vice president employed a market-driven approach to curb crime, helping individuals "find stable and well-paying employment" but paired that with "resources for housing, mental health treatment, parenting groups, mentoring, and other support services."[737] The whole philosophy is dignity based. One of the case managers puts it this way: "Success happens when an individual realizes that he/she has value and that their place in society is important, as this is realized, an individual becomes motivated...." Another effort helps juvenile offenders by rehabilitating them specifically to the people they have harmed and to their community.[738]

Civil society efforts play a huge part in making prison stints genuinely rehabilitative wherever possible. One program concentrates on the material and psychological needs of inmates' children, including bringing them to visit their parents, and is funded by the company that provides the inmates' snacks! Another program trains those in prison to become entrepreneurs, is entirely funded by the private sector, has a recidivism rate of 7 percent, and a 100 percent employment rate twelve months out from release. Recall that the average recidivism rate is 89 percent, and the unemployment rate for ex-offenders is 27 percent.[739] There are many educational programs for inmates, some even making it possible to complete a college degree. Inmates who pursue such opportunities are far less likely to land back in prison, with recidivism rates in the teens and some in the single digits. This is not just about getting a job. It's also about moral reflection, personal dignity, and accomplishment. Most inmates probably didn't land in prison because they valued their own lives and were building toward their future. But we can help them get to that place within themselves.

Finally, reentry efforts have skyrocketed as citizens returning to society have found themselves isolated, jobless, and confused by "life on the outside." Some businesses specialize in hiring ex-offenders, such as Dot Foods, Koch Industries, and Edwins Restaurant (and there are many more). By being prepared to deal with the struggles of returning citizens, these efforts have been successful. This outcome can be contrasted with legal efforts to ban the box (disallow employers from asking about criminal history until just before hiring). Counterintuitively, ban the box actually made employment for Black males *go down*, presumably because employers simply assume a criminal history if they're not allowed to ask about one.[740] But the intentionality involved in the efforts of programs like Homeboy Industries or Emerge Connecticut succeeds because everyone in the organization is trained to address the specific needs of ex-offenders. One wonderful thing about many of these efforts is that they pair resources for life with jobs and job training. Examples include trauma counseling, substance abuse treatment, parenting guidance, conflict resolution, and even just basic literacy and numeracy training. Finally, many nonprofits, like Families Against Mandatory Minimums (FAMM), focus on the policy changes that will lower unnecessary incarceration rates and ease transition for those who have been incarcerated.

We shouldn't underestimate how much the quiet, persevering, self-sacrificial efforts of these kinds of groups can change lives and change the system. It's so tempting to think that if we just got the right mix of policy changes in place, we'd solve our problems. Not only do these groups influence policy anyway, but truly, there are so many gaps that policy can never, ever fill. Struggling people need people—not just checks or vouchers or resource pamphlets—but real, flesh and blood people to walk with them through the struggle. If you are reading this book, we're willing to place a bet that you can mentor an at-risk teen, drive a child to visit her parent in prison, or hire an ex-offender at your place of business. But you probably won't unless you're plugged into one of these wonderful organizations, right? That's why we need you, and we need them. God bless all those doing this difficult and necessary work.

CONCLUSION

The claim of this book is that Black Americans have endured systemic exclusion from the otherwise just institutions of the American constitutional order. At the same time, Black Americans' shared experiences of oppression formed them into a community with rich civil society institutions, which allowed them to successfully fight for liberation from slavery and Jim Crow. Just when those overtly racist laws were rectified, other big government attempts to socially engineer the population arose, the (presumably) unintended consequences of which include disparate negative impacts on Black people. The difference here is that post–civil rights issues such as the rise of the welfare state, the drug war, and mass incarceration can affect anyone in American society. However, they have affected Blacks and other historically marginalized groups disproportionately because limited resources and networks make it hard for individual members of these groups to fight state-sponsored injustice. Unfortunately, many who attempt to solve such problems do so with the same kind of discriminatory, centralized, social engineering plans that caused them in the first place. Instead of making different versions of the same mistake, we ought to address the problem at the root from which it sprung: civil and economic exclusion.

By removing laws that needlessly criminalize and punish people, and by removing barriers to their economic participation, America can—in an outright rejection of the "white savior complex"—free already-existing Black social institutions from unnecessary constraints, thus empowering Black Americans to pursue full human flourishing. At the same time, certain approaches within civil society ought to be encouraged and others discouraged in our efforts to alleviate the consequences of systemic injustice. We draw attention to movements for "detoxing" philanthropy, investment in transitional justice to address the human rights violations of Jim Crow, and ways in which other churches can cooperate with and learn from the Black church to rebuild impoverished neighborhoods. We celebrate Black success and Black cultural inheritance without minimizing the Black struggle. We have striven to present a uniquely classical liberal account of the systemic oppression of Black Americans by drawing attention to the role of the state in creating and perpetuating Black oppression, the necessity of removing progressive efforts to socially engineer Black Americans, and the role of Black institutions of civil society in healing the wounds of Black America.

Epilogue on All
the Controversial Stuff

Critical Race Theory, Anti-Racism, Black "Conservatives," and Reparations

I t's hardly possible in this cultural moment to write a book about American race relations without being asked about certain controversial topics. Rather than leave you guessing, we'll quickly run down how we've thought through each of these as we've engaged with the American conversation on race, particularly over the last several years.

CRITICAL RACE THEORY

With so much confusion around the term, we ought to define critical race theory clearly before we proceed. To do so, we appeal to its founders, Derrick Bell and Richard Delgado:

> "Unlike traditional civil rights, which embraces incrementalism and step-by-step progress,

critical race theory questions the very founda-
tions of the liberal order, including equality theory, legal reasoning, Enlightenment rationalism,
and neutral principles of constitutional law."
—Richard Delgado

"[C]ritical race theory is a body of legal scholarship, now about a decade old, a majority of
whose members are both existentially people of
color and ideologically committed to the struggle against racism, particularly as institutionalized in and by law. Those critical race theorists
who are white are usually cognizant of and
committed to the overthrow of their own racial privilege.... Critical race theory writing and
lecturing is characterized by frequent use of the
first person, storytelling, narrative, allegory, in-
terdisciplinary treatment of law, and the unapologetic use of creativity. The work is often disruptive because its commitment to anti-racism goes
well beyond civil rights, integration, affirmative
action, and other liberal measures. This is not
to say that critical race theory adherents auto-
matically or uniformly 'trash' liberal ideology
and method (as many adherents of critical legal
studies do). Rather, they are highly suspicious
of the liberal agenda, distrust its method, and
want to retain what they see as a valuable strain
of egalitarianism which may exist despite, and
not because of, liberalism."
—Derrick Bell

It ought to be obvious by now that while we appreciate the
role of critical race theorists in uncovering various cases in which

liberal law was undermined in the service of racism, we can in no way join them in the deep suspicion of liberalism and liberal law that they inherited from critical legal theory. Rather, we have argued here that systems of liberal law, which are, let us remind ourselves, only a few hundred years old, have already been responsible for a sweeping revolution in human rights and material well-being—the greatest improvement in human flourishing in the history of the planet Earth. It can hardly be surprising that such a young political philosophy would stumble in its first inception upon the weight of preexisting circumstances such as slavery and ethnic hatreds. We simply do not believe that liberalism is hopelessly tied up with imperialism or other systems of oppression, simply because liberal societies have been by far the best in human history at eliminating these things (for instance, in a liberal society, you're perfectly free to be a critical race theorist!). That systems of oppression still remain is both perfectly predictable and deeply lamentable, and our strategy is to fight them tooth and nail. We do this not by pursuing a utopian goal untethered from the realities of human nature and state power, but rather by asking ourselves how we can more consistently carry out the liberal vision of individual rights, economic freedom, and minimal and balanced government. We believe that we have demonstrated through the evidence we have presented in this work that it is the state that has perpetrated and sustained a staggering percentage of the oppression that Black Americans have endured. Rather than rely on the same system that caused the problem to fix the problem, we recommend dismantling state-supported oppressions and turning to civil society and the market for solutions instead.

On the other hand, it ought to be mentioned that the classical liberal tradition counts as central to its identity both serious intellectual critiques of many of the phenomena that concern critical race theorists and practical activism against them: imperialism,[741] capitalism understood as cronyism,[742] sexism,[743] white supremacy,[744] and many other systems in which "power tends to corrupt."

ANTI-RACISM AND ANTI-RACIST POLICY

One might say that we're in a "racial reckoning" sort of moment, and the issue hasn't been this polarized in the last four decades. Conservatives insist that race is overplayed for ideological reasons, and progressives insist that it's underplayed for ideological reasons. We've argued in these pages that there's some truth to both of these positions, oddly enough, depending on what aspect of American life we're talking about: the minimization of racial oppression in history education, for instance, in service to the creation of a patriotic mythos, is well-documented; but we can also document the absurdities of political correctness in universities and now corporations. The reason we can't choose between the two narratives is that they're in different worlds. In the work-a-day world of, say, a white evangelical church, congregants and leaders alike may almost forget the existence of the Black church tradition in America, having no familiarity with it and no way of processing it in their theological and political categories. When asked to think about unity in the church across racial lines, they may respond with genuine confusion. In the ivory tower of academia, on the other hand, the purveyors of the latest trends in theory rarely discuss the fact that so many nonacademic Black Americans still adhere to the second-wave anti-racist rhetoric of universal human brotherhood, have socially conservative views on issues like sexuality and abortion, or are unapologetic market entrepreneurs who just want to have their chance to make it.

Here, we discuss three popular "solutions" to our racial tensions that we think are dead-ends, despite their ubiquity in the discourse: (A) race-based affirmative action, (B) implicit bias and diversity training, and (C) third-wave anti-racism. We will be almost painfully brief.

(A) Race-Based Affirmative Action

Self-proclaimed "cranky liberal" John McWhorter has been confusing people for decades with his heterodox pushback on our racial conversation. Affirmative action, he argues, made perfect sense in the wake of the civil rights movement, even if it did mean bending the rules a bit. That's because no one could deny that perfectly able Black people were quite forcefully kept out of positions and opportunities they ought to have had, and it was worth putting some effort toward righting the ship. But he also argues that currently such programs often only serve to move already successful Black people from great institutions to *really* great institutions. That doesn't actually sound that bad, until he explains the "mismatch" theory: a Black student is more likely to come from a background with less academic competition or training for the exact reasons of systemic injustice we've laid out in this book; if that student ends up at an institution at which it is impossible to succeed without that background training, this only makes it more likely for the student to fail out or drop down to a less sophisticated, and probably less financially rewarding, major. That means fewer Black economists, doctors, lawyers, engineers, or what have you, only because they were recruited away from the University of Michigan to go to MIT. McWhorter's point is that this doesn't help genuinely disadvantaged people—namely, the poor—since they had no path to college in the first place, and it doesn't help the Black middle class either, since it puts them on worse career tracks.[745] So, it doesn't help, and it's also insulting to Black people this far from the era of de jure racist policies to say that tests, teaching styles, and admission standards need to be adjusted for them because they just can't possibly do it. Instead, he says, pour your efforts into helping poor people—whatever their color—rise in the ranks. This will take real intentionality, not just recruiting; the poor will not only need financial assistance but also assistance with navigating a world with which they are entirely unfamiliar and being integrated into the relevant professional networks.[746]

(B) Implicit Bias and Diversity Training

"Wait!" the savvy reader will warn. "You're forgetting about implicit bias, which creates obstacles for Black people and other minorities at every turn." There's simply no doubt about this, as the famous, and oft-repeated, résumé experiments have shown.[747] If Michael and Jamal have the same exact résumé, Jamal's résumé is far more likely to be passed over because of his Black-sounding name. Therefore, it is insisted, we must institute implicit bias training in every workplace in order to overturn this clearly unfair tendency. Sadly, implicit bias and diversity training do not work. They do not reduce bias, and they do not increase diversity. This is not a conclusion based on a study or two, but on many, many studies, and meta-studies of studies, going back almost a century, as you can see in the Harvard-based article, "Why Doesn't Diversity Training Work?"[748] We continue to do these trainings, en masse, presumably because it seems like they should work, and doing them shows that we wish that they would work. Now that the ball is rolling, maintaining them also feeds a new industry of diversity trainers. But they don't work. This is also clear from studies focusing on police. A former member of the police force in Ferguson, Missouri, described to Rachel how the Department of Justice scolded the police department about the training that they needed to undertake in order to deal more fairly with the community. The officers only became angry, and some even walked out of the room. Is this because they were so inherently racist that they refused to listen to good advice? Perhaps, but the officer claimed that it was because they had already had all the training that the DOJ was suggesting.

(C) Third-Wave Anti-Racism

If such programs consistently make no difference, perhaps it's because we need to redouble our efforts and "do the work," as Ibram X. Kendi suggests in his book *How to Be an Antiracist*. In the summer of 2020, every city-dwelling, middle- or upper-income white progressive with a conscience was reading his book, or Robin DiAngelo's *White Fragility* (the two works are related but have different focuses; Kendi is thinking mostly about policy, DiAngelo about personal behavior). If only white people understood how deep their racism goes, the authors claim, we could move in the direction of a more equal society (but they probably won't). The problem isn't men at secret meetings wearing white sheets on their heads, but regular white people who simply unconsciously perpetuate our history of white supremacy by not thinking about Black people or their perspective much at all. There's definitely something to this. Half of business and civil society institutions is who you know, and professional networks are self-perpetuating. If we spent three and a half centuries making sure that Black people couldn't participate in markets and clubs dominated by white people, then it comes as no surprise that it will take more than fifty years to undo this dynamic. Kendi's claim is that merely being nonracist is not enough, since a nonracist person would be (even unconsciously) perpetuating the injustice by not consciously fighting against it. The logic of the argument makes sense, and if white people would stop denying systemic racism maybe they could help create more equal outcomes. Since we have acknowledged throughout this book that at least a significant part of Black inequality with whites today is due—directly or indirectly—to historic systemically racist policy (both de jure and de facto), then why aren't we on board with Kendi or DiAngelo?

There are three reasons we believe that promoting third-wave anti-racism won't work:

1. The third-wave anti-racists use an *overly broad definition of racism*. They condemn as racist the following sorts of claims: that class is now playing a larger role than race in racial inequalities; that strengthening fatherhood ought to be a main plank in any efforts to address racial inequality; or just the general view that Black people benefit more by celebrating themselves than focusing on their oppression. But there seems to be a *reductio ad absurdum* of this definition of racism. When asked about the Black Lives Matter movement, Denzel Washington (echoing, to some extent, the views of Malcolm X, whom he played in the biographical film) quickly replied that "it starts in the home" and claimed that he had better outcomes than his childhood friends because he had an involved father. Barack Obama used not only the bully pulpit but also federal support for fatherhood training programs to address the rising problem of fatherlessness. Zora Neale Hurston despised the celebration of victimhood and instead celebrated Black accomplishment, famously puzzling, "Sometimes, I feel discriminated against, but it does not make me angry. It merely astonishes me. How can any deny themselves the pleasure of my company? It's beyond me." If we want to say that Washington and Obama are wrong in their assessment or that Hurston is overly optimistic, fine. But it defies credulity to call such giants of Black excellence *racist* simply for having a different social scientific analysis of Black life than Kendi and DiAngelo.

2. The third-wave anti-racists *engage in one-thing-ism* when they claim that the best way to address inequality is to focus on white racism and historical racist policies. We've

argued extensively in this book that explicitly and egre-
giously racist policy has harmed the Black community
immensely. And even cultural factors like family structure and attitudes to education can often be the products
of bad policy, although as we've pointed out, many of
these issues arose after 1960. It's helpful to make a distinction between proximate and nonproximate causes
here. Even if a majority of separate outcomes between
Black and white people in America can be traced to racism and racist policies, some of what ails the most struggling subsets of the Black community is only distantly
related. For instance, even though we can trace high
levels of fatherlessness in the Black community to its
vulnerability to social changes because of prior oppression, addressing fatherlessness today may have little to
do with that history and far more to do with practical,
on-the-ground mentoring.

It is simply not often the case that the perpetrator of
a crime can fully make his victim whole. One of the most
painful parts of what it means to be a victim of abuse is
that one unjustly absorbs some of the responsibility for
the damage that someone else has done, since it is the
one who is damaged who must take the initiative to heal.
Similarly, the source of many cultural dysfunctions can
be genuinely traced to racist policies, but while those in
power must dismantle those policies, the communities
who have suffered are still stuck with the cultural consequences. It's wrong and, frankly, harmful to act as if these
cultural issues do not exist or that white people being less
racist now will somehow fix them completely. Of course,
we want to reduce racism as much as possible. But that
should not be set up as a contradictory position to addressing cultural issues that correspond with undesirable

educational outcomes, over-involvement in the criminal justice system, or underemployment.

3. Third-wave anti-racism offers *unwise solutions*. The definition of racism and assumptions about real solutions isn't just a matter of semantics or social scientific debate. Kendi wants to establish a Department of Anti-Racism, made up of unelected, unappointed officials who will have the power to punish legislators who present legislation that the department deems racist, which just means that the legislation fails to help close various white-Black gaps. There can be all sorts of reasons for passing legislation, and its effect on racial inequality may be impossible to predict. Even more disturbingly, by focusing on gaps, the Department of Anti-Racism might end up striking down legislation that would actually make positive changes. For instance, because of changes in the criminal justice system since 2001, the number of young Black men going to prison has plummeted, bringing the overall Black prison population down significantly. The number of white men also went down, however. That means that although the changes resulted in many fewer people going to prison, the Black-white ratio for ending up in prison actually went up at times. This did not result from Blacks doing worse, but from both Blacks and whites doing better, where whites were starting from smaller numbers in the first place. If more poor whites are imprisoned for their involvement in the opioid epidemic, this will make the Black-white ratio go down, but will Blacks be any better off? Clearly not—they may even be worse off, as the systems that support the War on Drugs become rejuvenated and solidified. Kendi's univocal attention to inequality over objective standards of well-being would, in many cases, be self-defeating in just this way.

4. Finally, and perhaps most relevant to our theme in this work, third-wave anti-racism is *anti-market*. Kendi wrongly insists that capitalism and racism are "conjoined twins." He indulges in the same confusion over the term "capitalism," and repeats many of the ideas we already spent time refuting in Chapter 2. Ultimately, the strong anti-market bias inherent in much of third-wave racism will perpetuate more poverty and inequality, not less. Black advancement through Black ownership ought to be our goal, but that would involve affirming that markets can be liberating.

BLACK "CONSERVATIVES"

We placed the term conservatives here in scare quotes because many of those Black thinkers often called Black conservatives are actually straightforwardly Black libertarians; this includes Thomas Sowell and Walter Williams. These economists, acolytes of Milton Friedman, are personally nonreligious men who are also loath to legislate morality wherever it can be avoided. It's a bit silly that terms like "conservative" or "right-leaning" are so often repeated about people who would end the drug war as soon as possible, minimize foreign military entanglements, or advocate for a generous immigration policy.

Others, like Zora Neale Hurston, Albert Murray, Stanley Crouch, Shelby Steele, and John McWhorter, are simply heterodox thinkers who are quite difficult to pigeonhole. This group in particular, but Williams and Sowell, too, are known for their anger over the insistence that the historical oppression of Black Americans means that Black individuals bear no responsibility for their failures or that white people should feel guilty or that America is currently hostile to Black achievement. Not unlike many Black nationalist thinkers, these writers focus more on Black empowerment than Black victimhood but, unlike the nationalists, have no concerns about pursuing a multiethnic future along with whites, Latinos, and Asians. Besides the fact that Hurston, Murray, Crouch, and McWhorter are not libertarian (Steele leans heavily libertarian but calls himself a conservative), there's also a difference in tone between them and the Sowell/Williams crowd; they are more culturally interested in the contributions of Black America and put a stronger emphasis on the way that Black people have shaped America into what it is today. It's notable, we think, that Murray and Crouch were both famous jazz music reviewers, as jazz is a particularly biracial musical tradition coming out of the uniqueness of an America created by racial mixing. McWhorter is also one of the leading scholarly experts on Black English, which he defends and celebrates.

There are, of course, those who are appropriately called Black conservatives, including Jason Riley, Glenn Loury, and Clarence Thomas. None of these men fit perfectly either: Jason Riley leans heavily toward a more open border position on immigration, for instance, while Loury favors a mixed economy with a fairly robust social safety net. And Clarence Thomas has consistently (far more consistently than Antonin Scalia) voted against the government when it comes to issues such as abuse of police power or eminent domain abuse, and has not hesitated to mention that poor Black citizens are often the ones to be targeted by such government overreach.[749]

We have learned an immense amount from all the thinkers listed above. Unlike the stereotype, these Black conservatives were not culturally white. These are men and women with deeply authentic Black American experiences. Clarence Thomas grew up Gullah-Geechee in Georgia and did not even speak English as child; he attributes his habit of listening silently to his avoidance of spontaneous speech in college and law school, lest he give away his impoverished origins. Thomas Sowell's mother was a maid whose poverty forced her to send him to his aunt's to be raised; he attended Howard University before matriculating to Harvard.

Walter Williams grew up in the projects of West Philadelphia and was court-martialed for fighting the racism he experienced in the army (he was found not guilty). John McWhorter's parents were avid civil rights activists—his mother deeply disliked white people. With Hurston's gorgeous novels and groundbreaking anthropological work on former slaves (*Barracoon*), she—also a Howard alum—was part of the Harlem Renaissance until her refusal to go along with the communist sympathies of Langston Hughes and others got her blackballed. She died penniless. We would beg the reader to see these thinkers as who and what they really were and are: unique and groundbreaking individuals generated from the very heart of the Black American community.

What's so controversial about all this is that some Black Americans argue that white conservatives have used these thinkers as a kind of cudgel against them (especially the thinkers with nationally syndicated op-ed columns, like Sowell and Williams). In common conversations, when Black Americans want to speak about the pain of racism, they are reminded by their white conservative friends of various points made by these Black conservatives: that slavery isn't unique to America, but shedding so much blood to end it might have been; that other groups around the world that experienced oppression still thrived; that the problems they're blaming on racism could be blamed on the welfare state instead, and so on. It seems like the stop-talking-about-race crowd is also saying that Black people should listen to this stuff because it's Black people who are saying it.

They are each brilliant in their own way and refreshingly heterodox. However, we would argue that there's a subtle balance to be struck between the genuine encouragement provided by belief in the effectiveness of individual endeavor and the realistic sociology of cultural and economic systems. Sowell and Williams understand how badly designed systems can create perverse incentives that encourage self-destructive group behaviors. The sense that many Black Americans get from their tone—that Black people are to blame for the discrepancies in their life outcomes—isn't really fair to the American story. Generations of economic exclusion made the Black community in America especially vulnerable to the tripartite shock we described in Chapter 9, a shock from which the central institutions of Black life suffered serious damage. Yes, part of this damage involved a change in moral expectations within some communities that only furthered the loss, but alas, this is just what it means for a community to become destabilized, and there are plenty such examples all over the world. We, too, believe that young, poor Black Americans today have many opportunities for success available to them. But it's silly to act as if these young people would simply make a better choice, they could do just as well as anyone else. Many of the "anyone else's" we have in mind already have the benefits of neighborhood stability, high employment rates in the community, extended social networks, and organic mentor relationships. This is why we unequivocally endorse the civil society solutions discussed in our section on neighborhood stabilization—the only solutions that we believe will be effective in truly connecting these youth to the opportunities we affirm genuinely do exist.

Furthermore, even if we grant Sowell and Williams's comparisons of other oppressed groups across the world to Black America, we are not talking about the world but about ourselves. We are interested in America's history, America's people, and America's pain. There are all sorts of other cultural tensions in others places, and we encourage those people also to pursue a strategy of appreciating healthy elements in struggling subcultures, finding areas of overlap among subcultures, and pursuing wise, limited government policy and commitment to neighborhood stabilization for poor communities. But beyond these broad and necessarily vague points, we have no comment on other places. But we do accept responsibility for own cultural institutions and attitudes. We are not mere social scientists, contemplating American conundrums from afar. We are fellow citizens and neighbors. We care about our fellow citizens in a special way because of our shared history and identity as Americans, and we are determined to do it justice. For these reasons, we eschew any and all denigrating rhetoric toward Black Americans or any other marginalized group. Conservatives do not serve the cause of human flourishing with this kind of simplistic blame and shame talk. Instead, we embrace the celebration of Black life that we find in authors like Zora Neale Hurston, John McWhorter, Anthony Bradley, and Esau McCaulley. If civil society is the answer, then conservatives ought to be pinpointing, praising, and supporting those aspects of Black culture that provide life-giving resources to its members. Instead of complaining that America's poor inner cities struggle with the same problems with which every country's poor inner cities struggle, we think Black and white conservatives could bring their insights to these problems in more powerful ways: by lending their fellow citizens their employment networks, mentoring in business, providing financial capital to inner-city entrepreneurs, assisting inexperienced parents, and working for racial healing—especially in the relationship between the Black and white church in America. To borrow an old phrase, if you're so worried about these communities, conservatives, then put your money where your mouth is.

Luckily, there is a group of Black conservatives doing just this: the Conscious Conservative Movement.[750] They complain about the failures of progressive policy for the Black community while staying honest about America's painful racial history. Although most members of this group are Christians, one of their slogans says, "My conservatism is Malcolm," referring, of course, to the way cultural conservatism and pro-Black identity can go together.

REPARATIONS

Finally, we come to the very practical political question of reparations. We hope that we're all agreed that the newly freed slaves ought to have gotten their land, ought to have benefitted from the Homestead Act, and ought to have been protected in their property and person by police and courts. That they suffered financially from the lack of access to basic justice is a certainty. Furthermore, we need not hearken all the way back to the days of slavery, if we think that's too far back to go, to find injustices. In the living memory of our friends and families we hear of those who were not allowed to pursue certain jobs, who were summarily swept out of their homes to make way for the urban planners, who were threatened with death over slights. That those who suffered under Jim Crow and its ilk did worse than they might have done financially is beyond dispute. Those of us who enjoy inheritances from our parents and grandparents might remember that our grandparents' Black compatriots could rarely take the same actions that our forebears took to accumulate wealth and pass it on to their children.

At the same time, we take exception to the claim often made in the reparations debate that white people benefitted from the oppression of Black people. Of course, some individual white people obviously did benefit, quite directly, when they were able to steal Black labor, cheat Black farmers, or pay low wages because their Black employees were not allowed to compete for other jobs. But we insist that any and all economic exclusion of a group certainly impoverishes the whole economy, as the rest of us are cheated out of all the missed potential for specialization in, and trade with, the excluded community. How much richer might we all have been if Black Americans had been free to learn, free to move, free to climb the corporate ladder, free to live among, marry, and work with whomever they chose? How much have we collectively wasted on the harassment, segregation, and persecution of Black people? White people as a group are most certainly not better off as a result of the oppression of Black Americans. We are worse off—by far.

Justice and consideration are the expectation of a free people, not a special benefit or a privilege. That white people sometimes receive these things when Black people do not does not mean that white people are benefitting in some exceptional way but that Black people are being excluded and oppressed. Let us not hope to create equality by dragging the majority down but rather by pulling the minority up.

Furthermore, particular groups of white people directly suffered from Black oppression as well, although, of course, not to the same extent. Poor white Southerners had their wages bid down because they were competing with slave labor. They were forced to run the slave patrols for white planters. Because their whole economy suffered from lack of competitive improvement, they were stuck with poorer infrastructure and a scattered and dwindling population. In fact, though it's uncomfortable to say so, open prejudice against "rednecks," "hillbillies," "white trash," or "trailer trash" has somehow persisted as a perfectly acceptable form of social contempt. Jokes implying that this group is incestuous, stupid, and lazy are commonplace. The more economically and culturally desperate this group has become, the more likely we are to blame them for the things we hate most about ourselves. The idea that this group somehow benefitted from Black oppression is especially absurd.

The only benefit that white people as a group could claim to gain from Black oppression was simply their feeling of superiority. If nothing else, they had the status of being white. That's it. It's important to note that status goods are based on envy. Not the desire to have what someone else has, but the desire to be above them, to take what they have for oneself, or to mitigate the pain of being below them by destroying what they have and bringing them down to one's own level. Envy is one of the most destructive and hateful of all human vices. It is incompatible with the character of a free people. Nor is a sick and twisted soul any true benefit to a person. Objectively, the encouragement of this sort of vice has been nothing but a spiritual cost to white America, and it should be seen as such.

What must be done then? We believe that it would indeed be unjust to coercively redistribute the wealth of everyone to Black people, since everyone else did not (on the whole) benefit from Black oppression. However, as we have argued, America's central government (and state and municipal ones as well) has seriously wronged Black people and does indeed owe them—particularly actual descendants of slavery, the vast majority of whom make up the exact same population traumatized by Jim Crow, since the first migration north was fairly small. On the other hand, many other people have also been harmed in their economic chances by some of these actions of the federal government, such as Latinos out west who were also ghettoized by highways. Nor do we desire to reignite racial tensions unwisely. Glenn Loury has wisely suggested that further racial distinction in benefits will only stoke the hatred of poor whites and Latinos, rather than build solidarity among fellow citizens. He's also agreed with Barack Obama that the paying of reparations to Black Americans will act as "an excuse for some to say we've paid our debt and to avoid the much harder work" of lifting up struggling Black communities. Finally, we have argued that market participation is essential for human flourishing and understand that a lack of capital can be a debilitating obstacle to economic growth. We have noted that many of the most pressing current issues caused by state intervention, like the drug war, incarceration, and family breakdown, increasingly affect all economically marginalized groups. We hear about these issues from Black people especially because they continue to be overrepresented below the poverty line and lag the white population in terms of wealth accumulation.

The question of reparations is a famously difficult one, both in terms of justice-related issues and in terms of realpolitik—how the move may actually work out. In the spirit of having a creative conversation around these matters, we would like to highlight two suggestions:

1. That funding for reparations come from the sale of federally held lands and other property, and
2. That reparations be given in the form of funding the capital investments of any poor entrepreneur, along with any actual descendant of slavery or enrolled tribal member.

The central government of the United States of America owns about 28 percent of this nation's land, worth about $1.8 trillion according to their own estimates.[751] According to the official way of measuring poverty, there are about thirty-four million Americans living below the poverty level. However, these numbers shrink drastically when various forms of income, such as government transfer payments, are included.[752] A more detailed debate could be had about how to draw the line exactly or perhaps to create a graduated system of some sort. Tracts of land differ, but dollars don't, so the central government could sell these lands to private interests directly and then distribute the funds. One imagines that logging, ranching, real estate ventures, and nature conservancies would be happy to make these purchases, converting these assets to cash, and as a bonus, reducing the size and wastefulness of the central government.

Deeply politically and socially conservative philosopher Rob Koons argues from his own Roman Catholic tradition for reparations. Citing multiple passages of scripture for each claim, he denies that individuals can be held responsible for the sins of their parents, but he acknowledges that whole nations can be held responsible for actions taken by the nation in the past. He actually puts more emphasis on the failed progressive policies of the last fifty years—up to and including the syphoning of successful Black people away from the best uses of their labor through affirmative action, so he escapes the charge that he's going too far back in history. This aligns well with our argument that it is governmental resources that ought to be expended, rather than raising the money through new taxation. He also argues that it is the Black community, not individual Black people, who are the appropriate object of efforts for repair. Koons argues that class differences always arise; even in a perfectly just system Black people would have sorted into upper, middle, and lower income, but along the same lines as whites and other groups rather than having a disproportionate representation in the lower-income bracket and diminished wealth in the upper-income bracket. And this is where we part ways with Koons's analysis. He argues that, rather than paying an even amount to all Black citizens, we should reward those who are already successful with large amounts with which to invest, thus building up the wealth builders in the community.

Alternatively, consider the suggestion of the founder of the Conscious Conservative Movement, "Coach" Felecia Killings, who argues that funds ought to be focused on business loans.[753] By supporting businesses with some basic history of success (she suggests two years) and requiring manageable repayment, we can support capital investment in wealth-building endeavors among those who do not already have access to capital. Repaid loans go right back into the pile to fund the next entrepreneur. One of the most frustrating problems for wealth building in poor communities is a lack of networks. These are the very resources upon which most entrepreneurs call when they are ready to scale up a small business but to which folks who are isolated, whether in urban or rural poverty, have no access. This plan would allow for them to access capital at that pivotal moment for a small business and to keep a lot of projects growing that might otherwise fail. As we've argued above, middle- and upper-income Black Americans will benefit greatly from things like transitional justice and educational freedom. But in general, this group is doing well. It's the subset of Black Americans who got stuck, even left behind, economically that need to be built back up again.

Killings may not agree with our suggestion to include poor entrepreneurs who are of other racial backgrounds than Black. But we think doing so has several advantages. First, it acknowledges that some of the injustices suffered since the 1950s affected others too. For instance, the racial consequences of the highway system were as bad for Latino communities out west and in Florida as they were for Black communities elsewhere. Discriminatory zoning laws have often been utilized to block high-density housing— the kind of housing that poor folks need—whether they were occupied by Black, Latino, Asian, white, or immigrant communities. Second, it unites Americans in the struggle to build wealth in communities that have become economically stuck. The acrimonious divide between poor white and poor Black Americans is itself a product of our white supremacist history, as elites (as well as some bad economic ideas) pitted these groups against one another, and we ought to push back against that legacy.

On the other hand, the whole conversation about reparations is being raised by the Black community in response to injustices aimed at American citizens entirely on the basis of the color of their skin. And if we propose to sell federal lands in order to address these injustices, we run into yet another set of injustices against Native Americans. Furthermore, journalist Matt Gruenig rightly points out that the Black-white wealth gap is actually a gap between the top 10 percent in both groups. By focusing on average wealth, we've missed the fact that poor and middle-class Black Americans are similarly situated to one another, while rich white Americans have fortunes many times that of rich Black Americans, taken as a group.[754] This matters because social networks have been built up separately, so that the poor and middle class of one group are more likely to draw upon the wealthy of their own group than of the other one, whether for business opportunities, investments, or nonprofit funding. So how can our suggestion for reparations satisfy legitimate concerns about current racial tensions with just as legitimate concerns about justice?

And because the constant historical obstacles have certainly contributed to the gap between the wealthy among Blacks and whites, boosting the capital of those who have already demonstrated serious business success remains an important element of true repair. Therefore, we suggest that while the federal funds will be available to all those entrepreneurs who qualify based on low income, anyone who can prove tribal membership or status as an actual descendant of slavery (which, as we said, will capture all those whose fortunes were affected by Jim Crow as well, which is probably more relevant for the wealth situation today) will have access to these funds no matter their income level.

Once again, this conversation is offered only as a creative contribution to an ongoing conversation about reparations.

We would be remiss to act as though government is the only entity in our society that bears responsibility to repair damage it has done. Another—and perhaps more painful, because it's a matter of spiritual family—is the white church. As we reviewed at the end of Chapter 5, the white church was not simply complicit in the story of American racism but central to it. First, American churches of all sorts ought to make intentional efforts to generate a better appreciation for the Black church and Black theology. Racial reconciliation is a separate task from poverty alleviation, so reconciliation between Black and white churches must come first. We find thoughtful approaches to racial healing in documents like the Atlanta Covenant out of the OneRace movement or the organization Civil Righteousness.[755] Then, *together*, the church as a united front can be the main driver of the neighborhood-stabilization movement, investing in real, transformative economic growth and stability in these places. These efforts can be undertaken in the spirit of repair, the repair of a deep and central wound in our history. This route to racial healing acknowledges that the heart of a nation is not its government but its civil society.

Atheists like John McWhorter, many centrist liberals, and conservative Christians have all noticed the strangely religious, even fundamentalist, attitudes of the radical left. Rather than laughing at this tendency, perhaps we ought to see it as the expression of a profound spiritual hunger, arising from a genuine sense that something is deeply missing from our life together as Americans. Turning to civil society, center-left, conservative, and libertarian Christians ought to see such repair within the church, not as a capitulation to radical leftism or, frankly, as something political at all. Rather, it's a positive and creative alternative that addresses genuine harm in the history of the American church.

Those who are willing to think outside tribal boxes can be countercultural but not reactionary. Rather than simply complaining about the excesses of hard left anti-racist discourse, offer a substantive alternative. Don't just react. Act.

Endnotes

1   Christopher Federico, "How People Organize Their Political Attitudes: The Roles of Ideology, Expertise, and Evaluative Motivation," American Psychological Association, September 2009, https://www.apa.org/science/about/psa/2009/09/sci-brief.

2   Kelly McGonigal, *The Willpower Instinct: How Self-Control Works, Why It Matters, and What You Can Do to Get More of It* (New York: Avery, 2013), 196.

3   Stephen Hawkins, Daniel Yudkin, Miriam Juan-Torres, and Tim Dixon, *The Hidden Tribes of America: A Study of America's Polarized Landscape,* 2018, Hiddentribes.us, https://hiddentribes.us/media/qf-pekz4g/hidden_tribes_report.pdf.

4   Mehrsa Baradaran, *How the Other Half Banks* (Cambridge, MA: Harvard University Press, 2018); Richard Rothstein, *The Color of Law: A Forgotten History of How Our Government Segregated America* (New York: Liveright, 2017), see our Chapter 7 on housing segregation.

5   Quentin Kidd, Herman Diggs, Mehreen Farooq, and Megan Murray, "Black Voters, Black Candidates, and Social Issues: Does Party Identification Matter?" *Social Science Quarterly,* Vol. 88, No. 1 (2007), 165–176, https://www.jstor.org/stable/42956177?seq=1; Amina Dunn, "5 Fact about Black Democrats," Pew Research Center, February 27, 2020, https://www.pewresearch.org/fact-tank/2020/02/27/5-facts-about-Black-democrats/; Ismail K. White and Chryl N. Laird, *Steadfast Democrats: How Social Forces Shape Black Political Behavior,* (Princeton, NJ: Princeton University Press, 2020).

6   David Beito and Marcus Witcher, *Rose Lane Says: Thoughts on Liberty, Equality, and Freedom* (Montgomery, AL: Huntingdon College, forthcoming), https://www.marcuswitcher.com/scholarship.

7   Clara Kaplan, *Zora Neale Hurston: A Life in Letters* (New York: Anchor Books, 2003); Valerie Boyd, *Wrapped in Rainbows: The Life of Zora Neale Hurston* (New York: Lisa Drew Books, 2004).

8   This is John Locke's famous argument from *The Second Treatise on Government*, particularly in Chapters I–V. Adam Smith makes similar points in *An Inquiry into the Nature and Causes of the Wealth of Nations*, edited with an introduction, notes, marginal summary, and an enlarged index by Edwin Cannan (London: Methuen, 1904), vol. 1, https://oll.libertyfund.org/title/smith-an-inquiry-into-the-nature-and-causes-of-the-wealth-of-nations-cannan-ed-vol-1#Smith_0206-01_527. "The property which every man has in his own labour, as it is the original foundation of all other property, so it is the most sacred and inviolable. The patrimony of a poor man lies in the strength and dexterity of his hands; and to hinder him from employing this strength and dexterity in what manner he thinks proper without injury to his neighbour, is a plain violation of this most sacred property. It is a manifest encroachment upon the just liberty both of the workman, and of those who might be disposed to employ him. As it hinders the one from working at what he thinks proper, so it hinders the others from employing whom they think proper. To judge whether he is fit to be employed, may surely be trusted to the discretion of the employers whose interest it so much concerns. The affected anxiety of the law-giver lest they should employ an improper person, is evidently as impertinent as it is oppressive."

9   David Hume discusses this in the third part of *The Treatise of Human Nature,* in the section on justice. Hume thinks that justice (meaning property, voluntary exchange, and promise-keeping) comes about as a matter of social evolution, as people in early societies realize its advantages. *A Treatise of Human Nature* by David Hume, reprinted from the original edition in three volumes and edited, with an analytical index, by L. A. Selby-Bigge, MA (Oxford: Clarendon Press, 1896), https://oll.libertyfund.org/title/bigge-a-treatise-of-human-nature#Hume_0213_1129. John Stuart Mill discusses his views in *On Liberty*, where he justifies classical liberalism explicitly from an ethically utilitarian perspective (meaning that he thinks it will bring about the greatest aggregate happiness within the society).

10   For Hayek, the term "just" or "unjust" can only refer to an action that someone chooses, because "justice" is a moral concept. Loosely, we

might say that it's unjust that someone was born with a birth defect, for instance. But unless one's mother knowingly did something that caused the defect, or something was knowingly done to her, that term isn't quite right. Rather, it's tragic when someone is born with a birth defect, but it's nobody's fault, and therefore it is not technically unjust. In order to focus on justice at the level of society, we're setting aside here questions of what we might call "cosmic justice"—whether there is a God and what responsibility a being like that might bear for tragic cases. A chance birth defect reminds us of questions of justice because we know that an innocent baby can never deserve the pain and burden that the defect might cause. But we also know that many such occurrences are random and that we all experience bad things we don't deserve, as well as good things we don't deserve either. So, it's important to make a distinction between questions of "cosmic justice," which is out of our hands, and the justice of a society, which addresses violations of the basic rules that allow us to live together in peace.

Just as we are tempted to refer to individual tragic cases as unjust, we are also tempted to refer to broad social outcomes that way, even if they aren't the result of any particular unjust choices. So, we might say that the inequality between rich and poor is unjust. Well, it probably is. But that all depends on whether anyone actually did something unjust that contributed to that outcome or whether some people simply turned out richer due to some mix of effort and luck, without harming anyone in the process. If the latter is the case, then the outcome is not unjust, even if we wish it were different.

Some critics of a market economy have argued that the whole set-up is unjust; that maybe even private property itself is a bad idea that makes tragic outcomes inevitable. And indeed, there's nothing *cosmically* just about the way property is distributed. After all, if we had a cosmically just set of institutions, I'd wager that the Saint Francises of the world would do better things with lots of wealth than the Kylie Jenners of the world do now. Why not simply take it from one and give it to the other?

This is where one of Hayek's great mentors, David Hume, comes in. Hayek never met Hume—they lived two centuries apart—but Hayek gives Hume credit for many of his insights about the way that the social order comes about. And here's the problem with our Saint Francis-Kylie Jenner conundrum that Hume's system highlights: if we take all the material productivity of a society as given, and then we try to decide how to distribute it, what system should we choose? We might immediately think of dividing it all up equally. However, people are diverse; they have diverse interests, talents, and abilities. Inevitably, their interactions and exchanges with one another will lead to diverse outcomes too, and then what will we do? Will we redistribute it all again, to try and keep things equal? It becomes quickly apparent that doing that creates one massive inequality: the one between the person with the power to do the redistributing and everybody else. In other words, Hume says, a perfectly equal distribution requires tyranny.

But there's another possibility as well. We might distribute property based on merit, like giving all of worldly Kylie's stuff to the saintly Francis. Unfortunately, we run into another tangle of problems here, since we can't agree at all on who counts as virtuous and deserving. Some would argue that Kylie actually does more for the world, by promoting her businesses and therefore providing goods, services, and jobs, than Francis, whose efforts help only one person at a time. Others would counter that Kylie's influence is corrosive to culture, while Francis's generosity represents and encourages everything that's best in human nature. And such arguments will go on interminably.

What's the solution, asks Hume? What we really need is a system of property that's *intuitive*, one that everyone can settle on so we can all just get on with our lives in peace. And so, property belongs to those who create it, as well as to whoever is currently in possession of it, or at least has been for a while. We know for sure that this isn't always fair: everything from petty family disputes to colonial oppression may have determined who owns what today. If there are specific thefts that we can track, they ought to be righted (we discuss the reparations debate in our "All the Controversial Stuff" section). But barring that, we've got nowhere else to start but right here.

We also snuck a big assumption into the thought experiments we just undertook. We said "if we take all the material productivity of a society as given" then we can contemplate how to distribute it all. But that's not actually how productivity works. In fact, a society's productivity depends a whole lot on how the gains from labor are distributed. If I see a lot of the benefit from working harder or smarter, I'm quite likely to do so. If the benefits of my harder or smarter work go to strangers, I'm not going to be very motivated at all. So, another great advantage of the intuitive system of property—that is, private property—is that it also encourages more productivity, by allowing people to benefit from their own work.

Once again, there's nothing cosmically just about this. Conrad Hilton may have deserved his wealth because of all the wonderful hotels he provided us with, but Paris Hilton doesn't deserve much, so far as we can tell. Nevertheless, part of our system is to allow Mr. Hilton to do whatever he wants to with his just gains. He actually left very little of his fortune to his children, but they gained more wealth by successfully running his hotel business. His son Barron also gave most of his wealth away but still left a small percentage (of a large fortune!) to his grandchildren, including Paris Hilton. As a society, we benefit because Conrad Hilton and his sons worked harder to make high-quality, affordable hotels for the rest of us. We may be fairly indifferent to someone like Paris Hilton or even roll our eyes at her posh lifestyle, but her being rich doesn't materially harm anyone. This is the deal we make when we let people keep what they produce, trade as they wish, and work where they will. (The case in which the wealth of the rich really does harm others is when they lobby the government for special favors for themselves; we discuss cronyism in Chapter 2 and "welfare for the rich" in Chapter 9.)

Ultimately, Hayek believes that the term "social justice" is mostly used to refer to a social outcome that embodies some notion of cosmic justice. Social justice advocates either want everyone to be equal in some material sense that goes beyond equality before the law or they want people to get what they truly deserve, or something else along the same lines. They fail to realize that most social outcomes are the result of an emergent order, a conglomeration of free interactions engaged in by a mass of diverse individuals and groups according to some basic legal rules. Specific exchanges may be just or unjust, but social outcomes are neither just nor unjust (assuming the rules were fair), even when they are tragic. They simply are.

Were we to apply the concept of justice to social outcomes, we'd end up right back where Hume described, in interminable debates over who has merit, who deserves what, and who gets to decide. These are not only insoluble debates; they also lead us into conflict and antagonism—often violent—over the most fundamental question that every society must answer: Who gets what? Conflicts over the basic rules are the very opposite of what every society needs at the most fundamental level: peace.

11   "Americans of all ages, of all conditions, of all minds, constantly unite. Not only do they have commercial and industrial associations in which they all take part, but also they have a thousand other kinds: religious, moral, [intellectual], serious ones, useless ones, very general and very particular ones, immense and very small ones; Americans associate to celebrate holidays, establish seminaries, build inns, erect churches, distribute books, send missionaries to the Antipodes; in this way they create hospitals, prisons, schools. If, finally, it is a matter of bringing a truth to light or of developing a sentiment with the support of a good example, they associate. Wherever, at the head of a new undertaking, you see in France the government, and in England, a great lord, count on seeing in the United States, an association." Eduardo Nolla, ed., *Democracy in America*, vol. 2, English edition, translated from the French by James T. Schleifer (Indianapolis: Liberty Fund, 2012), https://oll.libertyfund.org/title/democracy-in-america-english-edition-vol-2#Tocqueville_1593-02_902.

12   Marian Tupy, "The Most Important Graph in the World," *Reason*, December 13, 2016, https://reason.com/2016/12/13/the-most-important-graph-in-the-world/. The graph comes from "5 Graphs that Will Change Your Mind about Poverty" by Chelsea Follett, HumanProgress, https://www.humanprogress.org/five-graphs-that-will-change-your-mind-about-poverty/.

13   The World Bank expected the 2020 rate to hit 7.9 percent, but the COVID epidemic may have pushed it up past 9 percent. "COVID-19 to Add as Many as 150 Million Extreme Poor by 2021," World Bank press release, October 7, 2020, https://www.worldbank.org/en/news/press-release/2020/10/07/covid-19-to-add-as-many-as-150-million-extreme-poor-by-2021.

14   Homi Kharas and Kristofer Hamel, "A Global Tipping Point: Half the World Is Now Middle Class or Wealthier," Thursday, September 27, 2018, Brookings, https://www.brookings.edu/blog/future-development/2018/09/27/a-global-tipping-point-half-the-world-is-now-middle-class-or-wealthier/.

15   See Aristotle and Aquinas on money-lending or usury, especially. For Aquinas, see his question, " Is it a sin to take usury for the lending of money?" https://oll.libertyfund.org/page/aquinas-on-usury. And

for Aristotle, *The Politics of Aristotle*, trans. Benjamin Jowett (Oxford: Clarendon Press, 1885), book 1, chap. 10, p. 19.

[16] We draw here on the work of economic historian Deirdre McCloskey in the three-volume series *The Bourgeois Era*, as well as her *Why Liberalism Works* and *Leave Me Alone and I'll Make You Rich* (coauthored with Art Carden).Deirdre McCloskey, *The Bourgeois Virtues: Ethics for an Age of Commerce* (Chicago: University of Chicago Press, 2007); Deirdre McCloskey, *Bourgeois Dignity: Why Economics Can't Explain the Modern World* (Chicago: University of Chicago Press, 2011); Deirdre McCloskey, *Bourgeois Equality: How Ideas, Not Capital or Institutions, Enriched the World* (Chicago: University of Chicago Press, 2016); Deirdre McCloskey, *Why Liberalism Works: How True Liberal Values Produce a Freer, More Equal, Prosperous World for All* (New Haven CT: Yale University Press, 2019); Deirdre McCloskey and Art Carden, *Leave Me Alone and I'll Make You Rich: How the Bourgeois Deal Enriched the World* (Chicago: University of Chicago Press, 2020).

[17] We are appealing here to a vast literature on human progress, including the work of Hans Rosling in *Factfulness: 10 Reasons We're Wrong about the World—and Why Things Are Better Than You Think* (New York: Flatiron Books, 2018) and in his project at Gapminder.org. Also see Steven Pinker in *Enlightenment Now: The Case for Reason, Science, Humanism, and Progress* (New York: Viking Books, 2018). Also see the work with data being done at HumanProgress.org. And McCloskey's work cited above touches on this theme again and again.

[18] Jonathan Anomaly, "Public Goods and Government Action," *Politics, Philosophy & Economics* 2015, vol. 14(2) p. 111–112, citing Hume's *Treatise of Human Nature*, 1739: book 3, part 2, ch. 7, https://philpapers.org/archive/ANOPGA: "Two neighbours may agree to drain a meadow, which they possess in common; because it is easy for them to know each other's mind; and each must perceive, that the immediate consequence of his failing in his part, is, the abandoning the whole project. But it is very difficult, and indeed impossible, that a thousand persons should agree in any such action; it being difficult for them to concert so complicated a design, and still more difficult for them to execute it; while each seeks a pretext to free himself of the trouble and expence, and would lay the whole burden on others. Political society easily remedies both these inconveniences. Magistrates find an immediate interest in the interest of any considerable part of their subjects.

They need consult no body but themselves to form any scheme for the promoting of that interest. And as the failure of any one piece in the execution is connected, though not immediately, with the failure of the whole, they prevent that failure, because they find no interest in it, either immediate or remote. Thus bridges are built; harbours opened; ramparts raised; canals formed; fleets equipped; and armies disciplined every where, by the care of government, which, though composed of men subject to all human infirmities, becomes, by one of the finest and most subtle inventions imaginable, a composition, which is, in some measure, exempted from all these infirmities."

[19]   These insights arise from public choice theory. Classic works include James Buchanan and Gordon Tullock's *Calculus of Consent: The Logic of Constitutional Democracy* (Ann Arbor: MI: University of Michigan Press, 1960), and Mancur Olsen's *The Logic of Collective Action: Public Goods and the Theory of Groups* (Cambridge, MA: Harvard University Press, 1971).

[20]   John Tomasi, *Free Market Fairness* (Princeton, NJ: Princeton University Press, 2012), 130.

[21]   Tomasi, *Free Market Fairness,* 131.

[22]   The term "social justice" first appeared in a work by Luigi Taparelli, a Jesuit scholar writing in the 1840s who is considered one of the fathers of Catholic Social Thought. He was deeply influenced by Pope Leo XIII and his famous encyclical, *Rerum Novarum* (On the New Things). For Taparelli, social justice is both a personal virtue and a reference to the constitutional order of a well-framed polity. Social justice is not commutative justice, which deals with just exchange, nor is it distributive justice, which deals with the dissemination of some shared good, like honor. It's not legal justice either, since legal justice must arise *from* the constitutional order, which is logically prior to it. Social justice refers to "the actual arrangement of institutions, laws, and policies that operate to protect and promote the same exercise of rights and duties of the individuals that make up that society." Such an arrangement is just if it allows the individuals within that society to flourish in their strengths and abilities, in such a way that they contribute both to their own and to the common good. It follows then, that the virtue of social justice is the constant willingness to promote and protect this praiseworthy order. In particular, one commentator emphasizes, this virtue includes the willingness to do that on behalf of

any individual in the society, simply because he or she is a member of that society.

Taparelli held that there is a fundamental duty of any government to especially protect the weak, but was extremely careful in his analysis of how that ought to be done. Practically speaking, governments could care directly for a marginalized person as an "administratee," or by "furnishing them with the means to strengthen their own abilities to pursue their interests and to resist the violations of justice." Taparelli decries the first option, claiming that it would lead to "centralization, the injustice, inefficiency, and tyranny of which" he had already covered in much of his other writing. Rather, a well-formed polity should empower the most local institutions requisite for whichever problem is at hand: the family, the neighborhood, the municipality, etc. This is the famous decentralizing concept of "subsidiarity" in Catholic Social Thought. It assumes a background commitment of each citizen to the virtue of self-sacrificial charity, since even fulfilling the demands of every single type of justice perfectly will not eliminate every case of poverty or every issue of the downtrodden.

Taparelli contemplated the attitude a Christian should have toward any wealth one accumulates beyond what is needed to uphold one's station in life. He admits that, in the abstract, human beings are equals; that is, they all share a human nature as members of the same species. Therefore, justice requires a kind of equality among humans, especially legal equality. But in concrete reality, every individual varies from every other according to strength, intelligence, etc., so that in fact, human beings are naturally unequal, and owe each other different things. Taparelli makes the classic distinction between different types of justice—what Aristotle would have called numerical versus proportional justice. In exchanges between individuals, justice asks for equality. In a voluntary exchange between individuals, for instance, the goods exchanged should be of equal economic value, or an involuntary exchange such as theft, the punishment should be equal to the crime. But in the administration of some shared good—an endeavor such as a school or business, for instance—obviously justice must honor a person proportionally to their merit; that is, "equality consists here in equalizing the office to the person's capacity"; in other words, a business ought to promote its best salesman and a school ought to reward its best teacher.

Taparelli goes on to expound a view of one's involvement in the economy that rejects both the *homo economicus*, greed-is-good conception of liberal economics and the communist dismissal of private property that was gaining notoriety at the time. The "Catholic economy" he espouses would include paying a family wage, graciously accepting the natural hierarchy among people of different abilities, and dedication to virtuous and self-sacrificing public service. In other words, Taparelli is recommending a certain way of behaving morally in an economic system that doesn't stray too far from what Adam Smith—the father of economics—would recommend. Taparelli is quite explicit that, while economic science properly guides the relevant government policy, it must also acknowledge the role of "Catholic charity" in which "the shares of the capitalist and the proprietor return to a large extent into the hands of the worker as a balm, leveling through generosity the inequalities of fortune."

Taparelli wanted a social order that respected the principle of subsidiarity: smaller and more local authorities such as families and communities would be respected by the state and should in turn contribute to order within the state. Social justice, then, is a just arrangement of the legal and political institutions that allows for human flourishing to emerge because the arrangement accords with our nature as human beings (even though the outcome will certainly be materially unequal). But we also find helpful his discussion of the personal virtue of social justice. In cases in which the social order, either in its fundamental institutions or in particular laws and policies, fails to promote the flourishing of some citizen or group of citizens, the virtuous citizen fights hard to bring about changes that treat the disease itself and not just the symptoms.

Much of our critique of current efforts that fly under the banner of 'social justice' actually align quite well with Taparelli's concerns: we argue that they are often too centralized, too directly administrative of marginalized people's lives, and too focused on generating particular outcomes rather than fixing the government's failures at its own institutional roots. We hope that our suggestions in the final chapter of this book will inspire a discussion of institutional, legal, and policy changes that empower marginalized people to pursue their own flourishing in a just system. But we also hold up example of how we as citizens can contribute from our own abundance to empower these groups economically and culturally.

23 G. A. Cohen, *Why Not Socialism?* (Princeton, NJ: Princeton University Press, 2009), p. 76–77.

24 F. A. Hayek, "Competition as a Discovery Procedure," 1968 lecture at the University of Kiel, translated here: Quarterly Journal of Austrian Economics, vol. 5, no. 3 (Fall 2002), https://mises.org/library/competition-discovery-procedure-0.

25 Adam Smith, *An Inquiry into the Nature and Causes of the Wealth of Nations,* vol. I, ch. X, part II.

26 David D'Amato, "Abolition Was Actually a Free Market Cause," Libertarianism.org, February 6, 2020; Marc-William Palen, *The "Conspiracy" of Free Trade: The Anglo-American Struggle over Empire and Economic Globalisation, 1846-1896* (Cambridge, UK: Cambridge University Press, 2016).

27 "The Caning of Senator Charles Sumner," US Senate, May 22, 1856, https://www.senate.gov/artandhistory/history/minute/The_Caning_of_Senator_Charles_Sumner.htm.

28 David M. Levy and Sandra J. Peart, "The Secret History of the Dismal Science. Part I. Economics, Religion and Race in the 19th Century," the Library of Economics and Liberty, January 22, 2001, https://www.econlib.org/library/Columns/LevyPeartdismal.html.

29 Nicholas Buccola, ed., *The Essential Douglass: Selected Writings and Speeches* (New York: Hacking Publishing Co., 2016); Timothy Sandefur, *Frederick Douglass: Self-Made Man* (Washington, DC: Cato Institute, 2018). We recognize that conservatives have simplified Douglass's views over the years to try and claim him as one of their own. We believe that we offer a nuanced reading of Douglass that takes into account the important points that David Blight makes about Douglass's legacy in *Frederick Douglass: Prophet of Freedom* (New York: Simon and Schuster, 2018).

30 Frederick Douglass, "What to a Slave Is the Fourth of July?" speech delivered on July 5, 1852.

31 Quoted in Paul D. Moreno, *Black Americans and Organized Labor*, 37.

32 Timothy Sandefur, "Was Frederick Douglass a Libertarian?" *Cato at Liberty Blog*, Cato Institute, March 12, 2018.

33 Frederick Douglass, "Self-Made Men," speech delivered on various occasions, first in 1859.

34 Quoted in the American National Biography's entry on Villard, by Robert L. Gale. https://www.anb.org/view/10.1093/anb/9780198606697.001.0001/anb-9780198606697-e-1601698.

[35] See Burt Folsom's *New Deal or Raw Deal: How FDR's Economic Legacy Has Damaged America,* Threshold Edition, 2009; Jim Powell's *FDR's Folly: How Roosevelt and His New Deal Prolonged the Great Depression,* Crown Forum, 2004 (reprint); George Selgin's articles at https://www.alt-m.org/tag/great-depression/. Here is Powell on how the New Deal policies hurt Black Americans in particular: "Why Did FDR's New Deal Harm Blacks?" Cato Institute, December 3, 2003, https://www.cato.org/commentary/why-did-fdrs-new-deal-harm-blacks.

[36] David Beito and Linda Royster Beito, "Gold Democrats and the Decline of Classical Liberalism, 1896–1900," *The Independent Review,* vol. IV, no. 4 (Spring 2000), 555–575, https://www.independent.org/pdf/tir/tir_04_4_beito.pdf.

[37] Quoted in David T. Beito and Linda Royster Beito, "Isabel Paterson, Rose Wilder Lane, and Zora Neale Hurston on War, Race, the State, and Liberty," *The Independent Review,* vol. 12, no. 4 (Spring 2008), 555.

[38] David T. Beito and Linda Royster Beito, "Selling Laissez-faire Antiracism to the Black Masses: Rose Wilder Lane and the *Pittsburgh Courier,*" *The Independent Review,* vol. 15, no. 2 (Fall 2010), 279–294, https://www.independent.org/pdf/tir/tir_15_02_07_beito.pdf.

[39] Adam Ferguson: "Nations stumble upon establishments, which are indeed the result of human action, but not the execution of any human design." See the work of Don Lavoie, who coined the term "information problem" in *Rivalry and Central Planning: The Socialist Calculation Debate Reconsidered* (Arlington, VA: Mercatus Center at George Mason University, 2015, reprint from 1985).

[40] Thomas C. Leonard, *Illiberal Reformers: Race, Eugenics, and American Economics in the Progressive Era,* (Princeton, NJ: Princeton University Press, 2016).

[41] In 2018, Harvard's Donald Yacovone published in the *Chronicle of Higher Education* a review of 3,000 American-history textbooks stretching back into the 19th century. He was looking particularly for how these textbooks handled the subject of slavery—and was appalled (though not entirely surprised) that they depicted slavery as a benign institution where "untutored" blacks could "enjoy picnics, barbecues, singing, and dancing." https://www.educationnext.org/teaching-about-slavery-forum-guelzo-berry-blight-rowe-stang-allen-maranto/.

[42] Albert Murray, *The Omni-americans: Black Experience and American Culture* (Boston: Da Capo Press, 1990); quoted in Henry Louis Gates Jr.'s preface.

43   David D'Amato, "Abolitionism Was Actually a Free Market Cause," Libertarianism, February 6, 2020, https://www.libertarianism.org/columns/abolitionism-actually-free-market-cause. "It cannot be stressed enough that the period's most outspoken and principled free-traders consciously and explicitly did not identify their free-trade philosophy with capitalism or with capitalists and their interests. Cobden decidedly did not see free trade as 'a matter of advantage to the capitalists'—indeed the idea was 'anathema to [him].'"

44   Edward Baptist, *The Half Has Never Been Told: Slavery and the Making of American Capitalism* (New York: Basic Books, 2014).

45   John J. Clegg, "Capitalism and Slavery," *University of Chicago Press Journals*, vol. 2, no. 2 (Fall 2015), 295–296, https://www.journals.uchicago.edu/doi/abs/10.1086/683036?journalCode=chs.

46   Phillip Magness, "How the 1619 Project Rehabilitates the 'King Cotton' Thesis," *National Review*, August 26, 2019, https://www.nationalreview.com/2019/08/1619-project-new-york-times-king-cotton-thesis/. "And Baptist, to his discredit, has generally declined to answer the substantive criticisms of his work...."

47   H. Reuben Neptune, "Throwin' Scholarly Shade: Eric Williams in the New Histories of Capitalism and Slavery," *Journal of the Early Republic*, University of Pennsylvania Press, vol. 39, no. 2 (Summer 2019), 299–326, https://muse.jhu.edu/issue/40362; Richard C. Sutch, "The Economics of African American Slavery: The Cliometrics Debate," working paper 25197, DOI 10.3386/w25197, issue date October 2018, https://www.nber.org/papers/w25197. The latter paper by Sutch is also a good source for seeing some of the problems in *Time on the Cross*.

48   Jeffrey R. Hummel, *Emancipating Slaves, Enslaving Free Men: A History of the American Civil War* (McLean, VA: Open Court, 1996), 37. "The current consensus is that slaves did yield a return comparable to other investments at the time."

49   In 1860, 75 percent of slaves worked on plantations. Most worked in cotton, but there were also sugar and tobacco plantations. For brevity, I only refer to cotton here, but the same economic principles of marginal utility could be applied to other crops. Jeffrey R. Hummel, *Emancipating Slaves, Enslaving Free Men*, 45.

50   Hummel, *Emancipating Slaves, Enslaving Free Men*, 46.

51   Robert E. Wright, *The Poverty of Slavery: How Unfree Labor Pollutes the Economy* (London: Palgrave Macmillan, 2017), 124.

52 Gavin Wright, *Slavery and American Economic Development* (Baton Rouge, LA: LSU Press, 2006), 141–3.

53 Adam Smith, 1755 lecture on the need for "peace, easy taxes, and a tolerable administration of justice," Online Library of Liberty, https://oll.libertyfund.org/quotes/436.

54 Nathan Nunn, "Slavery, Inequality, and Economic Development in the Americas: An Examination of the Engerman-Sokoloff Hypothesis," National Bureau of Economic Research, October 2007, https://scholar.harvard.edu/files/nunn/files/domestic_slavery.pdf.

55 While I'm borrowing this phrase from Hummel's title, Cassius M. Clay, a convert from slaveholder to abolitionist, used the term "dead loss" in 1848 for some of the same considerations. Quoted in Woodman, 306.

56 Jeffrey Hummel, "Deadweight Loss and the American Civil War : The Political Economy of Slavery, Secession, and Emancipation," *Texas ScholarWorks*, https://repositories.lib.utexas.edu/handle/2152/10583. You can find a short summary here: https://www.aier.org/article/slavery-did-not-make-america-richer/. (Other economists taking issue with Fogel and Engerman's way of framing the question of plantation productivity include Gavin Wright, Peter Temin, Paul David, Richard Sutch, and Roger Ransom.)

57 Loren Schweninger, *Black Property Owners in the South, 1790–1915* (Champaign, IL: University of Illinois Press, 1990), ch. 2.

58 Robert William Fogel and Stanley L. Engerman, *Time on the Cross: The Economics of American Negro Slavery*, (Boston: Little, Brown and Company, 1974).

59 Wright, *The Poverty of Slavery*, 145–151.

60 Wright, *The Poverty of Slavery*, 145.

61 Wright, *The Poverty of Slavery*, 202–220.

62 Wright, *The Poverty of Slavery*, 223.

63 Jeffrey Glossner of the University of Mississippi provides a helpful overview of the development of the historical literature on this topic in "Poor Whites in the Antebellum U.S. South" for networks.h-net.org, the Humanities and Social Sciences online network. He cites important recent work on poor whites: Nancy Isenberg's *White Trash: The 400-Year Untold History of Class in America* (New York: Viking, 2016); and Keri Keigh Merritt's *Masterless Men: Poor Whites and Slavery in the Antebellum South* (Cambridge, UK: Cambridge University Press, 2017).

[64] James J. Feigenbaum, James Lee, and Filippo Mezzanotti, "Capital Destruction and Economic Growth: The Effects of Sherman's March, 1850–1920," National Bureau of Economic Research, December 2018, https://www.nber.org/papers/w25392.

[65] Gordon Tullock, "The Welfare Costs of Tariffs, Monopolies, and Theft," *Western Economic Journal*, 5:3 (June 1967), 224–32. The term "rent-seeking" was introduced in 1974 by Anne O. Krueger in "The Political Economy of the Rent-Seeking Society." Matt Mitchell clarifies how rent-seeking and its costs go far beyond mere lobbying, in *The Pathology of Privilege: The Economic Consequences of Government Favoritism* (Arlington, VA: Mercatus Center at George Mason University, 2014).

[66] Claudia D. Goldin and Frank D. Lewis, "The Economic Cost of the American Civil War: Estimates and Implications," *Journal of Economic History* 35(2): 299–326.

[67] Nathan Nunn, "The Long Term Effects of Africa's Slave Trades," *Quarterly Journal of Economics* 123 (1), 139–176, https://scholar.harvard.edu/nunn/publications/long-term-effects-africas-slave-trades. For a short summary of his research, see Paul Gleason's "Slavery's Sway" *Harvard Magazine* (November-December 2008), https://www.harvardmagazine.com/2008/11/slaverys-sway-html.

[68] Wright, *The Poverty of Slavery,* 156.

[69] Alexander Hammond, "What Can We Expect from Africa in the 2020s?" HumanProgress, January 23, 2020, https://humanprogress.org/article.php?p=2391.

[70] Frederick Douglass, *Narrative of the Life of Frederick Douglass,* 1845, ch. VI.

[71] Newton and Jefferson quoted in Wright, 117.

[72] Wright, *The Poverty of Slavery*, 162.

[73] Quoted in Robert E. Wright, *The Poverty of Slavery*, 163.

[74] See McCloskey's chart of the virtues, ranging from ancient, to medieval, to commercial: https://necessaryfacts.blogspot.com/2012/01/choose-your-virtues.html.

[75] Wright, *The Poverty of Slavery*, 165, 166.

[76] Wright, *The Poverty of Slavery*, 171.

[77] Wright, *The Poverty of Slavery*, 175.

[78] Homi Kharas and Kristofer Hamel, "A Global Tipping Point: Half the World Is Now Middle Class or Wealthier," Brookings, September 27, 2018, https://www.brookings.edu/blog/future-development/

2018/09/27/a-global-tipping-point-half-the-world-is-now-middle-class-or-wealthier/.

79   Per capita, Southern incomes were one-third lower than Northern, although some of this can be attributed to the effects of the harsh tariffs that fell disproportionately onto Southerners. Shockingly, the North maintained its lead in per capita income while its population was increasing at twice the rate of the Southern, due to the absorption of huge numbers of immigrants. Jeffrey R. Hummel, *Emancipating Slaves, Enslaving Free Men*, 50–51.

80   Hummel, *Emancipating Slaves, Enslaving Free Men*, 49.

81   D'Amato, "Abolition Was Actually a Free Market Cause."

82   Magness, "How the 1619 Project Rehabilitates the 'King Cotton' Thesis."

83   Phillip Magness, "The Anti-Capitalist Ideology of Slavery," American Institute for Economic Research, August 16, 2019, https://www.aier.org/article/the-anti-capitalist-ideology-of-slavery/.

84   Joyce Chaplin, *An Anxious Pursuit: Agricultural Innovation and Modernity in the Lower South—1730–1815*, (Williamsburg, VA: Omohundro Institute and the University of North Carolina, 1996), 54.

85   Chaplin, *An Anxious Pursuit*, 14.

86   See Clegg's extended discussion from "Slavery and Capitalism" 296–297.

87   Deirdre McCloskey, "Slavery Did Not Make America Rich," National Association of Scholars, September 16, 2019, https://www.nas.org/blogs/article/slavery-did-not-make-america-rich.

88   See the rough draft of the Declaration, https://www.loc.gov/exhibits/declara/ruffdrft.html.

89   The writers describe their own side of the tension: "The advocates for the constitution seemed to suppose, that this restriction being laid upon Congress only for a term of time, is the 'fair dawning of liberty.' That 'it was a glorious acquisition towards the final abolition of slavery.' But how much more glorious would the acquisition have been, was such abolition to take place the first moment the constitution should be established. If we had said that after the expiration of a certain term the practice should cease, it would have appeared with a better grace; but this is not the case, for even after that, it is wholly optional with the Congress, whether they abolish it or not."

90   Jones later softened this claim, after serious rebuffs from historians across the political spectrum. To the following sentence, "Conveniently left out of our founding mythology is the fact that one

of the primary reasons the colonists decided to declare their independence from Britain was because they wanted to protect the institution of slavery," she added "some of," as in "some of the colonists...."

91   Thanks to Phil Magness for pointing out that the people who did notice the Somerset decision in the colonies were generally anti-slavery. Benjamin Franklin wrote a letter to Anthony Benezet about the decision shortly after news reached North America. He expressed his disappointment that it did not go far enough since it only freed one slave. US abolitionists became very adept at using Somerset after the Revolution to mount a legal attack on slavery. Although it failed, the Dred Scott case was one such attempt (the dissent cites Somerset). See William Wiecek's *The Sources of Anti-Slavery Constitutionalism in America, 1760–1848* (Ithaca, NY: Cornell University Press, 2018). This is the classic work to cite on the Somerset decision but does not appear in the 1619 Project's references.

Relatedly, the earliest Northern voices for independence—e.g., James Otis—were vocally antislavery. Thomas Paine is often thought to be the author of the anonymous essay "African Slavery in America" in the *Pennsylvania Journal* in 1775, which got much wider circulation than the stuff NHJ invokes. See https://oll.libertyfund.org/title/ paine-the-writings-of-thomas-paine-vol-i-1774-1779#lf0548-01_ label_026.

92   Tom Mackaman, "An Interview with Historian Gordon Wood on the *New York Times'* 1619 Project," World Socialist Web Site, November 27, 2019, https://www.wsws.org/en/articles/2019/11/28/wood-n28. html.

93   Thomas Israel, *The Expanding Blaze: How the American Revolution Ignited the World,* 1775–1848 (Princeton, NJ: Princeton University Press, 2016), https://www.amazon.com/Expanding-Blaze-American-Revolution-1775-1848/dp/0691176604.

94   Schweninger, *Black Property Owners in the South*, 20. The Revolution actually led to the freeing of many Blacks, as the inspiration of the ideals of liberty and equality took hold—1782 Virginia legalized private manumissions, within eight years there were 12,766 free Blacks there. French-speaking Blacks fled from the Caribbean into the Gulf and lower Mississippi River Valley. By 1790 there were 32,357; by 1800, 61,241; by 1810, 108,265—one out of every twelve Blacks was free.

95   *Phillis Wheatley, Complete Writings*, "On the Death of General Wooster" and "Letter to Rev. Samson Occum" respectively.

96 "The Petition of a Grate Number of Blacks of this Province who by divine permission are held in a state of Slavery within the bowels of a free and Christian Country": An Appeal to Thomas Gage, Royal Governor of Massachusetts, May 25, 1774, Fordham University https://sourcebooks.fordham.edu/mod/1774slavesappeal.asp.

97 Douglass, "What to a Slave Is the Fourth of July?" https://teachingamericanhistory.org/library/document/what-to-the-slave-is-the-fourth-of-july/.

98 Lucas Morel, "America Wasn't Founded on White Supremacy," *The American Mind*, October 17, 2019, https://americanmind.org/essays/america-wasnt-founded-on-white-supremacy/.

99 Martin Luther King Jr., "I Have a Dream" speech, 1963, NPR, https://www.npr.org/2010/01/18/122701268/i-have-a-dream-speech-in-its-entirety.

100 Black academic critics include Lucas Morel, John McWhorter (who calls himself a "cranky liberal"), Glenn Loury, and Clayborne Carson. Historians criticizing the 1619 Project for the World Socialist Web Site include Victoria Bynum, Gordon Wood, James McPherson, and James Oakes.

101 Quoted in Loren Schweninger, *Black Property Owners in the South*, 144–5.

102 Joel Mokyr, *A Culture of Growth: The Origins of the Modern Economy* (Princeton, NJ: Princeton University Press, 2018).

103 We use the term "liberal" here in the global and philosophical sense (a system of government that defends individual freedoms), not in the sense in which the term is used in American politics.

104 This holds as long as there is no relevant difference between the groups. For instance, the law can make a distinction in application between children and adults, but only because children's wills are not fully formed. False claims to legally significant differences, such as the idea that Blacks and whites can be distinguished in the law for some pseudo-scientific reasons, are examples of unjust laws. Martin Luther King Jr. quoted Augustine on this matter: "An unjust law is no law at all," and then proceeded in the "Letter from Birmingham Jail" to give a classically Thomistic natural law justification for civil disobedience. To see the relevant section in Thomas Aquinas's "Treatise on Law," look at *Summa Theologiae*.

105 William Easterly's *The Elusive Quest for Growth* (Cambridge: The MIT Press, 2001).

[106] We realize that we are jumping into a longstanding historical debate here. We take the view that slaveholders, despite engaging in markets, were not capitalists because they did not share the bourgeois virtues that are essential for the culture of the market (we also take many of them at their word that they were not capitalists and that they deplored the emergence of what they deemed an impersonal economic system not based on patronage). Instead, slave holders were like past elites who engaged in markets, often begrudgingly, in order to support their social status as the new world's aristocratic elite. For a discussion of the new "republican" focus on egalitarianism and entrepreneurship and the retrenchment of Southerners, see Joyce Appleby, *Inheriting the Revolution: The First Generation of Americans,* (Cambridge, MA: Belknap Press, 2001). We also suggest Genovese's *The World the Slaveholders Made* (New York: Random House, 1969). These two "essays in interpretation" cover this feudalism vs. capitalism argument (although he frames it as seigneurialism vs. capitalism) in great detail.

[107] Sidney Mintz quoted in Loren Schweninger, *Black Property Owners in the South,* 11.

[108] For more on the character and evolution of slavery in the United States consult: John W. Blassingame, *The Slave Community: Plantation Life in the Antebellum South* (New York: Oxford University Press, 1972), particularly 250–51. Ira Berlin, *Many Thousands Gone: The First Two Centuries of Slavery in North America,* (Cambridge: Belknap Press, 1998). Berlin in particular traces the change over time. On women of the plantation see Elizabeth Fox-Genovese, *Within the Plantation Household: Black and White Women of the Old South* (Chapel Hill: UNC Press, 1988).

[109] Schweninger, *Black Property Owners in the South,* 14–15.

[110] Schweninger, *Black Property Owners in the South,* 52.

[111] Frederick Douglass, *My Bondage, My Freedom* (London: Penguin Classics, 2003), 239.

[112] Schweninger, *Black Property Owners in the South,* 42–43.

[113] Schweninger, *Black Property Owners in the South,* 80.

[114] C. C. Goen, *Broken Churches, Broken Nation* (Macon, GA: Mercer University Press, 1985), 82.

[115] Schweninger, *Black Property Owners in the South,* 40.

[116] Robert Higgs, *Competition and Coercion: Blacks in the American Economy 1865–1914* (Cambridge, UK: Cambridge University Press, reprint edition 2008), 38.

117 Black resistance during slavery included things like breaking of tools and other techniques. James Oakes, *Slavery and Freedom: An Interpretation of the Old South* (New York: Knopf, 1990), 138, 227; Peter Kolchin, *American Slavery, 1619–1877* (New York: Hill and Wang, 1993; reprinted in 2003), 157; Ira Berlin, *Generations of Captivity: A History of African-American Slaves* (Cambridge, MA: Harvard University Press, 2003), 175, 178.

118 This is in Schweninger's *Black Property Owners in the South.*

119 Robert W. Fairlie and William A. Sundstrom, "The Emergence, Persistence, and Recent Widening of the Racial Unemployment Gap," *Industrial and Labor Relations Review,* vol. 52, no. 2 (1999), https://people.ucsc.edu/~rfairlie/papers/published/ilrr%201999%20-%20racial%20unemployment.pdf.

120 Roy W. Copeland, "In the Beginning: Origins of African American Real Property Ownership in the United States," *Journal of Black Studies* 44, no. 6 (2013): 657, http://www.jstor.org/stable/24572860.

121 Copeland, "In the Beginning," 649.

122 *Swoll v. Oliver,* https://cite.case.law/ga/61/248/.

123 *Bryan v. Walton,* https://cite.case.law/ga/30/834/.

124 Copeland, "In the Beginning," 648–649.

125 Gates, 304.

126 Gates, 313.

127 Quoted in Copeland's "In the Beginning: Origins of African American Real Property Ownership in the United States," 654.

128 Higgs, *Competition and Coercion,* 52.

129 Higgs, *Competition and Coercion,* 78–80.

130 Kwame Anthony Appiah and Martin Bunzl, eds., *Buying Freedom: The Ethics and Economics of Slave Redemption* (Princeton, NJ: Princeton University Press, 2007), 218. Frederick Douglass published essays by Englishmen who tried to map England's compensated emancipation plan onto the S.

131 Higgs, *Competition and Coercion,* 45.

132 Higgs, *Competition and Coercion,* 45.

133 Higgs, *Competition and Coercion,* 57.

134 Higgs, *Competition and Coercion,* 49–50.

135 Higgs, *Competition and Coercion,* 45.

136 Quoted in Higgs's *Competition and Coercion,* 48.

137 Higgs, *Competition and Coercion,* 48.

[138] Adam Smith, *Wealth of Nations*: "People of the same trade seldom meet together, even for merriment and diversion, but the conversation ends in a conspiracy against the public, or in some contrivance to raise prices."

[139] Schweninger, *Black Property Owners in the South*, 157–9.

[140] Higgs, *Competition and Coercion*, 35.

[141] David Bernstein, *Only One Place of Redress: African-Americans, Labor Regulations, and the Courts, from Reconstruction to the New Deal* (Durham, NC: Duke University Press, 2001), 12.

[142] Higgs, *Competition and Coercion*, 117.

[143] Higgs, *Competition and Coercion*, 87 and 132.

[144] Higgs, *Competition and Coercion*, 86.

[145] Higgs, *Competition and Coercion*, 132.

[146] Higgs, *Competition and Coercion*, 133.

[147] Hamilton Lombard, "Black Households Earn More in the Mid-Atlantic, but There Is No Simple Explanation Why," StatChat, March 15, 2016, http://statchatva.org/2016/03/15/Black-households-earn-more-in-the-mid-atlantic-but-there-is-no-simple-explanation-why/.

[148] Higgs, *Competition and Coercion*, 120.

[149] Schweninger, *Black Property Owners in the South*, 282–284.

[150] Thad Sitton and James H. Conrad, *Freedom Colonies: Independent Black Texans in the Time of Jim Crow*, (University of Texas Press, 2005), 178.

[151] Thad Sitton Revised by Andrea Roberts, Grace Kelly, and Schuyler Carter, "Freedmen's Settlements," Handbook of Texas Online, accessed July 29, 2021, https://www.tshaonline.org/handbook/entries/freedmens-settlements.

[152] Gary Becker, *The Economics of Discrimination* (Chicago: University of Chicago Press, 1957, reprinted 1971).

[153] William Harold Hutt, *Economics of the Colour Bar* (London: Merritt & Hatcher, 1964).

[154] Jennifer Roback, "W. H. Hutt's *The Economics of the Colour Bar,*" *Managerial and Decision Economics*, vol. 9, Special Issue: A Collection of Essays Compiled as a Memorial to W. H. Hutt, https://www.jstor.org/stable/2487505; Art Carden (Samford University), Vincent Geloso (Free Market Institute at Texas Tech University), and Phillip W. Magness (Berry College), "Situating Southern Influences in James M. Buchanan and Modern Public Choice Economics,"

version: Tuesday, July 25, 2017, https://www.readcube.com/articles/10.2139%2Fssrn.3008867.

155 The debate over whether Reconstruction was a success or failure began during the 1870s and continues today. Much comes down to individual historians' conception of "success." For our part, we consider Reconstruction to have been a failure because although the sections came back together and some elements of Radical Reconstruction were successful, ultimately black Americans did not receive full citizenship. For a quick overview of the literature, see https://dailyhistory.org/Understanding_Reconstruction_-_A_Historiography.

156 For a detailed account of the Colfax Massacre consult LeeAnna Keith, *The Colfax Massacre: The Untold Story of Black Power, White Terror, and the Death of Reconstruction* (Oxford: Oxford University Press, 2008) and Charles Lane, *The Day Freedom Died: The Colfax Massacre, the Supreme Court, and the Betrayal of Reconstruction* (New York: Henry Holt, 2008).

157 Steven Hahn, *A Nation Under Our Feet: Black Political Struggles in the Rural South from Slavery to the Great Migration* (Cambridge, MA: Belknap Press, 2003), 292–295.

158 Hahn, *A Nation Under Our Feet*, 293–294.

159 Danny Lewis, "The 1873 Colfax Massacre Crippled the Reconstruction Era," *Smithsonian Magazine*, April 13, 2016, accessed on May 28, 2020, at https://www.smithsonianmag.com/smart-news/1873-colfax-massacre-crippled-reconstruction-180958746/; Michael Stop-Smith, "The Colfax Massacre," *Black Past*, April 7, 2011, accessed on May 28, 2020, at https://www.Blackpast.org/african-american-history/colfax-massacre-1873/.

160 Hahn, *A Nation Under Our Feet*, 294.

161 "House Report on the Condition of the South," Report Number 261, in Reports of Committees of the House of Representatives for the Second Session of the Forty-Third Congress (Washington, DC: US Printing Office, 1875), 11–14, accessed on May 28, 2020, at https://teachingamericanhistory.org/library/document/colfax-massacre-reports/.

162 "House Report on the Condition of the South," 11–14.

163 Eric Foner, *Reconstruction: America's Unfinished Revolution: 1863–1877* (New York: Harper Collins, 2011).

164 "House Report on the Condition of the South," 11–14.

165 Hahn, *A Nation Under Our Feet*, 295.

166 Lewis, "The 1873 Colfax Massacre Crippled the Reconstruction Era."

[167] Hahn, *A Nation Under Our Feet*, 295.

[168] Lewis, "The 1873 Colfax Massacre Crippled the Reconstruction Era."

[169] Richard Rubin, "The Colfax Riot: Stumbling on a Forgotten Reconstruction Tragedy, in a Forgotten Corner of Louisiana," *The Atlantic*, July/August 2003, accessed on May 29, 2020, at https://www.theatlantic.com/magazine/archive/2003/07/the-colfax-riot/378556/.

[170] For an in-depth account of how the Civil War has been remembered, see David Blight, *Race and Reunion: The Civil War in American Memory* (Cambridge: Belknap Press, 2002).

[171] Douglas A. Blackmon, *Slavery by Another Name: The Re-Enslavement of Black Americans from the Civil War to World War II* (New York: Anchor, 2008), 150.

[172] *Slavery by Another Name*, PBS documentary, 2012, accessed at https://www.pbs.org/show/slavery-another-name/.

[173] Blackmon, *Slavery by Another Name,* 53.

[174] Blackmon, *Slavery by Another Name,* 56.

[175] Blackmon, *Slavery by Another Name,* 99.

[176] Blackmon, *Slavery by Another Name,* 112.

[177] Blackmon, *Slavery by Another Name,* 55.

[178] Blackmon, *Slavery by Another Name,* 71.

[179] Blackmon, *Slavery by Another Name,* 64–65.

[180] Blackmon, *Slavery by Another Name,* 288.

[181] *Slavery by Another Name*, PBS documentary.

[182] Jonathan Bean, *Race and Liberty in America: The Essential Reader* (Lexington: University Press of Kentucky: 2009), 77.

[183] "History of Lynchings," National Association for the Advancement of Colored People, accessed at https://www.naacp.org/history-of-lynchings/.

[184] For a comprehensive analysis of lynching from many different perspectives, consult *Under the Sentence of Death: Lynching in the South*, edited by W. Fitzhugh Brundage (Chapel Hill: The University of North Carolina Press, 1997).

[185] Hahn, *A Nation Under Our Feet*, 426.

[186] Hahn, *A Nation Under Our Feet*, 427.

[187] "History of Lynchings," National Association for the Advancement of Colored People, accessed at https://naacp.org/find-resources/history-explained/history-lynching-america.

188 "History of Lynchings" National Association for the Advancement of Colored People, accessed at https://naacp.org/find-resources/history-explained/history-lynching-america.

189 Linda O. McMurry, *To Keep the Waters Troubled: The Life of Ida B. Wells* (Oxford: Oxford University Press, 1998), 130–131.

190 McMurry, *To Keep the Waters Troubled*, 130.

191 McMurry, *To Keep the Waters Troubled*, 131.

192 McMurry, *To Keep the Waters Troubled*, 131.

193 McMurry, *To Keep the Waters Troubled*, 132–133.

194 McMurry, *To Keep the Waters Troubled*, 133.

195 Paula J. Giddings, *A Sword Among Lions: Ida B. Wells and the Campaign Against Lynching* (New York: Amistad, 2008), 183.

196 Ida B. Wells, *Crusade for Justice: The Autobiography of Ida B. Wells*, edited by Alfreda M. Duster (Chicago: University of Chicago Press, 2020), 52; as quoted in Giddings, *A Sword Among Lions*, 189.

197 Wells herself was not completely enamored with Oklahoma. She spent three weeks visiting various cities in the territory and documenting her experience in the *Free Speech*. According to Giddings, however, Wells "had already determined to leave Memphis and seriously considered moving to Oklahoma and bringing the *Free Speech* there." Giddings, *A Sword Among Lions*, 197–199. McMurry, *To Keep the Waters Troubled*, 141–142.

198 Giddings, *A Sword Among Lions*, 193.

199 Giddings, *A Sword Among Lions*, 201.

200 Giddings, *A Sword Among Lions*, 213. Giddings recounts this movement in her chapter "Exodus" in her biography of Ida B. Wells. She quotes the *Indianapolis Freeman*, which declared that in the future, "the Negro race, weary of proscriptions and barbaric treatment in the South, migrated to the West, where, under kinder and more progressive conditions, it finally rises to the full height of complete citizenship." Giddings, *A Sword Among Lions*, 190. Linda O. McMurry also discusses the emigration at length in her chapter "The Memphis Lynchings." McMurry, *To Keep the Waters Troubled*, 140–141.

201 Giddings, *A Sword Among Lions*, 203.

202 Wells, *Crusade for Justice*, 64.

203 Frederick Douglass, "Lynch Law in the South," as quoted in David Blight, *Frederick Douglass: Prophet of Freedom* (New York: Simon and Schuster, 2018), 719–720.

204 As quoted in McMurry, *To Keep the Waters Troubled*, 146. As quoted in Giddings, *A Sword Among Lions*, 208.

205 As quoted in McMurry, *To Keep the Waters Troubled*, 146–147. As quoted in Giddings, *A Sword Among Lions*, 212.

206 As quoted in McMurry, *To Keep the Waters Troubled*, 148.

207 McMurry, *To Keep the Waters Troubled*, 148.

208 As quoted in McMurry, *To Keep the Waters Troubled*, 148.

209 As quoted in McMurry, *To Keep the Waters Troubled*, 148.

210 Giddings, *A Sword Among Lions*, 221.

211 As quoted in David Blight, *Frederick Douglass*, 722.

212 As quoted in Blight, *Frederick Douglass*, 733.

213 Patricia A. Schechter, *Ida B. Wells-Barnett and American Reform: 1880–1930* (Chapel Hill: University of North Carolina Press, 2001), 23.

214 As quoted in Giddings, *A Sword Among Lions*, 340–341.

215 "African Americans," Oklahoma Historical Society, accessed on January 2, 2021, https://www.okhistory.org/publications/enc/entry.php?entry=AF003.

216 Tim Madigan, *The Burning: Massacre, Destruction, and the Tulsa Race Riots of 1921* (New York: St. Martin's Griffin, 2001), 15.

217 For more on Blacks in Oklahoma, consult Jimmie Lewis Franklin, *The Blacks in Oklahoma* (Norman: University of Oklahoma Press, 1980), and Jimmie Lewis Franklin, *Journey Toward Hope: A History of Blacks in Oklahoma* (Norman: University of Oklahoma Press, 1982). For a description of Black towns, see Norman Crockett, *The Black Towns* (Lawrence: Regents Press of Kansas, 1979); Kenneth M. Hamilton, *Black Towns and Profit: Promotion and Development in the Trans-Appalachian West, 1877–1915* (Chicago: University of Illinois Press, 1991); and Karla Slocum, *Black Towns, Black Futures: The Enduring Allure of a Place in the American West* (Chapel Hill: University of North Carolina Press, 2019).

218 Madigan, *The Burning*, 16.

219 "African Americans," Oklahoma Historical Society.

220 Timothy Egan, *The Worst Hard Time: The Untold Story of Those Who Survived the Great American Dust Bowl* (Boston: Houghton Mifflin, 2006).

221 Madigan, *The Burning*, 16–17.

222 "November 10, 1898: Wilmington Massacre," Zinn Education Project: Teaching People's History, accessed on January 4, 2020, https://www. zinnedproject.org/news/tdih/wilmington-massacre-2/.

223 David Zucchino, *Wilmington's Lie: The Murderous Coup of 1898 and the Rise of White Supremacy* (New York: Atlantic Monthly Press, 2020), xvii.

224 "November 10, 1898: Wilmington Massacre."

225 For an overview on these and other racial massacres, consult Zinn Education Project's "Massacres in U.S. History," https://www.zinnedproject.org/collection/massacres-us/.

226 Madigan, *The Burning*, 11–12.

227 Madigan, *The Burning*, 20–22.

228 Madigan, *The Burning*, 18–22.

229 For more on the Red Summer of 1919, consult Cameron McWhirter, *Red Summer: The Summer of 1919 and the Awakening of Black America* (New York: St. Martin's Griffin, 2012); and Robert Whitaker, *On the Laps of Gods: The Red Summer of 1919 and the Struggle for Justice That Remade a Nation* (New York: Crown, 2009). For a quick summary of some of the massacres that occurred in 1919, see Zinn Education Project's "Massacres in U.S. History." https://www.zinnedproject.org/collection/massacres-us/, and Madigan, *The Burning*, 23.

230 Madigan, *The Burning*, 50–54.

231 Madigan, *The Burning*, 69–71.

232 Madigan, *The Burning*, 77–79.

233 Madigan, *The Burning*, 102–103.

234 Madigan, *The Burning*, 125.

235 Madigan, *The Burning*, 180–183.

236 Maggie Astor, "What to Know about the Tulsa Greenwood Massacre," *New York Times*, June 20, 2020, accessed on January 6, 2020, https://www.nytimes.com/2020/06/20/us/tulsa-greenwood-massacre.html.

237 David K. Li, "Nearly a Century Later, Tulsa Is Digging for Evidence of Mass Graves In Infamous Race Massacre," NBC News, July 14, 2020, https://www.nbcnews.com/news/us-news/nearly-century-later-tulsa-digging-evidence-mass-graves-infamous-race-n1233770.

238 Anthony Bradley, "Finally Healing the Wounds of Jim Crow," *Fathom Mag*, July 11, 2018.

239 Lisa Magarrell and Joya Wesley, *Learning from Greensboro: Truth and Reconciliation in the United States*, (Philadelphia: University of Pennsylvania Press, 2010).

[240] DeNeen L. Brown, "A White Republican Mayor Seeks the Truth about Tulsa's Race Massacre a Century Ago," *Washington Post*, March 13, 2020, https://www.washingtonpost.com/history/2020/03/13/tulsa-mayor-bynum-mass-graves/.

[241] The Associated Press, "Painting Looted by Nazis in 1933 Returned to Jewish Family," NBC News, October 15, 2020, https://www.nbcnews.com/news/us-news/painting-looted-nazis-1933-returned-jewish-family-n1243678.

[242] Albert J. Raboteau, *Slave Religion: The "Invisible Institution" in the Antebellum South*, updated edition (Oxford University Press, 2004), ch. 1.

[243] Black African is what was meant by the term "Ethiopian" in that historical context.

[244] Glenn Usry and Craig Keener, *Black Man's Religion: Can Christianity Be Afro-Centric?* (Westmont, IL: InterVarsity Press, 1996), 34.

[245] Thank you to historians Carey Roberts and Sam Smith for bringing this to our attention.

[246] Gina Zurlo, "The World as 100 Christians," Gordon Conwell Theological Seminary, January 29, 2020, https://www.gordonconwell.edu/blog/100christians/.

[247] Jemar Tisby, *The Color of Compromise: The Truth about the American Church's Complicity in Racism*, (Grand Rapids, MI: Zondervan, 2019), 20.

[248] Jeff Diamant and Besheer Mohamed, "Black Millennials Are More Religious Than Other Millennials," Pew Research Center, July 20, 2018, https://www.pewresearch.org/fact-tank/2018/07/20/Black-millennials-are-more-religious-than-other-millennials/.

[249] It might also be less surprising for those familiar with the history of Christianity, in which the church commonly attracted oppressed groups with its message of the inherent dignity and value of every individual, the raising up of the humble, and radical love. We know this in part because the church's detractors made fun of it for that very reason. For instance, in the second century, Celsus claimed that the church attracted only "the silly and the mean and the stupid, with women and children," and Bishop Cyprian reported that Christian women were so numerous it was difficult to get them Christian husbands. This dynamic also plays out powerfully in Chinua Achebe's classic historical novel, *Things Fall Apart,* as those with little standing in the Igbo community become the first converts of the missionaries.

250 Frederick Douglass, *The Narrative of the Life of Frederick Douglass and Other Works* (New York: Canterbury Classics, 2014), 212–213.

251 For a good introduction to the thought and writings of Frederick Douglass, see Nicholas Buccola's edited collection *The Essential Douglass: Selected Writings and Speeches* (Indianapolis, IN: Hackett Publishing Company, 2016).

252 Douglass, *The Narrative of the Life of Frederick Douglass and Other Works,* 95–98.

253 Raboteau, *Slave Religion,* 104–105.

254 Quoted in Raboteau, *Slave Religion,* 105.

255 Lauren F. Winner, *A Cheerful and Comfortable Faith: Anglican Religious Practice in the Elite Households of Eighteenth Century Virginia,* illustrated edition (New Haven, CT: Yale University Press, 2010).

256 Raboteau, *Slave Religion,* 103, 106–107.

257 Jeremiah 34:8–20: This passage describes not only a demand that all Hebrew slaves be freed, but a crushing punishment for failing to do so.

258 Jonathan Merritt, "Defining Evangelical," *The Atlantic,* December 7, 2015, https://www.theatlantic.com/politics/archive/2015/12/evangelical-christian/418236/.

259 Raboteau, *Slave Religion,* 132–133.

260 See the stories of Rebecca Protten and Jerena Lee, the mothers of the "Black Reformation," https://www.christianitytoday.com/history/2018/february/why-enslaved-african-americans-stayed-christian.html.

261 Nathan O. Hatch, *The Democratization of Christianity* (New Haven, CT: Yale University Press, 1991), 102.

262 Raboteau, *Slave Religion,* 149.

263 Hatch, *The Democratization of Christianity,* 105.

264 Raboteau, *Slave Religion,* 143–144.

265 At the Christmas Conference of 1784, the Methodists declared that they viewed slavery to be "contrary to the Golden Law of God."

266 Tisby, *The Color of Compromise,* 51.

267 Raboteau, *Slave Religion,* 147.

268 Raboteau, *Slave Religion,* 163–164.

269 Raboteau, *Slave Religion,* 141.

270 Raboteau, *Slave Religion,* 145.

271 Raboteau, *Slave Religion,* 165, quoting Southern missionaries Jones and Capers: "To benefit servants, evangelize the masters; to benefit masters, evangelize the servants."

[272] Raboteau, *Slave Religion*, 157.

[273] Raboteau, *Slave Religion*, 158.

[274] Augustine, *Confessions*, Book VIII.

[275] Aristotle, *Politics*, 1254b16–21.

[276] Abolition was impossible anyway, they argued, since they believed the newly invigorated cotton industry to be totally indispensable for the entire American—and even global—economy. We now know this claim to be simply false, as the textile industry successfully turned to Egypt and other markets to gain cotton during the Civil War. Jeffrey D. Grynaviski and Michael C. Munger, "Reconstructing Racism: Transforming Racial Hierarchy from "Necessary Evil" into "Positive Good," *Social Philosophy and Policy*, vol. 34, issue 1 (Summer 2017), 144163.

[277] Grynaviski and Munger, "Reconstructing Racism," 151.

[278] Raboteau, *Slave Religion*, 168.

[279] Quoted in Raboteau's *Slave Religion*, 168.

[280] Raboteau, *Slave Religion*, 170.

[281] Raboteau, *Slave Religion*, 171.

[282] Raboteau, *Slave Religion*, 183.

[283] Raboteau describes the minutes of a Virginia Portsmouth Baptist Association meeting wrapping up a few years of debate: "'What ought Churches to do with Members in their Communion, who shall either directly, or indirectly separate married Slaves, who are come together according to the custom as Man and Wife?' After another prolonged debate the question 'was thought by a Majority to be so difficult, that no answer could be given it.'" *Slave Religion*, 184.

[284] Raboteau, *Slave Religion*, 294–5.

[285] Raboteau, *Slave Religion*, 176.

[286] Albert J. Raboteau, *Slave Religion*, 294.

[287] Quoted in Raboteau's *Slave Religion*, 176.

[288] Raboteau, *Slave Religion*, 179

[289] Raboteau, *Slave Religion*, 179.

[290] Raboteau, *Slave Religion*, 195.

[291] Rev. H. H. Tucker of Mercer College, quoted in Albert J. Raboteau, *Slave Religion*, 195.

[292] Raboteau, *Slave Religion*, 204.

[293] Raboteau, *Slave Religion*, 214–215.

[294] Albert J. Raboteau, *Slave Religion*, 219.

[295] Raboteau, *Slave Religion*, 209–210.

296   2 Samuel 12.

297   I.e., Amos 5:18–24, Jer. 22:16, Is. 1:10–17, Is. 58:6–7, Ezek. 16:49, all
      quoted in Usry and Keener, p. 112–113. There are many more.

298   Raboteau, *Slave Religion*, 248.

299   Raboteau, *Slave Religion*, 307.

300   Donald G. Mathews, *Religion in the Old South (Chicago History of
      American Religion)* (Chicago: University of Chicago Press, 1979), 215.

301   Raboteau, *Slave Religion*, 318.

302   Raboteau, *Slave Religion*, 333.

303   Donald G. Mathews, *Religion in the Old South,* 229.

304   We distinguish here between "Black theology" as it might currently be
      practiced in elite academic institutions and seminaries, and the prac-
      tice of the historical black church. These two are by no means in sync
      with one another. See Esau McCaulley's *Reading While Black: African
      American Biblical Interpretation as an Exercise in Hope* (Westmont, IL:
      InterVarsity Press, 2020).

305   "Earth's crammed with heaven, And every common bush afire with
      God, But only he who sees takes off his shoes; The rest sit round and
      pluck Blackberries." —Elizabeth Barrett Browning

306   James Forbes, "Up from Invisibility," *New York Times*, December 23,
      1990, https://www.nytimes.com/1990/12/23/books/up-from-invis-
      ibility.html: "The Black church is still invisible to many whites..."

307   Quoted in C. Eric Lincoln and Lawrence H. Mamiya, *The Black
      Church in the African American Experience*, 8.

308   Lincoln and Mamiya, *The Black Church in the African American
      Experience,* 30.

309   Lincoln and Mamiya, *The Black Church in the African American
      Experience,* 28–29.

310   Kenneth B. Clark, *King, Malcolm, Baldwin: Three interviews*
      (Middletown, CT: Wesleyan University Press, 1985), 53.

311   Clark, *King, Malcolm, Baldwin,* 19.

312   Clark, *King, Malcolm, Baldwin,* 60.

313   Lincoln and Mamiya, *The Black Church in the African American
      Experience,* 7.

314   Albert J. Raboteau, *Slave Religion*, 311.

315   Both Douglass and Washington quoted in Raboteau's *Slave Religion*,
      248 and 249.

316   Sister Nancy Brooks, quoted in Raboteau's *Slave Religion*, 265.

317 Rachel grew up singing this spiritual, taught to her by her foster brother, Matt Brown. It assumes that the fourth person who appeared in the furnace with the three boys was Christ himself (the technical term for such an event is "theophany"): "Trouble in my way, I got to cry sometimes/ Trouble in my way, I got to cry sometimes/ I lay awake at night (lay awake at night), Tell me that's alright (that's alright)/ Cuz I know Jesus (Jesus, He will fix it) After while (after while)/ Stepped in the furnace (stepped in the furnace), a long time ago (a long time ago-o-o-o)/ Shadrach and Meshach (Shadrach and Meshach) and Abednego (and Abednego) [jokingly pronounced "a bad negro"]/Lemme tell ya they wasn't wary (they wasn't wary!)/ This I know! (this I know)/ Cuz I know Jesus! (Jesus, he will fix it)/ Cuz I know Jesus (Jesus He will fix it)/ Cuz I know Jesus! (Jesus, He will fix it)/ After while (after while)/ He fix it for my mama (Jesus He will fix it), he fix it for my papa (Jesus He will fix it), he fix it for my brothuh (Jesus He will fix it), he fix it for my sistah (Jesus He will fix it), and he'll fix it for you (Jesus He will fix it), after while (after whiiiiiiiiile)."

318 Daniel 6, Daniel 3, Jonah 2.

319 Anthony Bradley explains how Bavinck understands the Black Church advantage: "Black Church, Moses, Evangelical White church, Paul": http://www.whatisyoursalvationfor.com/blog/2017/1/7/black-church-moses-and-evangelical-white-church-paul.

320 Matthew 25:31–46. For instance, verses 41–46 read, "Then he will say to those on his left, 'Depart from me, you who are cursed, into the eternal fire prepared for the devil and his angels. For I was hungry and you gave me nothing to eat, I was thirsty and you gave me nothing to drink, I was a stranger and you did not invite me in, I needed clothes and you did not clothe me, I was sick and in prison and you did not look after me.' They will answer, 'Lord, when did we see you hungry and thirsty or a stranger or needing clothes or sick or in prison, and did not help you?' He will reply, 'Truly I tell you, whatever you did not do for one of the least of these, you did not do for me.' Then they will go away to eternal punishment, but the righteous to eternal life."

321 Raboteau, *Slave Religion*, 291.

322 Lincoln and Mamiya, *The Black Church in the African American Experience*, 18.

323 Lincoln and Mamiya, *The Black Church in the African American Experience*, 93.

324 Just as we had to clarify our use of the term "evangelical" earlier in this book, as it has taken on new meaning in recent decades in America, so too must we clarify the term "fundamentalist," which is used in a much broader sense in common parlance today than how we use the term here. Fundamentalists are a subset of evangelicals with a few definitive markers: 1) dispensationalism, the biblical hermeneutic in which God deals differently with humans in different ages, and 2) premillennial eschatology, in which Jesus is coming very soon, Christians will be raptured to heaven while the unbelievers experience terrible destruction, and there will be a thousand-year reign of Christ prior to the Judgment Day, 3) the special role of a literal Israel in biblical prophecy, and 4) as a result of their commitment to the imminent apocalypse, separatism—a kind of "fortress mentality" that is quick to isolate and declare cultural war. These ideas were laid out in *The Fundamentals*, a set of books that a wealthy benefactor sent to every white pastor in America in order to spread his theological views. The term "modernist," in this context, refers to a theological liberalism that denies the inerrancy of the Bible, denies the historical reality of some or all miraculous Christian claims, and emphasizes Christianity as an ethic instead.

325 Premillenial dispensationalism was the mid-nineteenth-century invention of John Nelson Darby, a British theologian whose ideas caught on in America. For most black Protestants, he had created a complex and innovative system of biblical interpretation that led to reading apocalyptic ideas into world events and making the Bible "say things it was not meant to reveal." Quoted in Mary Beth Swetnam Mathews's *Doctrine and Race: African American Evangelicals and Fundamentalism between the Wars (Religion & American Culture)*, first edition (University of Alabama Press, 2017), 73–74. Black Protestants generally "rejected the emphasis on biblical prophecies outright or were silent on it." Excepting the Pentecostals, the premillennial view was uncommon among Black Christians, who were loath to depart from the traditional view of most Protestants, that the kingdom of Jesus Christ has already begun but has not yet fully manifested. (Mary Beth Swetnam Mathews, *Doctrine and Race,* 70).

326 Mathews, *Doctrine and Race,* 77.

327 Quoted in Mary Beth Swetnam Mathews, *Doctrine and Race,* 76. It might be worth noting that some geographical and socioeconomic separation may have played a role as well: fundamentalism arose in northern and western cities, while most Blacks still lived in the rural

South between World Wars I and II; theological modernism was a project of the academy, rarely touching the lives of ordinary black worshipers.

[328] Mary Beth Swetnam Mathews, *Doctrine and Race,* 90.

[329] Mary Beth Swetnam Mathews, *Doctrine and Race,* 89.

[330] The term is somewhat imprecise; many adherents were theologically progressive, but some were also theologically conservative, such as the Pietists who led the Prohibition movement in hopes of alleviating the suffering of women and children subject to alcoholic husbands and fathers. Some leaned heavily toward socialism, while others emphasized voluntary movements to live with and identify with the poor.

[331] Mary Beth Swetnam Mathews, *Doctrine and Race,* 140.

[332] Mary Beth Swetnam Mathews, *Doctrine and Race,* 141. Some whites did this quite well, especially if they came from holiness traditions; consider that Oswald Chambers, the famous author of the deeply theologically conservative devotional *My Utmost for His Highest,* was a YMCA chaplain, one of the most profound social justice institutions of its day. (Chambers died when he refused to go to the hospital with appendicitis because he didn't want to take up a bed that a wounded soldier might need.)

[333] Quoted in Mary Beth Swetnam Mathews's *Doctrine and Race,* 140.

[334] The Black Church perspective anticipated academic analyses of this period in white American theology. Matthew Avery Sutton has argued that "[c]hristian fundamentalism and theological modernism were two sides of the same coin; both illustrated the all-consuming power of modernist thought." Fundamentalists unwittingly embraced a deeply modern perspective in many ways: assuming (in the evolution/creation debate) that God's action in nature was always interventionist rather than integral to the functioning of nature; dismissing the importance of the historical Christian creeds, communities, and historical theology; and taking a sort of engineer's perspective on the Bible—treating individual verses like cogs that could be cross-referenced, quantified, placed into taxonomies, and reassembled to form something new. "The Day Christian Fundamentalism Was Born." https://www.nytimes.com/2019/05/25/opinion/the-day-christian-fundamentalism-was-born.html.

[335] Esau McCaulley, *Reading While Black: African American Biblical Interpretation as an Exercise in Hope,* (Westmont, IL: InterVarsityPress, 2020).

336 Phillip Berryman, *Liberation Theology* (Philadelphia: Temple University Press, 1987), 138–139. Berryman claims that liberation theologians are not Marxists at all but rather merely utilize Marx's class analysis because so many Latin Americans are Marxist in their worldview.

337 Exodus 20:15; Deuteronomy 5:21, 19:14, 21:16, 27:17; Proverbs 3:16, 10:4, 13:4, 14:15, 14:23, 19:14, 22:28, 23:10; Job 24:2; and the powerful story of Naboth's vineyard in 1 Kings 21.

338 Tisby, *The Color of Compromise*, 85.

339 Zora Neale Hurston, *Dust Tracks on a Road* (New York: J. B. Lippincott, 1942).

340 Martin Luther King Jr., "I've Been to the Mountaintop," speech, April 3, 1968, Memphis, Tennessee, accessed July 12, 2021, at https://www.americanrhetoric.com/speeches/mlkivebeentothemountaintop.htm.

341 "This Is the Story of a People," exhibit at National Civil Rights Museum, Memphis, Tennessee.

342 "Many Paths, One Destination," exhibit at National Civil Rights Museum, Memphis, Tennessee.

343 For a full account of the creation of the evolution of the historiography, consult Robert J. Norrell's "Prologue" and his chapter "The Veil of History" in his recent groundbreaking biography of Booker T. Washington: Robert J. Norrell, *Up from History: The Life of Booker T. Washington* (Cambridge: The Belknap Press, 2009), 1–16 and 420–442.

344 Norrell, *Up from History*.

345 Booker T. Washington, *Up from Slavery* (Garden City, New York: 1901). As quoted in Norrell, *Up from History*, 20–21.

346 Washington, *Up from Slavery*, 23.

347 Norrell, *Up from History*, 24–27.

348 Norrell, *Up from History*, 27.

349 Washington, *Up from Slavery*, 27.

350 Norrell, *Up from History*, 28–35.

351 This is an unfair characterization of Washington. In fact, Washington was very interested in the political process. As Norrell asserts, "Booker's youthful participation in the Republican Party suggests an irresistible fascination with the political process, even though he knew from the 1869 Klan riot that politics was a dangerous business for Negroes. Like most recently freed slaves, he believed that democracy should ensure freedom for his people. The need to avoid racial conflict and the desire

to engage in the political process were competing instincts that would cause trouble for him all his life." Norrell, *Up from History*, 29.

352 Norrell, *Up from History*, 31.
353 Norrell, *Up from History*, 35–36.
354 Norrell, *Up from History*, 39.
355 Norrell, *Up from History*, 40–42.
356 Norrell, *Up from History*, 51–52.
357 Washington, *Up from Slavery,* as quoted in Norrell, *Up from History*, 62–63.
358 Norrell, *Up from History*, 69. As Norrell notes, "They successful efforts in brickmaking demonstrated to hostile whites that schooling made blacks valuable, not worthless. In fact, the enterprise added wealth and comfort beyond the campus boundaries, because the school sold its surplus brick to whites in the area."
359 Norrell, *Up from History*, 69.
360 Norrell, *Up from History*, 69–70.
361 Norrell, *Up from History*, 69–70.
362 Norrell, *Up from History*, 72–73.
363 Norrell, *Up from History*, 95.
364 As quoted in Norrell, *Up from History*, 74.
365 Ideas of colonizing Africa were promoted by Black leaders such as Marcus Garvey. For more on Garvey, see Colin Grant's *Negro with a Hat: The Rise and Fall of Marcus Garvey* (Oxford: Oxford University Press, 2010). Norrell, *Up from History*, 106–107.
366 Norrell, *Up from History*, 106–107.
367 Norrell, *Up from History*, 105.
368 Norrell, *Up from History*, 200.
369 Theda Skocpol, Ariane Liazos, and Marshall Ganz, *What a Mighty Power We Can Be* (Princeton: Princeton University Press, 2006), 13.
370 Skocpol et al, *Mighty Power*, 12.
371 Norrell, *Up from History*, 118.
372 Norrell, *Up from History*, 119.
373 Booker T. Washington, *The Story of My Life and Work* (Cincinnati, OH: W. H. Ferguson, 1900). As quoted in Norrell, *Up from History*, 122-123.
374 Booker T. Washington, "Atlanta Exposition Speech."
375 Washington, "Atlanta Exposition Speech."
376 Washington, "Atlanta Exposition Speech."
377 Washington, "Atlanta Exposition Speech."

378 Washington, "Atlanta Exposition Speech."

379 Norrell, *Up from History*, 124.

380 Norrell, *Up from History*, 126.

381 Norrell, *Up from History*, 128.

382 Norrell, *Up from History*, 132.

383 Norrell, *Up from History*, 130.

384 Norrell, *Up from History*, 141.

385 Norrell, *Up from History*, 170.

386 For more information about the streetcar boycotts in the late nineteenth and early twentieth centuries, see August Meier and Elliott Rudwick, "The Boycott Movement against Jim Crow Streetcars in the South, 1900–1906," in Meier and Rudwick, *Along the Color Line: Explorations in the Black Experience* (Urbana: University of Illinois Press, 1976), 267–289. Norrell, *Up from History*, 170.

387 For a detailed account of the origins of segregated streetcars, see Jennifer Roback, "The Political Economy of Segregation: The Case of Segregated Streetcars," *The Journal of Economic History*, vol. XLVI, no. 4 (December, 1986).

388 Norrell, *Up from History*, 145–146 and 302–308.

389 Norrell, *Up from History*, 260.

390 Norrell, *Up from History*, 302–308. For more on the life and appointment of William D. Crum, see William B. Gatewood, "William D. Crum: A Negro in Politics," *The Journal of Negro History*, vol. 53, no. 4 (October 1968), 301–320.

391 Booker T. Washington, *Up from Slavery*. As discussed in Norrell, *Up from History*, 219.

392 As quoted in Norrell, *Up from History*, 243.

393 As quoted in Norrell, *Up from History*, 246.

394 Norrell, *Up from History*, 246.

395 As quoted in Norrell, *Up from History*, 248.

396 As quoted in Norrell, *Up from History*, 250.

397 As quoted in Norrell, *Up from History*, 242.

398 Norrell, *Up from History*, 299.

399 Although Alabama was the last state to officially end convict leasing in 1928, there is evidence that many Southern counties continued the practice long afterwards. For more see Blackmon, *Slavery by Another Name*.

400 Norrell, *Up from History*, 261.

401 Norrell, *Up from History*, 298.

[402] As quoted in Norrell, *Up from History*, 268.

[403] Maceo Crenshaw Dailey Jr., "The Business Life of Emmett Jay Scott," *The Business History Review*, vol. 77, no. 4 (Winter 2003), 668–669.

[404] Dailey Jr., "The Business Life of Emmett Jay Scott," 670.

[405] Kenneth Hamilton, "Introduction," in the "Records of the National Negro Business League: A Guide to the Microfilm," *Black Studies Research Sources*, John H. Bracy Jr. and August Meier, eds., University Publications of America, accessed on July 18, 2021, http://www.lexisnexis.com/documents/academic/upa_cis/1559_natnegrobusleaguept1.pdf.

[406] Booker T. Washington, *The Negro in Business* (Boston and Chicago: Hertel, Jenkins & Company, 1907).

[407] "Junius G. Groves," Kansas Historical Society, April 2009, accessed July 18, 2021, https://www.kshs.org/kansapedia/junius-g-groves/12075.

[408] Booker T. Washington, *The Negro in Business*; "John S. Trower: Best Known and Probably the Wealthiest Negro in the Country," *Washington Bee*, April 29, 1911, accessed July 18, 2021, https://goinnorth.org/items/show/809.

[409] Garry Gray, "H.C. Haynes: Barber and Inventor," *Negro History Bulletin*, vol. 40, no. 5, 751–752. For more the history of black barbers see Douglas Walter Bristol Jr., *Knights of the Razor: Black Barbers in Slavery and Freedom*.

[410] "Samuel Raymond Scrottron," BlackPast, September 20, 2018, accessed July 18, 2021, https://www.blackpast.org/african-american-history/scrottron-samuel-raymond-1843-1905/. For more information on Scrottron's life consult his granddaughter, Gail Lumet Buckley: *The Hornes: An American Family* (New York: Alfred A. Knopf, 1986) and her more recent *The Black Calhouns: From Civil War to Civil Rights with One African American Family* (New York: Grove Press, 2017).

[411] Marcus M. Witcher, "Empowering Black Women, Madam C. J. Walker's Story," Libertarianism.org, Cato Institute, June 19, 2020, accessed July 18, 2021, https://www.libertarianism.org/articles/empowering-black-women-madam-cj-walkers-story. For a fuller description of the life of Madam C. J. Walker see A'Lelia Bundles, *On Her Own Ground: The Life and Times of Madam C.J. Walker* (New York: Scribner, 2001); republished as *Self-Made: Inspired by the Life of Madam C. J. Walker* (New York: Scribner, 2020). For more on Black millionaires who became wealthy in the face of racism and state-sanctioned discrimination, see Shomari Wills, *Black Fortunes: The Story*

of the First Six African Americans Who Survived Slavery and Became Millionaires (New York: Amistad, 2018).

[412] Hamilton, "Introduction," in the "Records of the National Negro Business League."

[413] DuBois, *The Souls of Black Folk* (1903). As quoted in Norrell, *Up from History*, 278.

[414] DuBois, *The Souls of Black Folk* . As quoted in Norrell, *Up from History*, 278.

[415] Norrell, *Up from History*, 279.

[416] Patricia Sullivan, *Lift Every Voice: The NAACP and the Making of the Civil Rights Movement* (New York: The New Press, 2009), 3.

[417] "The Niagara Movement: Declaration of Principles, 1905."

[418] "Niagara Movement (1905–1909)," BlackPast, December 16, 2007, accessed July 19, 2021, https://www.blackpast.org/african-american-history/niagara-movement-1905-1909/.

[419] Norrell, *Up from History*, 326.

[420] "The Niagara Movement: Declaration of Principles, 1905."

[421] Historian Robert Norrell disagrees with this point. He argues that the Niagara Movement was almost exactly the same as the statement of positions laid out at the Carnegie Hall meeting in 1904 where Washington, Du Bois, and others came together to determine how best to promote Black Americans political, social, and economic well-being. When comparing the Carnegie Hall platform to the Niagara Movement platform, Norrell insists that Niagara's "positions in effect reiterated the agenda" of the earlier meeting: "a defense of personal liberty, civil and voting rights, opportunity for education and jobs." Norrell concludes that the Niagara Movement's "manifesto differed only in an explicit embrace of open protest." Norrell, *Up from History*, 293–294, 321.

[422] "Springfield Race Riot, 1908," BlackPast, June 29, 2008, accessed July 19, 2021, https://www.blackpast.org/african-american-history/springfield-race-riot-1908/; Sullivan, *Lift Every Voice*, 5.

[423] Sullivan, *Lift Every Voice*, 5.

[424] Sullivan, *Lift Every Voice*, 6.

[425] Sullivan, *Lift Every Voice*, 8.

[426] As quoted in Sullivan, *Lift Every Voice*, 7.

[427] Sullivan, *Lift Every Voice*, 12–13.

[428] Sullivan, *Lift Every Voice*, 18.

[429] Sullivan, *Lift Every Voice*, xiv.

430 For more on *The Birth of a Nation* see Conrad Pitcher, "D. W. Griffith's Controversial Film, 'The Birth of a Nation,'" *OAH Magazine of History*, vol. 13, no. 3 (Spring 1999), 50–55.

431 "The First Great Migration (1910–1940)," National Archives, accessed July 20, 2021, https://www.archives.gov/research/african-americans/wwi/great-migration. For a complete analysis of the Great Migration, see Isabel Wilkerson's *The Warmth of Other Suns: The Epic Story of America's Great Migration* (New York: Random House, 2010).

432 "Racial Violence and the Red Summer," National Archives, accessed July 20, 2021, https://www.archives.gov/research/african-americans/wwi/red-summer.

433 "Red Summer: The Race Riots of 1919," The National World War I Museum and Memorial, accessed on July 20, 2021, https://www.theworldwar.org/learn/wwi/red-summer. For a complete history of the Red Summer, consult Cameron McWhirter, *Red Summer: The Summer of 1919 and the Awakening of Black America* (New York: Henry Holt, 2011); Robert Whitaker, *On the Laps of Gods: The Red Summer of 1919 and the Struggle for Justice That Remade a Nation* (New York: Crown, 2008); and David F. Krugler, *1919, The Year of Racial Violence: How African Americans Fought Back* (Cambridge: Cambridge University Press, 2014); and Nancy MacLean, *Behind the Mask of Chivalry: The Making of the Second Ku Klux Klan* (Oxford: Oxford University Press, 1994).

434 "Racial Violence and the Red Summer."

435 For more on the rise of the second KKK, see Linda Gordon, *The Second Coming of the KKK: The Ku Klux Klan of the 1920s and the American Political Tradition* (New York: Liveright, 2017).

436 "Red Summer: The Race Riots of 1919."

437 Sullivan, *Lift Every Voice*, xv.

438 As quoted in Daniel Okrent, *Last Call: The Rise and Fall of Prohibition* (New York: Scribner, 2010), 130.

439 As quoted in Sullivan, *Lift Every Voice*, 106.

440 Sullivan, *Lift Every Voice*, 109.

441 For a complete history of the amazing achievements that took place in Harlem during the 1920s, see Rachel Farebrother and Miriam Thaggert, *A History of the Harlem Renaissance* (Cambridge: Cambridge University Press, 2021). For a brief introduction, consult Cheryl A. Wall, *The Harlem Renaissance: A Very Short Introduction* (Oxford: Oxford University Press, 2016). For an in-depth exploration

of the New Negro movement and the life of Alain Locke, see Jeffrey C. Stewart, *The New Negro: The Life of Alain Locke* (Oxford: Oxford University Press, 2018).

[442] For a fuller account of the Brotherhood of Sleeping Car Porters, consult Larry Tye, *Rising from the Rails: Pullman Porters and the Making of the Black Middle Class* (New York: Henry Holt, 2004); and Beth Tompkins Bates, *Pullman Porters and the Rise of Protest Politics in Black America, 1925–1945* (Chapel Hill: University of North Carolina Press, 2001).

[443] "Brotherhood of Sleeping Car Porters (1925–1978)," BlackPast, November 24, 2007, accessed July 20, 2021, https://www.blackpast. org/african-american-history/brotherhood-sleeping-car-porters-1925-1978/.

[444] See Higgs's *Competition and Coercion,* cited extensively above for Chapter 3 on "Liberation Through the Freedom to Move: The Struggle for Black Property."

[445] Theodore Kornweibel Jr., "An Economic Profile of Black Life in the Twenties," *Journal of Black Studies,* vol. 6, no. 4 (June 1976), 311.

[446] Kornweibel Jr., "An Economic Profile of Black Life in the Twenties," 308–310.

[447] David M. Kennedy, *Freedom from Fear: The American People in Depression and War, 1929–1945* (Oxford: Oxford University Press, 1999), 765.

[448] "African Americans," The Living New Deal, accessed on July 20, 2021, https://livingnewdeal.org/what-was-the-new-deal/new-deal-inclusion/african-americans-2/.

[449] For a comprehensive treatment of A. Philip Randolph, see Cornelius L. Bynum, *A. Philip Randolph and the Struggle for Civil Rights* (Chicago: University of Illinois Press, 2010); Cynthia Taylor, *A. Philip Randolph: The Religious Journey of an American Labor Leader* (New York: NYU Press, 2005); and Andrew E. Kersten, *A. Philip Randolph: A Life in the Vanguard* (New York: Rowman & Littlefield, 2006).

[450] Kennedy, *Freedom from Fear,* 765–767.

[451] "Transcript of Executive Order 8802: Prohibition of Discrimination in the Defense Industry (1941)," Our Documents, accessed July 20, 2021, https://www.ourdocuments.gov/doc.php?flash=false&doc=72 &page=transcript.

[452] As quoted in Kennedy, *Freedom from Fear,* 768.

453   Euell A. Nielsen, "The Double V Campaign (1942–1945)," *Black Past*, July 1, 2020, accessed July 20, 2021, https://www.blackpast.org/african-american-history/events-african-american-history/the-double-v-campaign-1942-1945/. For a more detailed description of the Double V Campaign see Christopher S. Parker, *Fighting for Democracy: Black Veterans and the Struggle Against White Supremacy in the Postwar South* (Princeton: Princeton University Press, 2009).

454   Kennedy, *Freedom from Fear*, 768.

455   Skocpol et al., *Mighty Power*, 222. Another excellent book on the rise of fraternal societies in the United States is David T. Beito's *From Mutual Aid to the Welfare State: Fraternal Societies and Social Services, 1890–1967* (Chapel Hill: University of North Carolina Press, 2000).

456   Skocpol et al., *Mighty Power*, 135.

457   Skocpol et al., *Mighty Power*, 14.

458   Skocpol et al., *Mighty Power*, 13.

459   Skocpol et al., *Mighty Power*, 177–178. For more on the life of Thurgood Marshall, see Juan Williams, *Thurgood Marshall: American Revolutionary* (New York: Crown, 1998).

460   Skocpol et al., *Mighty Power*, 211–212.

461   Skocpol et al., *Mighty Power*, 137.

462   Skocpol et al., *Mighty Power*, 137.

463   Skocpol et al., *Mighty Power*, 14, 138.

464   Skocpol et al., *Mighty Power*, 178–179.

465   Skocpol et al., *Mighty Power*, 178.

466   Skocpol et al., *Mighty Power*, 225.

467   For the complete story of T. R. M. Howard's incredible life see David T. Beito and Linda Royster Beito, *T. R.M. Howard: Doctor, Entrepreneur, Civil Rights Pioneer* (Oakland: Independent Institute, 2018).

468   As quoted in Skocpol et al., *Mighty Power*, 15; David T. Beito and Linda Royster Beito, *T. R. M. Howard*, 89–91.

469   During the 1930s many prominent American intellectuals, both white and Black, rejected capitalism and praised the supposed merits of command economies under communist and other authoritarian regimes. This flirtation, along with some Black critiques of market capitalism, led segregationists to claim that at its core the civil rights movement was communist or perhaps even being backed by communist forces. For more on the international dimensions to the civil rights movement, see Mary L. Dudziak, *Cold War Civil Rights: Race and the Image of American Democracy* (Princeton: Princeton University Press,

2000). For more on the dubious connection of the civil rights movement to communism consult Jeff Woods, *Black Struggle, Red Scare: Segregation and Anti-Communism in the South, 1948–1968* (Baton Rouge: Louisiana State University Press, 2003).

[470] While Martin Luther King Jr. developed socially democratic views as time went on, he was always an adamant opponent of communism.

[471] Beito and Beito, *T. R. M. Howard*, 81–82.

[472] Sullivan, *Lift Every Voice*, 420.

[473] Beito and Beito, *T. R. M. Howard*, 104.

[474] Beito and Beito, *T. R. M. Howard*, 107–108.

[475] Beito and Beito, *T. R. M. Howard*, 109.

[476] Beito and Beito, *T. R. M. Howard*, 111.

[477] Beito and Beito, *T. R .M. Howard*, 112–113.

[478] Timothy Tyson, *The Blood of Emmett Till* (New York: Simon & Schuster, 2017).

[479] Devery S. Anderson, *Emmett Till: The Murder That Shocked the World and Propelled the Civil Rights Movement* (Jackson: University Press of Mississippi, 2015).

[480] Margena A. Christian, *Empire: The House That John H. Johnson Built* (Chicago: Doc.M.A.C. Write, 2018), 101–102.

[481] Beito and Beito, *T. R. M. Howard*, 132.

[482] Beito and Beito, *T. R. M. Howard*, 142, 165.

[483] For more on Howard's full role in the trial of Emmett Till, see Beito and Beito, *T. R. M. Howard*, 129-164.

[484] Beito and Beito, *T. R. M. Howard*, 144.

[485] Beito and Beito, *T. R. M. Howard*, 146–147.

[486] Beito and Beito, *T. R. M. Howard*, 154.

[487] Beito and Beito, *T. R. M. Howard*, 154–155.

[488] Beito and Beito, *T. R. M. Howard*, 155.

[489] Dudziak, *Cold War Civil Rights*.

[490] "Declaration of Independence: A Transcript," America's Founding Documents at the National Archives, accessed July 21, 2021, https://www.archives.gov/founding-docs/declaration-transcript.

[491] Leonard, *Illiberal Reformers*, 110.

[492] For an overview of Wilson's views on the presidency, consult Sidney M. Milkis and Michael Nelson, *The American Presidency: Origins and Development, 1776–2018* (Washington, DC: Sage Publishing, 2018). For a more critical appraisal, see Gene Healy, *The Cult of the Presidency:*

America's Dangerous Devotion to Executive Power (Washington, DC: Cato Institute, 2008).

493 Woodrow Wilson, "The Reconstruction of the Southern States," *Atlantic Monthly*, January 1901.

494 "File: Wilson-quote-in-birth-of-a-nation.jpg," Wikimedia Commons, https://commons.wikimedia.org/wiki/File:Wilson-quote-in-birth-of-a-nation.jpg.

495 For a comprehensive look at Otto von Bismarck's life, consult Jonathan Steinberg, *Bismarck: A Life* (Oxford: Oxford University Press, 2013).

496 Leonard, *Illiberal Reformers*, 8–9.

497 Leonard, *Illiberal Reformers*, 119.

498 Leonard, *Illiberal Reformers*, 110.

499 Quoted in Leonard, *Illiberal Reformers*, 165.

500 Lauren Weiner, "Making Sense of Oliver Wendell Holmes' Controversial Legacy," *The Federalist*, June 1, 2020, accessed at https://thefederalist.com/2020/06/01/making-sense-of-oliver-wendell-holmes-controversial-legacy/.

501 John Maynard Keynes, "Economic Possibilities for Our Grandchildren (1930)," in *Essays in Persuasion* (New York: Harcourt Brace, 1932), 358–373.

502 Phillip Magness and James Harrigan, "John Maynard Keynes, H. G. Wells, and a Problematic Utopia," *History of Political Economy*, forthcoming, SSRN, July 11, 2019, https://ssrn.com/abstract=3418380.

503 Keynes to Sanger, June 23, 1936, Sanger Papers, cited in Magness and Harrigan.

504 Magness and Harrigan, "John Maynard Keynes, H. G. Wells, and a Problematic Utopia."

505 Leonard, *Illiberal Reformers*.

506 Victoria Brignell, "When America Believed in Eugenics," *NewStatesman*, December 10, 2010, accessed 03/01/2020 at https://www.newstatesman.com/society/2010/12/disabled-america-immigration.

507 Brignell, "The eugenics movement Britain wants to forget," *NewStatesman*, December 9, 2010, accessed 03/01/2020 at http://www.newstatesman.com/society/2010/12/british-eugenics-disabled.

508 Leonard, *Illiberal Reformers*, 148.

509 Leonard, *Illiberal Reformers*, 116, 181.

510 Margaret Sanger's racism and eugenics views are well documented in her own writings. For example in her 1922 *The Pivot of Civilization* Sanger declared, "We are paying for, and even submitting to, the

dictates of an ever-increasing, unceasingly spawning class of human beings who never should have been born at all." In a 1919 article titled "Birth Control and Racial Betterment" she insisted, "Before eugenists and others who are laboring for racial betterment can succeed, they must first clear the way for Birth Control." In 1932, Sanger argued that the government should "give certain dysgenic groups in our population their choice of segregation or sterilization." Indeed, Sanger believed that eugenics was "the most adequate and through avenue in the solution of racial, political, and social problems." As quoted in M. K. Sprinkle, "Margaret Sanger's Legacy of Racism and 'Elimination of the Unfit,'" *Carroll County Times*, January 4, 2020, accessed at https://www.baltimoresun.com/maryland/carroll/opinion/cc-op-sprinkle-010420-20200104-opc3c76o4na47mtdtun4nvqw3y-story.html?outputType=amp. For a more sympathetic account of the complexities of Sanger's thought on eugenics and race, consult Jennifer Latson, "What Margaret Sanger Really Said about Eugenics and Race," *Time*, October 14, 2016, accessed at https://time.com/4081760/margaret-sanger-history-eugenics/.

[511] Leonard, *Illiberal Reformers*, 159.

[512] *Rerum Novarum*, sections 44 and 45.

[513] Gary S. Becker, *The Economics of Discrimination,* second edition (Chicago: University of Chicago Press Books, 1971), https://press.uchicago.edu/ucp/books/book/chicago/E/bo22415931.html.

[514] Leonard, *Illiberal Reformers*, 159.

[515] Leonard, *Illiberal Reformers*, 88.

[516] Leonard, *Illiberal Reformers*, 161–163.

[517] Mark J. Perry, "Milton Friedman in a 1966 *Newsweek* Op-Ed: The Minimum-Wage Law Is a 'Monument to the Power of Superficial Thinking,'" American Enterprise Institute, December 5, 2016, https://www.aei.org/carpe-diem/milton-friedman-in-a-1966-newsweek-op-ed-the-minimum-wage-law-is-a-monument-to-the-power-of-superficial-thinking/#:~:text=At%20the%20time%20of%20Friedman's,time%20since%20the%20late%201950s.

[518] BLS Reports, "Characteristics of Minimum Wage Workers, 2018," US Bureau of Labor Statistics, March 2019, https://www.bls.gov/opub/reports/minimum-wage/2018/pdf/home.pdf.

[519] Elizabeth S. Anderson, "What Is the Point of Equality?" *Chicago Journals*, vol. 109, no. 2 (1999), https://www.philosophy.rutgers.edu/joomlatools-files/docman-files/4ElizabethAnderson.pdf.

[520] David Neumark and Cortnie Shupe, "Declining Teen Employment: Minimum Wages, Other Explanations, and Implications for Human Capital Investment," Mercatus Working Paper, 2018, https://www.mercatus.org/system/files/neumark-teen-employment-mercatus-working-paper-v1.pdf.

[521] David Card and Alan B. Krueger, "Minimum Wages and Employment: A Case Study of the Fast-Food Industry in New Jersey and Pennsylvania," *American Economic Review,* vol. 84(4), 1994, http://davidcard.berkeley.edu/papers/njmin-aer.pdf.

[522] Jonathan Meer and Jeremy West, "Effects of the Minimum Wage on Employment Dynamics," National Bureau of Economic Research, working paper 19262, DOI 10.3386/w19262, issue date August 2013, revision date January 2015, https://www.nber.org/papers/w19262.

[523] Thomas Snyder and Marcus Witcher, "Minimum-Wage Rise Perilous," *Northwest Arkansas Democrat Gazette,* November 1, 2018, accessed at https://www.nwaonline.com/news/2018/nov/01/a-dark-history-20181101/?opinion.

[524] Amber Dance, "The Unemployment Crisis," American Psychological Association, March 2011, https://www.apa.org/monitor/2011/03/unemployment.

[525] Quoted in Paul D. Moreno, *Black Americans and Organized Labor: A New History* (Baton Rouge: LSU Press, 2008), 167.

[526] Moreno, *Black Americans and Organized Labor,* ch. 1.

[527] Becker, *The Economics of Discrimination.*

[528] Moreno, *Black Americans and Organized Labor,* 224.

[529] Becker, *The Economics of Discrimination.*

[530] Gail Heriot, "Don't Blame the Railroad for *Plessy v. Ferguson,*" *Reason,* May 18, 2018, https://reason.com/2018/05/18/dont-blame-the-railroad-for-plessy-v-fer/.

[531] Jennifer Roback, "The Political Economy of Segregation: The Case of Segregated Streetcars," *Journal of Economic History* 56, no. 4 (December 1986): 893–917.

[532] Moreno, *Black Americans and Organized Labor,* 5.

[533] Moreno, *Black Americans and Organized Labor,* Appendix: "Divide and Conquer": The Folklore of Socialism.

[534] Moreno, *Black Americans and Organized Labor,* 11. For more on the free labor ideology, see Eric Foner, *Free Soil, Free Labor, Free Men: The Ideology of the Republican Party before the Civil War* (Oxford: Oxford University Press, 1970).

[535] Moreno, *Black Americans and Organized Labor*, 12–13.

[536] Quoted in Moreno, *Black Americans and Organized Labor*, 37.

[537] Moreno, *Black Americans and Organized Labor*.

[538] Harold L. Cole and Lee E. Ohanian, "New Deal Policies and the Persistence of the Great Depression: A General Equilibrium Analysis," *Journal of Political Economy*, vol. 112, No. 4 (August 2004), 779–816.

[539] David Beito, forthcoming book on civil liberties and the New Deal, Independent Institute, forthcoming. We'd like to thank David for allowing us to access his manuscript early and share this incredibly important part of our history.

[540] Legal scholar David Bernstein argues this at Cato Unbound: "The Anglo-American common law, much beloved by libertarian legal scholars, required at least some public accommodations—particularly those granted exclusive government charters or otherwise exercising monopoly prerogatives—to serve all comers," https://www.cato-unbound.org/2010/06/16/david-e-bernstein/context-matters-better-libertarian-approach-antidiscrimination-law.

[541] Michael Tanner, *The Inclusive Economy: How to Bring Wealth to America's Poor* (Washington, DC: Cato Institute, 2018).

[542] James P. Bailey, *Rethinking Poverty: Income, Assets, and the Catholic Social Justice Tradition* (Notre Dame, IN: University of Notre Dame Press, 2010).

[543] William J. Collins and Robert A. Margo, "Race and Home Ownership from the End of the Civil War to the Present," *American Economic Review*, vol. 101, no. 3 (May 2011), 355–359.

[544] Rothstein, *The Color of Law*, 66.

[545] It's true that some libertarians, notably Robert Nozick, do argue that a contract for enslavement is possible, but this is not the traditional classical liberal position (for instance, John Locke argued explicitly against this). For a full discussion of this debate, see J. Philmore, "The Libertarian Case for Slavery," *The Philosophical Forum*, vol. XIV, no. 1 (Fall 1982), https://ellerman.org/wp-content/uploads/2012/12/Philmore-1982.scan_.pdf.

[546] It's also true that some libertarians argue for the legalization of euthanasia, and David Hume defended the choice to commit suicide. In general, however, traditional classical liberal thought acknowledges limits on what counts as a legitimate contract on a number of grounds. See the entry on euthanasia at libertarianism.org here: https://www.

libertarianism.org/topics/euthanasia. For the German case, see "Armin Meiwes," Wikipedia, https://en.wikipedia.org/wiki/Armin_Meiwes.

[547] David Schmidtz, "The Institution of Property," *Social Philosophy and Policy,* vol. 11 (1994): 42–62, https://philpapers.org/rec/SCHTIO-11.

[548] Rothstein, *The Color of Law,* 95.

[549] See Chapter 8 for our discussion of the 1964 Civil Rights Act.

[550] Louis Henkin, "*Shelley v. Kraemer*: Notes for a Revised Opinion," *University of Pennsylvania Law Review,* vol. 110 (February 1962), https://scholarship.law.upenn.edu/cgi/viewcontent.cgi?article=6893&context=penn_law_review.

[551] David Bernstein, "*Shelley v. Kraemer*: A Correct but Limited Decision," Cato Unbound, https://www.cato-unbound.org/2010/06/29/david-e-bernstein/shelley-v-kraemer-correct-limited-opinion.

[552] Rothstein, *The Color of Law,* 135.

[553] Rothstein, *The Color of Law,* 84–85.

[554] Rothstein, *The Color of Law,* 11.

[555] Rothstein, *The Color of Law,* 123–124.

[556] Rothstein, *The Color of Law,* 125–126.

[557] Rothstein, *The Color of Law,* 73–74.

[558] We see many of the regulators confused on this point. Here is Maxine Waters in the same discussion of Fannie and Freddie in which Barney Frank made his comments: "However, I have sat through nearly a dozen hearings where, frankly, we were trying to fix something that wasn't broke. Housing is the economic engine of our economy, and in no community does this engine need to work more than in mine." https://www.wsj.com/articles/SB122290574391296381.

[559] "What they said about Fan and Fred," *Wall Street Journal Opinion,* October 2, 2008, https://www.wsj.com/articles/SB122290574391296381.

[560] John Taylor, *Getting Off Track: How Government Actions and Interventions Caused, Prolonged, and Worsened the Financial Crisis* (Stanford, CA: Hoover Institution Press, 2009)—although some of his predictions about subsequent inflation haven't aged well.

[561] Anna Schwartz and Milton Friedman, *A Monetary History of the United States* (Princeton, NJ: Princeton University Press, 1963).

[562] Rob Williams, "Study: Economic Growth Is Spread Unevenly Among Cities," Economic Innovation Group, September 25, 2017, https://eig.org/news/study-economic-growth-spread-unevenly-among-cities.

[563]   Adam Smith, *The Theory of Moral Sentiments,* part VI, section II, ch. II, pp. 233–4, para 17.

[564]   "A Conversation with James Baldwin," 1963-06-24, WGBH, American Archive of Public Broadcasting (Boston and Washington, DC: GBH and the Library of Congress), accessed September 29, 2021, http://americanarchive.org/catalog/cpb-aacip-15-0v89g5gf5r.

[565]   Eric Avila, *The Folklore of the Freeway: Race and Revolt in the Modernist City* (Minneapolis: University of Minnesota Press, 2014).

[566]   Quoted in Avila, xi, from Jane Jacob's classic work, *The Death and Life of Great American Cities* (New York: Vintage Books, 1961).

[567]   "Story of Cities #32: Jacobs v. Robert Moses, battle of New York's urban titans." *Guardian,* available at https://www.theguardian.com/cities/2016/apr/28/story-cities-32-new-york-jane-jacobs-robert-moses.

[568]   For a comprehensive study of Robert Moses, see Robert A. Caro, *The Power Broker: Robert Moses and the Fall of New York* (New York: Knopf, 1974).

[569]   Deborah Talbot, "Why Jane Jacobs Still Leads in Urbanism," *Forbes,* April 14, 2019, https://www.forbes.com/sites/deborahtalbot/2019/04/14/why-jane-jacobs-still-leads-in-urbanism/#605102291f2a.

[570]   Boxofficemojo.com. 2017. *Cars (2006) - Box Office Mojo.* [online] Available at: http://www.boxofficemojo.com/movies/?id=cars.htm.

[571]   Freight by ship is also limited by the particularly deleterious Jones Act, which requires every aspect of any ship moving goods from one area of the US to another to be US made and manned. This drives up costs while delivering little of the promised benefit. (Colin Grabow, Inu Manak, and Daniel J. Ikenson, "The Jones Act: A Burden America Can No Longer Bear," Cato, June 28, 2018, https://www.cato.org/publications/policy-analysis/jones-act-burden-america-can-no-longer-bear.) The authors claim that "[w]hile the law's most direct consequence is to raise transportation costs, which are passed down through supply chains and ultimately reflected in higher retail prices, it generates enormous collateral damage through excessive wear and tear on the country's infrastructure, time wasted in traffic congestion, and the accumulated health and environmental toll caused by unnecessary carbon emissions and hazardous material spills from trucks and trains. Meanwhile, closer scrutiny finds the law's national security justification to be unmoored from modern military and technological realities."

[572] More resources: *Last Exit* is not the only recent book to recommend privatization as a way to improve transportation in the United States. Other worthy books on the topic include Walter Block's *The Privatization of Roads and Highways* (Auburn, AL: Ludwig von Mises Institute, 2009); Sam Staley and Adrian Moore's *Mobility First* (New York: Rowman & Littlefield, 2009); Randal O'Toole's *Gridlock* (Washington, DC: Cato Institute, 2009); and the most comprehensive compilation of the best research on the topic, Gabriel Roth's *Street Smart* (Oakland, CA: Independent Institute, 2006). These are from Semmens book review out of the Independent Institute: https://www.independent.org/publications/books/summary.asp?id=64.

[573] "The Civil Rights Implications of Eminent Domain Abuse," US Commission on Civil Rights, https://www.usccr.gov/pubs/docs/FINAL_FY14_Eminent-Domain-Report.pdf.

[574] *Susette Kelo, et al., Petitioners v. City of New London, Connecticut, et al.,* No. 04-108 (2005). https://www.law.cornell.edu/supct/html/04-108.ZD1.html.

[575] Ilya Somin, "The Political and Judicial Reaction to Kelo," *Washington Post,* June 4, 2015.

[576] Roy Cordato, "There Ain't No Economics in Economic Impact Studies," Mises Institute, May 28, 2017, https://mises.org/wire/there-ain%E2%80%99t-no-economics-economic-impact-studies.

[577] Matthew Mitchell et al., "The Economics of a Targeted Economic Development Subsidy," (Arlington, VA: Mercatus Center at George Mason University, forthcoming); Matthew Mitchell, Daniel Sutter, and Scott Eastman, "Political Economy of Targeted Economic Development Incentives," *The Review of Regional Studies,* vol. 48, no. 1 (2018): 1–9.

[578] Avila, *The Folklore of the Freeway,* 43.

[579] Rondo Avenue, "Who We Are," https://www.rondodays.net/.

[580] Avila, *The Folklore of the Freeway,* 45–46.

[581] Avila, *The Folklore of the Freeway,* 49.

[582] Martin Anderson, *The Federal Bulldozer: A Critical Analysis of Urban Renewal: 1949–62* (Cambridge: MIT Press, 1964).

[583] Peter H. Nash, "Anderson: The Federal Bulldozer," *Boston College Law Review,* vol. 6, issue 4 (July 1965), https://lawdigitalcommons.bc.edu/cgi/viewcontent.cgi?article=2989&context=bclr.

[584] Nash, 974.

[585] Nash, 974.

586 "Economic Benefits," Congress for the New Urbanism, https://www.cnu.org/resources/economic-benefits.

587 United States Census Bureau, "Historical Poverty Tables: People and Families—1959 to 2020," https://www.census.gov/data/tables/time-series/demo/income-poverty/historical-poverty-people.html.

588 W. Bradford Wilcox, "Black Men Making It in America: The Engines of Economic Success for Black Men in America," American Enterprise Institute, June 26, 2018, https://www.aei.org/research-products/report/black-men-making-it-in-america-the-engines-of-economic-success-for-black-men-in-america/.

589 David Hackett Fischer, *Albion's Seed: Four British Folkways in America* (Oxford: Oxford University Press, 1989).

590 John Gramlich, "Black Imprisonment Rate in the U.S. Has Fallen by a Third Since 2006," Pew Research Center, May 6, 2020, https://www.pewresearch.org/fact-tank/2020/05/06/Black-imprisonment-rate-in-the-u-s-has-fallen-by-a-third-since-2006/.

591 Stef W. Kight, "Incarceration of White Americans on the Rise," Axios, February 25, 2018, https://www.axios.com/african-american-incarceration-rates-falling-01382790-8fe4-43c2-a6be-035e267e98ab.html.

592 See Orlando Patterson, *Rituals of Blood: The Consequences of Slavery in Two American Centuries* (Washington, DC: Civitas/Counterpoint, 1998): "As I argued in *The Ordeal of Integration*, while 'race' is obviously the decisive factor in explaining the origins of the acute problems of the Afro-American poor, it is not at all clear that it has much to do with explaining contemporary poverty levels among either men or women. Latinos were never enslaved here; the majority of them are of European ancestry; and a substantial minority descended from slaveholders—uncomfortable facts too often glossed over in multicultural rhetoric—yet...their poverty levels are higher than Afro-Americans."

593 Matt Bruenig, "The Racial Wealth Gap Is About the Upper Classes," People's Policy Project, June 29, 2020, https://www.peoplespolicyproject.org/2020/06/29/the-racial-wealth-gap-is-about-the-upper-classes/.

594 Wendy Wang, "The Majority of U.S. Children Still Live in Two-Parent Families," Institute for Family Studies, October 4, 2018, https://ifstudies.org/blog/the-majority-of-us-children-still-live-in-two-parent-families.

595 Stephan Thernstrom and Abigail Thernstrom, *America in Black and White* (New York: Simon & Schuster, 1997), 238.

[596] W. Bradford Wilcox, "The Marriage Divide: How and Why Working-Class Families Are More Fragile Today," Institute for Family Studies, September 25, 2017, https://ifstudies.org/blog/the-marriage-divide-how-and-why-working-class-families-are-more-fragile-today.

[597] In 2014, what we would traditionally think of as welfare cost about $212 billion per year, while there were various sorts of programs that might also be categorized that way that cost another $456B. For the debate over the numbers, see Mike Konzcal, "No, We Don't Spend $1 Trillion on Welfare Each Year," *Washington Post*, January 12, 2014. In the meantime, Social Security, Medicare, and Medicaid cost a total of $2.25 trillion per year (in 2014).

[598] For instance, *When Work Disappears* by William Julius Wilson, pp. 94–96. Robert D. Mare and Christopher Winship estimate that 20 percent of the decline in marriage rates of Blacks between 1960 and 1980 can be explained by decreasing employment (https://www.brookings.edu/research/an-analysis-of-out-of-wedlock-births-in-the-united-states/).

[599] George A. Akerlof and Janet L. Yellen, "An analysis of out-of-wedlock births in the United States," Brookings, August 1, 1996, https://www.brookings.edu/research/an-analysis-of-out-of-wedlock-births-in-the-united-states/.

[600] Matthew J. Hill, "Love in the Time of the Depression: The Effect of Economic Conditions on Marriage in the Great Depression," Pompeu Fabra University, Barcelona, Spain, https://econ-papers.upf.edu/papers/1454.pdf.

[601] In *The Best of Intentions: The Triumph and Failure of the Great Society under Kennedy, Johnson, and Nixon*, Irwin Unger points to Charles Silberman's widely read 1964 book, *Crisis in Black and White*, for the first published appearance of the term "welfare colonialism," (p. 152, endnote on 375).

[602] Quoted in Robert Blauner, "Internal Colonialism and Ghetto Revolt," *Social Problems*, vol. 16, no. 4 (1969), 393–408, accessed August 5, 2021, https://www.jstor.org/stable/799949?read-now=1&seq=6#page_scan_tab_contents. Black communist radicals sometimes criticized the Black Power movement as too conservative, as just an updated "Bookerism" that wanted "race advancement" rather than a complete restructuring of economic relations. Adolph Reed Jr., "From Black Power to Black Establishment," *The New Republic*, April 28, 2020, https://newrepublic.com/article/157182/Black-power-manifesto-establishment-politics.

603   Blauner, "Internal Colonialism and Ghetto Revolt," 407.

604   Malcolm X, as told to Alex Haley, *The Autobiography of Malcolm X* (New York: Grove Press, 1965), chs. 1–2.

605   Royalty Media TV, "Killer Mike Agrees with Candace Owens against TI & GOES OFF," YouTube Video, 9:40, September 17, 2019, https://www.youtube.com/watch?v=4rBP90WeIxg.

606   Unger, *The Best of Intentions,* 155–157.

607   Steven Horwitz, *Hayek's Modern Family* (London: Palgrave Macmillan, 2015).

608   Plato's *Republic*, Book V, and Aristotle's response in his *Politics*, Book II.

609   Jean Twenge, "Marriage and Money: How Much Does Marriage Explain the Growing Class Divide in Happiness?" Institute for Family Studies, July 20, 2020, https://ifstudies.org/blog/marriage-and-money-how-much-does-marriage-explain-the-growing-class-divide-in-happiness.

610   W. Bradford Wilcox and Nicholas H. Wolfinger, "Then Comes Marriage? Religion, Race, and Marriage in Urban America," *Social Science Research*, vol. 36, issue 2 (June 2007), 569–589, https://www.sciencedirect.com/journal/social-science-research/vol/36/issue/2.

611   Wendy Wang and W. Bradford Wilcox, "Less Stable, Less Important: Cohabiting Families' Comparative Disadvantage Across the Globe," Institute for Family Studies, https://ifstudies.org/ifs-admin/resources/ifs-globalcohabbrief-final-1.pdf.

612   Hilary W. Hoynes, Marianne E. Page, and Ann Huff Stevens, "Poverty in America: Trends and Explanations," *Journal of Economic Perspectives,* vol. 20, no. 1 (Winter 2006), 47–68, https://pubs.aeaweb.org/doi/pdfplus/10.1257/089533006776526102.

613   To be clear, the recorded household income does not reflect government transfers. However, the authors did take this into account and created an alternative set of data that took transfers into account. While this did lower the poverty rates, it did not affect the overall trends or conclusions that we present here.

614   Hilary W. Hoynes, Marianne E. Page, and Ann Huff Stevens, "Poverty in America," *Journal of Economic Perspectives*, vol. 20, no. 1 (Winter 2006), 59–60, https://pubs.aeaweb.org/doi/pdfplus/10.1257/089533006776526102.

615   David T. Beito, *From Mutual Aid to the Welfare State* (Chapel Hill: University of North Carolina, 2000).

[616] William Julius Wilson, *When Work Disappears: The World of the New Urban Poor* (New York: Vintage, 1997); David Ellwood and Lawrence Summers, "Poverty in America: Is Welfare the Answer or the Problem?" National Bureau of Economic Research, working paper 17,11, issue date October 1985, https://www.nber.org/papers/w1711.

[617] CDC National Health Statistics Report, "Father's Involvement with Their Children: United States 2006–2010."

[618] We don't have good census information on Hispanic families prior to 1980, though.

[619] Anna Sutherland, "Yes, Father Absence Causes the Problems It's Associated With," The Institute for Family Studies, February 4, 2014, https://ifstudies.org/blog/yes-father-absence-causes-the-problems-its-associated-with.

[620] Tyler Cowen, *The Complacent Class: The Self-Defeating Quest for the American Dream* (New York: St. Martin's Press, 2017).

[621] Paul Jargowsky, "Architecture of Segregation: Civil Unrest, the Concentration of Poverty, and Public Policy," The Century Foundation, August 7, 2015, https://tcf.org/content/report/architecture-of-segregation/.

[622] Phil Harvey and Lisa Conyers, *Welfare for the Rich: How Your Tax Dollars End up in Millionaires Pockets and What You Can Do About It* (New York and Nashville: Post Hill Press, 2020).

[623] Tad DeHaven. "Enron: Dependent on Government," Downsizing the Federal Government, https://www.downsizinggovernment.org/enron-dependent-government. DeHaven drew on the work of employee Robert L. Bradley, who has published a trilogy based on his experiences with the Enron scandal.

[624] Troy Segal, "Enron Scandal: The Fall of a Wall Street Darling," Investopedia, https://www.investopedia.com/updates/enron-scandal-summary/.

[625] Hoynes, Page, and Stevens, "Poverty in America," table 3.

[626] Hoynes, Page, and Stevens, "Poverty in America," 53.

[627] Richard K. Vedder and Lowell E. Gallaway, *Out of Work: Unemployment and Government in Twentieth-Century America,* updated edition, (New York: NYU Press, 1997).

[628] Vedder and Gallaway, 279.

[629] George F. Will, "A Racist Vestige of the Past That Progressives Are Happy to Leave in Place," *Washington Post,* June 19, 2017, https://www.washingtonpost.com/

opinions/a-racist-vestige-of-the-past-that-progressives-are-happy-to-leave-in-place/2017/06/16/6d5cbbba-51f3-11e7-91eb-9611861a988f_story.html.

630 Vedder and Gallaway, *Out of Work*, 137.

631 Robert Higgs. "Why the Great Depression Lasted so Long and Why Prosperity Resumed After the War," *The Independent Review*, vol. 1, no. 4 (Spring 1997), 561–590, https://www.independent.org/pdf/tir/tir_01_4_higgs.pdf; James Grant, *The Forgotten Depression: The Crash That Cured Itself* (New York: Simon & Schuster, 2014).

632 Vedder and Gallaway, *Out of Work*, 137–143.

633 Robert Whapples, "Where Is There Consensus Among American Economic Historians? The Results of a Survey on Forty Propositions," *The Journal of Economic History*, vol. 55, no. 1 (March 1995), 139–154; Jeremy Horpedahl, Phil Magness, and Marcus Witcher, "Teaching the Causes of the Great Depression to College Students: Evidence from History, Economics, and Economic History Textbooks," *Journal of Economics and Finance Education*, forthcoming.

634 This same pattern was described in William Harold Hutt's The *Economics of the Colour Bar*, where he condemned the "coloureds" (mixed-race) for using the exact same monopolistic practices against the Africans that the whites were using against them both. Jennifer Roback puts it this way, "Racism can be thought of as rent-seeking" because even if there were no preference for discrimination in the first place, the possibility of creating 'rents' (unfair market advantages) would make it rational to create racism." https://www.jstor.org/stable/2487505?seq=3#metadata_info_tab_contents.

635 The mainstream view is that minorities and the poor are harmed by unnecessary occupational licensing. One paper has challenged this view but also been thoroughly critiqued. The critique here includes references to the major mainstream research as well. Daniel B. Klein, Benjamin Powell, and Evgeny S. Vorotnikov, "Was Occupational Licensing Good for Minorities? A Critique of Marc Law and Mindy Marks," *Econ Journal Watch*, vol. 9(3), (September 2012), 210–233, https://econjwatch.org/articles/was-occupational-licensing-good-for-minorities-a-critique-of-marc-law-and-mindy-marks.

636 Patterson, *Rituals of Blood*.

637 "Leadership and Staff," NAACP, https://www.naacp.org/naacp-legal-team/naacp-legal-history/.

638 Derrick Bell, *Silent Covenants:* Brown v. Board of Education *and the Unfulfilled Hopes for Racial Reform* (Oxford: Oxford University Press, 2005).

639 Zora Neale Hurston's letter to the editor of the *Orlando Sentinel*, August 11, 1955, BlackPast, https://www.blackpast.org/african-american-history/zora-neale-hurston-s-letter-orlando-sentinel-1955/.

640 Malcolm Gladwell, "Miss Buchanan's Period of Adjustment," *Revisionist History* podcast, Pushkin Industries, https://www.pushkin.fm/episode/miss-buchanans-period-of-adjustment/.

641 *Brown v. Board of Education*, 347 U.S. 483 (1954).

642 Thomas Sowell, "The Education of Minority Children," https://www.tsowell.com/speducathtml.

643 Stuart Buck, *Acting White: The Ironic Legacy of Desegregation* (New Haven, CT: Yale University Press, 2011).

644 John McWhorter, "The Origins of the 'Acting White' Charge," *The Atlantic*, July 20, 2019, https://www.theatlantic.com/ideas/archive/2019/07/acting-white-charge-origins/594130/.

645 Maya Angelou, *I Know Why the Caged Bird Sings* (New York: Random House, 2009).

646 Some Black conservatives made a similar argument at the time, but the NAACP didn't pursue that strategy. See Beito and Beito's *T. R. M. Howard*, 101–127.

647 Lisa Trei, "Black Children Might Have Been Better Off without *Brown v. Board*, Bell Says," Stanford Report, April 21, 2004, https://news.stanford.edu/news/2004/april21/brownbell-421.html.

648 Milton Friedman, "The Role of Government in Education," from *Economics and the Public Interest*, edited by Robert A. Solo, copyright © 1955 by the Trustees of Rutgers College in New Jersey, reprinted by permission of Rutgers University Press.

649 See the lengthy footnote from Milton Friedman's 1955 essay, "The Role of Government in Education," https://la.utexas.edu/users/hcleaver/330T/350kPEEFriedmanRoleOfGovttable.pdf.

650 Ben DeGrow, "Democratic Minority Voters Overwhelmingly Favor School Choice," Mackinac Center for Public Policy, January 6, 2020, https://www.mackinac.org/democratic-minority-voters-overwhelmingly-favor-school-choice.

651 Michael Strong, "Are Public Schools Causing an Epidemic of Mental Illness?" Medium, September 5, 2016, https://flowidealism.medium.

com/are-public-schools-causing-an-epidemic-of-mental-illness-1b37b6c0ef3e.

[652] Drew DeSilver, "U.S. Students' Academic Achievement Still Lags That of Their Peers in Many Other Countries," February 15, 2017, Medium.com.

[653] https://www.successacademies.org/results/#:~:text=Success%20Academy%20is%20the%20size,with%2041%25%20scoring%20a%204.

[654] Thomas Sowell, Thomas, *Charter Schools and Their Enemies* (New York: Basic Books, 2020).

[655] Jamie Davies O'Leary, "One of the Best Ways to Protect LGBTQ Students Might Be Fighting for School Choice," Thomas Fordham Institute, March 17, 2017, https://fordhaminstitute.org/national/commentary/one-best-ways-protect-lgbtq-students-might-be-fighting-school-choice.

[656] Matt Ladner, "Myth: School Choice Harms Children Left Behind in Public Schools," *School Choice Myths*, edited by Corey A. DeAngelis and Neal P. McCluskey (Washington, DC: Cato Books, 2020).

[657] See Nancy McLean's *Democracy in Chains*: *The Deep History of the Radical Right's Stealth Plan for America*, (New York: Viking, 2017).

[658] For a detailed and complete history of the debate over whether the Virginia voucher movement was pro-segregation see the links provided by Phil Magness in "Tarring School Vouchers with the Segregationist Brush" *Wall Street Journal*, October 22, 2021. https://www.wsj.com/articles/school-choice-vouchers-education-segregation-integration-virginia-11634855018.

[659] Tomas Monarrez, Brian Kisida, and Matthew M. Chingos, "Do Charter Schools Increase Segregation?" *Education Next,* July 24, 2019, https://www.educationnext.org/do-charter-schools-increase-segregation-first-national-analysis-reveals-modest-impact/.

[660] Including, but by no means limited to, Derrick Bell: Lisa Trei, "Black Children Might Have Been Better Off without *Brown v. Board*, Bell Says," Stanford Report, April 21, 2004, https://news.stanford.edu/news/2004/april21/brownbell-421.html.

[661] *Espinoza v. Montana Department of Revenue*, 18-1195, https://www.scotusblog.com/case-files/cases/espinoza-v-montana-department-of-revenue/; Tim Keller, "Myth: Private School Choice Is Unconstitutional," in Neal P. McCluskey's *School Choice Myths* (Washington, DC: Cato Institute, 2020).

662 Andrew J. Coulson, "Sweden and School Choice," Cato Institute, July 22, 2014, https://www.cato.org/publications/commentary/sweden-school-choice.

663 See David Dagan and Steven Teles, *Prison Break: Why Conservatives Turned Against Mass Incarceration, (Studies in Postwar American Political Development),* first edition (Oxford: Oxford University Press, 2016).

664 We drew extensively on John Pfaff's book *Locked In: The True Causes of Mass Incarceration and How to Achieve Real Reform,* illustrated edition (New York: Basic Books, 2017).

665 A whopping 27 percent of all currently incarcerated citizens are awaiting charges. Chris W. Surprenant and Jason Brennan, *Injustice for All: How Financial Incentives Corrupted and Can Fix the US Criminal Justice System,* first edition (Oxfordshire, UK: Routledge, 2019), 2.

666 Pfaff, *Locked In,* 2.

667 Pfaff, *Locked In,* 3.

668 https://www.nap.edu/catalog/18613/the-growth-of-incarceration-in-the-united-states-exploring-causes.

669 John Pfaff, *Locked In,* 191.

670 Surprenant and Brennan, *Injustice for All,* 69.

671 Surprenant and Brennan reference the literature here, including Kleiman, Kennedy, Durlauf, Nagin. John Pfaff also concurs in *Locked In.*

672 Surprenant and Brennan, *Injustice for All.*

673 Lydia Saad, "Black Americans Want Police to Retain Local Presence," Gallup News, August 5, 2020.

674 Ashley Nellis, "The Color of Justice: Racial and Ethnic Disparity in State Prisons," The Sentencing Project, June 14, 2016, updated October 13, 2021, https://www.sentencingproject.org/publications/color-of-justice-racial-and-ethnic-disparity-in-state-prisons/.

675 Dan Baum, "Legalize it All," *Harper's Magazine,* April 2016.

676 Pfaff, *Locked In,* 27.

677 James Forman Jr., *Locking Up Our Own: Crime and Punishment in Black America* (New York: Farrar, Straus and Giroux, 2017), 26.

678 Forman, *Locking Up Our Own,* 25–26.

679 "Drugs Win Drug War" from The Onion *Presents Our Dumb Century,* by Scott Dikkers and Mike Loew (New York: Three Rivers Press, 1999).

680 David Dagan and Steven Teles, *Prison Break,* 92.

[681] John Gray, "John Gray: Steven Pinker Is Wrong about Violence and War," *The Guardian*, March 13, 2015, https://www.theguardian.com/books/2015/mar/13/john-gray-steven-pinker-wrong-violence-war-declining.

[682] Michalangelo Landgrave and Alex Nowrasteh, "Criminal Immigrants in 2017, Their Numbers, Demographics, and Countries of Origin." Cato.org https://www.cato.org/publications/immigration-research-policy-brief/criminal-immigrants-2017-their-numbers-demographics

[683] Christopher Ingraham, "There's Never Been a Safer Time to Be a Kid in America," *Washington Post*, April 14, 2015, https://www.washingtonpost.com/news/wonk/wp/2015/04/14/theres-never-been-a-safer-time-to-be-a-kid-in-america/.

[684] Kim Parker et al., "The Demographics of Gun Ownership," Pew Research Center, June 22, 2017, https://www.pewsocialtrends.org/2017/06/22/the-demographics-of-gun-ownership/.

[685] Franklin E. Zimring and Gordon Hawkins, *Crime Is Not the Problem: Lethal Violence in America* (Oxford: Oxford University Press, 1999.)

[686] She's not kidding: see *Albion's Seed* by David Hackett Fischer, plus the comparison of rates of violent crime between the North and the South.

[687] Phillip Levine and Robin McKnight, "Three Million More Guns: The Spring 2020 Spike in Firearm Sales," Brookings, July 13, 2020, https://www.brookings.edu/blog/up-front/2020/07/13/three-million-more-guns-the-spring-2020-spike-in-firearm-sales/; Chloe Brown et al., "I'm a Black American. I Need a Gun to Feel Safe in This Country." New York Times, July 1, 2020, https://www.nytimes.com/2020/07/01/opinion/Black-gun-ownership.html?action=click&module=Opinion&pgtype=Homepage; Madison J. Gray, "Black Gun Ownership Surges Amid 2020 Racial Tensions, BET, August 4, 2020, https://www.bet.com/news/national/2020/08/04/gun-sales-african-americans.html.

[688] Steve Ekwall, "The Racist Origins of US Gun Control: Laws Designed to Disarm Slaves, Freedmen, and African-Americans," Sedgwick County, https://www.sedgwickcounty.org/media/29093/the-racist-origins-of-us-gun-control.pdf; Adam Winkler, "The Secret History of Guns," *The Atlantic*, September 2011, https://www.theatlantic.com/magazine/archive/2011/09/the-secret-history-of-guns/308608/.

[689] Will Van Sant, "The NRA's Unshakable Support for Police," The Trace, July 9, 2020, https://www.thetrace.org/2020/07/

the-nras-unshakable-support-for-police/. Notably, groups like Gun Owners of America are far more consistent.

[690] Mark Berman, "What the Police Officer Who Shot Philando Castile Said about the Shooting," *Washington Post*, June 21, 2017, https://www.washingtonpost.com/news/post-nation/wp/2017/06/21/what-the-police-officer-who-shot-philando-castile-said-about-the-shooting/.

[691] Jacob Sullum, "A Month Before Louisville Drug Warriors Killed Breonna Taylor, They Knew the 'Suspicious Packages' She Supposedly Was Receiving Came from Amazon," *Reason*, October 9, 2020, https://reason.com/2020/10/09/a-month-before-louisville-drug-warriors-killed-breonna-taylor-they-knew-the-suspicious-packages-she-supposedly-was-receiving-came-from-amazon/.

[692] Tim Stickings, Keith Griffith, and Karen Ruiz, "Cops Release Photos That Were Tagged 'Partners in Crime' from Breonna Taylor's Boyfriend's Phone That Show Them Both Holding Gun Believed to Be the One He Used to Fire at Police as Messages Also Suggest He Was Selling Drugs," *Daily Mail*, October 7, 2020, https://www.dailymail.co.uk/news/article-8816249/Louisville-police-release-details-Taylor-investigation.html.

[693] Logan Strother and Daniel Bennett, "Which Americans Support the Second Amendment? The Answer Depends on Whether Whites or Blacks Have the Guns," *Washington Post*, November 24, 2018, https://www.washingtonpost.com/news/monkey-cage/wp/2018/11/24/which-americans-support-the-second-amendment-the-answer-depends-on-whether-whites-or-blacks-have-the-guns/.

[694] Details from *The Deacons for Defense: Armed Resistance and the Civil Rights Movement*, Lance Hill in https://townhall.com/columnists/kenBlackwell/2007/02/06/second-amendment-freedoms-aided-the-civil-rights-movement-n1409414.

[695] Beito and Beito, *T. R. M. Howard*.

[696] Beito and Beito, *T. R. M. Howard*.

[697] Mark Engler and Paul Engler, "When Martin Luther King Gave Up His Guns," *The Guardian*, January 20, 2014, https://www.theguardian.com/commentisfree/2014/jan/20/martin-luther-king-guns-pacifism.

[698] Kim Parker et al., "The demographics of gun ownership."

[699] "Crime in the United States 2012," UCR Federal Bureau of Investigation, 2012, https://ucr.fbi.gov/crime-in-the-u.s/2012/

crime-in-the-u.s.-2012/tables/42tabledatadecoverviewpdf/table_42_
arrests_by_sex_2012.xls.

[700] L. N. Gase et al, "Understanding Racial and Ethnic Disparities in Arrest: The Role of Individual, Home, School, and Community Characteristics, *Race and Social Problems,* vol. 8 (2016), 296–312, https://www.aclu.org/sites/default/files/assets/141027_iachr_racial_disparities_aclu_submission_0.pdf.

[701] "Stop-and-Frisk Data," NYCLU, https://www.nyclu.org/en/stop-and-frisk-data.

[702] Mary F. Moriarty, "Traffic Stops as Criminal Investigations: Pretext Stops Should Be Disallowed in Minnesota," MinnPost, June 6, 2019, https://www.minnpost.com/community-voices/2019/06/traffic-stops-as-criminal-investigations-pretext-stops-should-be-disallowed-in-minnesota/; Frank R. Baumgartner, *Suspect Citizens: What 20 Million Traffic Stops Tell Us about Policing and Race* (Cambridge: Cambridge University Press, 2018).

[703] Surprenant and Brennan, *Injustice for All,* 108.

[704] O. Mitchell and M. S. Caudy, "Examining Racial Disparities in Drug Arrests," *Justice Quarterly,* vol. 32, issue 2 (2015), 288–313.

[705] L. N. Gase et al., "Understanding Racial and Ethnic Disparities in Arrest," 296–312.

[706] Taken from a real case, Surprenant and Brennan, *Injustice for All,* 135.

[707] Tom Jacobsaug, "Black Cops Are Just as Likely as White Cops to Kill Black Suspects," *Pacific Standard,* September 2018, https://psmag.com/social-justice/black-cops-are-just-as-likely-as-whites-to-kill-black-suspects.

[708] Bernadette Rabuy and Daniel Kopf, "Detaining the Poor: How Money Bail Perpetuates an Endless Cycle of Poverty and Jail Time," Prison Policy Initiative, May 10, 2016, https://www.prisonpolicy.org/reports/incomejails.html.

[709] Carlos Berdejó, "Criminalizing Race: Racial Disparities in Plea Bargaining," *Boston College Law Review,* vol. 59 (2018, forthcoming); Loyola Law School, Los Angeles Legal Studies Research Paper No. 2017-39, available at SSRN https://papers.ssrn.com/sol3/papers.cfm?abstract_id=3036726.

[710] Wendy Sawyer, "How Race Impacts Who Is Detained Pretrial," Prison Policy Initiative, October 9, 2019, https://www.prisonpolicy.org/blog/2019/10/09/pretrial_race/.

711 Christopher Ingraham, "Black Men Sentenced to More Time for Committing the Exact Same Crime as a White Person, Study Finds," *Washington Post*, November 16, 2017, https://www.washingtonpost.com/news/wonk/wp/2017/11/16/black-men-sentenced-to-more-time-for-committing-the-exact-same-crime-as-a-white-person-study-finds/.

712 Ingraham, "Black Men Sentenced to More Time."

713 ACLU, "Written Submission of the American Civil Liberties on Racial Disparities in Sentencing," Hearing on Reports of Racism in the Justice System of the United States, Submitted to the Inter-American Commission on Human rights, 153rd Session, October 27, 2014, https://www.aclu.org/sites/default/files/assets/141027_iachr_racial_disparities_aclu_submission_0.pdf.

714 Surprenant and Brennan, *Injustice for All.*

715 See the Mercatus Center's RegData project: https://www.mercatus.org/publications/regulation/regdata.

716 Douglas Husak, *Overcriminalization: The Limits of the Criminal Law* (Oxford: Oxford University Press, 2009).

717 Dick M. Carpenter et al., "License to Work: First Edition—A National Study of Burdens from Occupational Licensing," Institute for Justice, https://ij.org/report/license-to-work/.

718 Radley Balko, "The Militarization of America's Police Forces," *Cato's Letter,* vol. 11, no. 4 (Fall 2013), https://www.cato.org/sites/cato.org/files/pubs/pdf/catosletter-v11n4.pdf.

719 Emily Ekins, "Americans Don't Want to #Defund Police, Instead They Agree on Reform," Cato Institute, June 4, 2020, https://www.cato.org/blog/americans-agree-policing-reform.

720 Anthony Bradley, *Ending Overcriminalization and Mass Incarceration: Hope From Civil Society* (Cambridge: Cambridge University Press, 2018), 153.

721 Quoted in Bradley, 165.

722 Lea Hunter, "What You Need to Know About Ending Cash Bail," Center for American Progress, March 16, 2020, https://www.americanprogress.org/issues/criminal-justice/reports/2020/03/16/481543/ending-cash-bail/.

723 See *The Vanishing Trial*, a film by Families Against Mandatory Minimums.

724 Surprenant and Brennan, *Injustice for All,* 130.

725 Saad, "Black Americans Want Police to Retain Local Presence."

[726] Ekins, "Americans Don't Want to #Defund Police."

[727] Jay Schweikert, "Qualified Immunity: A Legal, Practical, and Moral Failure," Cato Institute, September 14, 2020, https://www.cato.org/publications/policy-analysis/qualified-immunity-legal-practical-moral-failure#null.

[728] Surprenant and Brennan, *Injustice for All.*

[729] J. Justin Wilson, "Federal Court Approves Historic Decree Ending 'Policing for Profit'" in Pagedale, Mo.," Institute for Justice, May 21, 2018, https://ij.org/press-release/federal-court-approves-historic-consent-decree-ending-policing-for-profit-in-pagedale-mo/.

[730] Surprenant and Brennan, *Injustice for All*, 101.

[731] Radley Balko, *Rise of the Warrior Cop* (New York: PublicAffairs, 2014).

[732] Balko, *Rise of the Warrior Cop.*

[733] Balko, *Rise of the Warrior Cop,* 210, 249; Surprenant and Brennan, *Injustice for All,* 38.

[734] Trevor Burrus, "Stopping Police Militarization," Cato Institute, https://www.cato.org/cato-handbook-policymakers/cato-handbook-policy-makers-8th-edition-2017/stopping-police. https://www.cato.org/publications/research-briefs-economic-policy/militarization-fails-enhance-police-safety-or-reduce.

[735] Christopher J. Coyne and Abigail R. Hall, *Tyranny Comes Home: The Domestic Fate of U.S. Militarism* (Stanford: Stanford University Press, 2018).

[736] Surprenant and Brennan, *Injustice for All*, 37.

[737] Bradley, *Ending Overcriminalization and Mass Incarceration*, 176–177.

[738] Bradley, *Ending Overcriminalization and Mass Incarceration*, 173–180.

[739] Lucius Couloute and Daniel Kopf, "Out of Prison & Out of Work: Unemployment Among Formerly Incarcerated People," Prison Policy Initiative, July 2018, https://www.prisonpolicy.org/reports/outofwork.html.

[740] Jennifer L. Doleac (Texas A&M) and Benjamin Hansen (University of Oregon), "The Unintended Consequences of 'Ban the Box': Statistical Discrimination and Employment Outcomes When Criminal Histories are Hidden," *Journal of Labor Economics*, vol. 38, no. 2 (April 2020).

[741] See "The Anti-Imperialism of Mises" https://mises.org/library/anti-imperialism-mises Coyne and Hall, *Tyranny Comes Home.*

[742] For a comprehensive understanding of Public Choice consult William F. Shughart II, "Public Choice" *Econlib*, accessed at https://www.econlib.org/library/Enc/PublicChoice.html.

[743] See John Stuart Mill's "The Subjection of Women;" Wendy McElroy's edited collection titled *Liberty for Women: Freedom and Feminism in the 21st Century* (New York: Ivan R. Dee, 2002). Other good resources include Jayme Lemke's numerous articles on libertarian feminism and Elizabeth Nolan Brown's scholarship on sex work.

[744] The entire Cobden school of abolitionists, including William Lloyd Garrison, Frederick Douglass, Oswald Garrison Villard, Moorfield Storey, and Nat Hentoff.

[745] John McWhorter, "Race and Admissions: Affirming Disadvantage," *The American Interest*, June 28, 2018, https://www.the-american-interest.com/2018/06/28/affirming-disadvantage/.

[746] John McWhorter, "The Demise of Affirmative Action at UC Berkeley: Dissecting the Stalemate," Edge, https://www.edge.org/3rd_culture/mcwhorter/mcwhorter_p2.html.

[747] David R. Francis, "Employers' Replies to Racial Names," National Bureau of Economic Research, The Digest, no. 9, (September 2003), https://www.nber.org/digest/sep03/w9873.html.

[748] Frank Dobbin and Alexandra Kalev, "Why Doesn't Diversity Training Work? The Challenge for Industry and Academia," *Uncommon Sense,* vol. 10 (2018), https://scholar.harvard.edu/files/dobbin/files/an2018.pdf.

[749] See the dissent in *Kelo v. New London* (https://supreme.justia.com/cases/federal/us/545/469/#tab-opinion-1961892), Thomas and O'Connor concurring.

[750] See ConsciousConservativeMedia.net.

[751] "New Estimates of Value of Land of the United States," April 2015, Bureau of Economic Analysis, https://www.bea.gov/research/papers/2015/new-estimates-value-land-united-states.

[752] John F. Early, "Reassessing the Facts about Inequality, Poverty, and Redistribution," Cato Institute, Policy Analysis, no. 839 (April 24, 2018), https://www.cato.org/policy-analysis/reassessing-facts-about-inequality-poverty-redistribution#conclusion.

[753] Felecia Killings, "The ADOS-BRO Initiative: A Conscious Conservative Response to Reparations," https://www.consciousconservativemedia.net/posts/16679492?utm_source=manual. Also see her book, *Conscious Black Conservatism: Building Social, Political, and Economic Empires Based on Kingdom Principles* (independently published, 2020).

754 Matt Bruenig, "The Racial Wealth Gap Is about the Upper Classes," People's Policy Project, April 29, 2020, https://www.peoplespolicy-project.org/2020/06/29/the-racial-wealth-gap-is-about-the-upper-classes/.

755 Atlanta Covenant, OneRace Movement, https://oneracemovement.com/atlanta-covenant/; "Reconciliation & Restorative Justice through Spiritual, Cultural, and Economic Renewal," Civil Righteousness, https://civilrighteousness.org/.

About the Authors

Rachel Ferguson is an economic philosopher at Concordia University Chicago. As director of the Free Enterprise Center there, she leads a nationwide, cross-disciplinary faculty network that engages questions of liberty and virtue through seminars, conferences, and pedagogy. Dr. Ferguson has been a visiting fellow at the Eudaimonia Institute and her work can be found in *Discourse*, the *Journal of Markets & Morality*, and the *Library of Economics and Liberty*. Ferguson lives in St. Louis, Missouri where she is actively involved in community building and empowering marginalized entrepreneurs through LOVEtheLOU and Gateway to Flourishing.

Marcus M. Witcher is an Assistant Professor of History at Huntingdon College in Montgomery, Alabama. He received his BA from the University of Central Arkansas in 2011, an MA from the University of Alabama in 2013, and completed his Ph.D. in history from UA in 2017. His first book, *Getting Right with Reagan: The Struggle for True Conservatism, 1980-2016*, was published by the University Press of Kansas in 2019. Dr. Witcher is also the co-editor of the three volume *Public Choice Analyses of Economic History* (2018, 2018, 2019) and is the co-editor of *Conversations on Conservatism: Speeches from the Philadelphia Society* (2021).

Acknowledgments

Five years ago, my friend and colleague, Patrick Walker, asked me to help get a bus full of college students to the grand opening of the Smithsonian Museum of African-American History and Culture. I did so, and helped to prepare the students for it through a five-week intrusion on one of their courses in which I presented the nascent ideas for this book—what I then called "A Classical Liberal Account of the Systemic Oppression of African-Americans." I must also thank Dana Klar and Karen Johnson for letting me have that time with their students and for an unforgettable time together in Washington D.C. In my last conversation with Patrick, his imagination was fired as we discussed the concept of transitional justice, one of the solutions described in this work. We were excited about future projects we could work on together. While Patrick and I differed on many matters of policy, we both agreed that, in his words, people can "do a lot of good and make money at the same time," and we wanted to encourage young Black entrepreneurs on our campuses. I cannot express the devastation that I felt when Patrick passed away from cancer this past year—far, far too young, at the age of forty-eight. His spirit of love, tolerance, and reconciliation was absolutely infectious. His encouragement of me in my work, despite our disagreements, was a testament to that. Patrick, I miss you so much, but I know we'll see each other again. Thank you for believing in me and in this project.

It would be ridiculous to begin listing all of those who helped with the writing of this book without first acknowledging my co-author, Marcus Witcher. While Marcus may not believe in such things, I cannot help but claim the intervention of divine providence in our pairing as co-authors. Not only is Marcus an excellent historian, but his enthusiasm for this project kept me going when Covid, family crises, and professional changes threatened to overwhelm me. Marcus's gift for details and organization are the perfect complement to my stereotypical "flighty professor" personality. Most of all, I truly believe that Marcus's work to survey atrocities against Black Americans and the history of Black entrepreneurship makes up the beating heart of this work. While I asked Marcus to work on this book with me for very specific reasons of scholarship, I could never have known in advance how wonderful this partnership would become. Here's to many more years of fruitful collaboration, my friend! You are a blessing.

More than anyone else, Jim Otteson is the person who made this project possible by offering me the opportunity to take a sabbatical at the Eudaimonia Institute at Wake Forest University in the spring of 2020. Our time together was interrupted by Covid, but having those months of concentrated focus was absolutely necessary for me to write this book. While Jim's move to Notre Dame sadly ended the Institute's existence, I am so thrilled that he is able to continue his good work as director of the Notre Dame/ Deloitte Center for Ethical Leadership. One of the hardest things about defending a liberationist account of markets is battling the general misconception that business itself is somehow a dishonorable activity. Thank God for Jim's excellent book, *Honorable Business*, and his work at Notre Dame. This is what colleges of business everywhere need.

We have to thank the wonderful Ben Klutsey and Devin Scanlon for organizing one of the most pivotal elements of our editing process. We are incredibly grateful to them and to the Mercatus Center at George Mason University for hosting a scholar manuscript roundtable as well as to Howard Wall and the John W. Hammond Institute for Free Enterprise at Lindenwood University, who funded it. Of course, the scholars themselves, Matt Mitchell, Anthony Bradley, and Kathaleena Monds, all did the hard work of reading through the manuscript and offering their feedback. Each scholar had profound effects on our final draft, including fundamental changes that we believe made this book far better than it might have otherwise been. At the same time, Kevin Hughes, Phil Magness, and David Beito provided comments independently, and each scholar improved the book immensely. I also benefitted greatly from long conversations with Carey Roberts, Sam Smith, and Rev. Carlos Smith. Then again, we cannot claim to have accepted all of their suggestions, and therefore all involved are released from any responsibility whatsoever for any misguided or ham-fisted elements that remain.

In writing this book, Marcus and I have experienced a level of generosity from others that can only be called supererogatory. The best example of this phenomenon is Garrett Brown, who worked tirelessly to help us navigate the publishing world, with no more incentive than his belief that the project was worthwhile. Garrett, someday we'll buy you lunch! We are thrilled to be working with Post Hill Press and Emancipation Books via his introduction, and have had a wonderful experience. Special thanks to Debra Englander and her whole team at Post Hill Press.

Early encouragers include David Schmidtz, who first suggested that I work a short presentation into something more substantive; Victor Claar and Christy Horpedahl, who invited me to their institutions to give talks on the research as it was progressing; and the aforementioned Howard Wall, who happily facilitated my criminal justice reform efforts at the Hammond Institute and championed my sabbatical opportunity. Thank you to David Masci at *Discourse* and Richard Reinsch at *Law and Liberty* for allowing me to hash out some of the ideas in their publications. I am entirely confident that I am forgetting many people whose words of encouragement and excitement about the project kept me going.

We want to thank the estate of Harlem Renaissance artist Jacob Lawrence for allowing us to use his wonderful image, "Builders, 1974" for our cover. The family he depicts, close together and moving forward, against the backdrop of the builders—Black and white together—making something new, seemed to us to be the perfect image of a hopeful future for Black America.

Finally, our own families endured much to see this book come to fruition. Less than two years into our marriage, my husband, Michael Ferguson, did not hesitate for a moment when I brought up the possibility of leaving for four months to live a thousand miles away so I could write a book. He communicated his determination to do whatever it took so that I would be able to take advantage of the opportunity. I will never forget that moment. Marcus's wife Takayla has also gone above and beyond, not merely as his partner in life but also often as an informal editor! My two young men, Asher and Solomon, fifteen and fourteen at the time, were pulled out of school and homeschooled in order to accommodate long periods out of town. While this turned out to be a blessing in disguise with the rise of Covid, they certainly didn't know that then, and had understandable anxieties. We all faced our fears together and had some interesting adventures along the way. Boys, remember the time we had to pack up the entire apartment plus ourselves into my tiny Hyundai and drive across country because Covid had shut down our living quarters in North Carolina? Solomon had a terrible crick in the neck because he was so jammed into the back, and I'm still finding shards of the Moravian star that got crushed under the seats! One especially gratifying moment for a mom was when Asher decided to get involved with LOVEtheLOU, one of the neighborhood stabilization organizations discussed in this book. I'm proud of his work as a tutor and "mulch man" in the community gardens. My heart is also warmed by my son Solomon's talent with kids and his interest in child psychology. If he pursues this route in life, I hope he will be a great healer. I hope they all know that we don't take these things for granted. Anyone who has experienced an unsupportive environment knows how much it can wear on the spirit. Instead, we were met with willingness, flexibility, and unflagging support and encouragement. My sincerest gratitude to Michael, Asher, and Solomon. I love you with all my heart. And Takayla, I can safely say that Marcus would echo these words of appreciation to you as well.

—Rachel Ferguson